State Failure
and State Weakness
in a Time of Terror

Other Brookings/World Peace Foundation Books
by Robert I. Rotberg

Ending Autocracy, Enabling Democracy: The Tribulations of Southern Africa 1960–2000 (2002)

Peacekeeping and Peace Enforcement in Africa: Methods of Conflict Prevention (2000)

Creating Peace in Sri Lanka: Civil War and Reconciliation (1999)

Burma: Prospects for a Democratic Future (1998)

War and Peace in Southern Africa: Crimes, Drugs, Armies, Trade (1998)

Haiti Renewed: Political and Economic Prospects (1997)

Vigilance and Vengeance: NGOs Preventing Ethnic Conflict in Divided Societies (1996)

From Massacres to Genocide: The Media, Public Policy, and Humanitarian Crises (1996)

State Failure and State Weakness in a Time of Terror

Robert I. Rotberg

Editor

WORLD PEACE FOUNDATION
Cambridge, Massachusetts

BROOKINGS INSTITUTION PRESS
Washington, D.C.

Copyright © 2003
THE WORLD PEACE FOUNDATION

State Failure and State Weakness in a Time of Terror
may be ordered from
BROOKINGS INSTITUTION PRESS
1775 Massachusetts Avenue, N.W.
Washington, D.C. 20036
Tel.: 1-800/275-1447 or 202/797-6258
Fax: 202/797-6004
www.brookings.edu

Library of Congress Cataloging-in-Publication data

State failure and state weakness in a time of terror /
Robert I. Rotberg, editor.
 p. cm.
Includes bibliographical references and index.
 ISBN 0-8157-7574-1 (cloth : alk. paper)—
 ISBN 0-8157-7573-3 (pbk. : alk. paper)
 1. Legitmacy of governments—Developing countries. 2. Political stability—Developing
countries. 3. Developing countries—Politics and government. 4. World politics—1989—
I. Rotberg, Robert I.
 JF60.S72 2003
 320'.01'1—dc21   2002151488

9 8 7 6 5 4 3 2 1

The paper used in this publication meets minimum requirements of the American National
Standard for Information Sciences—Permanence of Paper for Printed Library Materials:
ANSI Z39.48-1992.

Typeset in Times Roman

Composition by Stephen McDougal
Mechanicsville, Maryland

Printed by R. R. Donnelley
Harrisonburg, Virginia

Contents

Preface vii

1. Failed States, Collapsed States, Weak States:
   Causes and Indicators 1
   Robert I. Rotberg

Part One. Cases of Failure and Collapse

2. The Democratic Republic of the Congo: From Failure
   to Potential Reconstruction 29
   René Lemarchand

3. Sierra Leone: Warfare in a Post-State Society 71
   William Reno

4. The Sudan: A Successfully Failed State 101
   Gérard Prunier and Rachel Gisselquist

5. Somalia: Can a Collapsed State Reconstitute Itself? 129
   Walter S. Clarke and Robert Gosende

Part Two. Dangerously Weak

6. Colombia: Lawlessness, Drug Trafficking, and Carving
   Up the State 161
   Harvey F. Kline

7. Indonesia: The Erosion of State Capacity..................... 183
    Michael Malley

8. Sri Lanka: A Fragmented State........................... 219
    Erin K. Jenne

9. Tajikistan: Regionalism and Weakness 245
    Nasrin Dadmehr

Part Three. Safely Weak

10. Fiji: Divided and Weak................................. 265
    Stephanie Lawson

11. Haiti: A Case of Endemic Weakness 287
    Marlye Gélin-Adams and David M. Malone

12. Lebanon: Failure, Collapse, and Resuscitation................. 305
    Oren Barak

Contributors 341

Index... 345

Preface

From 1998 to 2002, the Harvard University Failed States Project attempted to analyze the post–Cold War phenomenon of nation-state failure and collapse. What caused developing-world nation-states to falter and fail? What distinguished weak from strong, failed from weak, and failed from collapsed states? What could best be recommended to prevent nation-states in the developing world from sliding rapidly from strength to weakness and then, in so many cases, to failure? Once failed and collapsed, should and could such states be restored to functionality and good governance?

These were among the many questions addressed by the project when it convened on regular occasions at Harvard University's John F. Kennedy School of Government, under the auspices of the World Peace Foundation and the Kennedy School's Program on Intrastate Conflict. More than forty gifted scholars and practitioners collaborated on the project, the results of which are presented in this volume and a companion volume forthcoming from Princeton University Press: Robert I. Rotberg (ed.), *When States Fail: Causes and Consequences*.

The present volume classifies and categorizes states according to criteria developed by the Failed States Project. The opening chapter distinguishes weak from failed and failed from collapsed states, providing the framework for the detailed examinations of states at risk that follow in the remainder of the volume. These separately authored studies cover failed states, the one contemporary collapsed state, and different varieties of weak and failing states.

The contributors to both volumes, the editor, and the Trustees of the World Peace Foundation all hope that this work will focus scholarly and policy attention upon the problem of failed and collapsed states. They intend these studies to illuminate examinations of the cases in question, and also to encourage UN and foreign policy engagement with the general issue, as well as how to help the specific cases, and others like them, as prevention of failure and nation-building increasingly preoccupy world attention.

In addition to his gratitude to the contributors to this book, all of whom labored hard and long to produce accessible and timely essays, the editor remains grateful to James Gow, Karin von Hippel, Nelson Kasfir, Robert Orr, Richard Ullman, and Leonard Wantchekon for their special contributions, to Deborah West and Tanjam Jacobson for their unfailing editorial assistance, to Graham Allison and the Kennedy School's Belfer Center for Science and International Affairs for their unwavering support, and to the Trustees of the World Peace Foundation for their strong backing.

—R. I. R.

State Failure
and State Weakness
in a Time of Terror

CHAPTER ONE

Failed States, Collapsed States, Weak States: Causes and Indicators

ROBERT I. ROTBERG

Nation-states fail because they are convulsed by internal violence and can no longer deliver positive political goods to their inhabitants. Their governments lose legitimacy, and the very nature of the particular nation-state itself becomes illegitimate in the eyes and in the hearts of a growing plurality of its citizens.

The rise and fall of nation-states is not new, but in a modern era when national states constitute the building blocks of legitimate world order the violent disintegration and palpable weakness of selected African, Asian, Oceanic, and Latin American states threaten the very foundation of that system. International organizations and big powers consequently find themselves sucked disconcertingly into a maelstrom of anomic internal conflict and messy humanitarian relief. Desirable international norms such as stability and predictability thus become difficult to achieve when so many of the globe's newer nation-states waver precariously between weakness and failure, with some truly failing, or even collapsing. In a time of terror, moreover, appreciating the nature of and responding to the dynamics of nation-state failure have become central to critical policy debates. How best to strengthen weak states and prevent state failure are among the urgent questions of the twenty-first century.

This book examines contemporary cases of nation-state collapse and failure.[1] It establishes clear criteria for distinguishing collapse and failure from generic weakness or apparent distress, and collapse from failure. It further analyzes the nature of state weakness and advances reasons why some weak states succumb to failure, or collapse, and why others in ostensibly more straightened circumstances remain weak and at risk without ever destructing. Characterizing failed states is thus an important and relevant endeavor, especially because the phenomenon of state failure is under-researched, hitherto with imprecise definitions and a paucity of sharply argued, instructive, and well-delineated cases. Further, understanding exactly why weak states slide toward failure will help policymakers to design methods to prevent failure and, in the cases of states that nevertheless fail (or collapse), to revive them and assist in the re-building process.

States are much more varied in their capacity and capability than they once were. They are more numerous than they were a half century ago, and the range of their population sizes, physical endowments, wealth, productivity, delivery systems, ambitions, and attainments is much more extensive than ever before. In 1914, in the wake of the crumbling of the Ottoman and Austro-Hungarian empires, there were fifty-five recognized national polities. In 1919, there were fifty-nine nations. In 1950, that number had reached sixty-nine. Ten years later, after the attainment of independence in much of Africa, ninety were nations. After many more African, Asian, and Oceanic territories had become independent, and after the implosion of the Soviet Union, the number of nations jumped to 191; East Timor's independence in 2002 brought that total to 192. Given such explosive numbers, the inherent fragility of many of the new recruits (fifteen of Africa's fifty-four states are landlocked), and the inherent navigational perils of the post–Cold War economic and political terrain, the possibility of failure among a subset of the total remains ever present.

Strength and Weakness

Nation-states exist to provide a decentralized method of delivering political (public) goods to persons living within designated parameters (borders). Having replaced the monarchs of old, modern states focus and answer the concerns and demands of citizenries. They organize and channel the interests of their people, often but not exclusively in furtherance of national goals and values. They buffer or manipulate external forces and influences, champion the local or particular concerns of their adherents, and mediate between the constraints and challenges of the international arena and the dynamism of their own internal economic, political, and social realities.

States succeed or fail across all or some of these dimensions. But it is according to their performance—according to the levels of their effective delivery of the most crucial political goods—that strong states may be distinguished from weak ones, and weak states from failed or collapsed states. Political goods are those intangible and hard to quantify claims that citizens once made on sovereigns and now make on states. They encompass expectations, conceivably obligations, inform the local political culture, and together give content to the social contract between ruler and ruled that is at the core of regime/government and citizenry interactions.[2]

There is a hierarchy of political goods. None is as critical as the supply of security, especially human security. Individuals alone, almost exclusively in special or particular circumstances, can attempt to secure themselves. Or groups of individuals can band together to organize and purchase goods or services that maximize their sense of security. Traditionally, and usually, however, individuals and groups cannot easily or effectively substitute private security for the full spectrum of public security. The state's prime function is to provide that political good of security—to prevent cross-border invasions and infiltrations, and any loss of territory; to eliminate domestic threats to or attacks upon the national order and social structure; to prevent crime and any related dangers to domestic human security; and to enable citizens to resolve their disputes with the state and with their fellow inhabitants without recourse to arms or other forms of physical coercion.

The delivery of a range of other desirable political goods becomes possible when a reasonable measure of security has been sustained. Modern states (as successors to sovereigns) provide predictable, recognizable, systematized methods of adjudicating disputes and regulating both the norms and the prevailing mores of a particular society or polity. The essence of that political good usually implies codes and procedures that together constitute an enforceable rule of law, security of property and inviolable contracts, a judicial system, and a set of values that legitimize and validate the local version of fair play.

Another key political good enables citizens to participate freely, openly, and fully in politics and the political process. This good encompasses the essential freedoms: the right to compete for office; respect and support for national and regional political institutions, like legislatures and courts; tolerance of dissent and difference; and fundamental civil and human rights.

Other political goods typically supplied by states (although privatized forms are possible) and expected by their citizenries include medical and health care (at varying levels and costs); schools and educational instruction (of various kinds and levels)—the knowledge good; roads, railways, harbors, and other physical infrastructures—the arteries of commerce; communications infrastructures; a money and banking system, usually presided over by a central bank and lubricated by a national currency; a beneficent fiscal and institutional context within which citizens can pursue personal entrepreneurial goals and potentially prosper; the promotion of civil society; and methods of regulating the sharing of the environmental commons. Together, this bundle of political goods, roughly rank ordered, establishes a set of criteria according to which modern nation-states may be judged strong, weak, or failed.

Strong states obviously perform well across these categories and with respect to each, separately. Weak states show a mixed profile, fulfilling expectations in some areas and performing poorly in others. The more poorly weak states perform, criterion by criterion, the weaker they become, and the more that weakness tends to edge toward failure, hence the subcategory of weakness that is termed *failing*. Many failed states flunk each of the tests outlined above. But they need not flunk all of them to fail overall, particularly since satisfying the security good weighs very heavily, and high levels of internal violence are associated directly with failure and the propensity to fail. Yet, violence alone does not condition failure, and the absence of violence does not necessarily imply that the state in question is not failed. It is necessary to judge the extent to which an entire failing or failed profile is less or more than its component parts.

Strong states unquestionably control their territories and deliver a full range and a high quality of political goods to their citizens. They perform well according to indicators like GDP per capita, the UNDP Human Development Index, Transparency International's Corruption Perception Index, and Freedom House's *Freedom of the World Report*. Strong states offer high levels of security from political and criminal violence, ensure political freedom and civil liberties, and create environments conducive to the growth of economic opportunity. The rule of law prevails. Judges are independent. Road networks are well maintained. Telephones work. Snail mail and e-mail both arrive quickly. Schools, universities, and students flourish. Hospitals and clinics serve patients effectively. And so on. Overall, strong states are places of enviable peace and order.

Weak states include a broad continuum of states that are: inherently weak because of geographical, physical, or fundamental economic constraints; basically strong, but temporarily or situationally weak because of internal antagonisms, management flaws, greed, despotism, or external attacks; and a mixture of the two. Weak states typically harbor ethnic, religious, linguistic, or other intercommunal tensions that have not yet, or not yet thoroughly, become overtly violent. Urban crime rates tend to be higher and increasing. In weak states, the ability to provide adequate measures of other political goods is diminished or diminishing. Physical infrastructural networks have deteriorated. Schools and hospitals show signs of neglect, particularly outside the main cities. GDP per capita and other critical economic indicators have fallen or are falling, sometimes dramatically; levels of venal corruption are embarrassingly high and escalating. Weak states usually honor rule of law precepts in the breach. They harass civil society. Weak states are often ruled by despots, elected or not.

There is a special category of weak state, as explored in Erin Jenne's chapter. That is the seemingly strong case, always an autocracy, that rigidly controls dissent and is secure but at the same time provides very few political goods. In extreme cases, such as North Korea, the regime permits its people to starve. Cambodia under Pol Pot also qualifies, as does contemporary Belarus, Iraq, and, possibly, Libya. Across recent times, the list of states that are fundamentally weak but appear strong is even more extensive.

Failed and Collapsed States

Failed states are tense, deeply conflicted, dangerous, and contested bitterly by warring factions. In most failed states, government troops battle armed revolts led by one or more rivals. Occasionally, the official authorities in a failed state face two or more insurgencies, varieties of civil unrest, different degrees of communal discontent, and a plethora of dissent directed at the state and at groups within the state.

It is not the absolute intensity of violence that identifies a failed state. Rather, it is the enduring character of that violence (as in Angola, Burundi, and the Sudan), the fact that much of the violence is directed against the existing government or regime, and the inflamed character of the political or geographical demands for shared power or autonomy that rationalize or justify that violence in the minds of the main insurgents.

The civil wars that characterize failed states usually stem from or have roots in ethnic, religious, linguistic, or other intercommunal enmity. The fear of the other that drives so much ethnic conflict stimulates and fuels hostilities between regimes and subordinate and less favored groups. Avarice also propels that antagonism, especially when greed is magnified by dreams of loot from discoveries of new, contested, sources of resource wealth, like petroleum deposits, diamond fields, other minerals, or timber.

There is no failed state without disharmonies between communities. Yet, the simple fact that many weak nation-states include haves and have-nots, and that some of the newer states contain a heterogeneous array of ethnic, religious, and linguistic interests, is more a contributor to than a root cause of nation-state failure. State failure cannot be ascribed primarily to the inability to build nations from a congeries of groups of diverse backgrounds. Nor should it be ascribed baldly to the oppression of minorities by a majority, although such brutalities are often a major ingredient of the impulse toward failure.

In contrast to strong states, failed states cannot control their borders. They lose authority over sections of territory. Often, the expression of official power is limited to a capital city and one or more ethnically specific zones. Plausibly, the extent of a state's failure can be measured by how much of its geographical expanse is genuinely controlled (especially after dark) by the official government. How nominal or contested is the central government's sway over peripheral towns and rural roads and waterways? Who really expresses power up-country, or in districts distant from the capital?[3]

Citizens depend on states and central governments to secure their persons and free them from fear. Unable to establish an atmosphere of security nationwide, and often struggling to project power and official authority, the faltering state's failure becomes obvious even before, or as, rebel groups and other contenders threaten the residents of central cities and overwhelm demoralized government contingents, as in Liberia and Sierra Leone.

In most failed states, regimes prey on their own constituents. Driven by ethnic or other intercommunal hostility, or by the governing elite's insecurities, they victimize their own citizens or some subset of the whole that is regarded as hostile. As in Mobutu Sese Seko's Zaire or the Taliban's Afghanistan, ruling cadres increasingly oppress, extort, and harass the majority of their own compatriots while privileging a more narrowly based party, clan, or sect. As in Zaire, Angola, Siaka Stevens's Sierra Leone, or pre-2001 Sudan, patrimonial rule depends on a patronage-based system of extraction from ordinary citizens. The typical weak state plunges toward failure when this kind of ruler-led oppression provokes a countervailing reaction on the part of resentful groups or newly emerged rebels.

Another indicator of state failure is the growth of criminal violence. As state authority weakens and fails, and as the state becomes criminal in its oppression of its citizens, so lawlessness becomes more apparent. Criminal gangs take over the streets of the cities. Arms and drug trafficking become more common. Ordinary police forces become paralyzed. Anomic behaviors become the norm. For protection, citizens naturally turn to warlords and other strong figures who express or activate ethnic or clan solidarity, thus offering the possibility of security at a time when all else, and the state itself, is crumbling. High rates of urban crime and the rise of criminal syndicates testify to an underlying anarchy and desperation.

Failed states provide only limited quantities of other essential political goods. They more and more forfeit to upstart warlords and other non-state actors their role as the preferred suppliers of political goods. A failed state is a polity that is no longer able or willing to perform the fundamental jobs of a nation-state in the modern world.

Failed states exhibit flawed institutions. That is, only the institution of the executive functions. If legislatures exist at all, they are rubber-stamping machines. Democratic debate is noticeably absent. The judiciary is derivative of the executive rather than being independent, and citizens know that they cannot rely on the court system for significant redress or remedy, especially against the state. The bureaucracy has long ago lost its sense of professional responsibility and exists solely to carry out the orders of the executive and, in petty ways, to oppress citizens. The military is possibly the only institution with any remaining integrity, but the armed forces of failed states are often highly politicized, devoid of the esprit that they once demonstrated.

Failed states are typified by deteriorating or destroyed infrastructures. Metaphorically, the more potholes (or main roads turned to rutted tracks), the more a state will exemplify failure. As rulers siphon funds from the state coffers, so there are fewer capital resources for road crews, equipment, and raw materials. Maintaining road or rail access to distant districts becomes less and less of a priority. Even refurbishing basic navigational aids along arterial waterways (as in the Democratic Republic of the Congo, the DRC) becomes typified by neglect. Where the state still controls such communications backbones as a land-line telephone system, that form of political and economic good betrays a lack of renewal, upkeep, investment, and bureaucratic endeavor. Less a metaphor than a daily reality is the index of failed connections, repeated dialings, and interminable waits for repair and service. If private entrepreneurs have been permitted by the state monopoly to erect cell telephone towers and offer mobile telephone service, such telephones may already have made the monopoly obsolete. Even, or particularly, because there is no state to interfere, in a *collapsed* state privately provided cell telephone systems prevail over what might remain of the land-line network, as in Somalia.

When a state has failed or is in the process of failing, the effective educational and health systems are privatized (with a resulting hodgepodge of shady schools and questionable medical clinics in the cities), or the public facilities become increasingly decrepit and neglected. Teachers, physicians, nurses, and orderlies are paid late or not at all, and absenteeism increases. Textbooks and medicines become scarce. X-ray machines break down and are not repaired. Reports to the relevant ministries are ignored. Citizens, especially rural parents, students, and patients, slowly realize that the state has abandoned them to their own devices and to the forces of nature. Sometimes, where a failed state is effectively split, as in the Sudan, essential services may be provided to the favored half, but not to the half in rebellion and engulfed in war. Most of the time the destroyed nation-state completely underperforms. Literacy rates fall, infant mortality rises, the AIDS epidemic overwhelms any health infrastructure that continues to exist, life expectancies plummet, and an already poor and battered citizenry becomes even poorer and more immiserated.

Failed states offer unparalleled economic opportunity—but only for a privileged few. Those around the ruler or the ruling oligarchy grow richer while their less fortunate brethren starve. Immense profits are available from an awareness of regulatory advantages and currency speculation and arbitrage. But the privilege of making real money when everything else is deteriorating is confined to clients of the ruling elite or to especially favored external entrepreneurs. The nation-state's responsibility to maximize the well-being and personal prosperity of all of its citizens is conspicuously absent, if it ever existed.

Corruption flourishes in many states, but in failed states it often does so on an unusually destructive scale. There is widespread petty or lubricating corruption as a matter of course, but escalating levels of venal corruption mark failed states: kickbacks on anything that can be put out to fake tender (medical supplies, textbooks, bridges, roads, and tourism concessions); unnecessarily wasteful construction projects arranged so as to maximize the rents that they generate; licenses for existing and nonexistent activities; and persistent and generalized extortion. In such situations, corrupt ruling elites mostly invest their gains overseas, not at home, making the economic failure of their states that much more acute. Or they dip directly into the coffers of the shrinking state to pay for external aggressions, lavish residences and palaces, extensive overseas travel, and privileges and perquisites that feed their greed. Military officers always benefit from these excessively corrupt regimes and imbibe ravenously from the same illicit troughs as civilian officials.

An indicator of failure, but not a cause of failure, are declining real national and per capita levels of annual GDP. The statistical underpinnings of most states in the developing world are shaky, but failed states—even, or particularly, failed states with vast natural resources—exhibit overall worsening GDP figures, slim year-to-year growth rates, and greater disparities of income between the wealthiest and poorest fifths of their populations. High official state deficits (Zimbabwe's reached more than 30 percent of GDP in 2001) fund extravagant security expenditures and the siphoning of cash by friendly elites. Inflation usually soars because rulers raid the central bank and print money. From the resulting economic insecurity, often engineered by rulers so as to maximize their own fortunes and their own political and economic power, there are many rents to be collected by entrepreneurs connected to the prevailing regime. Smuggling becomes rife. When state failure becomes complete, the local currency falls out of favor and one or more international currencies take its place. Money changers are everywhere, legal or not, and arbitrage becomes a steady international pursuit.

Sometimes, especially if there are intervening climatic disasters, the economic chaos and generalized neglect that is endemic to failed states leads to regular food shortages and widespread hunger—indeed, even to episodes of starvation and major efforts of international humanitarian relief. Natural calamities can overwhelm the resources even of non-failed, but weak, states in the developing world. But when state competencies have consciously been sucked dry by unscrupulous rulers and their cronies, as in failed states, unforeseen natural disasters or man-made wars can drive ignored populations over the edge of endurance into starvation. Once such populations have lost their subsistence plots and their sources of income, they forfeit their homes and their already weak support networks and are forced into an endless cycle of migration and displacement. Failed states provide no safety nets, and the homeless and the destitute become fodder for anyone who can offer food and a cause.

A nation-state also fails when it loses legitimacy—when it forfeits the "mandate of heaven." Its nominal borders become irrelevant. Groups within the nominal borders seek autonomous control within one or more parts of the national territory, or sometimes even across its international borders. Once the state's capacity to secure itself or to perform in an expected manner recedes, and once what little capacity remains is devoted almost exclusively to the fortunes of a few or to a favored ethnicity or community, there is every reason to expect less and less loyalty to the state on the part of the excluded and disenfranchised. When the rulers are perceived to be working for themselves and their kin and not for the state, their legitimacy, and the state's legitimacy, plummets. The state increasingly is conceived as being owned by an exclusive class or group, with all others pushed aside. The social contract that binds inhabitants to an overarching polity becomes breached. Various sets of citizens cease trusting the state. Citizens then naturally turn more and more to the kinds of sectional and community loyalties that are their main recourse in time of insecurity and their main default source of economic opportunity. They transfer their allegiances to clan and group leaders, some of whom become warlords. These warlords or other local strongmen can derive support from external as well as indigenous supporters. In the wilder, more marginalized corners of failed states, terror can breed along with the prevailing anarchy that naturally accompanies state breakdown and failure.

A *collapsed* state is a rare and extreme version of a failed state. Political goods are obtained through private or ad hoc means. Security is equated with the rule of the strong. A collapsed state exhibits a vacuum of authority. It is a mere geographical expression, a black hole into which a failed polity has fallen. There is dark energy, but the forces of entropy have overwhelmed the radiance that hitherto provided some semblance of order and other vital political goods to the inhabitants (no longer the citizens) embraced by language or ethnic affinities or borders. When Somalia failed in the late 1980s, it soon collapsed. Bosnia, Lebanon, and Afghanistan collapsed more than a decade ago, and Nigeria and Sierra Leone collapsed in the 1990s. When those collapses occurred, substate actors took over, as they always do when the prime polity disappears. Those warlords or substate actors gained control over regions and subregions within what had been a nation-state, built up their own local security apparatuses and mechanisms, sanctioned markets and other trading arrangements, and even established an attenuated form of international relations. By definition illegitimate and unrecognized, warlords can assume the trappings of a new quasi state, such as the internationally unrecognized Somaliland in the old north of Somalia. Despite the parceling out of the collapsed state into warlord fiefdoms, there still is a prevalence of disorder, anomic behavior, and the kinds of anarchic mentality and entrepreneurial endeavors—especially gun and drug trafficking—that are compatible with external networks of terror.

None of these designations is terminal. Lebanon, Nigeria, and Tajikistan recovered from collapse and are now weak. Afghanistan and Sierra Leone graduated from collapsed to failed. Zimbabwe is moving rapidly from being strong toward failure. Although a state like Haiti is termed endemically weak, most categorizations are snapshots. The quality of failed or collapsed is real, but need not be static. Failure is a fluid halting place, with movement forward to weakness and backward into collapse always possible. Certainly, too, because failure and collapse are undesirable results for states, they are neither inevitable nor unavoidable. Whereas weak states fail much more easily than strong ones, that failure is not preordained. Failure is preventable, particularly since human agency rather than structural flaws or institutional insufficiencies are almost invariably at the root of slides from weakness (or strength) toward failure and collapse.

Lebanon's experience is instructive. As Oren Barak suggests, the inability of Lebanon's feuding sectoral leaders to adapt a 1943 power-sharing agreement to altered political and social circumstances brought the divided state to its knees. During the nation's civil war of the mid-1970s, it collapsed. But once a cease-fire had been forged in 1990 and a new political compromise achieved through international mediation and the formal acceptance of Syria as a neighborhood hegemon, Lebanon could be revived as a functioning state, and slowly reconstructed. Without guarantees of human security, and the cooperation of dueling leaders, which Syria compelled, any resuscitation of the post-collapse Lebanese state would have proven impossible.[4]

Contemporary State Failure, Collapse, and Weakness

This decade's failed states are Afghanistan, Angola, Burundi, the Congo, Liberia, Sierra Leone, and the Sudan.[5] These seven states exemplify the criteria of failure sketched out above. Somalia is a collapsed state. Together they are the contemporary classical failed and collapsed states, but others were once collapsed or failed and many other modern nation-states now approach the brink of failure, some much more ominously than others. Another group of states drifts disastrously downward from weak to failing to failed. What is of particular interest is why and how states slip from weakness toward failure, or not. The list of weak states is long, but only a few of those weak and poorly governed states need necessarily edge into failure. Why? Even the categorization of a state as failing—Colombia and Indonesia, among others—need not doom it irretrievably to full failure. What does it take to drive a failing state over the edge into failure or collapse? Why did Somalia not stop at failure rather than collapsing?

These questions are answered in the country chapters that follow this opening essay. Because separate discussions of five failed and collapsed states are followed by examinations of seven weak states, two of which were once collapsed states, there is a wealth of empirical material on which to discriminate between the several categories of statehood in the developing world. Of the failed and collapsed cases, not each one fully fills all of the cells of the matrix of nation-state failure. However, to qualify for failure a state needs to demonstrate that it has met most of the explicit criteria. How truly minimal are the roads, the schools, and the hospitals and clinics? How far have GDP and other economic indicators fallen? How far does the ambit of the central government reach? Has the state lost legitimacy? Most important, because civil conflict is decisive for state failure, can the state in question still secure its borders and guarantee security to its citizens, urban and rural?

Walter Clarke and Robert Gosende ask how Somalia, a nation-state of about 9 million people with a strongly cohesive cultural tradition, a common language, a common religion, and a shared history of nationalism could fail, and then collapse. Perhaps, they say, it never constituted a single coherent territory, having been part of the colonial empires of two suzerains, with other Somalis living outside the boundaries of the two colonies. Then, as was often the experience elsewhere in Africa and Asia, the first elected, proto-democratic, post-independence civilian governments proved to be "experimental, inefficient, corrupt, and incapable of creating any kind of national political culture."[6] General Mohammed Siad Barre, commander of the army, decided that the politicians were ruining the country, so he usurped power in 1969, suspending the constitution, banning political parties, and promising an end to corruption. Twenty years and many misadventures later, Siad Barre had succeeded in destroying any semblance of national governmental legitimacy. Backed first by the Soviet Union and then by the United States, Siad Barre destroyed institutions of government and democracy, abused his citizens' human rights, channeled as many of the resources of the state as possible into his own and his subclan's hands, and deprived everyone else at the end of the Cold War of what was left of the spoils of Somali supreme rule. All of the major clans and subclans, other than Siad Barre's own, became alienated. His shock troops perpetrated one outrage after another against fellow Somalis. By the onset of civil war in 1991, the Somali state had long since failed. The civil war destroyed what was left, and Somalia collapsed onto itself.

The chapters on three failed states offer further exemplifications of the Somali theme. In each, a series of fateful decisions by rulers and ruling cadres eviscerated the capabilities of the state, separated the government from its subjects, created opposition movements and civil warfare, and ultimately ended the Potemkin pretense of international stature. William Reno shows how President Stevens (1968–1985) systematically reduced human security within Sierra Leone so as to maximize his own personal power, and how that increase in personal power permitted a quantum leap in his control over the country's rents and riches. Stevens "sold chances to profit from disorder to those who could pay for it through providing services."[7] He created a private military force to terrorize his own people and to aggrandize, especially in the diamond fields. As the official rule of law receded, the law of the jungle, presided over by Stevens, took its place. Institutions of government were broken or corrupted. The state became illegitimate, and a civil war over spoils, encouraged and assisted from outside, turned failure into a collapse. In 2002, after hideous atrocities, a brutal intervention by a West African peace enforcement contingent, much more war, and the arrival of British paratroopers and a large UN peacekeeping force, Sierra Leone recovered sufficiently to be considered failed rather than collapsed. It even held effective elections.

Mobutu used analogous tactics in the patrimony of Zaire. As his people's self-proclaimed *guide*, or as the personalist embodiment of national leadership during the Cold War, he deployed the largesse of his American and other Western patrons to enhance his personal wealth, to heighten his stature over his countrymen, and to weave a tightly manipulated web of loyalties across the army and into all aspects of Zairese society. Every proper political and democratic institution was an obstacle to the edifice that he created. So was civil society, politics itself in the broad sense, and economic development. Letting the country's Belgian-built infrastructure rot, maintaining a colonial type of resource extraction (of copper, other metals, and diamonds), rebuffing the rise of a real bourgeoisie, and feeding his people false glories instead of real substance and per capita growth accentuated his own power, wealth, and importance. As with Stevens and Siad Barre, the modernizing state was the enemy.

Mobutu had no sense of noblesse oblige. René Lemarchand says that for Mobutu's state, patronage was the indispensable lubricant. Ultimately, however, "the lubricant ran out and the Mobutist machine was brought to a . . . standstill. . . . The inability of the Mobutist state to generate a volume of rewards consistent with its clientelistic ambitions is the key . . . [to] . . . its rapid loss of legitimacy."[8]

The warring divisions of the failed Sudanese state, north and south, reflect fundamental ethnic, religious, and linguistic differences; Egyptian and British conquest and colonial administrative flaws and patterns; post-independence disparities and discriminations (the north dominating the south); and the discovery of oil in the south. A weak state in the north, providing political goods at minimal levels for its mostly Muslim constituents, became the nucleus of a truly failed state when its long war with the south (from 1955 to 1972 and from 1983 through 2002) entered the equation. The Sudanese war has the dubious distinction of having inflicted the largest number of civilian casualties (over 2 million) in any intrastate war, coupled with the largest internally displaced and refugee population in the world (about 4 million). Slavery (north against south) flourishes, as well. Moreover, in the south, the central government's writ rarely runs. It provides no political goods to its southern citizens, bombs them, raids them, and regards black southerners as enemy. As a result, the Sudan has long been failed. Yet, northerners still regard their state as legitimate, even though the southern insurgents do not and have sought either secession or autonomy for decades. As Gérard Prunier and Rachel Gisselquist suggest, however, so long as oil revenues shore up the north, the Sudan is unlikely to collapse entirely.[9] They also suggest that contemporary peace processes are unsustainable.

The paradigm of failure so well explored in the Somali, Sierra Leonean, Congolese, and Sudanese chapters holds equally well, with similar but differently detailed material, in Afghanistan, Angola, Burundi, and Liberia. (Reno's chapter contains material on Liberia.) Indeed, Angola's killing fields and internally displaced circumstances are almost as intense and certainly as destructive as the Sudan's. The wars in Afghanistan, Angola, Burundi, and Liberia have been equally traumatic for ordinary combatants and hapless civilians unwittingly caught up in a vicious and (until 2002 in Angola) interminable battle for resources and power between determined opponents. Burundi's majority-minority war has produced fewer deaths in recent decades, but it continues an enduring contest for primacy that antedates the modern nation-state itself. From birth economically weak and geographically limited, Burundi's capacity to perform has for a decade been fatally crippled by majority-backed insurgencies against autocratic minority-led governments.

Weakness and the Possibility of Failure

Collapsed and failed designate the consequences of a process of decay at the nation-state level. The capacity of those nation-states to perform positively for their citizens has atrophied. But, as the Lebanese and Tajikistani cases show, that atrophy is neither inevitable nor the result of happenstance. For a state to fail is not that easy. Crossing from weakness into failure takes will as well as neglect. Thus, weak nation-states need not tip into failure. Which ones do and which ones do not is the focus of the third section of this book.

There are several interesting cases that indeed test the precision of the distinction between weakness and failure:

Sri Lanka has been embroiled in a bitter and destructive civil war for nineteen years. As much as 15 percent of its total land mass has at times in the last decade been controlled by the rebel Liberation Tigers of Tamil Eeelam (LTTE), a Tamil separatist insurgency. Additionally, the LTTE with relative impunity has been able to assassinate prime ministers, bomb presidents, kill off rival Tamils, and in 2001, even destroy the nation's civil air terminal and main air force base. But, as incapable as the Sinhala-dominated governments of the island have been of putting down the LTTE rebellion, so the nation-state has remained merely weak (or fragmented, as Jenne's chapter posits), never close to tipping over into failure. For 80 percent of Sri Lankans, the government performs reasonably well. The roads are maintained and schools and hospitals function, to some limited extent even in the war-torn north and east. Since the early 1990s, too, Sri Lanka has exhibited robust levels of economic growth. The authority of successive governments extends securely to the Sinhala-speaking 80 percent of the country, and into the recaptured Tamil areas. For these reasons, despite a consuming internal conflict founded on intense majority-minority discrimination and deprivation and on pronounced ethnic and religious differences, Sri Lanka projects authority throughout much of the country, has suffered no loss of legitimacy among Sinhala, and has successfully escaped failure.

Indonesia is another case of weakness avoiding failure despite widespread insecurity. As the world's largest Muslim nation, its far-flung archipelago harbors separatist wars in Aceh in the west and in Papua (formerly Irian Jaya) in the east, plus large pockets of Muslim-Christian conflict in Ambon and the Maluku islands, Muslim-Christian hostility in northern Sulawesi, and ethnic xenophobic outbursts in Kalimantan. Given all of these conflictual situations, none of which has become less bitter since the end of the Soeharto dictatorship, it would be easy to conclude that Indonesia was approaching failure. Yet, as Michael Malley's chapter argues forcefully, only the insurgents in Aceh and

Papua want to secede and are contesting the state. The several other battles take place within the state, not against it. They do not threaten the integrity and resources of the state in the way that the enduring, but low-level, war in Aceh does. In Aceh and Papua, the government retains the upper hand. Overall, most of Indonesia is still secure. In most of the country the government projects power and authority. It manages to provide most other necessary political goods to most of Indonesia despite dangerous economic and other developments in the post-Soeharto era.

What about Colombia? An otherwise well-endowed, prosperous, and ostensibly stable state controls only two-thirds of its territory, a clear hint of failure. Three private armies project their own power across large zones carved out of the very body of the state. The official defense and political establishment has renounced or lost authority in those zones to insurgent groups and drug traffickers. Moreover, Colombia is tense and disturbed. It boasts the second highest annual per capita murder rate in the world. Its politicians and businessmen routinely wear armored vests and travel with well-armed guards, a clear indicator of the state's inability to ensure personal security. Even so, as Harvey Kline's chapter argues, the rest of Colombia as a state still delivers schooling and medical care, organizes a physical and communications infrastructure, provides economic opportunity, and remains legitimate. Colombia is weak because of its multiple insurgencies, but is comparatively strong and well-performing in the areas over which it maintains control. When and if the government of Colombia can re-insert itself into the disputed zones and further reduce the power of drug traffickers, the state's reach will expand. Then, a weak, endangered state will be able to move farther away from possible failure toward strength.

Zimbabwe is an example of a once unquestionably strong African state that has fallen rapidly through weakness to the very edge of the abyss of failure. All Zimbabwe lacks in order to join the ranks of failed states is a widespread internal insurgent movement directed against the government. That could come, particularly if the political and economic deterioration of the country continues unchecked. In 2000 and 2001, GDP per capita slid backward by 10 percent a year. Inflation galloped from 30 percent to 116 percent. The local currency fell against the U.S. dollar from 38:1 to 500:1. Foreign and domestic investment ceased. Unemployment rose to 60 percent in a country of 12 million. Health and educational services vanished. HIV infection rates climbed to 30 percent, with about 2000 Zimbabweans dying every week. Respect for the rule of law was badly battered and then subverted. Political institutions ceased to function fully. Agents of the state preyed on its real and its supposed opponents, chilling free expression and shamelessly stealing a presidential election. The government's legitimacy vanished. Corruption, meanwhile, flourished, with the ruling elite pocketing their local and Congolese war gains and letting most Zimbabweans go hungry. Real starvation appeared in mid-2002, despite food aid from abroad. All of this misery, and the tendency to fail, resulted (as it had earlier in the Congo and Sierra Leone) from the ruthless designs and vengeance of an omnipotent ruler.

Indonesia, Colombia, Sri Lanka, and Zimbabwe are but four among a large number of early twenty-first century nation-states at risk of failing. They each escape the category failed, but only for the time being, and only if they each manage to arrest their descent toward economic and political failure, accommodate their insurgency or insurgencies, and strengthen their delivery of political goods to all, or almost all, of their citizens. Tajikistan, examined in Nasrin Dadmehr's chapter, is a fifth state that harbors the possibility of failure, in this case, renewed failure. From 1992 to 1997, the government of Tajikistan projected power only in selected parts of the ramshackle nation; across vast areas, there was no government, war raged, and "the state lost its meaning."[10] Then Russia exerted itself in its former colony, claiming that its own security remained at risk because of lawlessness there. From 1999, Russia reinforced its major base in Tajikistan and increasingly became a force for stability against internal dissidence, as well as a buffer for the Tajikistan government against Taliban- and Uzbek-inspired adventurism. In this century, Russia has become the guarantor of Tajikistan's integrity.

A number of other nation-states belong in the category of weak states that show a high potential to fail. Nepal has been a clear case since its Maoist insurgency began again roiling the mountains and plains of the monarchist country. Already hindered by geography and poverty, Nepal has never been a robust provider of political goods to its inhabitants. The palace massacre of 2001 undermined the legitimacy of the monarchy, and thus of the ruling government. With the flare-up of a determined rural rebellion in 2002, and Nepal's demonstrated inability to cope effectively, security of persons and of regions became harder and harder to achieve, absent military assistance from India. Under these circumstances, Nepal can hardly project power or credibility. Failure becomes a distinct possibility.

So the potential for failure exists in those highly regimented states, such as Iraq and North Korea, that could implode as soon as a dictator or a dictatorial regime is toppled. Because, as Jenne suggests, such states are held together entirely by repression and not by performance, an end to or an easing of repression could create destabilizing battles for succession, resulting anarchy, and the rapid rise of non-state actors. In nation-states made secure by punishment and secret intelligence networks, legitimacy is likely to vanish whenever the curtain of control lifts.

Kyrgyzstan, Côte d'Ivoire, Kenya, and Nigeria all fit near Nepal on the continuum of weakness tending toward failure. Kyrgyzstan, with limited resources and arbitrary rule, has contended with a sharply contracted economy, poverty, and two forms of militant insurgency. Those militant rivals for power remain, respect for human rights and democratic processes has slipped, and Kyrgyzstan's ability to emerge from inherited weakness is questionable, even given the creation of a U.S. airbase and the arrival of free-spending Americans. Kenya is about to come to the alleged end of twenty-five years of single-man rule. Although Kenya is intrinsically wealthy, its fortunes have been badly managed, corruption is rampant, and a gang of ethnically specific thugs has distorted the rule of law, limited the supply of political goods, battered civil society and human rights, and privileged related ethnic minorities against larger, more central, but now marginalized ethnicities. Battles royal for spoils in the post-Moi era could lead to clashes between ethnic groups. A righting of scores could readily plunge Kenya into failure.

Nigeria is a democracy under President Olusegun Obasanjo, but the historic rivalries between east and west, south and north, oil-states and non-oil provinces, Christian and Muslim communities, democrats and autocrats, and soldiers and citizens that have bedeviled Africa's most populous state since independence in 1960 (and before) are still there, seething below a surface calmed or smoothed by the presence of Obasanjo. Military dictators could reemerge, intercommunal conflict could readily reoccur, and the north-south divide could once again become an obstacle to strengthening a state already softened by economic confusion, continued corruption, and mismanagement. Nigeria also performs poorly as a state, and provides political goods adequately at best across the vast mélange of poor and rich provinces that make up its little-unified and very unglued whole. Competition during the national election in 2003 could readily loosen the already tattered ties that keep Nigeria whole.

Other weak states that contain the incubus of failure because of serious intercommunal antagonisms but have managed effectively to come to terms with or to bridge their divisions include Fiji, as described fully in Stephanie Lawson's chapter; New Guinea; the Solomon Islands; Lebanon, as discussed in Barak's chapter; the Philippines; Bolivia; Ecuador; and Paraguay.

Lebanon had disintegrated almost entirely before Syria's intervention enabled the geographical expression that Lebanon had always represented to become a state once again, and to begin to function internally and internationally. Syria gave a sense of governmental legitimacy to what had been a bombed out shell of a polity. Lebanon today qualifies as weak rather than failed, because its state is credible, civil war is absent, and political goods are being provided in significant quantities and quality. Syria provides the security blanket, denies fractious warlords the freedom to aggrandize, and mandates cooperation between the usually antagonistic Muslim and Christian communities and between the battling groups within the Muslim community. The fear of being attacked preemptively by rivals, or losing control of critical resources, is alleviated by Syria's imposed hegemony. Within that framework of supplied security, Lebanon's traditional entrepreneurial spirit has transformed a failed state into a much stronger one.

Unlike many of the weak states discussed herein, Fiji is palpably a strong state. Yet it has become weak, being acutely "vulnerable to more serious failure in terms of its capacity to provide a secure social, political, and economic environment" for its two main antagonistic constituent peoples. Despite seventeen years of relatively stable post-colonial rule, Fiji experienced two coups in 1987 and another in 2000. Fiji, once considered a bastion of the rule of law in the Pacific, became a state with worrying centrifugal tendencies. Its weakness stemmed from ethnic rivalries, and the realization that democratic politics and constitutional processes were insufficient to bridge existing cleavages. Conflict and coups were propelled by unresolved fears among ethnic elites. Until those fears can be reduced, Fiji remains weak as a state and potentially prone (like the Solomon Islands) to renewed challenges to the state's authority and legitimacy.[11]

A third variety of weak state includes the enduringly weak. As the chapter by Marlye Gélin-Adams and David Malone suggests, Haiti has always been on the edge of failure, particularly during the nineteenth and twentieth centuries. But its entrenched weaknesses include no ethnic, religious, or other communal cleavages. There are no insurgent movements. Nor has Haiti experienced radical or rapid deflation in standards of living and national expectations, like Argentina in 2002 and Russia in the 1990s. Haiti has always been the poorest polity in the Western hemisphere.

Haiti's national capacity to provide political goods has always been compromised by autocratic and corrupt leadership, weak institutions, an intimidated civil society, high levels of crime, low GDP levels per capita, high rates of infant mortality, suspicion or outright hostility from its neighbors, and many other deficiencies. Narcotics trafficking has been a serious problem since the 1980s. The Haitian government has been unable or unwilling to interdict smugglers in general, and drugs transshippers in particular. Haiti, even under President Jean-Bertrand Aristide (1990–1991, 1994–1995, 2000–), is gripped in a vise of weakness. Yet, given very limited organized internal dissidence, almost no internal ethnic, religious, or linguistic cleavages within Haitian society except a deep distrust by the majority of the upper classes, and of mulattos because of their historic class affiliations, the ingredients of major civil strife are absent. Failure demands communal differences capable of being transformed into consuming cross-group violence. Haiti seems condemned to remain weak, but without failing.

Nation-states that, given their geographical and physical legacy (and future peril, in several cases, because of global warming and cataclysmic climatic change), can be considered inherently weak include (not a full list) Burkina Faso, Chad, Ghana, Guinea, and Niger, in Africa; Georgia and Moldova in the former Soviet Union, and Cambodia, East Timor, and Laos in Asia.[12] Each has its own distinguishing features, and Georgia and Moldova battle their own so far successful separatist movements. Chad at one time harbored a vicious civil war, and Burkina Faso, Niger, Cambodia, and Laos are all ruled by autocrats unfriendly to civil society and to participatory governance. East Timor is a very new state, having been rescued and resuscitated by the United Nations after two bitter and unrewarding colonial interludes and a brutal final Indonesian spree of destruction and death. East Timor, even with UN help, enters its full majority without a cadre of experienced professionals and bureaucrats and without much in the way of physical resources. The willingness of these weak states to provide political goods in quantity and quality is severely limited at the best of times. Almost any external shock or internal emergency could push them over the brink.

Indicators of Failure

As this chapter has suggested earlier, the road to nation-state failure is littered with serious mistakes of omission and commission. Even in the modern states with inherited weaknesses, failure is not preordained. Poor, arbitrary, absent-minded creations predisposed to failure need not fail. Indeed, Botswana, dirt poor at independence and a forlorn excuse for a state, under determined and visionary leadership created a state strong enough to take full advantage of a subsequent, and much unexpected, resource bonanza. Similarly, a sugar monoculture like Mauritius was transformed by determined visionary leadership into a thriving plural society based on manufacturing for export. In contrast, Malawi and Mali (two examples among many) remain weak and very poor, albeit democratic, having both been unable, in their different circumstances, to overcome the arbitrary configuration of their borders, a common absence of easily exploitable resources, geographical hindrances, and decades of despotism. Climatic change may hit both Malawi and Mali particularly hard, too.

Nation-states are blessed or cursed by the discovery or absence of natural resources, like oil or diamonds, within received borders. But it is not the accidental quality of their borders that is the original flaw; it is what has been made of the challenges and opportunities of a given outline that determines whether a state remains weak, becomes stronger, or slides toward failure and collapse. The colonial errors were many, especially the freeing of Africa south of the Sahara as forty-eight administrative territories instead of six or seven larger ones, and the abysmal failure to transfer the reins of authority much earlier and much more thoroughly to an indigenat. But it is not possible to predict this century's candidates for failure solely or even largely on the basis of colonial mistreatment.

Nor is it possible successfully to deploy the results of massive surveys of conflict and state collapse to predict failure. Esty et al. analyzed ethnic war leading to collapse, including 12 full collapses in 40 years and 243 "partial" state failures, conflicts, and crises between 1955 and 1994, but only in states larger than 0.5 million.[13] They called state failure and collapse "new labels for a type of severe political crisis exemplified by events of the early 1990s in Somalia, Bosnia, Liberia, and Afghanistan. In these instances the institutions of the central state were so weakened that they could no longer maintain authority or political order beyond the capital city. . . ."[14]

Three strong indicators emerged from their work (of seventy-five highly relevant variables): failure was likely when a nation-state favored a closed economic system—when openness to international trade was low or nonexistent; when infant mortality rates (a proxy measure for a society's quality of life) were high, that is, when the ratio of infant deaths per 1,000 live births rose above the international median; and when a nation-state was undemocratic, for lack of democracy feeds on itself. Esty et al. also concluded that GDP per capita levels were almost as robust an indicator of failure as infant mortality levels.

Unhappily, even though it is not implausible that high infant mortality rates are "associated with risk of state failure," for practical predictive purposes rises in infant mortality lag too far behind political and economic changes that, by themselves, are reasonable indicators of a propensity to fail. Likewise, as Esty et al. admit, infant mortality was a better indicator for democracies prone to failure than it was for less democratic cases—as this book shows, the more pressing category of states likely to fail. Closed economic systems, as in the extreme case of Burma after 1968, also predispose to failure; however, rapid falls in GDP per capita, purchasing power, domestic investment rates, and the like are surer and more readily apparent results and indicators of the possibility of failure. Esty et al. also report that trade openness works better for the less democratic regimes. As for the democracy indicator, Esty et al.'s findings are mostly tautological: a downward spiral of democracy obviously tends toward failure and, as they write, "partial democracies [especially in Africa] are indeed far more vulnerable to state failure-type crises than are either full democracies or autocracies."[15] The findings of this book dispute the very last point, but that difference may arise because the Esty et al. definition of failure is much narrower (being confined to wars, adverse regime transitions, genocides, and politicides) than the one used in this book. Furthermore, it is because democratic states respond to popular discontent and accommodate dissident political challenges while maintaining normative and institutional inhibitions against massive human rights violations that they fail to fail. Failing and failed states do not respond or accommodate effectively. That is what failure is about.

Three kinds of signals of impending failure—economic, political, and deaths in combat—provide clearer, more timely, and more actionable warnings. On the economic front, Indonesia in 1997–1999, Nigeria in 1993–1999, Lebanon in 1972–1979, and Zimbabwe in 2001–2002, each provide instances of how rapid reductions in incomes and living standards indicated the possibility of failure early enough to be noted and for preventive measures to have been attempted. Once the downward spiral starts in earnest, only a concerted, determined effort can slow its momentum; corrupt autocrats and their equally corrupt associates usually have few incentives to arrest their state's slide, since they find clever ways to benefit from impoverishment and misery. As foreign and domestic investment dries up, jobs vanish, and per capita incomes fall, the mass of citizens in an imperiled state see their health, educational, and logistical entitlements melt away. Food and fuel shortages occur. Privation and hunger follow, especially if a climatic catastrophe intervenes. Thanks to foreign exchange scarcities, there is less and less of everything that matters. Meanwhile, in the typical failing state, ruling families and cadres arrogate to themselves increasing portions of the available pie. They systematically skim the state treasury, take advantage of official versus street costs of foreign exchange, partake of smuggling and the rents of smuggling, and gather what little is available into their own sticky palms. If it were possible reliably to calibrate the flow of illicit funds into overseas accounts, nation by nation, robust early warnings would be available. Absent detailed reports of such theft, the descriptors in this paragraph become very suggestive indicators that can be watched, in real time, and can forecast serious trouble, if not an end state of failure.

Politically, the available indicators are equally clear, if somewhat less quantifiably precise. A leader and his associates begin by subverting democratic norms, greatly restricting participatory processes, and coercing a legislature and the bureaucracy into subservience. They end judicial independence, block civil society, and suborn the security forces. Political goods become scarce or are supplied to the leading class only. The rulers demonstrate more and more contempt for their peoples, surround themselves with family, clan, or ethnic allies, and distance themselves from their subjects. The state becomes equated in the eyes of most citizens with the particular drives and desires of a leader and a smallish group. Many of these leaders drive grandly down their boulevards in motorcades, commandeer commercial aircraft for foreign excursions, and put their faces prominently on the local currency, on airports and ships, and on oversize photographs in public places.

The third indicator is the level of violence. If it rises precipitously because of skirmishes, hostilities, or outright civil war, the state can be considered crumbling. As national human security rates fall, the probability of failure rises. Not every civil conflict precipitates failure, but each offers a warning sign. Absolute or relative crime rates and civilian combat death counts above a certain number cannot prescribe failure. But they show that a society is deteriorating and that the glue that binds a new (or an old) state together is becoming fatally thin.

No single indicator provides certain evidence that a strong state is becoming weak or a weak state is heading pell-mell into failure. But a judicious assessment of the several available indicators discussed in this section, taken together, should provide both quantifiable and qualitative warnings. Then avoidance maneuvers can occur and efforts at prevention can be mounted.

That said, research on failed states is insufficiently advanced for precise tipping points to be provided. It is not yet correct to suggest that if GDP falls by X amount in a single year, rulers dismiss judges or abuse the human rights of their subjects by X, soldiers take a state house, or civilian death rates rise more than X per year, the state in question will tip for sure from weak to failing to failed. All we know is that all of those actions suggest that all is not well in the depths of Ruritania, misery is spreading, and the future shape and fate of the state is at serious risk.

The Hand of Man

State failure is largely man made, not accidental. Institutional fragilities and structural flaws contribute to failure, but those deficiencies usually hark back to decisions or actions of men (rarely women). So it is that leadership errors across history have destroyed states for personal gain; in the contemporary era, leadership mistakes continue to erode fragile polities in Africa, Asia, and Oceania that already operate on the cusp of failure. Mobutu's kleptocratic rule extracted the marrow of Zaire and left nothing for the mass of his national dependents. Much of the resource wealth of that vast country ended up in his or his cronies' pockets; over four decades, hardly any wealth was devoted to uplifting the Congolese people, improving their welfare, building infrastructures, or even providing more than rudimentary amounts of human security. Mobutu's government performed only for Mobutu, as Lemarchand's chapter so thoroughly documents, not for Zaire.

Likewise, oil-rich Angola remains failed following three decades of war and, within the territory now fully controlled by the government of President Jose Eduardo dos Santos, also because he and his associates have long refused to deliver more than limited political goods to their fellow countrymen.[16] President Stevens decapitated the Sierra Leonean state in order to strengthen his own power amid growing chaos. Sierra Leone, as Reno's chapter describes, has not yet recovered from Stevens's depredations. Nor has Liberia been resuscitated in the aftermath of the slashing neglect and unabashed greed of Samuel Doe, Prince Johnson, and Charles Taylor, which Reno also discusses. In Somalia, as Clarke and Gosende show, Siad Barre arrogated more and more power and privilege to himself and his clan. Finally, there was none left for other pretenders to power and its rewards. The Somali state had been gutted willfully, the abilities of the Somali government to provide political goods endlessly compromised, and the fall into failure and then into full collapse followed inexorably.

President Robert Gabriel Mugabe personally led Zimbabwe from strength to the precipice of failure, his high-handed and seriously corrupt rule having bled the resources of the state into his own pockets, squandered foreign exchange, discouraged domestic and international investment, subverted the courts, and driven his country to the very brink of starvation. In Sri Lanka, Solomon and Sirimavo Bandaranaike, one after the other, drove the LTTE into reactive combat by abrogating minority rights and vitiating the social contract on which the country had been created as Ceylon. In Afghanistan, Gulbuddin Hakmatyar and Burrhan ul-din Rabani tried to prevent Afghans other than their own Pashtun and Tajik fellow nationals from sharing the perquisites of governance; their narrowly focused, self-enriching decisions enabled the Taliban to follow them in triumph and Afghanistan to descend into all-out terror.

Wherever there has been state failure or collapse, human agency has engineered the slide from strength or weakness and willfully presided over profound and destabilizing resource shifts from the state to the ruling few. As those resource transfers accelerated and human rights abuses mounted, countervailing violence signified the extent to which states in question had broken fundamental social contracts and become hollow receptacles of personalist privilege, personalist rule, and national impoverishment. Inhabitants of failed states understand what it means for life to be brutish and short.

In earlier, less interconnected eras, state weakness and failure could be isolated and kept distant from the developed world. Failure once held fewer implications for the surrounding regions and for the peace and security of the globe.

Now, however, as much as their citizens suffer, the failings of states also pose enormous dangers beyond their own borders. Preventing nation-states from failing, and resuscitating those that have failed and will fail, have thus become the critical, all-consuming, strategic and moral imperatives of our terrorized time. The chapters in this book demonstrate how and why states have failed and will fail, and how weak states have in several cases been spared the descent into despair and destruction.

Notes

1. This book and this opening chapter emerged from a five-year project of the World Peace Foundation and Harvard University's Program on Intrastate Conflict on all aspects of state failure. More than forty collaborators, including all of the contributors to this volume, were involved in formulating the direction of the research and in reviewing the conclusions presented in this chapter and in the individual chapters that follow. A companion volume, *When States Fail: Causes and Consequences*, will also appear in 2003. The present chapter draws on concepts developed in my articles "The New Nature of Nation-State Failure," *Washington Quarterly*, XXV (2002), 85–96, and "Failed States in a World of Terror," *Foreign Affairs*, LXXXI (2002), 1–13. With respect particularly to this chapter, I am very appreciative of the helpful and unstinting advice and ideas of Michael Ignatieff, Nelson Kasfir, and Susan Rose-Ackerman.

2. For political goods, see J. Roland Pennock, "Political Development, Political Systems, and Political Goods," *World Politics,* XVIII (1966), 420–426, 433.

3. Some of these points were earlier made by I. William Zartman, "Introduction: Posing the Problem of State Collapse," in idem (ed.), *Collapsed States: The Disintegration and Restoration of Legitimate Authority* (Boulder, 1995), 3. Zartman's overall definition, "Collapse means that the basic functions of the state are no longer performed, as analyzed in various theories of the state" (5), parallels what has been suggested here. This book, however, parses *failed* and *collapsed,* distinguishing them. It also details the "functions," suggesting which ones are critical. The Failed States project at Purdue University defines failed states "by the patterns of governmental collapse within a nation which often bring demands (because of the refugees they foster, the human rights they abridge and their inability to forestall starvation and disease) which threaten the security of their surrounding states and region." The Purdue definition appears much less specific than the one employed herein. For the Failed States website at Purdue University, see www.ippu.purdue.edu/failed_states. Earlier, Gerald B. Helman and Steven R. Ratner, "Saving Failed States," *Foreign Policy*, LXXXIX (winter 1992–93), 3, defined failed nation-states as entities "utterly incapable of sustaining" themselves as members of the international community. Civil strife, government breakdown, and economic privation were proximate causes of state failure.

4. Oren Barak, "Lebanon: Failure, Collapse, and Resuscitation," chapter 12 in this volume, 305–339.

5. In 1995, Jennifer Widner suggested that the same states, plus Chad, Togo, and Congo-Brazzaville, had experienced "the collapse of political order" and authority had "disintegrated completely into civil war." Widner, "State and Statelessness in Late Twentieth-Century Africa," *Daedalus,* CXXIV (1995), 136–137.

6. Walter Clarke and Robert Gosende, "Somalia: Can a Collapsed State Reconstitute Itself," chapter 5 in this volume, 129–158.

7. William Reno, "Sierra Leone: Warfare in a Post-State Society," chapter 3 in this volume, 75.

8. René Lemarchand, "The Democratic Republic of the Congo: From Failure to Potential Reconstruction," chapter 2 in this volume, 37.

9. Gérard Prunier and Rachel Gisselquist, "The Sudan: A Successfully Failed State," chapter 4 in this volume, 101–127.

10. Nasrin Dadmehr, "Tajikistan: Regionalism and Weakness," chapter 9 in this volume, 245.

11. Stephanie Lawson, "Fiji: Divided and Weak," chapter 10 in this volume, 265–288.

12. Timothy Docking, "Responding to War and State Collapse in West Africa" (21 January 2002), a United States Institute of Peace Special Report, calls Guinea a collapsed state.

13. Daniel C. Esty, Jack A. Goldstone, Ted Robert Gurr, Barbara Harff, Marc Levy, Geoffrey D. Dabelko, Pamela T. Surko, and Alan N. Unger, "State Failure Task Force Report: Phase II Findings" (31 July 1998). Earlier, most of the same authors produced "Working Papers: State Failure Task Force Report" (30 November 1995). The Esty et al. definition of failure in both versions of the report is much narrower than the definition used in this book.

14. Daniel C. Esty et al., "The State Failure Project: Early Warning Research for U.S. Foreign Policy Planning," paper on the Failed States website, Purdue University (West Lafayette, February 25–27, 1998).

15. Esty et al, "State Failure Task Force Report" (1998), 9.

16. IMF report on Angola, cited in Justin Pearce, "IMF: Angola's 'Missing Millions,'" BBC News (18 October 2002), http://news.bbc.co.uk/2/hi/world/africa/2338669.stm; Global Witness report, "All the President's Men" (2002), cited in "West 'Creates' Conditions for Corruption," BBC News (25 March 2002), http://news.bbc.co.uk/2/hi/business/1892790.stm; "The Oil Diagnostic in Angola: An Update," Human Rights Watch (March 2001), www.hrw.org/backgrounder/africa/angola/index.htm.

PART ONE

Cases of Failure and Collapse

The Democratic Republic of the Congo: From Failure to Potential Reconstruction

RENÉ LEMARCHAND

The African continent is littered with the wreckage of imploded polities. From Guinea Bissau to Burundi, from Congo-Brazzaville to Congo-Kinshasa, from Sierra Leone to Guinea and Côte d'Ivoire, failed or failing states confront us with an all too familiar litany of scourges—civil societies shot to bits by ethno-regional violence, massive flows of hapless refugees across national boundaries, widespread environmental disasters, rising rates of criminality, and the utter bankruptcy of national economies.

In its most recent avatar—the Democratic Republic of the Congo (DRC)—this former Belgian colony was not just a failed state in 2002; it was the epitome of the failed state, whose descent into hell has loose a congeries of rival factions fighting proxy wars on behalf of six African states. In a sense, stateless-ness conveys a more realistic picture of the rampant anarchy in many parts of the country. Carved into four semi-autonomous territorial enclaves, three of which were under the sway of rebel movements, it was the most fragmented and violent battleground in the continent. The scale of human losses was staggering. According to the International Rescue Committee, the death toll since 1998 could be as high as 3 million. In comparative terms this is roughly the equivalent of the human losses of 11 September on a daily basis over a three-year period. Meanwhile, disease, starvation, and homelessness were said to have affected 16 million out of a total population of approximately 50 million.[1] The economy was in ruins, with approximately half of the country's mineral wealth mortgaged to President Joseph Kabila's allies, the other half looted by invaders.

There is no precedent for the multiplicity of external forces involved in the destruction of the state and the plundering of the country's human, economic, and environmental resources. In 2001, at least six states were militarily involved, officially or unofficially: Rwanda, Uganda, and Burundi on the side of the rebellion, and Angola, Zimbabwe, and Namibia on the side of the Kabila government in Kinshasa. Putting the pieces back together was all the more problematic because of the extent to which intervenors were using the chaos to serve their own interests. Even though their objectives may have differed, each had a stake in perpetuating the breakup of the state.

The two key players, Rwanda and Uganda, once united in a common crusade against President Mobutu Sese Seko's dictatorship, were in 2002 at daggers drawn over the loot in eastern Congo, in the process dragging their respective client factions into violent turf battles. Born in a suburb of Kigali (Kabuga) in August 1998, with the blessings of Rwandan President Paul Kagame, the Congolese Rally for Democracy (Rassemblement Congolais pour la Démocratie [RCD]) was split into two rival factions: one based in Goma, in North Kivu— the pro-Rwanda RCD-Goma, led by Adolphe Onusumba Yemba; and the other in Bunia, in the Kibali-Ituri province—the pro-Uganda RCD-Bunia, recently led by Ernest Wamba dia Wamba, and in 2002, by Mbusa Nyamisi. Both wings were torn by violent struggles for leadership, confronting their external patrons with difficult choices. Also supported by Uganda, a third rebel movement, led by Jean-Pierre Bemba, the Mouvement de Libération du Congo (MLC)— renamed Front de Libération du Congo (FLC), following its merger with the RCD-Bunia in January 2001—fought pitched battles against Laurent Kabila's rag-tag army in the Equateur province in the north and claimed, implausibly, to control some 900,000 square kilometers "from Zongo on the Ubangi river all the way to Kanyabayonga in North-Kivu."[2] In 2002 approximately half of the DRC was under the fragile control of rebel movements kept alive by substantial infusions of direct military assistance from their respective sponsors. When the Rwanda Patriotic Army (RPA) and the Uganda People's Defense Forces (UPDF) were not fighting each other, the key strategic positions, including those in the border area between Rwanda and Uganda, were held by units of these two forces. The DRC was the only country in Africa with approximately half of its national territory under foreign military occupation.

As if to complicate further the task of reconstruction, foreign-linked factionalism goes far beyond the three rebel movements currently tied to Rwanda and Uganda. A plethora of loosely knit factions have emerged in the interstices of the three-cornered struggle between Kinshasa, Kampala, and Kigali. One group, the Mai-Mai, tactically linked to Kabila, brought together a loose assemblage of local warlords, all vehemently opposed to the RCD-Goma and its

Rwandan patron. Another consisted of Hutu-armed groups from Rwanda and Burundi, the former generally identified with the remnants of Rwanda's militias, the Interahamwe; the latter, with the Burundi-based Forces pour la Défense de la Démocratie (FDD). A third (and more ambivalent) faction, the Forces Républicaines Fédéralistes (FRF), led by Manasse "Muller" Ruhimbika, drew its support from a small segment of the Tutsi community indigenous to South Kivu (the so-called Banyamulenge); while openly critical of the presence of the Rwandan army in the DRC, it can hardly be described as pro-Kabila. In this extraordinarily fluid, deeply fragmented environment, the only glue holding together this disparate group of counterinsurgents was their common hatred of the Rwandan occupying forces and their local allies.

Laurent Kabila's assassination on 16 January 2001, followed by an impromptu transfer of presidential authority to his twenty-nine-year-old son, Joseph, raised further questions. What hidden hand, if any, lay behind the bodyguard's bullet? Kabila père had made enough enemies at home and abroad to be at risk of an attempt on his life. Whether Kabila fils can avoid his father's egregious mistakes—his utter insensitivity to the demands of the civil society, his sheer ruthlessness in dealing with his suspected opponents within and outside the army, his stubborn refusal to implement the Lusaka accords and cavalier dismissal of the UN-appointed facilitator, Sir Ketumile Masire (derisively called the "complicator")—and in time chart a new course toward peace and reconstruction, remains, in 2002, to be seen.

What accounts for the failure of the state in the DRC? Plausible though it is to detect historical continuities between the horrors of the Léopoldian system and Mobutu's brutally exploitative dictatorship, or between the sheer oppressiveness of Belgian rule and the excesses of the successor state, in the last analysis Mobutu himself must be seen as the determining agent behind this vertiginous descent into the abyss.[3] What set Mobutu apart from other neo-patrimonial rulers was his unparalleled capacity to institutionalize kleptocracy at every level of the social pyramid and his unrivaled talent for transforming personal rule into a cult and political clientelism into cronyism.[4] Stealing was not so much a perversion of the ethos of public service as it was its raison d'être. The failure of the Zairian state was thus inscribed in the logic of a system in which money was the only political tool for rewarding loyalty, a system that set its own limitations on the capacity of the state to provide political (public) goods, institutionalize civil service norms, and effectively mediate ethno-regional conflicts.

Only through the concerted efforts of the Western troika—the United States, Belgium, and France—(and after the United States and Belgium had secretly orchestrated the assassination of Patrice Lumumba) could Mobutu come to power and rule the Congo for thirty-two years with such an appalling combination of brutality, cunning, and manipulative perversity.[5] Although the massive infusions of financial assistance from the International Monetary Fund (IMF) and the World Bank contributed in no small way to satisfying Mobutu's incessant demands for cash, once confronted with their reluctance to oblige, it took all of the pressures that the United States could bring to bear on both institutions to ensure that the aid money would keep flowing into Mobutu's private pockets.[6] For decades, maintenance of the state system overruled reason.

Seen through the prism of the crises of the 1990s, the end of the Cold War emerged as a watershed in the unraveling of the Mobutist state. In 1990, after accumulating arrears of $70 million, the IMF, no longer facing U.S. veto, suspended its loans to the country, while other donors cut off their assistance. Mobutu responded to the advent of multiparty democracy by buying off opposition parties. The urgent need for cash was met by printing wads of paper money. Spiraling inflation inevitably followed, driving the economy further into the ground.

From then on the cancer spread rapidly, paralyzing one sector after another. As the delivery of political rewards beyond Kinshasa became increasingly uncertain, the control of the state shrank correspondingly. And when the salaries of the military could no longer be paid, the more disaffected troops took to the streets and went on looting sprees through the capital city, killing hundreds. If internal security was nonexistent, so was the capacity of the state to meet external threats. As the Rwandan army crossed into eastern Congo in October 1996, preparing the ground for Kabila's triumphant march to Kinshasa, the state had already ceased to exist.

On 17 May 1997, eight months after its creation, the victorious Alliance des Forces Démocratiques pour la Libération du Congo (AFDL) marched into Kinshasa. Its spectacular success in carrying the banner of "liberation" to the gates of Kinshasa is a commentary on the extent of disaffection generated by the Mobutist dictatorship; more to the point, it speaks volumes for the degree of institutional paralysis that afflicted the apparatus of the state.

Anatomy of Disaster: Failure, Collapse, and Fragmentation

As the history of the Congo shows, the failure of one set of institutions is not enough to explain systemic collapse. The unraveling of the armed forces in 1964–1965, after the Muleliste insurrection, did not bring about the disintegration of the state. External military assistance, coupled with substantial infusions of financial aid from the United States, made it possible for the state to recover, if only momentarily, from what could have been an insurmountable challenge. By the early 1990s, however, the Congo had lost its strategic significance to the West and the costs of an external rescue operation seemed greatly to outweigh the benefits. At a time when multiparty democracy was in vogue in Africa, bolstering Mobutu's dictatorship had ceased to be a realistic option. Moreover, the multiplicity of opposition forces released by the National Sovereign Conference (CNS) in 1991–1992, and the continuing tug-of-war between the transitional institutions and the Mobutist state, forced donors (primarily France, Belgium, and the United States) to question how best to assist the transition, or indeed whether any assistance, short of military intervention, could make a difference.

Donors' inaction meant a continuing deadlock over the pace and manner of the transition. The resulting paralysis of decision-making mechanisms ushered in one crisis after another. None of the seven prime ministers appointed in 1991 and 1992 proved equal to the task of restoring governmental authority. The economy went into a tailspin when the rate of inflation jumped from 261 percent in 1990 to 6,800 percent in 1994.[7] Mobutu's insistence on printing new paper money against the advice of Prime Minister Etienne Tshisekedi led to the latter's resignation in December 1992. When local traders refused to accept the newly minted 5 million zaire banknotes, several units of the armed forces responded by going on looting sprees through Kinshasa and elsewhere. The most violent and extensive of a series of pillages by the army occurred in January 1993, when devastation spread to several areas in the Lower Congo and the Kivu provinces. Faced with major ethno-regional conflicts in North Kivu and Shaba (now renamed Katanga), by 1993 the Mobutist state had lost all capacity to mediate the crises effectively. Rather than serving as an instrument for the state, the army had become a loose cannon, and at times an active participant in local insurrections. From 1991 to 1993, failure metastasized from one institutional sector to another, reducing the Zairian state to utter impotence.

It is difficult to pinpoint precisely when the Mobutist state failed. In 1992, a senior U.S. diplomat noted that Zaire had all the earmarks of a hollowed-out state.[8] But if failure were already patent in 1992, it did not become conclusive until late 1996, with the destruction of the Hutu refugee camps of eastern Zaire by the Rwandan Patriotic Army and the emergence of Laurent-Désire Kabila as the self-proclaimed leader of the Alliance des Forces Démocratiques pour la Libération du Congo. That it took only six months for the poorly equipped and poorly led anti-Mobutist coalition to reach the gates of Kinshasa demonstrated the weakness of the Zairian Armed Forces (ZAF), rather than the strength of the AFDL.

Mobutu's appalling performance from one crisis to the next suggests the strongest reservations about structural explanations in any attempt to account for the demise of the Zairian state. More than the carryover of the Bula Matari

syndrome into the post-independence years—evocative of underlying historical continuities between the ruthlessness of the Léopoldian regime and the autocratic features of the Mobutist state—Mobutu must be seen as the chief archi-
tect of disaster.[9] Mobutu's unrelenting efforts to thwart democratic opposition
forces, his highly personalized style of rulership, built partly on repression and
partly on extensive patronage networks, his scandalous squandering of the
Congo's wealth, his megalomaniac obsession with grandiose development
schemes at the expense of public goods for the masses, and his pathetic *sauve-
qui-peut* attitude in the face of the relentless march of the AFDL on Kinshasa,
were critical factors in the ultimate collapse of his Bula Matari kingdom.

Herbst's thesis, that state failure in Africa is traceable to the generalized
inability of African states to control their hinterland effectively, owing to the
artificiality of state boundaries combined with low population densities, raises
questions about whether the weakness of the state (as defined in terms of its
ability or inability to raise taxes, to provide public services, or to protect its
citizens) can conceivably be treated as a constant.[10] The convenient "ceteris
paribus" qualifier does not take us very far in our quest for explanation. Even
where the inability of the state to "broadcast power," to use Herbst's terminol-
ogy, is patent, as in the Mobutist state, the significance of intervening variables
cannot be excluded.

Just as we need to recognize that not all state systems are equally vulnerable,
it is no less important to avoid the trap of brute functionalism. In an otherwise
inspiring essay, Zartman makes surprisingly short shrift of what others have
termed "critical junctures," or decisive events, on processes of state collapse.
His use of metaphors is revealing: "What is notable in these scenarios [of state
collapse]," he writes, "is the absence of clear turning points, warning signals,
thresholds or pressure spots. . . . The slippery slope, the descending spiral, and
the downward trend are the marks of state collapse rather than deadlines and
triggers."[11] The least that can be said of this curiously ahistorical construction is
that it is difficult to reconcile with the evidence at hand (not unlike trying to
explain the collapse of the French monarchy without reference to the seizure of
the Bastille, the Tennis Court Oath, or the flight to Varenne . . .). Elsewhere
Zartman asks, "Why do states collapse?" Because, we are told, "they can no
longer perform the functions required for them to pass as states" (not unlike
explaining the death of a patient by saying that he or she could no longer perform the functions required to stay alive).[12]

If triggering events, thresholds, or critical junctures cannot be ignored, neither can the long-term forces of decay and decomposition be dismissed. It is
anybody's guess how much longer the Congolese state could have lasted had it
not been for the decisive blows administered by the Rwandan assault against

refugee camps in October 1996; what is beyond question is that by 1996 the Congolese state was already a pushover, thoroughly undermined by its long-standing prebendal involution, declining legitimacy, and the near disintegration of its armed forces. The crisis of 1996 was the triggering event that brought the state to its knees.

The Regional Context

State collapse is contagious. Although the seeds of failure are inseparable from failed leadership, the risks of disintegration are significantly greater where the proximity of a failing state threatens to contaminate its neighbor. Just as the civil war in Liberia decisively hastened the destruction of Sierra Leone (and vice versa), the flow of refugees generated by the civil strife in Sierra Leone posed a clear and present danger to Guinea. Nowhere, however, is the contagiousness of failure more dramatically illustrated than in the rapid spread of ethnic violence from Rwanda to eastern Congo in the aftermath of the Rwandan genocide. Of the many unanticipated consequences of that bloodbath, none has had more profoundly destabilizing consequences than the massive exodus of over 1 million Hutu refugees across the border into the Kivu provinces of eastern Congo.

To grasp the spin-off effects of the Rwandan carnage, attention must be paid to several features common to the Great Lakes region (Rwanda, Burundi, Uganda, and eastern Congo). One is the absence of coincidence between ethnic and geographic maps. The presence of Tutsi and Hutu communities in Uganda, Tanzania, and eastern Congo bears testimony to the arbitrariness of state boundaries. Although many peoples arrived during and after the colonial era, the Tutsi and Hutu presence reaches back to pre-colonial times. It is estimated that there are approximately 10 million people speaking Kinyarwanda in the Great Lakes region, and 15 million if speakers of Kirundi (a language closely related to Kinyarwanda) are included. In North Kivu alone, about half of the total population of some 3.5 million were identified as Kinyarwanda-speaking in 1993, and of these about 80 percent were Hutu and 20 percent Tutsi. The significance of this regional ethnic configuration is best captured by Huntington's concept of "kin country syndrome," a situation in which ethnic fault lines tend to replicate across national boundaries, thus creating a deadly potential for conflict to expand and escalate.[13]

Another major characteristic is the very high population density and resulting pressure on land throughout the region. Rwanda claims the highest population density in Africa, with Burundi and North Kivu close behind. With an estimated 1 million people in the late nineteenth century, Rwanda claimed 7.6

million on the eve of the genocide, and an average of 336 inhabitants per square kilometer. The figures for North Kivu indicate similar densities in the high-lying areas of the Congo-Nile crest. It is not a coincidence that the most densely populated areas—Masisi and Rutshuru—are also the places where the most intractable land disputes have arisen.[14] Herbst describes a very different situation for most of pre-colonial Africa: "In pre-colonial Africa, land was plentiful and populations thin on the ground. . . . As a result there were few areas where territorial competition was the central political issue because land was plentiful. . . . Control over territory was often not contested because it was often easier to escape from rulers than to fight them."[15] The land issue in North and South Kivu has been, and remains, at the heart of ethnic violence through much of the region.

A third factor relates to the presence of sizable refugee populations from neighboring states. The process began in Rwanda in the early 1960s, when tens of thousands of Tutsi refugees sought asylum in Uganda (70,000), Burundi (60,000), and eastern Congo (22,000). A nightmarish cycle of tit-for-tat ethnic violence followed the cross-border raids of armed refugees into Rwanda, culminating in the massacre of thousands of Tutsi civilians in 1963. That, in turn, caused a further exodus of Tutsi refugees to neighboring states. In Burundi (which, unlike Rwanda, acceded to independence under Tutsi rule) the heightening of tension caused by the presence of Tutsi refugees from Rwanda reached boiling point in 1972, with the genocidal massacre of at least 100,000 Hutu (some say 200,000) at the hands of the all-Tutsi army, again causing the exodus of tens of thousands of Hutu refugees to Rwanda, Tanzania, and eastern Congo (South Kivu).[16]

The most devastating illustration of "refugees as vectors of violence" occurred in eastern Congo in the wake of the Rwandan genocide in 1994, when 1.2 million Hutu refugees poured across the border into North and South Kivu. As many as 100,000 refugees were members of Interahamwe militias and remnants of the Forces Armées Rwandaises (FAR). There was no precedent in the history of the region for such a massive irruption of armed refugees into a host country, or for the seriousness of the threats that they posed to their country of origin. Such exceptional circumstances brought forth an exceptional response from the Rwandan government, in the form of a surgical pre-emptive strike against the refugee camps. The destruction of the camps by the Rwandan Patriotic Army in October 1996 marked a watershed in the decomposition of the Mobutist state. Besides triggering the virtual disintegration of the Congolese Armed Forces (FAC), the search-and-destroy operations conducted by the RPA quickly snowballed into a popular crusade against Mobutu.[17]

From Integral State to Shell State: The Costs of Self-Cannibalization

Intimations of the mortality of the Zairian state were felt long before its downfall. Failure is a relative concept, and so, also, are the challenges posed to a failed state. From the beginning, Mobutu's rule embodied a neo-patrimonial polity. The extreme personalization of authority built around the presidential palace had as its corollary a systematic effort to thwart the development of a responsive and efficient bureaucracy. At no time was an effective institutional mechanism forged for resolving conflicts among competing constituencies. The scale of the challenges posed by the end of the Cold War was more than could be handled by the "lame Leviathan." By the early 1990s, lameness had given way to utter paralysis.[18]

For years after Mobutu's second coming in November 1965, the Zairian state tried to project the image of an all-embracing, hegemonic apparatus, dedicated to transforming the institutions of the state into an engine of development. What Young calls the "integral state" was the ideological hallmark of Mobutu's autocracy.[19] On closer inspection, a different reality emerges. Control over the civil society, though ostensibly mediated through the ruling party, the Mouvement Populaire pour la Révolution (MPR), involved the extension of clientelistic nets to all sectors of society, including the army. As in every patrimonial state, the Mobutist state owed its stability to its capacity to "service" the networks; patronage was the indispensable lubricant of the state machinery. Eventually, however, the lubricant ran out and the Mobutist machine was brought to near standstill. By 1975, Mobutu was faced with a catastrophic decline of his sources of revenue. Copper prices plummeted, debt servicing increased dramatically, and the megalomaniac projects destined to usher in economic prosperity—the Inga-Shaba power line, the Makulu steel mill, the Tenge-Fugurume copper mines—proved unmitigated disasters. The inability of the Mobutist state to generate a volume of rewards consistent with its clientelistic ambitions is the key element behind its rapid loss of legitimacy.

With the end of the Cold War the integral state came to look more and more like a "shell state."[20] The erosion of state capacity increased in proportion to Mobutu's growing inability to keep up the flow of external funding from donors, leading in turn to a further shrinkage of patronage networks. The result set in motion a process of involution centered around a handful of venal, rent-seeking cronies. What Young has described as "self-cannibalization" vividly captures the hollowing out of state institutions under Mobutu's prebendal rule.[21]

For a quarter of a century, the Mobutist state was able to compensate for its lack of internal legitimacy by drawing huge dividends from its international status as the United States' staunchest ally in Africa. As has been noted time and again, what one French official described as "a walking bank account in a leopard-skin cap" was a creature of the U.S. Central Intelligence Agency (CIA). The end of the Cold War sharply increased the Congo's international isolation and legitimacy deficit; bartering its anti-communist credentials for external assistance was no longer a feasible option. Just as Mobutu owed his rise to power to the penetration of East-West rivalries in the continent, the collapse of the Zairian state must be seen as a casualty of the Cold War's end.

Trajectories of Collapse: Thresholds and Triggers

By any of the conventional yardsticks—declining institutional performance, military indiscipline, harassment of civilians, inability to collect taxes, and governmental spending on public services, notably health and education—Zaire in the early 1990s stood at the top of the list of Africa's failed states. By then, three basic indicators of failure mapped out the road to failure: (1) a sharp decline of institutional capabilities, matched by a corresponding lack of responsiveness to the demands of the citizenry for "more democracy"; (2) widespread indiscipline and looting of private property by the armed forces and the police; and (3) major eruptions of civil violence, notably in Shaba (1992–1993) and North Kivu (1993).

Each of the foregoing, in turn, draws attention to certain critical junctures or thresholds in the decomposition of the state: (1) the (dis)organization of the CNS in 1991, and the rise of multiparty competition; (2) the looting sprees of the army and presidential guard in 1993, marking the virtual dissolution of the state's "legitimate monopoly of force"; and (3) the North Kivu emergency of 1993.

The CNS and the Aborted Transition to Multiparty Democracy

Yielding to domestic and international pressures, in April 1990 Mobutu formally announced the advent of "political reform" and the opening of multiparty competition; a year later the CNS met in Kinshasa to lay the constitutional groundwork for multiparty democracy. Bringing together some 3,400 representatives of political parties and members of the civil society, the aim was to lay the groundwork for a reconfiguration of the state, but, as one observer noted, "it dramatically accelerated its disintegration."[22]

The conference made clear Mobutu's determination to use "divide and rule" strategies to pull the rug from under the feet of the main opposition forces, notably Tshisekedi's Union pour le Progrès Social et la Démocratie (UPSD).

Mobutu's talent for buying off members of the opposition and bankrolling the birth of friendly factions led to a phenomenal proliferation of political parties. More than 200 parties were registered at the end of the year. Meanwhile, the volume of cash funneled into floating satellite parties translated into a further shrinking of public spending on social services, while seriously compromising the chances of a broad consensus among participants at the conference.

The imperative of divide and rule inexorably encouraged the rise of local and regional fiefdoms and the entrenchment of pro-Mobutu forces in some provincial arenas, as in Shaba, where Karl I. Bond's Union des Fédéralistes et Républicains Indépendents (UFERI) soon emerged as the staunchest opponent of Tshisekedi's UPSD, and in South Kivu, where pro-Mobutu politicians, mostly of Bembe origins, took systematic steps to denigrate and deny rights of citizenship to long-established communities of ethnic Tutsi—the so-called Banyamulenge. The same scenario could be seen in North Kivu, where Tutsi "59ers" (refugees of the 1959–1962 revolution in Rwanda) were openly branded as "foreigners" working hand in hand with the Rwanda Patriotic Front (RPF) guerillas in neighboring Rwanda. Under the pretense of the "géopolitique" argument set forth by Mobutu's client parties—whereby positions of authority in the provincial administration should be reserved for those originating from that province—"indigeneity" was now brandished as the key priority of provincial reconfigurations.

Competition between pro- and anti-Mobutu parties led to violent ethnic eruptions in Shaba and North Kivu. In Shaba, the efforts of the pro-UFERI governor to consolidate his grip on provincial institutions took the form of systematic pogroms against the Kasaian populations, mostly Luba immigrants suspected of sympathies for the Kasaian-led UPSD. Hundreds were killed at the hands of the UFERI *jeunesse* groups, while thousands fled to Luba-dominated areas of the Kasai province.

Significantly, ethnic cleansing of Luba immigrants occurred shortly after Mobutu dismissed Tshisekedi, the Kasaian-born UPSD leader, from the prime-ministership, in October 1991. His tenure in office lasted exactly six days and came to an abrupt end after he insisted on controlling the central bank. Tshisekedi's dismissal only increased his popularity among Luba elements, in turn prompting UFERI to unleash a campaign of indiscriminate violence against the immigrant communities of southern Katanga.[23]

In North and South Kivu, neither ethnic Tutsi nor Banyamulenge were able to gain representation in the CNS, causing serious tensions vis-à-vis the self-proclaimed "native Congolese."[24] In May 1993, North Kivu exploded, with ethnic violence sweeping across several rural localities. By willfully encouraging ethnic confrontation as a means of controlling the forces released by the

CNS, Mobutu created the very conditions that accelerated failure. Not only did the apparatus of the state prove utterly incapable of mediating the competing claims of social actors, the army virtually disintegrated.

The Failure of the Security Forces

In the catalogue of afflictions suffered by the state, none looms larger than the appalling performance of the Zairian armed forces; its "rabble" character remained almost constant throughout the Mobutu years. The history of Zaire demonstrates—and this truth is even more cruelly evident in the case of Laurent Kabila's RCD—the inability of the regime to make effective use of its security forces to deal with the threat of regional, externally supported, insurrections.

Like the state itself, the Forces Armées Zairoises (FAZ) can best be seen as a political machine lubricated by strong doses of corruption, clientelism, and ethnic favoritism. Numbering approximately 150,000 in 1993, Mobutu's army consisted of two core units, the Division Spéciale Présidentielle (DSP) and the Garde Civile (GC), headed respectively by his brother-in-law, General Etienne Nbgale Kongo Nzimbi, and General Philemon Kpama Baramoto, both of Ngbandi origins, like Mobutu himself. Approximately half of the sixty-two FAZ generals came from Mobutu's region (Equateur), and one-third were of Mobutu's Ngbandi. They were overwhelmingly concentrated in the DSP and the GC. Recruitment into the higher ranks can best be described as a patronage operation designed to reinforce the loyalty of the officer corps to the supreme patron. Kinship played a key role in strengthening loyalty, and merit and competence were of secondary importance to personal devotion to Mobutu. In return for their political loyalty, the army high command was given a free hand to engage in lucrative commercial activities. While some were involved in smuggling operations, others sold military equipment, spare parts, and military fuel on the black market. Embezzling salaries intended for the troops was a standard practice among officers, a fact that goes a long way toward explaining the exactions and indiscipline of the troops.

Already in 1964–1965, during the Muleliste insurrection in eastern Congo, the poor performance of the Congolese army had been made painfully clear. Had it not been for the assistance proffered by South African and European mercenaries (and the bombing missions flown by Cuban exiles in the pay of the CIA), Mobutu's second coming, in November 1965, might not have materialized. Again, only through the timely intervention of French and Moroccan troops during the Shaba I and Shaba II insurrections in 1977 and 1978 was the Mobutist state saved from its self-inflicted doom.

The danger posed by the absence of even a minimally disciplined army was dramatically revealed during the looting sprees that swept across the country from 1991 to 1993. Resentful of not being paid salaries comparable to those of the CNS delegates, and further angered by the refusal of local traders to accept Mobutu's worthless banknotes, bands of soldiers went on a rampage in Kinshasa in September 1991, stealing, and killing anyone who stood in their way. The same scenario unfolded in Lubumbashi in October 1991, in Mbanza-Ngungu in January 1992, in Goma in December 1992, in Mbandaka in September 1992, in Kisangani, Goma, and Rutshuru in January 1993, and in Lisala in August 1993. In each locality millions of dollars worth of property were destroyed by rampaging soldiers. The extensive "pillages" brought into sharp relief the extreme fragility of a security apparatus largely built on ethnic clientelism and the degree to which the absorption of financial wealth by the Mobutu clique conspired to destroy the army's morale and heighten its indiscipline.

By 1993, the FAZ was spinning out of control. With the prospect of Mobutu running out of cash, bitter rivalries emerged among different factions of the officer corps, notably between the Mbudja and Ngbandi subgroups, headed respectively by Generals Bumba and Babia. As the latter's faction eventually gained the upper hand, the security forces came increasingly under the control of the all-Ngbandi "gang of four," Generals Mavua, Eluki, Baramoto, and Nzimbi, respectively minister of national defense, chairman of the chiefs of staff, commander of the GC, and head of the DSP. By 1996 the gang of four had become a collective loose cannon, and Mobutu was at the mercy of his generals.

Mobutu, whom one observer referred to as the cowboy of generals and the progenitor of factions and godfathers, caused the FAZ to unravel. "Unfortunately Mobutu failed to read the message sent by the mutinous troops. The latter were simply fed up with the mafia operating within the army. The troops were paid irregularly, poorly fed, [and] poorly led, while their commanding officers were abusively swelling the size of their units and embezzling their [troops'] salaries with impunity."[25] To compensate for their unpaid salaries, the officers gave their troops a blank check to ransom and loot; meanwhile the loyal clienteles built around the Ngbandi-dominated Division Spéciale Présidentielle proved just as adept at engaging in plunder and theft. When the time came to take on Kagame's "refugee warriors" and their Congolese allies in the east in October 1996, all that Mobutu could summon was a band of armed thugs masquerading as an army.

The Kivu Emergency, 1993–1996

Long before the attacks on the refugee camps in October 1996, North Kivu had become a calabash of seething political and ethnic tensions, for which

Mobutu bears much of the responsibility. By first favoring the Tutsi community, and more specifically the first generation of 59ers, against native Congolese, and then turning against them, and by declaring all Banyarwanda foreigners and denying them the rights of citizenship, Mobutu sowed the seeds of his own undoing.[26]

The roots of the Kivu crisis revolve around land issues. These issues are traceable in part to the legacy of Belgian policies, and in part to the critical role played by one of Mobutu's most trusted advisers and chief of staff, Bisengimana, a Tutsi 59er. Land hunger in the Kivu would never have reached such critical dimensions had it not been for (1) the long-term effects of Belgian policies in "facilitating" the immigration of tens of thousands of Rwandan families to North Kivu in order to meet the labor demands of European planters, along with the designation of hundreds of thousands of acres as "vacant lands" in order to turn them into protected parklands; and (2) the crucial role played by Tutsi refugees from the Rwandan revolution (1959–1962) in appropriating large tracts of land at the expense of the "indigenous" communities. This is where Bisengimana—himself, like many of his kinsmen, one of the largest landowners in the Kivu—bears considerable responsibility for heightening tensions between the Banyarwanda and native Congolese.

By 1981, the land problem and the nationality question had become two sides of the same coin. Citizenship rights meant the right to vote and the right to buy land. Until then, the Banyarwanda could exercise both, thanks to a 1972 law pushed through parliament at the request of Bisengimana. By 1977, he had fallen out of grace and anti-Banyarwanda sentiment was growing throughout the region. The nationality law of 1981 in effect withdrew citizenship rights from all Banyarwanda, including those whose roots in the Kivu went back to pre-colonial times. From then on, citizenship only applied to "those persons who could show that one of their ancestors was a member of a tribe, or part of a tribe, established in the Congo prior to 1908," when the Congo ceased to be a "Free State" and became a Belgian colony.[27] Behind the palpable ineptitude of this stipulation lay a clear intention to deprive all Banyarwanda of their citizenship.

While some Banyarwanda had hoped that the nationality issue would be resolved at the CNS, this was not to be the case. The party delegations representing the interests of the "foreigners" were refused admission to the conference; the civil society delegates likewise. The "géopolitique" argument received widespread support among the majority of the participants, thus ratcheting up the ethnic tension in eastern Congo.

The nationality issue came to a boil in May 1993, when anti-Banyarwanda violence suddenly erupted in Masisi and Walikale (North Kivu), causing an estimated 10,000 deaths (mostly Hutu) and the displacement of some 250,000 people. Although the evidence concerning the immediate circumstances of the rioting is sketchy, certain basic facts are reasonably clear. "Violence was directed against all Banyarwanda irrespective of their ethnic identity (Hutu or Tutsi); it was instigated by indigenous 'tribes' (Hunde, Nande, and Nyanga), assisted by Mai-Mai and Bangilima warriors; the killings occurred in response to a widespread campaign of civil disobedience organized by the Magrivi, a pro-Hutu *mutuelle*, in large part directed against indigenous traditional authorities"—the latter suspected of being in league with Tutsi land-owners.[28]

Hutu-Tutsi tensions had yet to reach the point of no return. For a while this surge of xenophobic violence caused the two ethnic fragments of the Banyarwandan community to develop closer ties. Some spoke of an emergent "Hutu-Tutsi coalition." The least that can be said is that it proved extremely short-lived. Already, many young ethnic Tutsi in both North and South Kivu had gone over to the RPF, and were actively engaged in the civil war next door, causing suspicions of "disloyalty" among local politicians. With the capture of power in Rwanda by the RPF in July 1994, followed by the huge flood of Hutu refugees into North Kivu, the stage was set for a major reshuffling of ethnic alliances. From then on, the Hutu-Tutsi split emerged as the critical frame of reference in Kivu politics, only to be supplanted, after the destruction of the camps in 1996, by a growing polarization between "Tutsi"—the all-encompassing label designating Rwandan Tutsi, descendants of the early migrants to North Kivu, the 59ers, and the long-established Banyamulenge communities of South Kivu—and "native" elements. The turning point came on 7 October 1996, when the South Kivu governor urged all Tutsi to leave the country within a week or face "appropriate" sanctions. A week later the RPA troops unleashed the full force of their assault on the refugee camps.

The 1996 Watershed: From Zaire to DRC

The nemesis visited upon the refugee camps radically altered not just the political landscape in eastern Congo, but the fate of the successor state. With the emergence of Laurent Kabila at the head of the AFDL, the stakes were raised far beyond the immediate objective of eliminating the threats posed to Rwanda by armed refugee groups; the aim was to wrestle the Mobutist monster to the ground and make the whole of the Congo safe for Rwanda. The first was achieved with relative ease by Kagame's troops, though at a horrendous cost in refugee lives; the second proved immensely more difficult.

Orchestrated by Kagame, assisted by troops from Rwanda, Uganda, and Angola, applauded by almost every nation in the continent, the AFDL campaign against Mobutu was harnessed to a common will—to overthrow dictatorship and prepare the ground for democracy. The Rwandan army played a decisive role in the undoing of Mobutu.[29]

There are few parallels for the popular legitimacy of a self-styled revolutionary leader soaring and collapsing in such a brief interval. Laurent Kabila's ineptitude in handling the demands of civil society must be seen as one of the main reasons behind his plummeting popularity in the months following the fall of Kinshasa. Another factor stemmed from his overwhelming military and political dependence on Banyamulenge and Rwandan elements.

That Laurent Kabila would not stand as the apostle of democracy was made clear in his inaugural speech, on 29 May 1997. The CNS was ruled out as the basis for a new constitutional order; it belonged to a Mobutist past that had to be rejected completely. So, too, were opposition political parties. If any doubts remained about Kabila's dictatorial dispositions, these were quickly dispelled by the arrest and incarceration of dozens of civil society leaders and journalists in the months following his inauguration. True to his paleo-Marxist nurturing, in 1999 Kabila dissolved the AFDL and established People's Power Committees (PPCs) aimed at giving power to the masses—a thinly veiled attempt to place police informants in strategic positions so as to have opponents arrested. Ominously, on 14 November 1999, he authorized the PPCs to carry weapons, an operation supervised by the People's Self-Defence Force (FAP), a private militia officially said to be an extension of the army. On the eve of the millennium, the DRC had all the earmarks of a police state. Summarizing the parallel with Mobutu's Zaire, Joseph Oleghankoy—who first rallied to and then promptly defected from the RDC-Goma—commented, "Kabila and Mobutu are like Pepsi and Coca-Cola: you can't taste the difference."[30]

Nor could this "Mobutisme sans Mobutu" syndrome leave the international community indifferent. The visit of U.S. Secretary of State Madeleine Albright to Kinshasa in December 1997 turned out to be a near-disaster as Laurent Kabila took advantage of a press conference to come down hard on the opposition, ending his tirade with a mocking smile and a cynical "Vive la democratie!"[31] While other donors remained equally wary of providing financial assistance, the United Nations became involved in a long and inconclusive struggle with Kabila over the fate of tens of thousands of Hutu refugees allegedly killed by AFDL and Rwandan troops in the course of their exodus. The UN investigatory commission headed by Special Rapporteur Roberto Garreton ran into endless problems. Following one complication after another, in March 1998, a year after it had been appointed, the Garreton commission left Kinshasa, empty-handed.

Laurent Kabila's stonewalling could not have made clearer his utter dependence on Kigali. Whatever evidence there is about the circumstances surrounding the massacre of refugees suggests that the RPA was far more involved than the AFDL. In blocking the work of the commission, Kabila was evidently taking his marching orders from Kigali.

If further proof were needed, one could point to the growing influence of certain key Rwandan and Banyamulenge personalities in his entourage: Kagame's army chief of staff, James Kabarehe; Bizima Karaha, minister of foreign affairs; Deogratias Bugera, minister of presidential affairs and former secretary general of the AFDL; and Moise Nyarugabo, his personal secretary (the last three would eventually surface as key members of the RCD-Goma). Nor could one fail to notice the commanding presence in Kinshasa of many Tutsi-looking, Kinyarwanda-speaking elements. As anti-Tutsi feelings intensified in the capital, Kabila could not be seen otherwise than as a stooge of Kagame. As 1997 drew to a close, the choice he faced was either to hang on to his Rwandan protectors and suffer an even greater loss of legitimacy, or to free himself of their embrace and face the consequences. By mid-1998 Kabila had made his choice—and the results proved fatal to his regime.

The Road to Hell: The 1998 Rebellion and Its Aftermath

The crunch came on 27 July 1998, with Laurent Kabila's announcement that all foreign troops would be expelled from the DRC. The next day, six planeloads of Tutsi and Banyamulenge troops hurriedly flew out of Kinshasa, leaving hundreds of others to their own devices.[32] Meanwhile, hundreds of Tutsi residents of Kinshasa (and not a few Tutsi-looking Africans) were massacred by what was left of Kabila's army and angry mobs of Congolese. By yielding to the mounting anti-Tutsi sentiment, the Congo's new king turned the kingmakers into his bitterest enemies.

Kagame's sense of outrage struck a responsive chord among several Congolese opposition figures whose distaste for Kabila exceeded their grievances against the Rwandans. The crisis gave them a unique opportunity to turn the tables on Kinshasa. Like Kabila in 1996, they knew that the road to Kinshasa passed through Kigali; like Kabila, they quickly realized the need for a home-grown, authentically Congolese vehicle to lend credibility to their plans. Thus the RCD came into existence in Kigali on 16 August. By then a full-scale rebellion was already under way in eastern Congo; in Kinshasa, the FAC braced for a decisive confrontation with Kagame's troops.

In early August, with an unerring aim for the jugular, Kagame airlifted some 600 troops from Goma to Kitona, a major military airbase about 200 kilometers west of Kinshasa. There they linked up with the local FAC garrison (then undergoing "re-education"). The key towns of Moanda and Matadi were seized almost immediately. By 17 August, the huge hydroelectric dam at Inga was under rebel control. With the flick of a switch, Kinshasa was plunged into darkness and its water supply cut off. Then, precisely when Kinshasa seemed about to cave in, Angola saved the day. On 22 August, an estimated 3,500–4,000 Angolan troops surged from the Cabinda enclave and, with tanks and heavy artillery, attacked Kagame's men from the rear. Fleeing the Angolan assault from the west, on 26 August Kagame's men made a last-ditch effort to seize Kinshasa, only to concede defeat.

Despite its setback in the west, the rebellion quickly picked up momentum in the east. After the recapture of Kisangani by the Rwandan army, rebel troops struck out north and west and, with the backing of the Ugandan army, took one town after another: Bunia, Buta, Bumba, Isoro, and Aketi.[33] With the fall of Kindu, the capital of the Maniema, on 12 October, the rebellion scored a major victory. Besides giving the rebels and their Rwandan allies free access to the mineral resources of the region, the path was now clear for a further advance south toward Kasongo, Kabalo, Kabinda, and the diamond-rich Kasai province.

1998: A Replay of 1996?

On the surface, the 1998 rebellion had all the earmarks of a replay of the 1996 anti-Mobutist insurrection. In both instances the initiative came from Kigali, with the support of Kampala. The points of ignition, logically enough, were Goma and Bukavu, with the Banyamulenge acting as the spearhead of the rebellion. The insurgents had relatively little in common, however, besides their shared aversion to the Kinshasa regime.

In 1998, however, Angola switched sides, a critical difference. The key to this decisive turnaround lies in the Angolan civil war. All too aware of the absolute necessity of retaining Laurent Kabila's support in his fight against Jonas Savimbi's Uniao Nacional para a Independencia Total de Angola (UNITA), and seeking to destroy their rear bases in the DRC, Angolan President Eduardo dos Santos did not hesitate to throw his weight behind Kabila. Had he acted differently, the DRC would probably no longer exist.

In 1998, as in 1996, the senior partner in the coalition became the source of enduring hatred among the insurgents, but with different implications. The pattern of alliances stitched together from Kigali was far more fragile than in 1996. In late 1998, thoroughly exasperated by Kigali's efforts to control the RCD, Ernest Wamba dia Wamba, an exile academic of Bakongo origins, decided to set up his own rebel faction—the RCD-Bunia —and turned to Uganda for support. Equally distrustful of Rwanda's intentions, a third rebel movement emerged in Equateur province, the Mouvement de Libération du Congo led by Jean-Pierre Bemba, son of a well-known businessman and former supporter of Mobutu.

Seemingly endless factional struggles subsequently plagued each rebel movement. The most violent, in late 2000, virtually ripped apart the RCD-Bunia when a dissident faction led by Mbusa Nyamesi turned against Wamba and forced him to seek refuge in Uganda.

Anti-Rwandan sentiment drove a deep wedge not only between the two wings of the RCD, but also between their external sponsors, Rwanda and Uganda. Competition between their respective clients over access to the Congo's mineral wealth was one of the underlying factors behind the trial of strength between the UPDF and the RPA for control of Kisangani. In August 1999, following an armed confrontation between two RCD factions, Rwandan and Ugandan troops jumped into the fray, and for four days fought each other tooth and nail on behalf of their respective allies in Kisangani, leaving some 200 soldiers and civilians dead. An even bloodier confrontation erupted in May 2000, for much the same reasons, resulting in the death of an estimated 1,000 local residents. Many more were left wounded and homeless.

The battle for Kisangani was more than a case of external patrons reluctantly drawn into a factional struggle. More than anything else, it reflected a deadly rivalry for the rich deposits of gold, timber, diamonds, and coltan (columbite-tantalite ore, used in the manufacture of cell phones, computers, and jet engines) of eastern Congo. After 1996, the stakes involved in the struggle changed dramatically. The security imperative invoked by Kigali in 1996 was of secondary importance to the huge profits drawn by Rwanda and Uganda from the plunder of the Congo's mineral resources.[34] Not all of this wealth ended up lining private pockets; much of the war effort was financed by exports from eastern Congo.

Except for the violence in the Kivu, which remained constant—and constantly horrendous—and the killings of tens of thousands of fleeing Hutu refugees by the RPA, the 1996 insurrection did not involve major bloodshed among Congolese. The same cannot be said of the 1998 rebellion. The cost in human lives was without precedent. Both sides were responsible for unspeakable atrocities against civilian populations. The slaughter of Tutsi in Kinshasa and Lubumbashi (in the name of what some government-controlled media referred to as the Hamitic threat to Bantu people) has been matched by the innumerable revenge killings committed by Rwandan troops against the civilian communities of North and South Kivu.

A major source of violence stems from the incessant attacks launched by Mai-Mai militias against RPA soldiers and their RCD allies, in turn bringing devastating retaliatory strikes against civilians. Cases in point include the massacres in Kasika (South Kivu) in August 1998, where more than 1,000 Congolese were killed at the hands of the RPA or Banyamulenge soldiers, and in Makobola (also in South Kivu) in January 1999, where an estimated 500 villagers were wiped out in similar circumstances. Similar atrocities were reported in Butembo, Cidaho, Kalehe, Kilambo, Luberezi, Lulingu, Lurbarika, Lusenda-Lubumba, Ngenge, Shabunda, and Uvira; in Mwenga in November 1999, fifteen women are said to have been buried alive after being tortured. The overall picture conveyed by Garreton's 1999 report to the UN Human Rights Commission is one of unmitigated horror. Between December 1998 and November 1999, some thirty-five massacres of civilians were reported as reprisals for Mai-Mai attacks against RPA soldiers and/or their RCD allies, causing thousands of casualties, all of which were at first denied by the RCD and later acknowledged as "unfortunate mistakes."[35]

The Hema-Lendu Tragedy

Just as lethal in its effects is the extension of the Hutu-Tutsi conflict to areas inhabited by populations sharing cultural affinities with Tutsi and Hutu. The most dramatic illustration of this phenomenon occurred in a remote corner of the newly created Kibali-Ituri province, near Bunia, in June 1999, when violent clashes suddenly erupted between Hema and Lendu, resulting in an estimated 10,000 people killed and over 50,000 displaced.

The Hema are pastoralists who have much in common, culturally, with the Tutsi of Rwanda and Burundi, the Banyamulenge of eastern Congo, and the Hima of the Ankole district in Uganda. The Lendu, in contrast, are settled agriculturalists and hunters; many identify with the Hutu, largely because of their anti-Hema feelings.[36] Despite long-standing tensions between them, the savagery that has attended more recent clashes is unparalleled in their history. The flare-up in 2001 transformed the area in and around Bunia into a human abattoir. Graphic descriptions of the atrocities committed by both sides were reported in the press. One observer commented on how the head of a young boy was hacked off and then "skewered on the tip of a spear and paraded on the back of a pick-up truck . . . while soldiers on the truck sang a soccer song."[37] Although the exact number of lives lost will never be known, there is general agreement that the spark that ignited the killings was a dispute over land in Djugu, involving Hema contesting a farm owned by Lendu. Soon, the conflict took on ominous proportions. According to a humanitarian source, "it has now become a conflict over power and money. . . . The presence of various Congolese and foreign armed groups, the easy availability of weapons, the war-ravaged economy, and a rise in 'ethnic ideology' in the area have provided dangerous fodder for the conflict's rapid extension and ferocity." More specific circumstances also played a role, notably the decidedly pro-Hema attitude of Adele Mugisha, the provincial governor, herself a Hima from Ankole. Ethnic sympathies seem largely responsible for her decision to authorize elements of the UPDF to back local Hema militias in their efforts to drive the Lendu from their land.

In addition to its terrible cost in human lives, the Hema-Lendu strife had a profoundly disruptive impact on the intramural struggle going on within the RCD-Bunia. While Wamba dia Wamba cast his lot with the Lendu, his vice-president, John Tibasima (a Hema), and prime minister, Mbusa Nyamwesi (a Nande), both tended to support the Hema. After a violent fire fight between the rival subfactions, Wamba was hastily summoned to Kampala and urged to resign from the presidency of the movement, thus paving the way for the merger of the Nyamusi-Tibasima faction with Bemba's MLC, now renamed the Front de Libération du Congo. Despite the hopes raised by the Hema-Lendu peace accord brokered by the FLC in February 2001, ethnic killings continue unabated through much of the Ituri province. In February 2002, attacks by Lendu militias left 200 people dead and thousands displaced in a Hema village north of Bunia, prompting Human Rights Watch (HRW) to urge the UN Secretary-General to send military and civilian observers to the strife-torn Ituri province.

The Banyamulenge: A Genocide Waiting to Happen?

Next in line on the list of "minorities at risk" are the Banyamulenge of South Kivu, whose fate, like that of the Hema and Lendu, is deeply intertwined with the politics of foreign-linked factionalism, in this case the RCD-Goma. Although the term *Banyamulenge* is often used indiscriminately to refer to all ethnic Tutsi in North and South Kivu, they form a group apart, whose history is rooted in the mists of pre-colonial history.[38] The date of their migration into the region is a matter of controversy, but most historians would agree that they settled in the high-lying plateau of the Itombwe long before the advent of colonial rule. As such, they have every right to Congolese citizenship. Their ethnic profile is Tutsi, their language is Kinyarwanda, their traditional homeland is the Itombwe plateau, but they all insist, with reason, that their national identity is Congolese. This is what many of their Congolese neighbors contest, arguing that they are Tutsi who recently entered the country from Rwanda, and that Rwanda is where they belong.[39]

The fight over citizenship rights masks a conflict over memory. Selective memory, or selective forgetting, only serves to harden the edges of ethnic enmities. Each side sees itself as a victim of the other. Central to the collective memory of the Banyamulenge is the story of their pre-colonial migrations, a well-established historical fact which their Congolese opponents strenuously contest. While the latter reproach them for their involvement on the side of Kinshasa during the 1964 Muleliste rebellion, the Banyamulenge retort that they initially joined forces with the rebels and only switched sides after seeing their cattle stolen and slaughtered to feed the rebel army.[40] When reviled for sending their young men to fight with the RPF as early as 1981, they argue that they had few other choices, given that they were treated as foreign interlopers in their own land and denied citizenship rights. When questioned about their involvement in the destruction of refugee camps in South Kivu in late 1996 and their subsequent rallying to the AFDL, they are quick to respond that they were pushed into the arms of the Rwandans by the threats posed to their people; few, indeed, have forgotten the withering verbal attacks of Shweka Mutabazi, the Uvira Zone Commissioner, in July 1996, encouraging the "authentic" Congolese to "hunt down the Banyamulenge snake." Nor have they forgotten the request of a leading human rights group—ironically labeled the Collectif d'Actions pour le Développement des Droits de l'Homme (CADDHOM)—to the governor of South Kivu to expel "as quickly as possible" these "Rwandan immigrants" who show "no respect for the laws and authorities of this country." But if anything will be forever etched in their collective memory it is the wanton killing of hundreds of Banyamulenge in Kinshasa and Lubumbashi in the wake of the 1998 war, when the Kabila government declared open season on them. For many of their enemies, however, the one layer of memory that eclipses all others is the auxiliary role played by the Banyamulenge in making the Kivu a colony of Rwanda.

While grappling with a past that evokes conflict and hatred on both sides, the Banyamulenge are faced with hard choices: either to cast their lot with the RCD-Goma and enjoy the continued protection of the RPA, or to distance themselves from both in the interest of national reconciliation. Several leading Banyamulenge leaders have chosen the first option, notably Azarias Ruberwa, currently secretary-general of the RCD-Goma, and Bizama Karaha, serving as minister of interior. Others, arguing that they have been all along "instrumentalized" by Rwanda, insist that there is no other solution to the Kivu crisis than to combat Rwandan expansionism and seek a modus vivendi with the people of the Kivu, north and south. This is the position taken by Ruhimbika, head of the Forces Républicaines Féderalistes.

Founded in Uvira in January 2000, the FRF summed up its key objective in a letter of 20 January 2000 to the UN secretary-general: "In the face of this double threat—extermination by the Kabila government or instrumentalization by the allies of the RCD-Goma—the Congolese Tutsi, in concert with other peace-loving Congolese, have taken the decision to organize themselves into a movement [*collectif*] designed to negotiate a peace agreement in eastern Congo between the Congolese Tutsi and their neighbors."[41] Since then, Banyamulenge politics have become more complex, with the emergence of a guerilla movement in the Itombwe led by a certain Masunzu, determined to hold his ground against both the RCD-Goma and the Rwandans. The net result of the leadership crisis faced by the Banyamulenge has been to split their movement into a host of warring factions.

The dilemma facing the Banyamulenge remains unchanged, however: if and when the Rwandan occupying forces are withdrawn from eastern Congo—a key objective of the Lusaka accords—what are the guarantees that they will not be the target of a wholesale massacre by the self-styled "authentic" Congolese, or that they will not be forcefully expelled to Rwanda? And while there is little question that the overwhelming dependence of the RCD-Goma on Rwanda has been the source of major discords among the Banyamulenge, what is one to make of Rwanda's argument that they are the only safety net available to their kinsmen in North and South Kivu?

Managing conflict within their respective client factions is a burden which both Kagame and President Yoweri Museveni have to bear, and so far neither can claim much success. The same could have been said of Laurent Kabila as he vainly tried to impart some degree of internal cohesion and coordination to a congeries of semi-autonomous satellites—Mai-Mai warlords, Interahamwe bands, and FDD militias—while at the same time fending off plots, real or imagined, within his own politico-military apparatus. In the end, Kabila failed on both counts.

What is beyond dispute is that in his three and a half years in office, Laurent Kabila outdid Mobutu in taking his country into the abyss. Measured by the familiar yardsticks of the Mobutu dictatorship—extreme personalization of power and nepotism, corruption and rent seeking, neglect of public services, and indifference to the demands of the civil society—his performance is arguably even worse than that of his predecessor. Although Mobutu must bear full responsibility for sponsoring the failure of the state, Laurent Kabila's ineptitude is what precipitated its dismemberment. Where Mobutu refused to share power while resisting the breakup of the state, Laurent Kabila "preferred sharing the country to sharing power."[42] His early aura of legitimacy as the man who toppled Mobutu was mortgaged at the outset by heavy dependence on his Rwandan backers, but this factor is not enough to explain his inability to build up the power base needed to challenge his former allies. At no time was a serious attempt made to come to terms with the opposition, give voice to civil society, reorganize the army into a viable fighting force, or reallocate the country's resources with an eye to the crying needs of the rural sectors. His style of governance was that of a warlord not a statesman, reminiscent in many ways of "the methods of leadership he practiced as a militia leader in Fizi-Baraka or while running his many Tanzanian businesses."[43] For all his avowed enmity to the Mobutist dictatorship, Laurent Kabila's ramshackle regime was an institutional clone of its predecessor.

Enter Kabila Fils

"Despite widespread discontent with his rule, Kabila's regime is not threatened by internal unrest, or even a coup."[44] Less than a month after the publication of this assessment in an otherwise excellent report by the International Crisis Group (ICG), Laurent Kabila was shot dead by one of the child soldiers (kadogo) in charge of his security. The exact circumstances of the assassination are still murky. What were the assassin's motives? Was the hand that pulled the trigger guided by Angolans? If so, why? What is the connection between Laurent Kabila's order to execute Masasu Nganda, one of his key lieutenants in the Katanga, on 27 November 2000, and the kadogo's bullet? One can only venture the most tentative answers. The most plausible hypothesis points to a convergence of two separate sets of factors. The decision to eliminate Kabila most probably came from dos Santos or his chief of staff, General Jogo Baptista de Matos; according to a well-informed source, the kadogo, one of several involved in the assassination, was the instrument chosen by the Angolans.[45] But compliance would not have been forthcoming had it not been for Laurent Kabila's callous indifference to the fate of the kadogo while fighting the RPA and its domestic allies. In brief, the kadogo and the Angolans had different sets of grievances, yet they both converged on the same target.

The growing frustration of the Angolans stemmed in part from the extraordinary inefficiency of the Laurent Kabila establishment in getting its act together on the battlefield and in building a viable power base in Kinshasa. Nepotism and corruption were another source of disillusionment. The last straw came when dos Santos realized that Laurent Kabila was conniving with UNITA rebels—via a group of Lebanese intermediaries based in Kinshasa—in channeling into his hands the benefits of the illicit trade in diamonds. This realization, in turn, explained the gunning down, gangland-style, of the eleven Lebanese involved in the diamond deals, along with their immediate relatives, in the days immediately following Kabila's assassination. That the order to kill the Lebanese came from Colonel Eddy Kapend, Kabila's aide-de-camp, confirmed his pro-Angolan leanings. A Lunda from the Katanga, Kapend was seen by the

Angolans as their safest ally in their fight against the penetration of the Popular Movement for the Liberation of Angola into the Katanga. Significantly, Kapend was put in jail, a move suggestive of Joseph Kabila's determination to resist manipulation by the Angolans.

That the kadogo were unhappy with Laurent Kabila is easy to understand; poorly trained, poorly fed, and seldom paid, most of them were used as cannon fodder against Rwanda's crack units in the Katanga. Hundreds were killed while fighting RPA and RCD soldiers on the eastern front. Many felt outraged upon learning of the execution of their beloved "patron," Masasu Nindaga, in November 2000, near Pweto (Katanga). Nindaga, Kabila's first chief of staff, and former leader of the Mouvement Révolutionnaire pour la Libération du Congo (MRLC), was one of the four original parties who formed the AFDL. From the Kivu region like the vast majority of the kadogo, his father was a Mushi and his mother a Munyamulenge. His political credentials notwithstanding, his maternal ties were enough to raise doubts about his loyalty to the AFDL, and, in November 1997, Kabila had him arrested; not until April 2000, after an amnesty was declared, was he released. Once again suspected of conniving with the Tutsi enemy, he was arrested and executed on 27 November 2000, on the eve of the Pweto battle, which saw the rout of Laurent Kabila's army at the hands of the RPA and RCD troops and the flight of an estimated 10,000 kadogo into Zambia.

Although the presidential succession leaves many important items of contention unresolved, by mid-2002 the performance of Kabila fils was not nearly so negative as had been initially foreseen. No sooner was the new incumbent anointed than the strongest doubts were expressed within and outside the Congo about his ability to lead his country out of the mess inherited from his father. Commentators pointed to his youth, his lack of experience, his poor French, and his unfamiliarity with the arcane politics of Kinshasa, all of which presumably disqualified him for the job.[46] Nonetheless, his subsequent achievements, modest as they may be, call for a more nuanced assessment. Where his father made a mockery of the Lusaka accords, consistently resisted calls to negotiate with the rebels and their allies, and heaped scorn on the UN-appointed facilitator, Joseph Kabila showed himself surprisingly receptive to the implementation of the accords. Masire was called back to the Congo, the ban on political parties was lifted, a national dialogue was called, and, in a significant sign of goodwill, Kagame and Museveni pulled back some of their troops. Furthermore, the impression Joseph Kabila made on his interlocutors during visits to European capitals and Washington was generally favorable. More importantly, he made every effort to distance himself from the old-guard politicians surrounding his father, as well as from his Angolan allies. Nonetheless, one can hardly overlook the constraints imposed by his father's legacy on his ability to reconstruct the Congolese state.

The troubled circumstances of Joseph Kabila's rise to power throw into stark relief two obvious handicaps: his dependence on external patrons, especially Angola, and the collapse of his army. In the absence of a soldiery worthy of the name, reliance on Angolan and Zimbabwean troops was his only option. The price to be paid was a continued abdication of sovereignty, not only because of the limits thus placed on his strategic options, but because it provided justification for the presence of Rwandan and Ugandan troops in eastern Congo. Withdrawal is a two-way street, and the initial limited pullback of Rwandan and Ugandan troops was not matched by similar moves by his allies.

The kadogo factor raises other problems. Besides being a metaphor for the appalling inefficiency of the Congolese army, it could also become a synonym for further unrest. With tens of thousands of child soldiers left to their own devices, most of them thoroughly disillusioned, when not facing starvation and death, the prospect of a massive influx of kadogo back to their home provinces (North and South Kivu) and into the Mai-Mai nets is by no means unlikely. Were a kadogo shift of allegiance to materialize on a substantial scale, the result would be to ratchet up the threats posed to Rwanda and give Kagame further reasons to maintain a military presence in eastern Congo. Yet security is not the only reason for the occupation of North and South Kivu. The enormous profits derived from the exploitation of the region's mineral wealth, and the variety of interested parties on the receiving end of the line, were not the least of the obstacles to the implementation of the Lusaka accords.

"Continuation of Economics by Other Means"

Keen's twist on the Clausewitzian aphorism focuses attention on the relationship between violence and economics, and between the vicious struggle among parties to the conflict as they try to extract maximum benefits from the Congo's mineral resources and the role of foreign buyers overseas.[47]

Consider the following incident, one among many never reported in the media. On 7 November 2000, a group of Mai-Mai commandeered a Ugandan pick-up truck loaded with $70,000 worth of coltan coming from Manguredjipa, a small locality in the northeast of the DRC, near the Ugandan border. The following day a group of UPDF soldiers, accompanied by a tank, was sent to neighboring villages in hope of recovering the loot. As they came to Kikere, where a wedding was taking place, they opened fire on the assembled crowd near the church, killing seventeen; one house nearby was set on fire, while others were emptied of all furniture. A total of thirteen people were reported burned to death; a number of villagers, including women and children, were taken prisoners and sent to jail in Rughenda. Thirty people, including three Mai-Mai, were said to have been killed.[48]

The killings in Kikere were cruelly emblematic of what Jackson describes as "the perniciously symbiotic relationship between economic activity and violence." As he observes, "violence provides the cover for the economic exploitation of the Kivus by elites at home and in neighboring Rwanda. In turn, part of the massive economic profits underwrites the violence of the actors."[49] The "incident" also raises important questions about other foreign participants, unknown to the people of Kikere. Rwandan and Ugandan invaders would have few stakes in the conflict were it not for the willingness of Western corporate interests to act as their business partners, or, better still, as their partners in crime.

A complex chain of transactions and intermediaries links the local diamond and coltan miners to trading posts in Kisangani, Goma, and Bukavu, and from Kigali and Kampala to foreign business interests in Europe and the United States. The last play a dominant role in channeling profits into African hands. Rwanda, not exactly known for its diamond production, now has several diamond marketing agencies (*comptoirs*). Uganda, likewise, has exported millions of dollars worth of gems in the last few years. Museveni's half brother, General Salim Saleh, had a major stake in the weekly shipment of gold from the Office des Mines d'Or de Kilo-Moto and the Société Miniere et Industrielle du Kivu (Sominki). According to one eyewitness account, "in Kilo-Moto the Ugandans have kicked out all Congolese; every Tuesday and Friday a Ugandan jet lands in Durba and takes the loot to Kampala."[50] Nor were Rwanda and Uganda the worst offenders. Zimbabwe was deeply implicated in the same sort of transactions.

Particularly damning are the findings of the 2001 UN report on the illegal exploitation of natural resources in the DRC.[51] The report laid to rest the notion of security imperatives as the sole or primary reason for the presence of RPA and UPDF forces in the Congo. With information collected in the course of an extended visit to eastern Congo, Rwanda, and Uganda, the authors conclusively implicated top-ranking officers from Rwanda and Uganda in the looting of natural resources, the huge profits derived by their respective client factions in the Congo, and the deep involvement of Western and non-Western corporate interests in the export of coltan and other commodities, including timber, ivory, gold, diamonds, and coffee.

The same report describes Presidents Kagame and Museveni as "the godfathers of the illegal exploitation of natural resources and the continuation of the conflict in the DRC."[52] It draws attention to the close ties between the Rwandan president and "the business community operating in the DRC, the army and the structures involved in the illegal activities." (In eighteen months, Rwanda was estimated to have made $250 million in profits from the export of coltan alone.) As for Museveni, "when he appoints the very people who carry out criminal activities, and when his family members get away with criminal activities, it becomes overwhelming that the president has put himself in the position of accomplice." The subaltern individual actors identified as playing a crucial role in "providing support, entertaining networks or facilitating the exploitation of natural resources" include, on the Ugandan side, Museveni's brother, Salim Saleh; his wife; General James Kazini, former chief of staff of the UPDF; and Colonel Tikamanyire. On Rwanda's side, the names most frequently mentioned are those of Colonel James Kabarebe, former chief of staff of the RPA; Tibere Rujigiro, a key member of the RPF; and Aziza Kulsum Gulamali, described as a "unique case," in part because of her uncanny ability to survive the shifting sands of factional realignments. After serving as a major business partner of the FDD, the Burundi-based Hutu rebel faction, she became heavily involved in coltan, gold, and ivory trafficking on behalf of the Rwandans and their RCD ally in Goma.

The importance of these "facilitators" cannot be overemphasized. Through their close personal contacts with the leadership of the Congolese rebellions, they act as privileged intermediaries between the local factions and their external patrons. Many are major shareholders in companies created to siphon off mineral and timber resources. A case in point is the Victoria Group, owned by Museveni's son, Muhoozi Kainerugabe, and his sister-in-law, Jovia Akandwanaho. It deals in diamonds, gold, and coffee, has buyers in every major locality in the Orientale province, and pays taxes to Bemba's MLC. Or take the case of Trinity, described as a fictitious company and a conglomerate of various businesses owned by Salim Saleh and his wife; the "manager" of the company is none other than Ateenyi Tibasima, second vice-president of the RCD-Bunia.

A similar pattern emerges on the Rwandan side. Rwanda Metals and Grands Lacs Metals both deal in coltan, both have close ties to the RPA, and their shareholders include RPA officers as well as RCD politicians. "A myriad of small companies were created and their shareholders are invariably powerful individuals in the Rwandan nomenklatura or RCD structures." Where Rwanda differs from Uganda is in the closer integration of its business interests with its client faction in eastern Congo, and the presence of a "financial bridge" between them and the Kigali-based Banque du Commerce, du Développement et de l'Industrie (BCDI). "This financial bridge is statutory; indeed, the RCD statute indirectly recognizes the role of Rwanda in overseeing the finances of the movement and its participation in decision-making and control/audit of finances."[53]

Though it has received less attention than Uganda or Rwanda, Zimbabwe's participation in the looting is amply chronicled. Much of Mugabe's war effort was sustained by the profits derived from mining concessions and joint ventures with Congolese companies. Among Zimbabwean companies doing business in the Congo, pride of place goes to the state-owned Zimbabwe Defense Industries (ZDI), run by retired military officers and party officials, and Zvinavashe Investment, a holding company owned by Gen. Vitalis Zvinavashe, the head of Zimbabwe's military and commander of the joint southern African forces fighting in the Congo.[54] A major source of profit for the Zimbabweans is the copper parastatal Générale des Carrieres et des Mines (Gécamines), managed by Zimbabweans; another is Société Miniere de Bakwanga (MIBA), which holds a virtual monopoly on diamond extraction in the Kasai. To procure Zimbabwe's military support, a large portion of Gécamines' mining rights were transferred to a Zimbabwean company, Ridgepoint, without compensation. In a similar arrangement, diamond mining concessions were transferred from MIBA to the Zimbabwean Defense Forces (ZDF), until it became apparent that the recipient did not have the required capital or technical skills to draw maximum advantage from the deal. It was at this point that the controversial mining start-up Oryx Zimcom, with a $1 billion twenty-five-year concession in the DRC, entered into a joint venture with COSLEG, a Zimbabwean company, and MIBA, to provide the needed expertise.[55] The pattern that emerged from these transactions was one of a tight imbrication of private and corporate interests, with the major shareholders in COSLEG being none other than top-ranking Zimbabwean army men and politicians. In 2000, as many as 500 Zimbabwean companies were said to be operating in the DRC as a result of insider deals between Mugabe and Kabila.

Not the least significant of the UN report's findings was the active participation of Western and non-Western corporate interests in the export of the Congo's mineral wealth. Out of a sample of thirty-four companies exporting minerals from the DRC, thirteen are based in Belgium, five in Germany, another five in Holland, two in Great Britain, one in Russia, one in India, and another in Malaysia. Reflecting on such unprecedented plundering of the Congo's wealth, one commentator wrote: "The Congo has become a carcass being chewed at by its elite and its neighbors. They have looted and sold its natural resources on a scale without precedent. This, with the direct or tacit complicity of pious governments and corporations around the world."[56]

If the presence of foreign armies in the DRC brings to mind the "soldiers without borders" phenomenon, its counterpart is the smuggler, for whom borders are a necessary condition of trade. Secret shipments of arms to the region come from many sources, some in South Africa, others from as far as Bulgaria, described by one observer as "the arms bazaar for rebels and terrorist organizations of every political, ethnic and religious persuasion . . . including the Hutu militia who were responsible for mass killings in Rwanda."[57] Whereas the Bulgarian state marketing agency, Kintex, along with the country's largest arms manufacturer, Arsenal, are reported to have sold weapons to Hutu militias, much of Joseph Kabila's military hardware comes from ZDI. In short, much of the DRC became a free trade area for arms merchants, drug traffickers, gold and diamond smugglers, and plain thugs, transforming the region into a prime example of a criminalized economy.[58]

The Essence of Failure

"Victims of their own wealth" is the title of a Canadian newspaper article on the war in the DRC.[59] Suggestive as it is, greed is not the only force driving local factions to turn against each other; despair is the price paid by the Congolese for the greed of their neighbors. None of the huge profits extracted from the Congo is plowed back into the local economy. The result has been the utter collapse of infrastructures and the near evaporation of social services. The school system is in a shambles, and what few schools still operate are hardly enough to meet the growing demand for education or professional training. As Garreton reported in 1999, "in Kisangani schools are open only a few days a week, while other have been closed; school enrollment has declined to alarming levels, and since students cannot be reunited with their families, some have ended up joining the army."[60]

For younger generations of Congolese, joining one Mai-Mai faction or the other offered the only hope of salvation. The phenomenon lies at the heart of factional violence sweeping across North and South Kivu. As Vlassenroot showed, the social marginalization of youth is the single most important factor underlying the proliferation of armed militias collectively referred to as Mai-Mai.[61]

While there can be no doubt about their intense hatred of the foreign invader, youth's willingness to engage in factional violence must be seen as a rational option where professional opportunities are almost nil. Confronted with a situation where traditional safety nets have disintegrated, and in the absence of meaningful employment alternatives, joining the Mai-Mai becomes a "viable employment option." Analyzing the circumstances that led to the flowering of the militias, Vlassenroot traces their birth to the emergence of "marginalized youngsters and school drop-outs [who] formed groups of underage combatants acting against every representative of modern political authority." Whether called Kasindiens, Bangilima, Katuku, Batiri, Simba, or Mai-Mai, he writes, "these are nothing more than different names for the same phenomenon."[62] They were the political expression of a diffuse sense of hopelessness in the face of social and economic circumstances that were totally beyond their control. For many, recourse to magic was the only source of psychic reassurance. Belief in their own invulnerability through the intercession of witch doctors provided the clearest symbolic link to their Mai-Mai predecessors of 1964–1965. Like the Mai-Mai of the Muleliste rebellion, their strategies were dictated by short-term interests, and so, also, their tactical alliances. All shared the conviction that they owed their misery to the invasion of their country by foreign armies. The conditions created by looting Kivu's economy drove them to seek redemption in violence. The perverse effects of the global economy summoned back into existence some of the most intractable forces encountered in the continent: warlordism fueled by immiseration and xenophobia.

What Paths to Reconstruction?

As if driven by a desire to avoid his father's mistakes, Kabila the younger did more in his first six months to move the peace process forward than Kabila the elder had done in three years. Although the full implementation of the Lusaka accords was still distant in 2002, on several key issues substantial progress had been registered. The principle of an inter-Congolese dialogue had been accepted, along with Masire's presence in Kinshasa. In a move that went far beyond the terms of the Lusaka accords, in 2001 Rwanda pulled its troops back 125 miles from its frontline position at Pweto (Katanga); Uganda followed suit, withdrawing some 1,500 troops from Buta (Orientale province) in the north. Meanwhile, the UN Mission in the Congo (MONUC) deployed some 3,000 peacekeepers in the buffer zone separating the combatants. Further contributing to the relaxation of tension, Joseph Kabila was willing to give serious attention to Rwanda's security concerns. (In August 2002, the bulk of Rwanda's troops remained in the Congo, Uganda began removing the remainder of its troops, and Zimbabwe started withdrawing token numbers.)

Between the revival of the Lusaka accords and the reconstitution of Congolese statehood lie a huge distance and some formidable hurdles: the restoration of a legitimate government, the reassertion of Congolese sovereignty, and the reconstruction of a disciplined and efficient military. All three are closely interrelated. None can be resolved without peace, yet the terms on which peace is based will spell the difference between success and failure.

For peace to be achieved, there must be a sustainable cease-fire agreement, the withdrawal of all foreign troops and the full deployment of UN peace keepers, the disarmament of "negative forces" (i.e., Interahamwe and Mai-Mai), and the installation of a transitional government brought into existence by an inter-Congolese dialogue. The logic of this scenario, compelling as it is, makes unduly short shrift of the realities on the ground. Despite indications to the contrary, a complete withdrawal of foreign troops is improbable so long as their strategic and economic interests dictate otherwise. Neither Kinshasa nor the UN has the capacity to bring the "negative forces" under control, and so long as Kigali can legitimately claim that they pose a threat to its security, their presence in the Kivu serves as a convenient pretext for the continuation of war by other means. The same is true of Uganda, even though the threat posed by the Alliance of Democratic Forces (ADF) to its security is benign compared to the Mai-Mai and Interahamwe. Although Angola and Zimbabwe both derive substantial material benefit from their involvement, for Luanda, strategic considerations are far more significant. In view of the cozy relationship between Bemba's MLC and UNITA, and the latter's continuing close ties with Rwanda, it was easy to see why dos Santos had second thoughts about pulling Angola's remaining 5,000 troops out of the Congo. But he did remove nearly all of them in 2002.

Given the obstacles in the way of the full implementation of the Lusaka agreements, one must give serious consideration to the alternative path explored by Herbst: the decertification of the Congolese state through a redrawing of its geographical boundaries.[63] Concretely, doing so would translate into the international recognition of new territorial entities, corresponding roughly to the areas presently under the control of rebel and foreign forces. North and South Kivu would thus become a separate state, and the broad swathe of territory running from Bunia in the east to Gbadolite in the west would form another independent entity. The Congo would thus morph into three states (or possibly four, if the Bunia-based RCD decided to go it alone).

Whether the breakaway states would provide a more appropriate basis for resolving the Congo's woes is very doubtful, however. To begin with, none of the domestic rebel factions is willing to settle for less than the capture of power in Kinshasa; secession is simply not part of their agendas. Furthermore, as far as eastern Congo is concerned, Rwanda would not be prepared to recognize the breakaway state (or states) unless it had the option to exercise substantial military and economic control over the area, a development likely to arouse the fiercest opposition not only from "native" Congolese but from a great many Banyamulenge, who feel that they have been "instrumentalized" by Rwanda. Another major drawback is that the creation of smaller state systems does not in itself guarantee internal harmony. The shrinking of political arenas may do little more than displace the focus of conflict without enhancing the mediating capacity of the breakaway state. Or it may create new sources of tension between pro- and anti-secessionist forces. Herbst's contention that "it is hard to see that the creation of smaller units is inherently bad" is not necessarily wrong. In the case of the Congo, however, it is less than ideal, not out of reverence for the old Belgian slogan—"*Congo uni, Congo fort*"—but because of the potential for renewed conflict that such an arrangement would create. Intense rivalries likely would arise over the hoarding of the Congo's wealth by the richest states (North and South Kivu), and hegemony by Rwanda, and possibly Uganda, over the newly created states would likely continue.

There is no magic formula for the reconstruction of a Congolese state, only tentative, piecemeal measures designed to limit the costs of anarchy and facilitate the step-by-step implementation of the Lusaka accords. For all of their drawbacks, those accords offered the most hopeful solution. Yet, in order to become reality the accords need strong support from the international community. Such support should recognize that the proper sequencing of initiatives is of crucial importance if they are to be workable, that nothing constructive can be accomplished unless a modicum of peace is achieved, and that peace, in turn, requires a far heavier investment in the deployment of peacekeepers as well as the strongest pressures upon international and non-state actors to induce compliance with the peace process.

There are also lessons to be learned from the past. After the near disintegration of the Congolese state in 1965, the recipe for reconstruction included three major ingredients: the appointment of a strongman at the helm, massive infusions of financial and technical assistance, and the reorganization of the armed forces. Although the strongman turned out to be an unmitigated disaster for the country, there is little question about Mobutu's role in restoring stability. As history demonstrates only too well, long-term stability requires legitimacy, and this factor is even more true today than in the 1960s.

The immediate priority in today's Congo is the reconstitution of a legitimate state system within the limits of its present boundaries; only then can one envisage moving on to the next stages, i.e., the reassertion of territorial sovereignty, the creation of a viable military force, the neutralization of "negative forces," and the expansion of political participation. Only by giving sustained attention to the organization of a broad, cross-cutting inter-Congolese dialogue, involving rebel groups as well as representatives of civil society, notably churches, can a measure of transitional legitimacy be restored to what is left of the state. The dialogue is a key element of the Lusaka peace process, in effect committing the Kinshasa government, the main unarmed opposition parties, civil society (*forces vives*), and rebel factions to agreement on a new political order. Key items to be discussed include a timetable for holding multiparty elections, a transitional power-sharing agreement designed to bring "dissident" elements into the government, provisions for the disarming of militias, the reorganization of the armed forces, and citizenship rights for the Banyamulenge.

Hammering out a political formula for restoring a measure of legitimacy to a transitional order promises to be a daunting task, however, a fact made cruelly obvious by the seemingly endless tiffs and discords surrounding the dialogue in April 2002, held at the unlikely site of Sun City, South Africa.[64] The problems facing the 360 participants revolved around three basic issues: Who was qualified to participate in the dialogue? How much power, if any, should Kabila retain for himself during the transition period? How could a cease-fire be maintained long enough to allow the participants to reach agreement on basic constitutional, military, and security issues?

The representation of unarmed opposition parties provoked immediate disagreement between the Kinshasa delegation and Bemba's MLC, the latter arguing that many of the dozen or so political parties attending the dialogue were stooges of the government. After the MLC delegation walked out of the talks, it was the turn of the RCD-Goma to call into question the representation of some Mai-Mai militia leaders (Karendo Padiri and Madoa-Madoa) as part of the civil society, and the decision of Masire to increase the quota of delegates for the RCD-Bunia from nine to sixteen. Meanwhile, following the arrest of several of his supporters in Kinshasa, the UPSD leader, Tshisekedi, adamantly refused to take part in the dialogue. Only days after the opening of the talks, a number of opposition parties joined Bemba's MLC and the RCD-Goma in contesting the government's choice of unarmed opposition groups. Whether Kabila should remain in office during the transition or surrender power to a collegial executive, as advocated by the MLC and the RCD, was yet another source of discord; and so, also, was the question of defining the powers of the interim executive authority, collegial or otherwise.

The extreme fragility of the cease-fire made the outcome of the dialogue all the more problematic. Thus, when the news broke out on 15 March 2002 that the Rwanda-backed RCD had taken the strategically located towns of Moliro and Pweto in Katanga, the Kinshasa delegation pulled out—only to resume its participation a few days later after the UN Security Council unanimously demanded that rebel forces withdraw from both localities. The attacks on Moliro and Pweto made plain the role of external "spoilers" in the peace process. Rwanda, rather than the RCD, was the main culprit, yet acted hand in glove with the RCD to make military gains at the expense of the Kinshasa government while the dialogue was under way, and at the same time hoped to create further divisions among the delegates. On the other hand, the immediate and unanimous reaction of the Security Council made equally plain the determination of the international community to set limits to Rwanda's efforts to manipulate the peace process to its advantage.

Much more, however, must be done to help the Congo reinvent itself. The international community needs to reassess the political implications of its assistance. Far more pressure than in the past must be brought to bear on the belligerents, domestic and foreign, in order to strengthen their commitment to peace. Among the more urgent moves, the following should receive immediate attention:

1. A sustained effort to inform public opinion of the interests involved in the looting of the mineral wealth of the DRC must be carried out, with a view to shedding light on the responsibilities of private interests in perpetuating the balkanization of the country.

2. Western corporations doing business in the DRC must become part of the solution. Home countries must develop codes of conduct consistent with the peace process, including conditions under which they may operate in the DRC.

3. International institutions, notably the World Bank and the IMF, must be persuaded to bring their financial assistance programs in line with the need for a "tough love" approach, meaning "an absolute refusal to lend and donate in the absence of the rule of law, good governance and sensible economic policy."[65]

4. Western donors, notably France and the United States, must unify their strategy for dealing with the crisis.[66]

Although Great Britain, the United States, and Sweden have been most reluctant to rein in Rwanda's military incursions in eastern Congo, arguing that its security interests are paramount, others, notably France and Belgium, are far more prepared to detect other motives in the continuing and systematic looting of the Congo's wealth. Much the same diplomatic line-up applies to Uganda; despite its overwhelmingly negative role in fueling violence in the Ituri province, donors prefer to look the other way and call attention to its impressive economic performance, totally oblivious to the fact that much of its wealth comes from the Congo. The time has come to recognize that none of the above measures can succeed unless a concerted and systematic effort is made at the highest levels—the European Union, the United States, and Canada—to support the peace process.

Only the wildest optimist would pretend that peace is around the corner. Deep and lasting hatreds have been sown among the people of the Congo toward foreign invaders and their domestic allies, and those suspicions will not go away any time soon. Nor has the potential for a resumption of hostilities vanished overnight.

Notes

1. For some moving African testimonies of how the ongoing civil war affects grassroots communities, see the contributions of Alphonse Maindo Mongo Ngonga, Leonard N'Sanda Buleli, and Jacques Kabulo, in "RCD: La guerre vue d'en bas," in the special issue of *Politique Africaine*, LXXXIV (December 2001).

2. FLC, "Les cent premiers jours du Front de Libération du Congo," mimeo (Beni, 12 May 2001).

3. For some Belgian historians, like Jean Stengers, the absence of memories of the Congo Free State among Congolese is sufficient proof of its negligible impact on present-day developments. But this misses the point, argues Wrong in her brilliant account of Mobutu's demise: "I, too, had been surprised by how few of these horrors had ever been mentioned to me by Zairian friends. But it wasn't necessary to be an expert on sexual abuse to know it was possible to be traumatized without knowing why; that, indeed, amnesia—whether individual or collective—could sometimes be the only way of dealing with horror, that human behavior could be altered forever without the cause being openly acknowledged. The spirit, once comprehensively crushed, does not recover easily. For seventy-five years, from 1885 to 1960, Congo's population had marinated in humiliation. No malevolent witch-doctor could have devised a better preparation for the coming of a second Grand Dictator." Michela Wrong, *In the Footsteps of Mr. Kurtz: Living in the Congo on the Brink of Disaster* (New York, 2001), 59, 60. For an outstanding, painstakingly researched treatment of the horrors of the Léopoldian system, see Adam Hochshild, *King Leopold's Ghost* (New York, 1998).

4. The man President Reagan referred to as "the voice of good sense and good will" was also the self-proclaimed Guide, the Messiah, the Helmsman, the Leopard, the Sun-President, the cock who jumped on anything that moved. His adopted full name, Mobutu Sese Seko Kuku wa za Banga, can be loosely translated as "the all powerful warrior who goes from conquest to conquest leaving fire in his wake." See Bill Berkeley, *The Graves Are Not Yet Full* (New York, 2001), 109.

5. See Ludo De Witte, *L'Assassinat de Lumumba* (Paris, 2000)

6. The point is convincingly argued by Thomas Callaghy in his review of Wrong's *In the Footsteps of Mr. Kurtz*, "Life and Death in the Congo," *Foreign Affairs*, LXXIX (2001), 143–149.

7. In Kinshasa the black-market exchange rate reached 2.5 million zaire to the U.S. dollar in 1993; in Lubumbashi it went from 12 million to 24 million. See Berkeley, *The Graves*, 113.

8. Cited in Crawford Young, "Zaire: The Shattered Illusion of the Integral State," *Journal of Modern African Studies,* XXXII (1994), 247.

9. For a fuller discussion of this phenomenon see Crawford Young, *The African Colonial State in Comparative Perspective* (New Haven, 1994), 1–12.

10. Jeffrey Herbst, *States and Power in Africa: Comparative Lessons in Authority and Control* (Princeton, 2000), 14.

11. I. William Zartman (ed.), *Collapsed State: The Disintegration and Restoration of Legitimate Authority* (Boulder, 1995), 9.

12. Ibid., 5.

13. Samuel Huntington, *The Clash of Civilizations and the Remaking of World Order* (New York, 1996), 272.

14. Bucyalimwe Mararo, "Land, Power and Ethnic Conflict in Masisi (Congo-Kinshasa), 1940–1994," *International Journal of African Historical Studies,* XXX (1997), 503–538.

15. Herbst, *States and Power in Africa*, 37–39.

16. Lemarchand, *Burundi: Ethnic Conflict and Genocide* (New York, 1995).

17. See Kisangani Emizat, "The Massacre of Refugees in the Congo: A Case of UN Peacekeeping Failure and International Law," *Journal of Modern African Studies,* XXXVIII (2000), 163–202.

18. The phrase is borrowed from Thomas Callaghy, *The State-Society Struggle: Zaire in Comparative Perspective* (New York, 1994), passim.

19. Young, "Zaire: The Shattered Illusion of the Integral State," 247–263.

20. "The Heart of the Matter," *The Economist* (13 May 2000), 25.

21. Crawford Young, "Reflections on State Decline and Societal Change in Zaire," typescript (Madison, 1997), quoted in Lemarchand, "Patterns of State Collapse and Reconstruction in Central Africa: Reflections on the Crisis in the Great Lakes Region," *Spectrum*, XXXII (1997), 184.

22. John F. Clark, "Zaire: The Bankruptcy of the Extractive State," in Leonardo Villalon and Philip Huxtable (eds.), *The African State at a Critical Juncture: Between Disintegration and Reconfiguration* (Boulder, 1998), 113.

23. In September 1993, I interviewed Gabriel Kyungu wa Kumwanza, the UFERI governor, who claimed that the UFERI jeunesse was a "totally uncontrolled, self-recruiting group," but neglected to mention that he had himself played a key role in fanning the flames of ethnic hatred, never missing an opportunity to hold the Kasaians collectively responsible for the sufferings of the "native Katangans."

Berkeley, one of the few journalists present in the Katanga at the time, recalled that "in a series of public rallies and radio speeches the governor railed against the 'enemy within' the *bilulu* (insects in Swahili). 'The Kasaians are foreigners,' he declared. 'Their presence is an insult'." By April 1992, in the wake of systematic attacks against their homes, hundreds of Kasaians were forced to return to their province of origin, including those who were born in the Katanga. Berkeley, *The Graves,* 122.

24. The history of the Banyamulenge, both extremely complex and tragic, lies outside the scope of this discussion. The term has been the source of considerable confusion because it became increasingly used as an omnibus label to designate all Tutsi living in North and South Kivu. It came into usage in 1976, as a result of the efforts of the late Gisaro Muhoza, a member of parliament from South Kivu, to regroup the Banyamulenge populations of the Mwenga, Fizi, and Uvira zones into a single administrative entity. Although his initiative failed, the name stuck, and by 1996 it was often used by ethnic Tutsi and Congolese to designate all Tutsi residents of North and South Kivu. The Banyamulenge (literally, the "people of Mulenge") are Tutsi pastoralists who live on the high-lying plateau of the Itombwe region of South Kivu; they came to this

area long before the advent of colonial rule. Estimates of their numerical importance vary, but consensus of opinion among scholars points to some 60,000 to 100,000 as a reliable figure. They are socially and culturally distinct from both the long-established Tutsi of North Kivu and the Tutsi refugees of the 1959–1962 revolution in Rwanda (the so-called 59ers); indeed, many Banyamulenge do not speak Kinyarwanda. Whereas many 59ers joined the eastern rebellion in 1964–1965, the Banyamulenge did so reluctantly, and then quickly switched sides (largely because the pro-Mulele Bafulero of South Kivu plundered their cattle during the rebellion). Despite assertions to the contrary, they did not form the bulk of the FPR fighters recruited in eastern Congo, even though a few hundred joined the FPR in the early 1990s; the bulk of the fighting force from the Congo was drawn from among the sons of 59ers and ethnic Tutsi from North Kivu. By 1996, however, a large number joined Kabila's AFDL in eastern Congo; they suffered heavy casualties during the anti-Mobutist campaign and after the 1998 crisis, as shown by the inordinately large number of Banyamulenge widows in Bukavu. Today a number of Banyamulenge hold important positions in the RCD-Goma (including Bizima Karaha, minister of foreign affairs), but it would be profoundly misleading to assume that they are all solidly behind the rebellion. Many share Ruhimbika's view that they were "instrumentalized" by Kagame, in the same way as the RDC was being manipulated by Kigali to promote Rwandan interests in the Congo. For further information, see Joseph Mutambo, *Les Banyamulenge* (Limete, 1997); Manasse Muller Ruhimbika, *Les Banyamulenge* (Paris, 2001); Jean-Claude Willame, *Banyarwanda and Banyamulenge* (Paris, 1997). For evidence of the pre-colonial presence of Banyamulenge in South Kivu, see Jean Hiernaux, "Note sur les Tutsi de l'Itombwe: la position anthropologique d'une population émigrée," *Bulletins et Mémoires de la Société d'Anthropologie de Paris*, VII (1965), 361–379. I am grateful to Etienne Rusamira, Sanson Muziri, and Manasse Muller Ruhimbika for sharing with me their excellent grasp of the Banyamulenge problem.

25. Honore N'Gbanda Nambo Ko Atumba, *Ainsi Sonne le Glas! Les Derniers Jours du Maréchal Mobutu* (Paris, 1998), 50. Also known as the Terminator for his role during the violent repression of "la marche des Chretiens" on 16 February 1992, Atumba served as Mobutu's special adviser on security from 1992 to 1997, until replaced by General Nzimbi. During these years he served as Mobutu's key intermediary to UNITA and is widely reported to have made a huge fortune by "facilitating" the sale of Angolan diamonds for Mobutu.

26. By lumping together under the same label all Tutsi subgroups, irrespective of their date of arrival in the region, including the long-established Banyamulenge of South Kivu and those Tutsi of North Kivu whose roots went back to the early colonial and pre-colonial days, the 1981 nationality law had a catalytic effect on their common self-awareness as a victimized community. By stripping them of their nationality, Mobutu made them potentially receptive to the appeals of the RPF in the 1990s. Technically, the term Banyarwanda also included Hutu migrants from Rwanda; in fact, however, it increasingly came to be used primarily to designate Tutsi elements.

27. For a more detailed commentary, see René Lemarchand, "Ethnic Violence, Public Policies and Social Capital in North Kivu: Putnam Revisited," a paper presented at

the workshop organized by the Center for Development Studies (Antwerp, 4–5 December 1998).

28. Ibid., 12.

29. "Rwanda was the Godfather of the Congolese rebellion." Schatzberg's statement encapsulates the central factor behind the ensuing struggle for power leading to the 1998 crisis. Michael G. Schatzberg, "Beyond Mobutu: Kabila and the Congo," *Journal of Democracy,* XVIII (1997), 81.

30. Quoted in Corinna Sculer, "Slippery Slope to Humiliation," *National Post* (21 August 2000), D2.

31. See Peter Rosenblum, "Kabila's Congo," *Current History,* XCVI (1997), 195.

32. This fact will neither be forgotten nor forgiven soon by many Banyamulenge survivors, who make no secret today of their profound dislike of their Rwandan "protectors." Interview with Clément Ngirabatware (Montreal, September 2000).

33. That Kisangani was taken by Rwandan and not Ugandan troops is an important element in the background of the subsequent confrontation between Rwanda and Uganda: the standard Rwandan argument is that the capture of the city by the Rwandan army entitled them and their RCD ally to proprietary rights over the city and the mineral resources of its environs. Another source of distrust between them stems from the fact that Kampala was never informed of Kagame's decision to launch the August 1998 raid on Kitona; yet after the raid fizzled, Kagame immediately turned to Museveni to request that Ugandan tanks be sent to North Kivu. Interview with Etienne Rusamira (Montreal, December 2000).

34. See Stephen Jackson, "Criminalised Economies of Rumor and War in the Kivus, DRC," paper presented at the annual conference of the American Association of Anthropology (San Francisco, 2000).

35. See Roberto Garreton, UN Special Rapporteur, *Report on the Situation of Human Rights in the Democratic Republic of the Congo* (New York, 2000), 33–34. See also the devastating report of the Brussels-based NGO, Rassemblement pour le Progres, *Pour que l'on n'oublie jamais* (Brussels, 1999).

36. IRIN report (15 November 1999). For further details on the Hema-Lendu conflict, see "Conflit sanglant Hema-Lendu," *Justice-Plus* (Bunia, 23 June 1999). On the more recent clashes, in August 2000, that caused 142 deaths, see *New Vision* (Kampala, 21 August 2000).

37. Ian Fisher, "Congo's War Turns a Land Spat into a Blood Bath," *New York Times* (29 January 2001), 6.

38. For an outstanding analysis, see Koen Vlassenroot, "Conflict and Identity Formation in South Kivu: The Case of the Banyamulenge," *Review of African Political Economy* (forthcoming).

39. The issues surrounding the nationality issue are ably discussed in Manasse Muller Ruhimbika, *Les Banyamulenge (Congo-Zaire) entre deux guerres* (Paris, 2001)

40. As Vlassenroot perceptively noted, the decision of the Banyamulenge to fight the rebels at the side of the Armée Nationale Conglaise (ANC) marks their entry into modernity, in large part because of the social benefits that they received for having picked the "right" side: "For many young Banyamulenge, their conscription into the

ANC meant the start of a military career. As a recompense for their war effort on the Haut Plateau the central government also offered them full access to education, social services and employment opportunities." "Conflict," 5.

41. Unpublished document from the author's collection. For an illuminating semi-autobiographical account of the circumstances leading to the creation of the FRF, see Ruhimbika, *Les Banyamulenge*.

42. International Crisis Group (ICG), *Scramble for the Congo: Anatomy of an Ugly War* (Brussels, 2000), 40.

43. Ibid., 47.

44. Ibid., 40.

45. For the views in this paragraph and the next, I am indebted to Gérard Prunier; I have also drawn from Stephen Smith's insights in "Ces enfants-soldats qui ont tué Kabila," *Le Monde* (9 February 2001).

46. Norimitsu Onishi and Ian Fisher, "Doubts on Whether Kabila's Son Can Lead the Congo," *New York Times* (21 January 2001), 8.

47. David Keen, "The Economic Functions of Violence in Civil Wars" (London, 2000), cited in Jackson, "Criminalised Economies," 12.

48. Fax from Groupe de Réflexion des Sans Voix (Butembo, 28 November 2000).

49. Jackson, "Criminalised Economies," 7.

50. Quoted by the Brussels-based NGO, Réseau Congolais d'Information (Brussels, 1999). Also see Ingrid J. Tamm, *WPF Report 30: Diamonds in Peace and War: Severing the Conflict-Diamond Connection* (Cambridge, 2002).

51. United Nations Security Council, *Report of the Panel of Experts on the Illegal Exploitation of Natural Resources and Other Forms of Wealth of the Democratic Republic of the Congo*, S/200/357 (12 April 2001). In view of the crushing evidence supplied in this document, it is with no little astonishment that one reads that among Rwanda's "direct and indirect objectives behind its continuing involvement in the Congo" are "security promotion," "nation-building, in order to leave behind a structure in the Congo that can fill the current vacuum," "economic expansion and commercial development," and "human rights promotion." John Prendergast and David Smock, "Putting Humpty Dumpty Together: Reconstructing Peace in the Congo," United States Institute of Peace (Washington, D.C., 31 August 1999), 4.

52. Ibid., 41; other quotes in this paragraph are from pages 39, 40, 41, 17, 18.

53. Ibid., 17.

54. See Robert Block, "Zimbabwe's Elite Turn Strife in Nearby Congo into a Quest for Riches," *Wall Street Journal* (12 October 1998), 1.

55. COSLEG was born of a partnership between Operation Sovereign Legitimacy (OSLEG) and the Congolese Compagnie Mixte d'Import-Export (COMIEX). Among the key shareholders in OSLEG are General Vitalis Musungwa Zvinavashe, minister of defense; Job Whabira, former permanent secretary in the Ministry of Defense; Onesimo Moyo, president of Minerals Marketing Corporation of Zimbabwe; and Isiah Rusengwe, general manager of Zimbabwe Mining Development Corporation. UN Security Council, *Report of the Panel of Experts*, 34.

56. Richard Hottelet, "The Plundering of the Congo," *Christian Science Monitor* (16 May 2001), 9.

57. Quoted in Raymond Bonner, "Bulgaria Becomes a Weapons Bazaar," *New York Times* (3 August 1998), 3.

58. For excellent explorations of this theme, see William Reno, *Warlord Politics and African States* (Boulder, 1998); Jean-Francois Bayart, Stephen Ellis, and Béatrice Hibou, *The Criminalization of the State in Africa* (Bloomington, 1999).

59. Patrick Graham and Finbarr O'Reilly, "Victims of Their Own Wealth," *National Post* (21 August 2000), D11.

60. Garreton, *Report on the Situation of Human Rights in the DCR*, 32. Elsewhere in the report, Garreton informs the reader that "the special rapporteur took advantage of his trip from Goma to Kinshasa during his second mission to bring copies of the 1998 examination taken by the South Kivu candidates back for correction," 40.

61. Koen Vlassenroot, "Identity and Insecurity: Building Ethnic Agendas in South Kivu", in Ruddy Doom and Jan Gorus (eds.), *Politics of Identity and Economics of Conflict in the Great Lakes Region* (Brussels, 2000), 281.

62. Ibid., 282.

63. Herbst, *States and Power in Africa*, 264.

64. Sun City was a metaphor for permissible interracial sex in the days of apartheid, and remains to this day a major playground for Africans and expatriates. This is how Norimitsu Onishi described the surreal qualities of this African Las Vegas at the beginning of the dialogue: "Today's ceremony was held in the Entertainment Center's Superbowl arena, a stone's throw from the Jungle Casino and the Fast Food Village on one side, and the huge sculptures of elephants and monkeys at the Bridge of Time on the other side. The Lake of Peace was a long way away though . . . ." "Congo Factions Gather for Peace Talks," *New York Times* (26 February 2002), A8.

65. Robert I. Rotberg, "Africa's Mess: Mugabe's Mayhem," *Foreign Affairs*, LXXIX (2000), 60.

66. See ICG, *Scramble for the Congo*, 83.

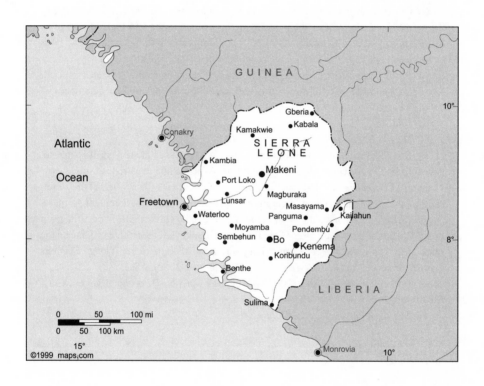

GUINEA

Gberia
Kabala
Kamakwie
SIERRA
LEONE
Kambia
Makeni
Port Loko
Magburaka
Lunsar
Masayama
Panguma
Kailahun
Pendembu
Moyamba
Sembehun
Bo
Kenema
Koribundu
Bonthe

Atlantic

Ocean

Conakry

Freetown
Waterloo

LIBERIA

Sulima

0   50   100 mi
0   50 100 km

15°

Monrovia
10°

©1999 maps.com

10°

8°

CHAPTER THREE

Sierra Leone:
Warfare in a Post-State Society

WILLIAM RENO

Sierra Leone easily fits the definition of a failed state by virtue of its declining ability to provide order and security, much less social services. As noted in the definition of state failure in the introduction to this volume, Sierra Leone is and has been "palpably incapable of delivering political goods." Furthermore, Sierra Leone is a case in which rulers intentionally destroyed state capacity to provide public goods. Conflict developed in that context, but did not fundamentally threaten the political power of those whose actions generated the conflict. In fact, political authorities used violence and insecurity in place of bureaucratic state institutions to control their people. These techniques included manipulating access to remaining economic opportunities, especially clandestine ones, and instigating local tensions and factional splits—using disorder as a political instrument—to divide potential challengers.[1] This manner of rule tolerated, and even promoted, the decentralized exercise of violence via proxies and the intentional weakening of the capacity of state administrations to act. It sacrificed these capabilities in exchange for the ability to prevent people from organizing themselves, undermining any "civil society" distinct from the state. Viewed in this light, Sierra Leone's official state bureaucracies were failing well before the Revolutionary United Front (RUF) appeared in 1991.

Many people in Sierra Leone, especially the youth, view themselves as victims of corrupt and venal politicians. Yet the political economy of violence creates formidable obstacles to collective action among those who might otherwise become social bandits or revolutionaries.[2] This fact explains why even groups, like the RUF, that fight the government do not develop a revolutionary or reformist ideological alternative, create "liberated zones," or convert themselves into a coherent political party in the context of peace agreements. Instead, marginalized youth, even those who articulate clear political programs and grievances, find that the best way to improve their personal situation is to force their way into the social system, whether as clients of state officials or as rebels. This clamor for security in the interstices of the informal networks of the collapsed bureaucratic state further excludes ideological critics who view such behavior as anti-social or corrupt, and undermines already blurry distinctions between corrupt officials and armed gangs.

To those outside Sierra Leone, headlines such as "The Hell That Was Sierra Leone" and "Voyage to Hell" confirm Sierra Leone as a failed state in popular imagination.[3] At war with insurgents since March 1991, the government's internal resources totaled about $10 million in 1999, compared to roughly $250 million annually in the mid-1970s.[4] This paucity of official capacity reflects the fact that what RUF spokesman Gibril Massaquoi called "the Government of Freetown" controlled only about a quarter of the territory of Sierra Leone in late 2000. Even this level of control depended upon protection from about 600 British military trainers and 12,500 peacekeepers of the United Nations Mission in Sierra Leone (UNAMSIL). By mid-2001, formal government control extended to include nearly all of the country, but only as the UNAMSIL force approached its authorized strength of 17,500 and British trainers continued to assist Sierra Leone's army. Despite the turn toward relative peace, other armed groups operated alongside the Sierra Leone Government, UN, British, and RUF forces. These include several hundred Gbethi, Tamaboro, and Kapra fighters, and several thousand Kamajor home guards. Added to this number were several hundred fighters originally called West Side Boys, a breakaway segment of the official Sierra Leonean government's army who joined other groups and preyed upon the population on their own account.

After 1997, RUF forces invaded the capital twice, once holding it for nine months. Insecurity had forced 510,000 Sierra Leoneans to flee abroad as of the end of 2001. Another quarter million (of a pre-war population of 4 million) were internally displaced.[5] One million remained in RUF-controlled areas. "Reports from those areas" observed a UN official, "indicate that severe food shortages and unchecked infectious diseases are taking their toll on the civilian population," a situation that continued to cause concern even after a return to relative peace in mid-2001.[6] These miserable conditions earned the country a position at the bottom of the United Nations Development Program's (UNDP) Human Development Index.[7] The propensity of RUF fighters to amputate limbs of noncombatants ensured that Sierra Leone became widely associated in Africa and the rest of the world with the notion of the collapse of order, connected to the failure of state institutions.

Despite these disastrous consequences of conflict, disorder and violence actually served the interests of rebels and some among the elite who created the social structure out of which the rebels arose. Such a situation persists alongside disarmament and integration exercises and internationally monitored elections, at least until fighters find other pursuits in a growing legitimate economy. State failure in this context is not only a failure of policy and bureaucratic capacity; it is a consequence of a conscious political strategy, akin to that in the Congo described by Lemarchand in chapter 2 of this volume. Contemporary conflict resolution strategies and diplomatic norms assume that these developments signal a departure from "normal" politics. In fact, external conflict resolution strategies in Sierra Leone have often reinforced the connection between politics, violence, and accumulation.

Failures of States versus Failures of Public Authorities

Sierra Leone, and other countries such as the Central African Republic, Guinea, Liberia, the Congo, Congo-Brazzaville, and Nigeria, long exhibited very weak bureaucratic capacities. By 1985, for example, the Congo (former Zaire) had 12,000 miles of usable roads, down from 88,000 miles at independence in 1960.[8] Congo-Brazzaville's government in 1987 allocated 2 percent of its expenditures to agricultural services in a country where most people farm for a living, while civil service employment jumped 2,300 percent over twenty years.[9] These and numerous other examples suggest that many states in Africa have been candidates for state failure for some time. Others, such as Chad, arguably began their independent existence as failed states.[10]

Despite this poor bureaucratic record, the people in some of these countries enjoyed extended periods of civil order, if not economic prosperity and state services. The façade of sovereignty protected rulers as they built informal systems of personal rule that sustained order, fulfilled informal cultural and social obligations to subjects, and in many instances enjoyed some popular legitimacy. In the absence of bureaucratic institutions, political authority has rested upon controlling markets and manipulating access to economic opportunities. The ruler's capacity to privatize state assets plays a key role in the exercise of authority in this regard. A Sierra Leonean politician with a substantial following highlighted this link between political authority and the ruler's personal control over wealth in his plea to then-President Siaka Stevens: "I face strain as a result of defending myself in the continuing two year VOUCHERGATE [corruption] trial. I restrain and console myself with your fatherly advice to keep calm. . . . We wait anxiously that the recent release of Alluvial Diamond Mining Lands in Kono . . . will be humbly received and will shower your Excellency's blessings on us," indicating that he expected to receive a diamond license and a pardon in a politically motivated corruption trial in exchange for his support of the president.[11]

A key feature of this strategy of personal rule lies in the ruler's interest in undermining security for individuals, including the corrupt politician above, and in weakening impersonal bureaucratic institutions of the state. Meanwhile, existing global recognition of the state's sovereignty facilitates the ruler's access to foreign aid and foreign business partners standing in for diminished state capacity to collect revenues or to support the productivity of citizens. Bureaucracies are targets because institutional autonomy and efficiency might generate independent perspectives among effective state officials, particularly if their agency performed well amid overall bureaucratic weakness, corruption, and economic scarcity. These fears proved realistic as military officers started challenging rulers in sub-Saharan Africa.

African rulers during the 1970s and 1980s who cared to make the calculation could anticipate that they faced a 72 percent chance that they would be forced from office amid violence. This percentage fell to 41 percent in the 1990s, as more countries held multiparty elections.[12] Yet, even after 1990, rulers faced considerable personal threats. Of six elections in 2000, for example, opposition parties boycotted two (the Sudan, Côte d'Ivoire), one reelected president was later removed by force (Côte d'Ivoire), a main opposition figure died in violent circumstances (Guinea-Bissau), and another campaign aggravated separatist violence (Tanzania). In 1999–2000, in Algeria, Angola, Burundi, Congo, Congo-Brazzaville, Guinea-Bissau, Sierra Leone, Somalia, and the Sudan—nine of Africa's fifty-four states—armed groups fought incumbent regimes. Elements of national armies and former security heads fought their former bosses in six states.[13] These threats have encouraged rulers to weaken and divide bureaucracies, especially those able to exercise coercion. Rulers create numerous parallel informal militaries, palace guards, and special anti-crime units. Liberia's President Charles Taylor at various times maintained the Armed Forces of Liberia, Special Security Unit, Security Operations Division, "Demon Force," Anti-Terrorist Unit, Joint Security Forces, National Bureau of Investigation, and "Charlie's Angels," a female bodyguard unit.

To the extent that rulers keep some popular support and provide order, they can tolerate the end of a state monopoly on coercion and increasingly feeble bureaucratic capacity. The collapse of state institutions and the war in Sierra Leone are better understood in the context of a broad definition of state failure that emphasizes the inability to provide public (political) goods. The most basic public good—order—is a primary target of elites' instrumental uses of disorder and violence to divide and control rivals. Order is a central element in Hobbes's classic definition of a sovereign as embodying an interest that exceeds the sum of the private interests of agents staffing an organization.[14] In practical terms, Hobbes's sovereign protects people in a society, whether they want protection or not. By contrast, a racketeer creates disorder so that he can charge individuals for exemption from the harm that he creates. A racketeer and his gang fail to fulfill even this most basic element of the definition of a state, regardless of how its leader styles himself. It is not the weakness or configurations of specific institutions, but rather *the uses and organization* of coercion that define state failure in the broader sense of failure of public authority.

Could racketeers or armed gangs become more state-like in behavior? This is a critical question in analyzing state collapse in Sierra Leone, since officials of the UN and the U.S. government put great stock in the capability of peace negotiations to encourage insurgent leaders and politicians to take more interest in providing public goods such as order and economic development. This approach conflates weak institutions and conflict with the specific phenomenon of the intentional suppression and disappearance of public goods—the essence of state failure in this category of cases. The critical feature that distinguishes these organizations from nascent public authorities lies in the cumulative effects of particular uses of violence. In Sierra Leone, the country's rulers intentionally made life for their subjects less secure and more materially poor. They became personally wealthy as a consequence of this disorder, then sold chances to profit from disorder to those who could pay for them by providing services—as experts in violence, for example—and to those local and expatriate businessmen who traded their access to commercial networks. This imposition of negative externalities, when taken to an extreme, defines the failure of states in places like Sierra Leone, where violent personalist politics predominated.

President Taylor's organization in Liberia provides an exemplary case of a violent group that failed to become more state-like even when bestowed with sovereignty. Popular attention in late 1999 focused on his government's efforts to return the first post-war traffic signal to service in busy Monrovia—a quintessential public good. It would be expensive and cumbersome to sell access to its benefits to selected passers-by. The signal lasted for three weeks, while 80 percent of the government's budget that year was devoted to providing personal security to Taylor and unpaid "civil servants" preyed upon local inhabitants.[15]

It is useful to conceive of the complete absence of public authority as an "ideal" type, in Weber's sense of providing an analytical absolute against which to measure actual practice. Even Sierra Leone and Liberia exhibit minimal bureaucratic features. One finds elements of governance at times in a variety of organizations, including in groups that have no formal roles in state administration. Attention to degrees of governance also recognizes the possibility that organizations do change the structure of their relationships with people under their control, and reveals how they use coercion and actual violence. Olson notes that some predatory "roving bandits" become "stationary bandits," who promote the productivity of their victims so that they can extract more.[16] Likewise, Volkov found that OPS-Uralmash in Russia evolved from a karate club for youth into a racketeering gang, then a predatory business syndicate, a soccer club, and finally, a political party, using coercion and fostering relationships with those who were variously clients, victims, and customers.[17]

This minimalist definition of state failure as the failure to provide public goods in Sierra Leone is less concerned with determining at what point weak bureaucratic capability signals state failure, since political authority in many African countries at present is not constructed primarily on such a basis. It also confronts the issue of norms. Many regimes are odious and fail to do for all what one thinks a state should do. But they may have supporters and provide non-excludable benefits to at least some in society. Most politicians in Sierra Leone chose not to provide public goods to most people.

Failure of the Bureaucratic State in Sierra Leone

Officials in the late 1950s complained that institutions of higher learning were expanding too quickly, but lauded the increased frequency and punctuality of government bus service to rural communities and looked forward to the arrival of daily papers from the capital in time for their lunch breaks, courtesy of expanded internal passenger flights.[18] These developments read as fantastic, utterly unlikely propositions by the 1990s. Yet even in the thirty years before the start of the war in 1991, the country was not devoid of social services. Budgets allocated 6 percent of expenditures to health services and about 20 percent to education up to the late 1980s, with much of the rest spent on civil servants' salaries.[19] An observer noted: "Poorly paid doctors in government service used hospital facilities and working time for their own private practices. . . . In the supply sector, the availability of drugs was adversely affected by the deteriorating economy which led to outrageously corrupt practices by government officials."[20] But teachers met students, police (occasionally) pursued criminals, and civil servants complained of traffic (on some paved roads) on their way to offices.

This situation underwent a qualitative change in the late 1980s. Government could no longer pay most civil servants. Some bureaucrats abandoned their posts and others engaged in "Mammy Cokerism" (the use of state property for private enterprises such as beauty salons and restaurants in the manner of Mammy Coker, a mythical archetype of the shrewd and savvy Freetown businesswoman) as the political elite turned away from running a government. Permanent blackouts gripped most of the capital. Television ended in 1987, when the minister of information sold the transmitter to a "Kuwaiti investor." Radio disappeared in 1989 when the broadcasting antenna fell over. More revealing, by 1993, only 3 percent of the (much diminished) official budget was spent on education, while a meager 4 percent was earmarked for other "socially oriented" spending.[21]

War then caused the most severe recession in state capabilities, despite the president's efforts to try to mobilize defense against the RUF and bolster the capabilities of state agencies. This development also helped to shift the priorities of social services vis-à-vis other tasks. Most damaging were RUF attacks on the facilities of two foreign firms, Sierra Ore and Mineral Company and Sierra Rutile, Ltd., in January 1995, causing the loss of an annual $12 million in tax payments to government, 57 percent of the previous year's internally generated revenues.[22] During the same year, the minister of finance reported that the expenses of fighting the RUF absorbed 75 percent of official spending, forcing the government to lay off one-third of its employees.[23] Pressure to make token payments on the country's foreign debt may have also encouraged civil service layoffs and cuts in social service spending. Greater de facto layoffs occurred as fewer civil servants actually received salaries. Foreign observers sometimes complain that African states employ fake "ghost" workers to pad civil service rolls so that officials can pocket the extra salaries. In fact, this occurs alongside a different kind of "ghost" worker, the (virtually) unpaid civil servant who nonetheless struggles to perform essential tasks out of a personal sense of duty and community service.

The recession of state resources in the late 1980s and 1990s not only further weakened state capacity to provide services to citizens. More important, state officials increasingly abjured their roles as patrons, while they still used their power to make themselves personally wealthy. The 1985 retirement of Stevens, president since 1968, quickened this change. Throughout his rule, Stevens laid the groundwork for this development by weakening the political centrality of the bureaucratic state as a provider of public goods. In its place, he built a patronage-based political system that used extra-legal violence, looting, and domination of the entire economy, formal and clandestine alike, to acquire resources. As the petitioner quoted above indicates, enterprising individuals could expect that they would be integrated into his political network if they supported his authority and were prepared to use violence to do so. Over time, this political network was built more upon Stevens' personal domination of economic opportunities and less on any state agency's capacity to generate resources.

Stevens was not a common racketeer. Most racketeers work in countries where government agencies protect people while racketeers try to behave as free riders. They create local disorder and sell exemption from it. They may even subvert agents of the state to their enterprise. But the racketeer benefits from a wider provision of order, since that helps his victims remain productive. Sierra Leone and other truly failed states differed in that they lacked a broader framework of order. Stevens found it more politically and financially rewarding to create disorder, despite the fact that his victims became much less productive as a result. Stevens did so within the framework of his All Peoples Congress (APC) single-party regime, and because of the faltering bureaucratic state. This separation of political authority from the formal structures of the state insulated Sierra Leone's political elite from the political impact of bureaucratic decline, and the sovereign status of Sierra Leone as a state insulated Stevens and his associates from many of the negative economic consequences of their predation.

Most Sierra Leoneans blamed Stevens and the APC for economic decline and disorder.[24] Disorder, insecurity, and poverty grew out of Stevens' control of the country's diamond mining sector and his use of it to mobilize and accentuate the violence of clandestine commercial networks that supported his hold on power. Stevens interfered in local disputes to accentuate local grievances and recruited violent groups to intervene on behalf of loyal supporters. This instrumental use of violence, down to a personal micro-level, dominated the country's economic and political life throughout the 1970s and 1980s. Stevens' political network eventually monopolized even clandestine economic opportunities. Stevens provided limited opportunities for some outside this political class. For young men especially, this provision required that they participate in violence against other Sierra Leoneans on behalf of patrons, a transaction that lacked social reciprocities of patronage organized around legitimate, recognized social values. Instead, young men's work resembled a commercial transaction based upon violence.

Violent Commerce and Instrumental Disorder

Diamonds have played a prominent role in Sierra Leone's political culture since the discovery of local alluvial deposits in 1931. Unlike oil in Nigeria and Gabon or copper in the Congo and Zambia, alluvial diamonds are accessible to large numbers of people and are easily smuggled. Sierra Leone's diamonds have been one of the few entrepreneurial outlets for enterprising people, especially young men. One scholar estimates that approximately 35,000 people were engaged in legal and illicit diamond mining (IDM) throughout the 1950s and early 1960s.[25] IDM has been a continuous concern for officials in Sierra Leone since the 1930s. Local people, including some officials, viewed IDM as a source of local conflict.[26]

Popular claims of ownership of resources appear elsewhere, such as in Nigeria's Niger Delta, where most of Nigeria's oil is produced. But Sierra Leone's diamonds do not offer governments an easy monopoly on rent-seeking exploitation of natural resources, contrary to suggestions in recent literature.[27] In Sierra Leone (as with alluvial diamonds in Congo and Angola), state officials and their associates had to fight local people and popular local politicians for control over diamonds.

IDM not only challenges official state and politicians' informal control over resources, but also shapes local politics. Diamonds therefore played a central role in Sierra Leone's politics from the 1930s. Colonial officials complained that unregulated economic opportunity attracted the "worst and toughest characters" and "undesirables from French Guinea and even further abroad." These "tough characters"—unemployed urban youth and rural fortune seekers from much the same social origins as those who would populate Sierra Leone's armed groups in the 1990s—often teamed up with local notables to challenge the colonial administration of the 1950s. "Mr. Carter, Assistant Superintendent of Police, Special Constabulary, raided an area near Yomandu and was captured by illicit miners, and they, the illicit miners, threatened to cut his throat," reports an official. "Some of the African employees were severely man-handled, and Mr. Carter was lucky to be allowed to go free."[28] Even earlier, an agent of a foreign diamond mining company observed that "the illegal miners are armed with swords and machetes and the leaders are beginning to exhort their men to resistance."[29] It was to these "tough characters" that Stevens turned in the 1970s and 1980s when he was looking for ways to intimidate his rivals.

British colonial and early independent administrations saw legalization and licensing of IDM as a way not only to increase revenues and spur local economic development, but also to limit the chance that IDM operators would side with more radical nationalist politicians, whose charges that the state and private foreign mining firms were exploiting local people and the resources that rightfully belonged to them were attracting multi-ethnic followings among the poor. Officials worried that IDM gangs intimidated local politicians and chiefs who supported British administration. These concerns became more acute in the mid-1950s, as armed uprisings across Sierra Leone targeted local African colonial officials whom rioters accused of corruption and other abuses of power. Officials were convinced that IDM gangs were a security threat to the state, "the opinion being that unless visible results are produced very soon, the Kono people will again become restive."[30]

Most licenses were distributed according to patronage concerns. Zack-Williams discovered that by the early 1970s, associates of the ruling APC received most of the licenses. He shows how Stevens, the APC's head, used mining licenses to incorporate local rulers into the APC power structure and undermine local opponents who included both traditional elites and a new political class of Western-educated indigenes.[31] In doing so, Stevens replicated the favoritism of his predecessor, only with different people and more intensively.

Stevens' own road to power was rough. A military coup after his election in 1967 blocked him from taking office until a counter-coup in 1968 restored him to power. Stevens then used the army to track down illicit miners who still supported officials who had favored his predecessor. But Stevens was wary of making the army too strong. Armed IDM gangs offered Stevens a useful alternative, since he could use them to attack opponents while requiring gangs to align themselves with local politicians who supported him. Now local notables who benefited from IDM owed their wealth to Stevens via these armed youth.

Armed youth were not only mining diamonds and beating up opposition supporters. Parliament condemned APC "thugs," and warned the public about those who "under the cloak of the youth section of the All Peoples Congress intimidate the inhabitants and extort money."[32] The behavior of the regular military, however, confirmed for Stevens the benefits of fielding armed followers to protect him and to attack his critics. In April 1971, coup plotters managed to enter Stevens' residence. (Cpl. Foday Sankoh, the future head of the RUF, played a minor role in this affair, for which he was imprisoned for several years.) A new paramilitary force, the Internal Security Unit (ISU), drew recruits from young APC supporters. The ISU went into action during the 1973 election and helped the APC secure 84 of 85 contested seats. This entrenched a pattern of creating private armed groups to protect political factions, a practice that in large part created the conditions leading to Sierra Leone's state failure and civil war.

Armed APC youth and the ISU attacked Fourah Bay College students in 1977, after students called for more attention to the country's poor socio-economic condition. These attacks led to widespread looting in Freetown and the declaration of a state of emergency. Given license for predation by Stevens outside the law, the ISU demonstrated behavior that Sierra Leoneans now call "Operation Pay Yourself." Commenting on the ISU activities to suppress riots, a local journalist noted: "There have been several reports of members of the Internal Security Unit capitalizing on their position to harass innocent traders at night, [making] attempted assault on women and even [going] to the extent of store breaking."[33] Students later commemorated their repression as an annual "All Thugs Day," in recognition of the link between Stevens and predatory armed youth gangs.

Stevens made unprecedented use of armed supporters to manipulate local disputes and to increase the APC's hold on power. Even APC supporters questioned this interference in local political matters: "A delegation from Kono comprising APC supporters called on the Acting Minister to enquire whether there was truth in the allegation that the 'big men' in the Party had decided to put up a particular candidate for a Kono chieftaincy election to the exclusion of all others."[34] Chieftaincy succession (about 30 of Sierra Leone's 146 chieftaincies are in diamond mining areas) led to conflicts over access to mining, licit and illicit alike. Local subjects documented and complained to the president that, along with "inhuman treatment," the new chief over five years had misappropriated about $150,000 in chiefdom revenues related to diamond mining activities.[35] The local favorite, who had been denied his office as chief, and his supporters responded with violence. The chief relied upon armed mining gangs that operated with his approval and on youthful APC activists to defend his economic and political interests and to attack local rivals.

This particular chief actively supported his patrons' interests. When, in 1982, a dissident challenged the APC's choice of a parliamentary candidate in single-party elections, the chief shot the candidate's most prominent local backer. The chief's violent act renewed political grievances dating from his own selection, since the injured candidate was from a local rival's family. Even though the chief was charged with a crime, the president's cabinet dropped the charges, as "his opponents may capitalize on his fate and cause chaos in the Chiefdom with a view to deposing him."[36]

The tight connection between that chief and his patrons in Freetown undermined the rule of law and tied governmental administration more closely to the private gain of favored individuals. Meanwhile, most citizens faced economic decline and personal insecurity as local disputes became more violent and as they reflected national-level power struggles. Nonetheless, the willingness of citizens in 1982 to attempt to use the institutions and laws of the state, and the willingness of judges and other civil servants to hear such cases, shows how Sierra Leone's bureaucratic state (corrupt though it was) was a victim of Stevens' use of power.

Stevens' political strategy contradicted the primary admonition of a commission of inquiry that investigated causes of violence across Sierra Leone in 1955 and 1956: "Firstly the Paramount and other chiefs should not be associated with any party, and that party platforms should not be used in local affairs. . . . They cannot perform their functions properly—any more than can civil servants—if they serve, or might be made to appear to serve, only those people who have the same political faith as themselves."[37] Stevens' aim was precisely to divide local factions and cause conflict between them, by recruiting individual chiefs and local strongmen to a particular party and supplying them with opportunities in the formal and clandestine economies and with access to violence to use against their rivals, and even to settle personal scores. This anthropology of violence and incorporation of multiple grievances and personal competition foreshadowed the RUF's organizational strategy, while also creating what Sierra Leoneans would later call "town rebels."

Although disorder and impoverishment undermined the legitimacy of the state in the eyes of most people, the APC's monopolization of the country's most accessible significant economic opportunity changed the nature of resistance and undermined possibilities for mobilizing ideological alternatives. This centralization of power through the mobilization of armed gangs to militarize local conflicts extended to the 1982 single-party parliamentary elections. Local university students warned of the consequences of this tactic: "It is anybody's guess what will be the magnitude of the catastrophe that follows."[38] Young men who engaged in IDM to improve their personal situations had to deal with local chiefs and politicians who, now with tacit permission from State House, counted control over IDM and its armed gangs as a perquisite of power. This is especially significant because it directed the energies of illicit miners toward integrating themselves into the informal political system that many rightly blamed for the country's impoverished condition and their own personal distress. Doing so made it difficult for them to back opposition politicians who argued for local control over natural resources, since such opponents now faced the superior firepower of politicians' militias.

Bettering oneself also meant jettisoning ideology, aligning oneself according to the dictates of personalist politics, and perhaps serving as an armed supporter of a local strongman in return for access to a bit of diamond wealth. Informal and clandestine markets in this context were not and still are not venues for "civil society" groups to organize outside the purview of the dominant political authority.[39] Thus, even as Sierra Leone's state agencies declined and its own high officials undermined the rule of law, violent informal channels of power tied to Stevens' authority grew stronger. In contrast to Kaplan's depiction of Sierra Leone's state failure as a vacuum of political authority, alternative authority structures replaced state power.[40] From this perspective, agents and structures that promoted bureaucratic state failure proved to be very powerful and operated according to a predictable logic. They disrupted other people's efforts to organize alternative political structures and forced existing institutions to respond to their interests.

Failure and the Global Economic Dimension

Stevens relied upon foreigners and local ethnic Lebanese businessmen, many constitutionally prohibited from becoming citizens, to help him exploit diamonds and other commodities as personal property, outside the control of state agencies. He and a local Lebanese partner, Jamil Mohamed (known simply as "Jamil" or "the White President"), became board members of the state diamond marketing company in 1976. The company was the sole legal channel for the export of diamonds, accounting for over 75 percent of the value of the country's exports. This put Stevens and his partner in control of the bulk of the foreign exchange earnings of the formal economy, even though the company was nominally state owned. This trade was valued between $150 million and $200 million annually, on the basis of official exports at the height of maximum suppression of IDM in the 1960s.[41] Appointment to the company's board then became patronage for loyal strongmen and politicians who ran IDM operations. This development further integrated IDM into the central structures of power at the expense of state institutions and the formal economy. In fact, a future RUF leader found a job in 1982 as a security guard for Stevens' business, putting him at the center of the violent politics of the mining area and giving him what he claimed was valuable military experience and connections.

Showing enthusiasm for creditor prescriptions to reduce state control over the economy, Stevens "privatized" agricultural marketing in 1979 for the benefit of himself and his associates. Stevens and Jamil used their private commercial positions to import oil, while the president used his official power to insist that the Central Bank pay for the oil at street market rates. The partners then exchanged local currency earned through sales at the much more favorable (for them) official rate. Over the course of one year in the mid-1980s, the partners gained a windfall of $27 million, or about 3 percent of recorded GDP at the time.[42] Likewise, the president became a major private importer of rice, which he sold to the state. As president, he then distributed state rice to political supporters, undercutting local commercial food production. Almost no aspect of the state escaped Stevens' mania for personal appropriation. Other failed deals included a proposal to import toxic wastes and to sell an island to the Palestine Liberation Organization.[43]

These activities severely undermined the fiscal resources of what remained of state bureaucracy in Sierra Leone. Spending deficits jumped from about 50 percent of revenues in the 1970s to over 100 percent by the mid-1980s.[44] Corrupt and inefficient though it was, Sierra Leone's state bureaucracy succumbed to Stevens' predations. Figures cited above suggest that, earlier, civil servants at least paid lip service to the notion of providing services to citizens. Citizens also suffered from the loss of clandestine opportunities, whether in diamond mining, customs evasion, or currency trading. As with diamonds, individuals wishing to better their personal condition amid this economic wreckage and concentration of privilege found in clandestine markets the very same individuals who were responsible for their plight in the first place. Some ended up in urban areas, *rarray* men awaiting employment as muscle for political bosses and commercial big men, or as petty thieves. They then became candidates for recruitment to the armed groups in the Sierra Leonean conflict after 1991.

Foreign borrowing helped bolster formal state structures through the 1980s. IMF assistance in the early 1980s (despite the early termination of a 1981 agreement) sustained some state services. But by the late 1980s—when payments on arrears fell behind—creditors ended their support. By then, there was little of Sierra Leone's indigenous revenue base that was not in the hands of Stevens, or, after he retired in 1985, the political network that he had created. By 1988, official diamond exports were only $2 million, just 5 percent of the previous year, as well-connected entrepreneurs smuggled stones out of the country. Exports fell to just 12 carats for the first four months of 1989. Export duty collection fell an astounding 98.3 percent in 1987.[45]

These developments signaled the extent to which Stevens' hand-picked successor, General Joseph Momoh, in 1985 inherited a nearly stateless regime. This is the point of serious state failure, from a bureaucratic perspective. It also highlights that corruption within Sierra Leone's civil service was not the primary culprit in the creation of conditions leading to the collapse of public order in Sierra Leone following the March 1991 RUF invasion from Liberia, despite the tendency of creditors to ascribe dwindling bureaucratic capacity to bureaucratic corruption. Many countries have corrupt administrations, but corruption alone does not make states fail. What distinguished Stevens was that he not only destroyed Sierra Leone's formal state institutions, he also turned his back on his social obligations as a patron and instead invaded most avenues of political opposition, including informal markets, and created the social basis for the fragmentation and militarization of politics by his sponsorship of armed gangs that owed personal loyalty to him.

Town Rebels and Bush Rebels

Momoh struggled to hold power. To do so, he had to prevent Stevens' associates from monopolizing the exploitation of the clandestine economy, given that the formal economy barely existed. But Stevens had chosen Momoh as his successor precisely because he was Force Commander of a military that Stevens had intentionally kept very weak. Loyal, not particularly energetic, and himself implicated in corruption, Momoh was a safe bet to leave undisturbed the private commercial activities of Stevens (who died soon after leaving office) and his associates. Through the late 1980s, the army had only 3,000 personnel, who attracted popular derision because of the army's low level of training and subordination to the ISU and to the armed youth gangs under Stevens' protection.

Momoh turned to foreign entrepreneurs to wrest diamonds from the hands of Stevens' old political associates. Regaining some control over diamonds was also a key creditor condition for loans, since doing so offered the only promise of even minimal payments on the country's foreign debt. Momoh had to battle elements of the APC and the armed gangs that backed them, since attracting new foreign investors required removing these violent commercial networks. Foreign firms were a good political alternative to direct army occupation for Momoh— especially given the weakness of the army—since he could use those firms to gain control over his own associates, control the access of others to clandestine opportunities, and dole out such opportunities to his own loyalists.

The first attempt to control diamonds in this manner lasted for several months in 1987. Momoh's first partner, an Israeli businessman, turned out to be a sanctions-buster for South Africa's apartheid government and was arrested in the United States on felony charges. The next investor arrived in 1989, also an Israeli businessman. He turned out to be an alleged drug money launderer. He made his own deals with strongmen in diamond mining areas, rather than winning back control for the president. He left Sierra Leone after spending time in prison in Freetown for "economic sabotage." The next entrepreneur helped to precipitate the collapse of order in the country's diamond mining area and later appeared in other war zones in Africa, where he interested desperate governments in his plans to seize mine sites by force.

A mining consortium proposed to invest in a large kimberlite diamond mining operation, provided that it would be given a comprehensive concession to operate alluvial mining operations too. The firm insisted that the area had to be cleared of IDM gangs, most of which owed some allegiance to local strongmen. Momoh's government had also reached a critical point in negotiations with creditors, and needed to generate income to pay arrears. Accordingly, in mid-1990, the Sierra Leonean army launched "Operation Clean Sweep" and "Operation Clear All." These operations removed up to 30,000 miners. But the army was not as efficient as first appeared. Soldiers began mining diamonds together with local APC strongmen and gangs who had no intention of allowing Momoh or a foreign firm to exclude them from the country's major source of wealth.

While there is no direct military link between the March 1991 RUF invasion from Liberia and Momoh's diamond policy, Momoh's actions helped to change the social framework of violent commerce by alarming armed gangs at odds with State House over control of resources. Momoh expanded the army to 6,000 men to meet the RUF threat. His foreign minister admitted that recruits consisted "mostly of drifters, rural and urban unemployed, a fair number of hooligans, drug addicts and thieves."[46] Nonetheless, the more charismatic junior officers among them actually organized the country's defense against the RUF. They also recognized that corrupt senior officers stole supplies meant for soldiers on the front lines. Sergeant Valentine Strasser and his associates, most in their early twenties, marched from the front lines to Freetown in April 1992, forcing Momoh to flee. Strasser's immediate complaint centered on the absence of medical care in the army—he was allegedly injured when RUF fighters overwhelmed his unit while they mined diamonds. Strasser set up the National Provisional Ruling Council (NPRC) and promised to defeat the RUF. By 1994, the NPRC had increased the army's strength to 14,000 soldiers, many recruited from unemployed youth and those with experience in armed gangs.

Rather than an end to the war, "there developed," wrote Arthur Abraham, a former NPRC minister, "an extraordinary identity of interests between NPRC [regime] and RUF [rebels]." As new senior officers helped themselves to diamonds and war supplies, less privileged soldiers found ways to help themselves, too. "This," continued Abraham, "was partly responsible for the rise of the *sobel* phenomenon, i.e., government soldiers by day become rebels by night."[47] War gave these soldiers an opportunity to loot and mine diamonds while redressing their exclusion from patronage networks of Stevens' era. Soldiers' predations became so serious that the NPRC warned that 20 percent of the army was disloyal.[48]

This unpopular insurgency turned into an intractable rebel war once the appearance of RUF fighters provided the opportunity for other armed men to take advantage of opportunities to loot and settle local scores. These activities were thus not a rebellion against an old order. Instead, they offered to marginalized youth the prospect that they could renegotiate (or force a change in) their position vis-à-vis an existing political network that controlled economic opportunity. Kandeh examines this political class as the product of the collapse of the formal economy and of politicians' mobilization of what he calls "lumpen" groups.[49] Once Momoh was unable to recentralize patronage, violent political networks began to fragment. This gave "armed marginals" more diverse points of access through armed gangs and the army to violent commercial networks, now in ways that posed greater threats to what remained of public order.

Sierra Leone is distinctive in that "armed marginals" succeeded in 1992 in overthrowing a regime, partly through forming significant alliances with numerous surviving politicians and strongmen. Many Sierra Leoneans recognized the common features that these rulers and RUF insurgents shared, especially the connection between violence, looting, and politics. A Freetown journalist equated the two categories, "bush rebels" and "town rebels." "Bush rebels are made up of young and old people (including children), all under the influence of hard drugs and always shabbily dressed," he wrote. His description of "town rebels" is more revealing and points directly to the link between Stevens' strategies of rule and contemporary warring parties:

> This is perhaps the largest category. . . . They are in constant help and communication with bush rebels. They are always neatly dressed and so are not easily identified. They live in towns, just next door to you. . . . They work for the established government. They work in offices close to the seat of the President. They are present in all spheres of work. Private business as well. Even in the churches and mosques. They are always neatly dressed especially in coats and ties. This class of rebels is responsible for the ugly state (and pleasant state) you are in today. . . . With just a signature they robbed your country of billions. They give you right when you are wrong and wrong when you are right. . . .[50]

Sankoh, the RUF's leader until jailed in Freetown in 2000, also equated the predations of town rebels and his bush rebels and linked them to APC styles of rule in his own justification for fighting against Sierra Leone's government:

> They ask us why we mine diamonds. Why didn't they ask Jamil or Shaki [Siaka Stevens] that when the APC was in power? Yeah, we mine! We in RUF believe in wealth, arms, and power in the hands of the people. . . . We're not going to give up diamonds or our guns to anybody. And we will get POWER right now![51]

Many local communities attempted to oppose the RUF. Starting in 1994, local notables began recruiting what in southern Sierra Leone's Mende language are known as "unruly youth"—village school dropouts, some who had earlier welcomed the violence of the RUF as an opportunity to settle local scores and tilt an alienating rural social order in their favor. These "unruly youth" instead became the core of home guard units. Alpha Lavalie, a history professor at Fourah Bay College in Freetown, helped to organize these units into an army, realizing that the official army could not fight the RUF.[52] Though soldiers shot him, his group became the nucleus of the Kamajors later in the war. These units scored successes against the RUF, especially after they received training from Executive Outcomes, a South African outfit that the NPRC hired to fight on Freetown's side in the war. These successes, combined with international diplomatic pressure, created an opportunity for local activists to call for long-promised multiparty elections. Ahmed Tejan Kabbah, a former UN administrator, won the election, and was installed as president in March 1996.

Executive Outcomes' stay, however, was brief. The firm departed under diplomatic pressure and due to the government's inability to pay its fees. By 1997, Kabbah was left with what appeared to be a defeated rebellion, along with an army harboring many sobels, some of whom were responsible for three coup attempts in the first nine months of Kabbah's administration. Kabbah and Hinga Norman, his deputy defense minister, turned to the Kamajors to protect their regime.

Even loyal soldiers suspected that Kabbah was building a private army to advance the interests of his political party. Acting with impunity, some Kamajors took advantage of their positions to better their personal lots. "If they are not beating senior police officers and civilians or extorting monies," wrote a Freetown journalist, "they will be engaging in shootouts killing innocent civilians."[53] External observers complained of abuses, some of which resembled those of the RUF (though not of the same intensity). These included arbitrary detentions and extortions of money and property at checkpoints, evidence that Kamajors increasingly operated as a freelance group, especially when deployed outside their home areas.[54]

The army took power again on 25 May 1997. The RUF welcomed the coup and formed an alliance, the Armed Forces Ruling Council (AFRC), with the army's Major Johnny Paul Kormoh as its head. Kormoh named Sankoh his deputy. Human rights abuses, already considerable before the coup, increased. The AFRC and the RUF singled out Kabbah supporters and others for mutilation. Many eyewitnesses and victims reported that amputees were often instructed to deliver messages to others that the AFRC and the RUF would resist international pressure to give up power.[55] The AFRC did not attempt to administer regions it controlled, even in the capital, beyond appointing heads of state agencies. Civil servants were urged to "donate" their time, and were forced at gunpoint to go to work while fighters looted the city. When faced with opposition from a West African (primarily Nigerian) expeditionary force that held the western reaches of the city, AFRC spokesmen threatened to kill citizens and raze the city in "Operation No Living Thing."[56]

That West African expeditionary force of Nigerian troops forced the AFRC out of Freetown in February 1998. In July 1998, the United Nations authorized a small detachment, the United Nations Observer Mission in Sierra Leone (UNOMSIL), to serve alongside the West African force. Meanwhile, ex-army and RUF rebels continued their campaign against Kabbah's government. They recruited new fighters by kidnapping them, forcing them to commit atrocities in their communities to ensure that they could not easily return.[57] AFRC and RUF fighters, for example, kidnapped 2,700 children during an incursion into Freetown in January 1999.[58] They continued the practice of mutilating civilians. One RUF fighter was reported to have said to his victim: "Since you civilians are not here for us, we are here to destroy you."[59] UN observers underscored that "these incidents underlined the problems related to the effectiveness of command and control within the rebel groups. . . ."[60] They also showed the extent of fighters' anger at authorities and social structures not just of the state, but of larger society. A survey of the damage in Freetown shows that rebels targeted cultural monuments; churches; headquarters of human rights, development, and women's organizations; pharmacies; courts; and law offices. This targeting was apparent enough to the local population that unexplained gunfire in April 2001 was sufficient to cause workers at some non-governmental organizations to destroy identifying signs, lest rebels attack them.[61]

Kabbah again negotiated with the RUF when it became clear that Nigerian soldiers would leave Sierra Leone after elections in Nigeria in 1999. On 7 July 1999 Sierra Leone's government and the RUF signed the Lomé peace agreement. That agreement named Sankoh chairman of a diamond resource commission and national vice president. The RUF would turn itself into a political party, and other RUF leaders would receive state offices. The UN Security Council replaced the observer mission with UNAMSIL. But this agreement collapsed in May 2000, when UNAMSIL forces attempted to enter the mining areas. The RUF kidnapped over 500 UN soldiers, sparking a British military intervention, which continued into 2001. Johnny Paul Koroma's forces from the AFRC regime switched sides to support Kabbah. Thus the Lomé agreement rested upon unfounded optimism that the RUF and other factions would abide by the terms of the agreement and evolve into something like political parties, and that their leaders would conclude that their success in a democratic coalition government required gaining public support and confidence.

The Homogenization of Political Resistance

This context of state failure, where economic opportunities are welded to the exercise of political authority, offers little room for ideological insurgents to take time and resources to build support through administering liberated zones. Instead, contested militarized patronage networks provide young men (and women) who already play roles in violent economies the chance to improve their economic and social standing. Often the most marginalized members of society find that freelancing or joining a rebel group offers them opportunities to remedy their situation and settle old scores. Nonetheless, economic grievances are more likely to prevail in violent political networks, as in Sierra Leone, where political power and wealth are tied to maximizing displays of violence.

In the pre-war context, violent groups were more successful in political competition. Youths were recruited into APC militias and the paramilitaries of local strongmen on this basis, which further destroyed formal and informal institutions of rule and made people less secure. Sierra Leone's violent political structures—both rebel and "official"—placed premiums on violence and private gain. If any of these groups had tried to supply public goods in the short term, it is likely that they would have lost out to rivals. During APC rule, such activity would threaten the president. Local APC strongmen who did tend to the concerns of local people faced attacks. This was the case in 1986 in eastern Sierra Leone during the *Ndogboyosoi* uprising, when APC politicians and local leaders who asserted popular grievances against the Freetown regime were confronted by armed APC supporters from outside and from young men recruited locally.

Building popular bases of support and reconstructing Sierra Leone as a state will require that those with arms forego looting and instead divert scarce resources toward improving the welfare of local people. In the context of violent accumulation, this fact leaves political organizers militarily vulnerable to rival gangs, or to rivals within their own organization. Internationally mediated negotiations that focus on armed groups reinforce this context, since the surest way to power is to grab guns, cause disruption (and get some loot), and receive a seat at the bargaining table as a result. Kamajor militias initially appeared to take on state-like tasks, such as providing security to communities and enforcing social norms that most people considered legitimate. But outside core areas of ethnic support, these militias found that they, too, had to contest control over diamonds if they were to protect themselves. Once armed, their members attracted attention from strongmen and factions in the capital. Likewise, members of the poor people's movement that bothered British and Sierra Leone officials in the 1950s and 1960s in mining areas also faced formidable firepower from gangs affiliated with incumbent politicians. Its supporters also found that they could remedy their poverty through association with those whom they criticized—the politicians whose behavior had created poverty and disorder in the first place.

No ideological statement emerged from the RUF except a pamphlet, *Footpaths to Democracy*, written by a businessman who helped to handle RUF diamond sales.[62] The RUF made no apparent sustained attempt to administer occupied areas, nor to advertise a political program to recruit members. Likewise, groups such as the West Side Boys did not offer a political program to recruit members. In fact, its head left the group to become a government official, attracting criticism and envy from members for his fancy office, nice clothes, and political connections, and suspicions that he would run for president. This shift underscored the extent to which these groups resembled the political structures that they fought.

Former Yugoslavia helps shed light on the specific nature of the relation of Sierra Leone's state failure to protest and private violence. There, armed gangs included individuals who performed clandestine economic and military services for the collapsed regime and recruited followers from among economically marginalized youth. One gang leader, Zeljko Raznajatovic ("Arkan"), doubled as official head of the Belgrade soccer team's fan club. Arkan robbed banks in Western Europe, then, as fan club director, organized a paramilitary group with close ties to Serb politicians and clandestine economy figures.[63]

A captured RUF fighter in 1991 explained that his task was to attack civilians, but not to kill them. He said, "that way, towns will be thrown into chaos and there will be breakdown of law and order."[64] Economic motives are compatible with this use of force to settle old scores, punish corrupt politicians, and serve the ambitions of war leaders. Many concluded that having a gun and joining an armed gang was the best way to remedy their poor situations. A Nigerian commander observing warfare in neighboring Liberia noted that fighters there were eager to loot a town that the Nigerians were guarding. "From discussions with them, it was quite clear that most of them believed that Buchanan was their prize for several years of combat. They planned to use loot acquired in Buchanan to start off business or advance their education after the war."[65]

The West Side Boys, some of whom later fought their former RUF allies, also incorporated concerns of youth in the collapsed state as they set up roadblocks and collected numerous "taxes" from surrounding communities. Their name comes from the hip-hop culture popular among urban youth. It refers to the rivalries between two gangsta rap studios located on opposite coasts of the United States. This business rivalry resulted in the murders of "West's" most popular artist, Tupac Shakur, and "Biggie" Smalls (Notorious B.I.G.), the CEO of "East."[66] This association was not "anti-system" in Sierra Leone's context, where youth admire two enterprising and clever alleged drug dealers who used violence to make a lot of money in the legitimate music business. While not selling crack cocaine, APC politicians operated in much the same fashion, though with far less cultural appeal.

AFRC members share this preference for "West" with RUF members. In October 1998, for example, more than 100 AFRC and RUF members joined to attack Tonko Limba Chiefdom. They reportedly wore T-shirts bearing the picture of Shakur, which were cheap and readily available. Eyewitnesses report many that rebels attacking Freetown in January 1999 wore similar T-shirts. In February 1999 AFRC/RUF fighters again appeared in Shakur T-shirts during their attack on the provincial capital of Kenema.[67] By May 2000, however, it had become apparent to most young people that West Side Boys head Koroma backed the Sierra Leonean government against the RUF and had traded rap for music more compatible with his conversion as a born again Christian.

The Role of Outsiders in Sustaining the Failure of Public Order

Outsiders have played a major role in promoting the failure of public order in Sierra Leone. In neighboring Liberia, Taylor played a very direct role through his support of the RUF from 1991. Taylor visited Sierra Leone in 1988 to recruit support from Momoh to overthrow Liberia's president at that time, Samuel Doe. Momoh had Taylor jailed while he attempted to sell Taylor to Doe. Taylor escaped from prison and fled. Harboring a grudge against Momoh, Taylor was rumored to have threatened to "do a RENAMO" on Momoh—to support a predatory rebel group to remove Momoh from power by destroying the institutions and infrastructure of societal order in Sierra Leone, as the rebel group RENAMO had done in Mozambique in the 1980s. More pressing strategic reasons for Taylor's actions by 1991 included Momoh's support and aid to an anti-Taylor coalition based in Sierra Leone, and because Momoh-based elements of the West African expeditionary force opposed Taylor's unilateral bid for power in Liberia on Sierra Leone's territory.

Taylor's assistance to the RUF remained a consistent feature throughout the war, reducing incentives for the RUF to rely on the support of Sierra Leoneans to survive. Diamonds marketed via Taylor's international business connections, combined with the RUF's control of Sierra Leone's Kono diamond fields, generated considerable income for all involved. An investigation revealed that diamond exports involved sums on the order of $300 million annually.[68] Diamonds played an important role both in financing the RUF and sustaining Taylor's political network in Liberia.

International approaches toward conflict resolution played a large role in sustaining warfare in the region and were structured in ways that helped Taylor's and the RUF's exploitation of natural resources. Despite his ties to the RUF, Taylor succeeded in securing international recognition as president of Liberia in 1997. The key to Taylor's success lay in his participation in internationally mediated peace talks, starting in 1990, just as the RUF participated in talks concerning Sierra Leone after 1996. Liberia's negotiations culminated in a 1995 peace plan that made provisions for a coalition government and a joint military command that included members of all major warring factions. The rationale was that negotiations had to include groups that had guns, otherwise they would disrupt efforts to resolve the conflict. Once inside Liberia's capital, Taylor was able to use armed fighters from the National Patriotic Front of Liberia (NPFL) to eliminate rivals. Amid this insecurity, assassination attempts were made against NPFL dissidents and the Catholic archbishop, while non-NPFL media were attacked.[69]

Taylor accurately guessed that international organizations, such as the UN, that were eager to disengage from the conflict would overlook repression in Liberia or his assistance to insurgents like the RUF, since they had no credible means of coercing him to cooperate. Taylor was also able to intimidate Liberia's voting population. He won more than 75 percent of the votes in the 1997 election. Destitute and traumatized, Liberians voted for a strongman who could prevail over the other factions and end the incessant violence. The reality was that the way in which Taylor exercised authority underwent little change, despite his shift from faction leader to president. His relationship to the RUF and by 1999 to a Guinean insurgent leader, and his backing in 2000 of a former president of Côte d'Ivoire, destabilized countries surrounding Liberia through intensifying violent commercial and military ties between these men and Taylor.

Taylor's links to the RUF remained strong. An team of observers sponsored by the UN Security Council reported that "most of the mission's interlocutors, including those at the most senior levels, had no doubt that President Taylor exercised strong influence, even direct control, over RUF."[70] James Cunningham, a U.S. representative to the UN, said: "We think that President Taylor and his government bear a special responsibility with regard to the RUF, and that they haven't broken off support."[71]

Despite these shortcomings, the July 1999 Lomé agreement, signed by RUF and Sierra Leonean government officials, resembled the 1995 Liberian agreement. The 1999 agreement called upon the RUF to transform itself into a political party. A foreign official who helped write the agreement asserted that Sankoh would thereby be forced to confront the demands and interests of Sierra Leone's people, and become more "governance oriented" in his approach. The official suggested that including him in a coalition government as head of the Strategic Mineral Resources Commission to manage diamond resources would change his views toward serving the public interest—reconstructing Sierra Leone rather than looting it. Unlike the Liberian agreement, the Sierra Leonean agreement also recognized the need to increase the number of the 12,000 UN observers who were meant to oversee disarmament by all sides.[72]

RUF participation in the UN-sponsored disarmament program that predated the 1999 agreement was minimal. By the time the 1999 agreement collapsed, only 12,500 weapons had been collected. These were generally "low quality" arms, and the UN suspected that the RUF was holding on to its best weapons.[73] The RUF even managed to retrieve 400 of the collected rifles from a storage site in April 2000. Weaker groups were disarmed in greater numbers, partly because they were less able to keep fighters from unilaterally appearing for their $300 bounties. Overall, uneven disarmament had the effect of increasing the premium on violence as a strategy for groups to remain competitive in Sierra Leone's tumultuous political economy.

Throughout the life of the agreement, RUF forces did not allow UN observers or Sierra Leonean government officials to enter areas under RUF control, except in small numbers. Indeed, RUF fighters armed themselves with more than 500 automatic weapons, truck loads of ammunition, and armored personnel carriers that they captured from UNAMSIL contingents in January 2000, and additional weapons captured in the May 2000 kidnapping of UN forces.

Meanwhile, Sankoh used his official position as commissioner of diamond resources to market RUF diamonds. Violating a UN travel ban, Sankoh visited a business associate of the Liberian president in South Africa in February 2000, allegedly to sell diamonds. He imported eight dump trucks, explaining: "I want to be adequately prepared for full-fledged campaigning."[74]

Sankoh was captured and arrested on 16 May 2000 after fleeing from his residence in Freetown. Although he was removed from the scene, UN officials insisted that negotiations with the RUF continue and therefore demanded that the RUF "elect" a new leader, Issa Sesay. The effort to find an interlocutor appeared to fragment the RUF. A spokesman for one RUF faction said: "General Issa has betrayed them [the fighters] and they now have nothing to do with him."[75] Fighting broke out between another faction and Sam Bockarie, a RUF commander who probably still enjoyed Taylor's protection in 2002.[76]

On the one hand, attempts to resolve these conflicts by military means failed. Failed states tend to be of scant strategic importance to powerful states. Thus, there usually is little political will among outsiders to intervene directly, as in conflicts in the Balkans. Nor is there any long-term international effort to help deal with the poverty and violent rule of states like Sierra Leone. On the other hand, negotiations absolve human rights violators. Sankoh was branded a war criminal under UN Resolution 1132 of 1997, yet in 1999 he occupied a central role in the UN-mediated process under the Lomé agreement. It thus appears that groups based upon violent commercial exploitation of resources are not easily "evolved" into groups interested in providing public goods.

In a departure from past international approaches to Sierra Leone, British military forces sought a military solution to Sierra Leone's state failure after the collapse of the Lomé agreement in 2000. As of 2002, British military forces were protecting Kabbah's civilian government and equipping what was supposed to be a new Sierra Leonean army. British officials made clear their conviction that the RUF had no intrinsic reason to negotiate for peace so long as it retained a commercial and political link to Liberia's president. British military exercises were timed to coincide with UN attempts to negotiate with the RUF. Facing UN criticism, a British official replied: "It is as if the UN learned nothing from previous experiences. They are using the same language that led to their humiliation a few months ago." A senior UN military officer's reply is instructive: "If the British want war, they can have it and we will leave."[77]

The British and UN positions highlight the divide over approaches toward resolving disorder in failed states. Negotiations are critical for dealing with the problem of violence where the political will for a military solution is lacking. Deploying a large army for frontal assaults is not very effective against multiple and autonomous opponents who alternately oppose and ally with one another at critical moments. Where there is no "army" that can surrender, pacification requires physical occupation and administration. In addition, defeating groups like the RUF, the Civil Defense Forces (CDF), the West Side Boys, and various associated factions on the battlefield would likely require attacks on families of fighters, taking hostages, and the use of force at levels that would violate multiple conventions of warfare and international agreements.

The British method offers a different approach for fighting wars and pacifying stateless regions that draws upon the institutional legacy and administrative memory of the British Empire. Former colonial officers contribute to discussions concerning British strategies. A former district commissioner returned to Sierra Leone to consult with chiefs to gain a micro-level understanding of the multiple grievances that lead people to take up arms and to build support for Kabbah's regime among local notables. This political effort draws upon the experience and personnel connected to the 1956 report cited above that examined violence in the Protectorate prior to independence. Many Sierra Leoneans recognize this link, and several thousand demonstrated in Freetown in October 2000 to call for a restoration of British rule.

This approach contrasts with those of the UN, and other states, that do not address the realities of conflict in collapsed states. Starting in late 2000, British-trained fighters, the CDF, and Guinea's army (which has received help from foreigners) attacked the RUF in the east of the country, while UN demobilization camps were set up to receive fighters who did not want to risk their lives for the RUF. By July 2001, RUF fighters, along with CDF members, were surrendering arms to UN peacekeepers in the Kono diamond mining region. The war appeared to have come to an end.

In 2002, there remained the problem of finding jobs and educational opportunities for ex-fighters in Sierra Leone's wrecked economy. A solution was essential, so that they and youths would not be tempted to return to war if politics became unstable or if they could not feed themselves.

The elections in May 2002 resulted in Kabbah's reelection. At the same time, the UN reported that an unexpectedly large number—78,000—of fighters had been demobilized. Of these, only 6,500 had completed a reintegration process that included job training.[78] However, even for those who had received training, there was little in the way of a viable economy into which to integrate.

UN forces left to themselves are hobbled by limited mandates. U.S. officials, in particular, tend to look for general solutions, such as the Lomé agreement patterned on Liberia's agreement. Despite continuing allegations of Taylor's connections to the RUF in 2002, the international community relaxed its condemnations of Taylor, especially when it appeared in early 2002 that a Liberian rebel force might challenge his hold on power. It seemed better to keep quiet about Taylor's role in promoting violence, lest he lose his grip on power and Liberia return to factional fighting and spoil disarmament and elections in Sierra Leone. The $722 million budget for UNAMSIL from 1 July 2001 to 30 June 2002 gave added incentives to declare victory in Sierra Leone and depart.[79] The 11 September attacks on the United States, the subsequent departure of almost 5,000 Pakistani peacekeepers from Sierra Leone as the India-Pakistan military confrontation worsened, and looming UN concerns about possible deployments in Afghanistan increased the urgency of finding a way to wrap up UNAMSIL.

These approaches also are rooted in assumptions about the universal predictability of behavior, divorced from local cultures and languages, and have great difficulty in grasping how societies work. They downplay the social damage of state failure: the creation of a class of unemployed, desperate youth who have been abandoned by elite political classes, who see joining armed gangs as one of the few remaining ways to improve their personal situations, and who then become the means of advancing the interests of organizers, who pursue their own objectives. So long as these approaches predominate, it is unlikely that the international community can address the concerns of Sierra Leoneans. Ideologues and would-be state builders will be forced to struggle in a context that remains extremely hostile toward any alternative vision of politics in failed states.

Notes

1. The term is from Patrick Chabal and Jean-Pascal Daloz, *Africa Works: Disorder as Political Instrument* (Bloomington, 1999).

2. In contrast to conceptions of revolution in Eric Wolf, *Peasant Wars of the Twentieth Century* (Norman, 1999); Eric Hobsbawm, *Bandits* (New York, 2000); James Scott, *Weapons of the Weak: Everyday Forms of Peasant Resistance* (New Haven, 1987).

3. Norimitsu Onishi, "The Hell That Was Sierra Leone," *New York Times* (31 March 2000), A2; Rafiu Mohammed, "Voyage to Hell," *Tell* [Lagos] (2 October 2000), 15.

4. International Monetary Fund, *Balance of Payments Statistics Yearbook* (Washington, D.C., 1990), 243, for figures from the 1970s, which I have adjusted for inflation. The 1999 figures are from Government of Sierra Leone, *Bulletin of Economic Trends* (Freetown, 2000).

5. United Nations, *Twelfth Report of the Secretary-General on the United Nations Mission in Sierra Leone* (New York, 13 December 2001), 10.

6. United Nations, *Seventh Report of the Secretary-General on the United Nations Mission in Sierra Leone* (New York, 31 October 2000), 7.

7. United Nations, *Human Development Report 2000* (New York, 2000), 149.

8. John Ayoade, "States without Citizens," in Donald Rothchild and Naomi Chazan (eds.), *The Precarious Balance: State and Society in Africa* (Boulder, 1988), 106.

9. Michael Radu and Keith Sommerville, "People's Republic of Congo," in Chris Allen et al., *Benin, the Congo, Burkina Faso* (London, 1989), 159.

10. Mario Azevedo, *Roots of Violence: A History of War in Chad* (London, 1998).

11. Letter of a Kono politician to His Excellency, Dr. Siaka P. Stevens (17 January 1983).

12. Author's calculation.

13. Margareta Sollenberg et al., "Major Armed Conflicts, 1999," *SIPRI Yearbook 2000: Armaments, Disarmament and International Security* (New York, 2000), 52–55.

14. Thomas Hobbes, *Leviathan* (New York, 1996, rev. std. ed.), 110–118.

15. "Liberia Allocates 40m for Army," *Jane's Defense Weekly*, 33:10 (8 March 2000), 14.

16. Mancur Olson, "Dictatorship, Democracy, and Development, *American Political Science Review*, LXXXVII (1993), 567–576.

17. Vadim Volkov, "The Political Economy of Protection Rackets in the Past and the Present," *Social Research*, LXVII (2000), 1–36. Uralmash can be visited at www.ops-uralmash.ru.

18. Governor's Office, "Confidential, No. 13383/517" (12 February 1959).

19. Bank of Sierra Leone, *Economic Review, July–December 1988* (Freetown, 1988), A11.

20. C. Magbaily Fyle, "The State and Health Services in Sierra Leone," in Fyle (ed.), *The State and the Provision of Social Services in Sierra Leone since Independence, 1961–91* (Dakar, 1993), 59.

21. John Karimu, *Government Budget and Economic and Financial Policies for the Financial Year, 1996* (Freetown, 29 December 1995), 12.

22. Sheku Saccoh, "Capital Flight in Sierra Leone," *Africa Economic Digest* (13 February 1995), 14.

23. John Karimu, *Government Budget and Economic and Financial Policies for the Fiscal Year 1995/1996* (Freetown, 29 June 1995), 10; Economist Intelligence Unit, *Sierra Leone*, first quarter (London, 1995), 26.

24. For popular views on this subject, see National Constitutional Review Commission, *Report of the National Constitutional Review Commission* (Freetown, March 1991).

25. H. L. van der Laan, *Sierra Leone Diamonds* (Oxford, 1965), 10–11.

26. Chief Inspector of Mines, "Interim Report on the Alluvial Diamond Mining Scheme" (18 June 1956) [MD 11/36(v)].

27. Paul Collier and Anke Hoeffler, *Greed and Grievance in Civil War* (Washington, D.C., 2000).

28. Letter of Area Superintendent of Mines, Kono, to Area Superintendent of Mines, Kenema (Kenema, 6 March 1957).

29. Letter from Maroc, Ltd., to Provincial Commissioner, Northern Province (3 January 1935).

30. Cabinet Minute Paper, 954/58/358 (18 June 1958).

31. Alfred Zack-Williams, *Tributors, Supporters and Merchant Capital* (Aldershot, 1995), 164–166, 231.

32. Minute Paper [Freetown] (14 January 1969).

33. "Halt Deteriorating Situation," *Daily Mail* [Freetown] (4 February 1977), 8.

34. Minute Paper (30 July 1971).

35. "Petition against Paramount Chief Alhaji Sahr Thorlie" (19 November 1982).

36. Minute Paper (14 July 1982).

37. Government of Sierra Leone, *Report of the Commission of Inquiry into Disturbances in the Provinces* (London, 1956), 147.

38. For example, Thomas Cole, "Sierra Leone's Election: Post Mortem," *Awareness* [Freetown] (October 1982), 5–32. *Awareness* was a pan-Africanist political journal produced by University of Sierra Leone students during the 1980s.

39. This contrasts with the findings of Janet MacGaffey et al., *The Real Economy of Zaire* (Philadelphia, 1991).

40. Robert Kaplan, "The Coming Anarchy," *Atlantic Monthly,* CCLXXIII (1994), 44–76.

41. Partnership Africa Canada, *The Heart of the Matter: Sierra Leone Diamonds and Human Security* (Ottawa, 2000), 40–43.

42. Details of transactions from documents of the National Development Bank, Freetown, accessed December 1989.

43. "U.S. Dumping Demonstration," *West Africa* (25 February 1980), 377.

44. International Monetary Fund, *Balance of Payments Statistics Yearbook* (Washington, D.C., 1990), 173.

45. Government Gold and Diamond Office, *Annual Report* (Freetown, 1988, 1989, 1990).

46. Quoted in Lansana Gberie, "The May 25 Coup d'Etat in Sierra Leone: A Militariat Revolt?" *Africa Development*, XXII (1997), 153.

47. Arthur Abraham, "War and Transition to Peace: A Study of State Conspiracy in Perpetuating Armed Conflict," *African Development*, XXII (1997), 103.

48. Gberie, "The May 25 Coup d'Etat," 154.

49. Jimmy Kandeh, "What Does the Militariat Do When It Rules? Military Regimes: The Gambia, Sierra Leone and Liberia," *Review of African Political Economy,* XXIII

(1996), 387–404. See also Ibrahim Abdullah and Patrick Muana, "The Revolutionary United Front of Sierra Leone," in Christopher Clapham (ed.), *African Guerrillas* (Oxford, 1998), 172–193; Jimmy Kandeh, "Ransoming the State: Elite Origins of Subaltern Terror in Sierra Leone," *Review of African Political Economy,* XXVI (1999), 349–366.

50. As Nasralla, "Types of Rebels," *For di People* [Freetown] (5 February 1999), 2.

51. "What Foday Sankoh Really Said in Makeni," *For di People* (1 February 2000), 3 [my translation].

52. Alpha Lavalie analyzed the connection between officials' uses of armed gangs and societal violence in his "Government and Opposition in Sierra Leone, 1968–1978," mimeo (Freetown, 1985).

53. Krugba Ndevuyama, "The Kamajor Menace," *For di People* (4 October 2000), 2.

54. United Nations, *Seventh Report,* 3, 5.

55. Human Rights Watch, *Sowing Terror, Atrocities against Civilians in Sierra Leone* (New York, 1998).

56. U.S. Department of State, "Sierra Leone Rebel Atrocities against Civilians," (Washington, D.C., 12 May 1998); United Nations, *Second Progress Report of the Secretary-General on the United Nations Observer Mission in Sierra Leone* (New York, 18 October 1998).

57. Human Rights Watch, *Forgotten Children of War: Sierra Leonean Refugee Children in Guinea* (New York, June 1999).

58. United Nations, *Fifth Report of the Secretary-General on the United Nations Observer Mission in Sierra Leone* (New York, 4 March 1999), para. 26.

59. Human Rights Watch, "Fresh Reports of RUF Terror Tactics" (26 May 2000).

60. United Nations, *Eighth Report of the Security Council on the United Nations Observer Mission in Sierra Leone* (New York, 23 September 1999), para.7.

61. Personal observation.

62. Revolutionary United Front, *Footpaths to Democracy: Toward a New Sierra Leone* (1995).

63. United Nations Commission of Experts, *Final Report of the United Nations Commission of Experts Established Pursuant to Security Council Resolution 780 (1992),* Annex III.A, *Special Forces* (New York, 28 December 1994), paras. 100–101.

64. Janet Mba, "All-Out War," *Newswatch* [Lagos] (22 April 1991), 33.

65. Major I. A. Nass, *A Study in Internal Conflicts: The Liberian Crisis and West African Initiatives* (Enugu, 2000), 166.

66. AFRC fighters admired Tupac Shakur of Death Row Records (in Los Angeles, i.e., "West") because he claimed to have been betrayed by his former business partner, Biggie Smalls, at Bad Boy Records (in New York, i.e., "East"). Shakur claimed that Smalls tried to kill him and bragged that he had sex with Smalls' wife. The Sierra Leonean parallel involves efforts of Kabbah (the former business partner) to replace the Sierra Leone army with Kamajor irregulars in 1996–1997.

67. Interview with a human rights worker, Freetown (9 May 2001).

68. Partnership Africa Canada, *The Heart of the Matter,* 29.

69. *Africa Confidential* (10 May 1996).

70. United Nations, *Report of the Security Council Mission to Sierra Leone* (New York, 16 October 2000), 5.

71. Barbara Crossette, "Behave or Face a Diamond Ban, Security Council Tells Liberians," *New York Times* (8 March 2000), A6.

72. *Peace Agreement between the Government of Sierra Leone and the Revolutionary United Front of Sierra Leone*, author's copy of original.

73. United Nations, *Third Report of the Secretary-General on the United Nations Mission in Sierra Leone* (New York, 7 March 2000), para. 24.

74. Augustus Mye Kamara, "Sankoh's Vehicles Arrive at Quay," *Pool* [Freetown] (5 April 2000), 1.

75. "Massive Recruitment," *Standard Times* [Freetown] (1 August 2000), 1.

76. UN Office for Coordination of Humanitarian Affairs, "Sierra Leone Humanitarian Situation Report" (6 December 2000). UN sources suspected that Taylor harbored Bockarie until mid-2002. United Nations, *First Report of the Secretary-General Pursuant to Security Council Resolution 1343 (2001) Regarding Liberia* (New York, 30 April 2001), para. 27.

77. Quoted in Douglas Farah, "A Separate Peacekeeping," *Washington Post* (10 December 2000), A42.

78. United Nations, *Fourteenth Report of the Secretary-General on the United Nations Mission in Sierra Leone* (New York, 19 June 2002), para. 20.

79. United Nations, *Twelfth Report*, para. 83.

CHAPTER FOUR

The Sudan:
A Successfully Failed State

GÉRARD PRUNIER
RACHEL M. GISSELQUIST

The category of failed state covers a variety of cases. How failed a state is depends not only on its current degree of territorial control, effective administration, legitimacy, and so on, but also on the historical resilience of the state. A related question concerns whether the state will transition from failure to collapse. The Roman Empire in the fifth century A.D. was a case of state collapse. France was largely a failed state between its defeat at the hands of British armies at Poitiers in 1346 and its final recovery from the Hundred Years' War at Castillon in 1450. Between its birth as a nation state in 221 B.C. and October 1949 A.D. China failed about five or six times as a state, although it never collapsed.

Any discussion of how an African state has failed has to be carried out with these parameters in mind. The case of the Sudan is unusual within the broader category of African states because, unlike the vast majority of states on the continent, it is not a product of European colonialism, nor is it a purely "home-grown" country like neighboring Ethiopia. The Sudan, uniquely on the continent, is the product of colonialism by Ottoman Egypt. That particular characteristic is more pregnant with consequences than most observers of the modern Sudan have cared to reflect upon.

The Sudan today is indeed a failed state but is not collapsed, nor likely on the verge of becoming so. For most of the years since its independence, the Sudan has been convulsed by civil war. In the Sudan's south, sovereignty is contested by the Sudanese Peoples' Liberation Movement/Army (SPLM/A).

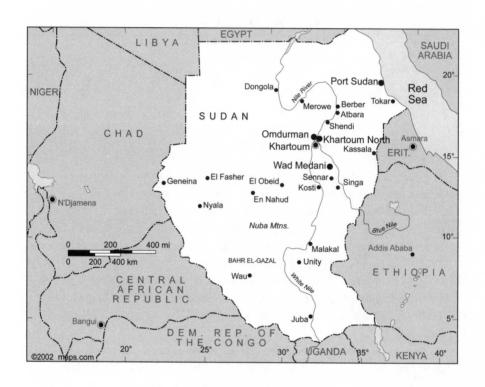

Since the second civil war began in 1983, at least 2 million Sudanese have died and more than 400,000 have fled to neighboring countries. Four million have been internally displaced, making the Sudan's the largest displaced population in the world.[1] In the course of the war, the Sudanese state has routinely used terror against its own civilian population.

Although the state exercises authority and provides some public services in the north, it does not do so in large parts of the country. Particularly in the south (where most of the war-related fighting has occurred) and the Nuba Mountains, the Sudanese state does not provide security and public order, logistical and communications infrastructures, or basic medical and educational services. As evidence of its failure to provide security, one can look not only to the number of war-related deaths and displaced people, but also to the practice of slavery and abduction. As many as 15,000 women and children have been abducted and enslaved in the Sudan since 1983, mainly from the southern province of Bahr-el-Ghazal.[2] As other evidence of failure, a large portion of the population—about 8 percent, or nearly 2.4 million people—are dependent on food aid, most of it provided by the UN-led Operation Lifeline Sudan.[3] In recent years, the southern Sudan experienced famine in 1988–1989 in Bahr-el-Ghazal, 1992–1993 in Upper Nile, and 1998 again in Bahr-el-Ghazal.

Nevertheless, the Sudanese state as a whole is not about to collapse. State bureaucracy in the north, at least, is adequate, and in spite of power struggles since 1999, the National Congress (NC)—known as the National Islamic Front (NIF) until 1999—maintains its hold on the northern section of the state. Economic factors, in particular, suggest that the ruling party will continue to hold power. Although the Sudan's GDP per capita (about $377) and human development indicators are hardly impressive, its annual GDP per capita growth, which was –2 percent in the 1980s, was 5.9 percent in the 1990s and is estimated at a respectable 3.9 percent for 2000–2004.[4] Growth is due in large part to the oil sector, which the government is working with foreign partners to develop. The state's share of oil revenues will increase from 40 percent during the first five years of production to as much as 80 percent thereafter.[5]

There is substantial opposition to the government, but it seems unlikely that opposition groups will overthrow it. On the one hand, the ruling party can draw on the substantial economic profits from the oil sector in order to fund its activities. On the other, the National Democratic Alliance (NDA), SPLM/A, and other smaller opposition groups have all been highly factionalized and ineffective in mounting strong challenges. Most observers argue that it is unlikely that either side in the civil war can score a decisive military victory. Barring substantial outside intervention, this situation is unlikely to change. Further, the primary objective of the SPLM is to secure self-determination for the south, not necessarily to take control of the Sudanese state. In short, the Sudan seems trapped in a low-level equilibrium of state failure.

It is clear that the Sudan is failed, but why is it "successfully" failed? As this chapter argues, although the state per se has failed, the system that the influential Muslim Brotherhood and its political wing, the National Islamic Front, installed through a coup in 1989 has been largely successful as measured against its own parameters and judged by the standards of its own political program. Thus, a state's political leaders may knowingly create state failure in the process of achieving their own narrow objectives. A state's failure, in fact, may be an integral part of meeting those objectives. A second main point of this chapter is that in order to characterize fully the failure of the Sudanese state and to begin to grasp its causes, it is necessary to look to the state's history.

The Second Civil War and the Current Failure of the Sudanese State

Since independence in 1956, the Sudanese state has been either failed or failing. Its current status as a failed state is inextricably linked to the ongoing second civil war and the related lack of state authority in the south. The second civil war between the Sudan's "Arab-identified" northern government and its Christian and animist African south began in 1983, continuing the first civil war, which began in 1955 and lasted until 1972.

Two factors, in particular, fuel the second civil war and remain obstacles to any peace process. First, there are conflicts over identity. While non-Arabized northerners represent about 26 percent of the population and southerners another 34 percent, the northern-run state has attempted to impose an Arab, Islamic identity throughout the country.[6] Second, there are long-standing conflicts over the control of resources—first, water, and more recently, oil, discovered in Bentiu in the south in the early 1980s.

Founded in 1983 with Egyptian assistance, the SPLM/A, led by Colonel John Garang, is the main southern opposition movement. Its stated goal is self-determination for the south within a united, secular Sudan. Early on, its main southern rival was the Anyanya II. While the SPLM/A sought self-determination, the Anyanya II initially sought southern secession. While the SPLM/A was perceived to be dominated by Garang's tribal group, the Dinka, the Anyanya II was perceived as a Nuer organization. Thus, the two main southern organizations were at war with each other perhaps more regularly than with the north. The Anyanya II, in fact, allied with the government against the SPLA at various points in the war. Eventually, in 1988, the Anyanya II merged with the SPLA, although some forces continued to fight on the government side. Throughout this period, the SPLA also fought against various tribal militias, which the northern government, playing on ethnic divisions, courted and supported.[7]

Nevertheless, the SPLM/A enjoyed some significant popular support and external backing, including from Ethiopia's Mengistu Haile Mariam, backed by the Soviet Union; from Cuba, in the training of troops; and from Eritrea and Uganda. Between 1988 and 1990 the civil war intensified, but the SPLA suffered no major defeats and eventually controlled at least two-thirds of the south, lacking only Bahr-el-Ghazal province and the towns of Juba, Malakal, Wau, Bentiu, and Aweil.[8]

In 1991, however, three related events changed the course of the war, plunging the south into further chaos. First, in Ethiopia in May, the Mengistu government lost power. One effect was the loss of important external support. Another was the influx of thousands of southern Sudanese refugees back into the south. In early June, the deputy governor of Upper Nile reported that an average of 300 migrants per day were arriving in the state.[9] Hutchinson estimated that eventually there were 370,000 refugees around Nasir.[10] In the midst of the humanitarian emergency, the resources of the northern-controlled Sudanese state were devoted to bombing and otherwise intimidating these refugees.[11]

Second, the Khartoum government stepped up its offensive. On the diplomatic front, it launched a new series of efforts, successfully courting an alliance with the Ethiopian People's Revolutionary Democratic Front. On the military front, it launched attacks in Equatoria around Juba and built up a stock of weapons in Malakal.

Finally, on 28 August 1991, Dr. Riek Machar, the SPLA zonal commander in western Upper Nile, and Dr. Lam Akol, a commander in northwestern Upper Nile, formed a breakaway SPLA-Nasir faction, largely with Nuer support. Akol and Machar's stated goals were to democratize the SPLA and change its objectives to southern secession if the "ideal goal" of the "unity of the Sudan under a secular federal system" could not be achieved.[12] They also expressed dissatisfaction with Garang's "undemocratic" leadership and reported on human rights abuses by the SPLA, including the use of child soldiers. For the most part, these criticisms seem to have been based on fact, but it also seems likely that, as the SPLA alleges, the northern government "encouraged" the Nasir faction to defect in order to destabilize the SPLA. In 1996, in fact, Machar's new organization, the Southern Sudan Independence Movement, and a number of other smaller southern opposition groups, signed a political charter with the Khartoum government.

Throughout the remainder of 1991, SPLA-Nasir forces raided a series of Dinka villages in Kongor and Bor in Upper Nile province. During these raids, 2,000 to 5,000 people were killed, numerous villages destroyed, and hundreds of thousands of civilians displaced.[13] The region between Waat, Ayod, and Kongor in Upper Nile became known among aid agencies as the "Hunger Triangle." Intertribal violence continued throughout the 1990s between Dinka and Nuer groups and among Nuer subgroups. In the late 1990s, there was some progress toward intertribal peace as a result of a series of peace conferences facilitated by the New Sudan Council of Churches.

Meanwhile, peace talks between the north and south were unsuccessful. Both a Nigerian-led initiative and the Intergovernmental Authority on Development (IGAD) initiative led by Kenya stalled on key issues, including the role of religion in society, the boundaries of the south, the specifics of a referendum on southern self-determination, interim political arrangements, and the sharing of water and oil resources. Another problem with the IGAD talks was that important actors like the National Democratic Alliance and Egypt and Libya, Sudan's neighbors, were excluded. As clashes between the ever-changing southern factions continued, the NDA, an alliance of northern opposition parties and Garang's SPLM/A-"Mainstream," took up arms in 1995. Uncertain of the IGAD process, Egypt and Libya introduced their own initiative.

Throughout the war, the northern government has pursued a "scorched earth" policy, particularly around the southern oil fields. The Sudan's oil pipeline, which was completed in 1999 and runs from oil fields in Unity and Heglig, via the Al-Jalia refinery in Khartoum, to Port Sudan and the shipping routes of the Red Sea, displaced thousands of southerners. In the late 1990s, oil became even more central to the conflict. Oil revenues allowed the government to double its military expenditures between 1998 and 2001.[14]

As part of its war effort in the south, the northern government regularly bombed civilian and humanitarian sites, such as camps for displaced persons. The U.S. Committee for Refugees reported 113 bombings in 2000. Although the number of bombings seems to have since decreased, bombings of civilians continued throughout 2002. Human rights agencies further have charged that the government has used oil company–built airplane runways and roads to launch such attacks.[15] In addition to attacking Sudanese civilians, the Sudanese state (as well as the SPLM/A) has prevented the delivery of humanitarian assistance to civilians by denying flights to certain locations. Government support of and participation in slave raids also has been alleged. In any case, while slavery is illegal in the Sudan and the government has made some public efforts to enforce the law, the practice has continued. For instance, as the Canadian Harker commission reported: "The Governor, or Wali, of Bahr El Ghazal is said to have told a German parliamentary delegation bluntly that although he is governor and head of security, his decisions are only hypothetical—the Sudanese Army and security do what they want."[16]

Recent Political Developments in the North

The National Congress, the current Sudanese ruling party, has been in power since 1989. In June 1989, Brigadier-General Omar Hassan Ahmed al-Bashir, the leader of a radical Islamic faction of the military, launched a coup that toppled the government of Gaafar Nimeiry and installed himself as president, forming a cabinet dominated by the NIF. Hassan al-Turabi, the NIF's militant leader, was widely believed to be the force behind the government. The following year, the government officially declared the Sudan an Islamic state. During the 1990s, under Turabi's militant leadership, the Sudan supported Islamic fundamentalists in Algeria, rebels in Uganda, and the Iraqi occupation of Kuwait. It refused to turn over Islamic militants accused of attempting to assassinate Egyptian President Hosni Mubarak, which led to sanctions by the UN Security Council. It also was linked to plots to bomb the Lincoln and Holland tunnels and the UN headquarters in New York. In 1993, the United States placed the Sudan on its list of states that sponsor terrorism and cut off all foreign assistance except humanitarian aid. In 1998, it bombed a pharmaceutical factory in Khartoum suspected of manufacturing chemical weapons.

On the economic front, in 1990, unable to make payments on the substantial debt that it had accumulated during the 1970s, the Sudan was declared non-cooperative by the IMF. It took until 1999 for the IMF to lift the declaration of non-cooperation and until 2000 to restore the Sudan's voting rights. In 1997, the United States imposed economic sanctions on financial transactions.

In December 1999, there was an important change in Sudanese politics. Just two days before a scheduled vote on legislation introduced by Turabi's supporters that would have decreased Bashir's presidential powers, Bashir declared a three-month state of emergency, disbanded parliament, and appointed a new government. The state of emergency was later extended through 2000, 2001, and 2002. Presidential and legislative elections were held a year after Turabi's ouster, although rebel-held areas were excluded and the main opposition parties boycotted them. Bashir was reelected president with 86 percent of the vote. The new government has the backing of the influential Muslim Brotherhood. Some observers think that factions within the Brotherhood and the NIF/NC were involved in pushing out Turabi.

With the new focus on terrorism and failed states after 11 September 2001, the Sudan gained new international attention. The United States strongly pressured the government to cooperate against terrorism and, at the same time, became more involved in the peace process. The outcome of these efforts remains to be seen, especially since Bashir is struggling to retain the support of the Sudan's Islamic hard-liners. The International Crisis Group, for one, argued that the "shock effect" of 11 September affected debates in Khartoum and created a unique opportunity for the resolution of the war.[17] Yet, in 2002, the Sudan remained a state at war and a failed state. How did it fail?

The Historical Antecendents of the Current Sudanese State

The country now called the Sudan is in fact an arbitrarily demarcated chunk of the African continent whose borders are loosely derived from the limits of Ottoman Egyptian expansion from 1821 onwards. When he invaded what later became the Sudan, Muhammad 'Ali, viceroy of Egypt, was in theory a nominal vassal of the Ottoman Empire. In reality he was the largely autonomous head of a province that was neither an Arab nation like modern Egypt nor simply a subdivision of the Turkish-led multinational empire. In the aftermath of the French invasion of Egypt in 1798, Muhammad 'Ali had pried the area loose from Ottoman control. And it is that curious semi-independent province of a multinational empire that, in turn, had conquered the Sudan.[18] During the period known in Sudan as the *Turkiyya* (the time of the Turks), a vast piece of northeastern Africa was loosely occupied by Ottoman administrators leading largely African mercenary troops. The name of the occupied territory was derived from the old appellation medieval Arab geographers gave to Africa south of the Sahara: *beled as-sudan* (the land of the blacks). During those sixty-plus years, the position of *hikimdar* (governor general) was held by an ethnically bewildering array of people ranging from Armenians to Syrians by way of Greeks and Kurds. Colonel Charles Gordon, the famous British Victorian hero, was hikimdar of the Sudan between 1877 and 1879, in the service of Ottoman Egypt and not of Great Britain. But there were no Arab Egyptian governors, thus making the term "Egyptian colonization" somewhat misleading.[19]

The "Sudanese" territory was in itself highly imprecise. It comprised the whole of today's Sudan plus northern Uganda, large chunks of Ubangi-Shari (part of today's Central African Republic), the fringes of eastern Chad, the whole Somali Red Sea coast all the way down to Kenya, parts of Eritrea, and the region of Harrar in today's Ethiopia. These various territories are not part of the Sudan today because the Sudan exploded in 1885 when Ottoman rule was overthrown by the indigenous revolt known as the *Mahdiyya*.[20] When this vast territory was reoccupied in 1898, this time by the British, who had colonized Egypt in 1882, they limited themselves to the present-day borders. By then, the colonial scramble was on and all the surrounding territories were being occupied by various powers, not least by Britain itself.[21]

The legacy bequeathed by history to the independent Sudan is one of political ambiguity, cultural heterogeneity, and territorial imprecision. Each of these three problems has affected the nature of the modern Sudan's crisis.

Political Ambiguity

The first "modern" state pattern to which the Sudanese were forced to adapt was that of nineteenth century Ottoman power. The Ottoman Empire had some features of the modern state, in that it minted currency, raised taxes, established customs, and maintained a professional army and an organized civil service. But it was also an expression of the old pillage state which the Turks had projected upon enormous areas of North Africa, the Middle East, the Balkans, and Central Europe. In many ways, for all its administrative sophistication, the Ottoman Empire was a gigantic tribute-levying machine, surviving by exploitation and capable of maintaining its large military establishment only by continuing to conquer new territory.[22] In many ways, the Sudan was (by proxy) the last conquest of the Ottoman Empire, in an age when it had gone to sleep everywhere else. Thus, in the Sudan the state became *al-hukum*, a word that connoted raw power rather than administrative efficiency. The state never focused on economic development, which is another reason why the expression "Egyptian colonialism" does not apply. Between 1821 and 1885, the emphasis was on levying taxes and asset stripping, particularly through the slave trade.

Slave trading runs like a red thread throughout the history of the region. Egyptian historians have done their best to wash their own country of this blemish, but have yet to succeed.[23] It is important to remember that the slave trade was not a byproduct of Ottoman occupation; it was its raison d'être.[24] Later, anti-slavery treaties notwithstanding (and they were always violated), Ottoman Egyptian power in the Sudan created a pattern where pillage (of men, cattle, and mineral resources) was seen as the normal way for the hukum to raise money.

The economy was seen as a zero-sum game. The concept of development, which one or two governors tried to apply by growing cotton, was considered strange. Despite its subsequent colonization by the British, who attempted economic development, the Sudan was never seen as a rich colony like Ghana, Kenya, or India. It was a strategic colony, desirable in order to keep the Nile flow open and to keep the French from challenging British control of the Red Sea route to India. The Sudan was colonized not for itself but to keep others out, as the Fashoda incident of 1898 between France and Britain exemplified.[25] As a result, the British administered at a very limited level and delegated much of the work to Egyptian and Sudanese clerks, thus involuntarily passing on the notion of hukum to further generations. The Sudan, perhaps even more than Nigeria, was the almost perfect field of application for Lord Lugard's theories of indirect rule.[26] It was largely left to its own devices, and lightly supervised by London. In many ways, British colonization left less of an imprint upon the political consciousness of the Sudanese than did the old Turkiyya.[27]

Cultural Heterogeneity

The Sudanese, with their dry sense of humor, call their own country *laham ras,* or sheep's head, because every single morsel in a sheep's head looks and tastes different. The implication is, and rightfully so, that the country is a hodge-podge of cultures, races, and languages. Unlike neighboring Ethiopia, which in many ways is just as heterogeneous as the Sudan, there is no unifying historical factor, no independent state tradition, and no nationally accepted concept of what constitutes the country. The Sudan is not the only ethnically mixed country on the continent, but its situation is unique in that the differences between its various components are not simply tribal. They are civilizational. The country is divided into three (or arguably three-and-a-half) cultural groups whose daily lives (dress, family matters, food, language group, and world outlook) are radically different.

The perception that the Sudan is torn between Christians and Muslims is untrue. The real conflict in the Sudan today is not between a Muslim north and a Christian and animist south, but between the approximately 30 percent of the population who are Arab-identified and everyone else. The term "Arab-identified" refers to people whose mother tongue is Arabic and who are racially almost similar to the populations of the old historical Abyssinian heartland of Ethiopia. They share their state with two completely different groups: (a) Muslim blacks from the western part of the country, who are the easternmost extension of the south Sahelian/Sudanic populations stretching from Nigeria all the way to Darfur and Kordofan; and (b) Nilotic Christian and animist populations of southern Sudan. One can almost add an additional half family, the Cushitic Beja, who are neither Arabs nor African blacks and who, despite being Muslims, are racially different from their "Arab-identified" fellow countrymen.

Across the cultural families there is a modicum of cooperation and cultural understanding. However, a huge rift was created when the Sudanese Arabs decided that they embodied the truth, the heart, the core, the soul, and the reality of the Sudan, rendering all others second class. This is not a South African–type apartheid division. There is a fair amount of good-natured social exchange, cross-cultural banter, and casual shoulder-rubbing, but there is hardly any inter-group matrimony. The Arabs control the state and the economy. With very few exceptions, doctors, engineers, civil servants, lawyers, and university professors are Arabs. The Sudanese Arabs are proud of their Arabic culture and look down upon the rest of the country. This racism has never been systematized, nor given a biological base like European racism. The result has been to promote a tightly-knit elite group that has monopolized political and economic power. The Sudan is basically, gently, hopelessly schizophrenic. Some of the best minds in the country, such as the late Mohamed Omar Beshir or Francis Deng, have long recognized this tragic state of affairs.[28]

The perceived history of the slave trade is a perfect example of this form of intellectual alienation. For the Sudanese Arabs, it is a much-exaggerated phenomenon which lasted for only a limited number of years and should be ascribed to Egyptian domination. For the southerners, it is a burning memory of massacres and humiliation. The northerners deny it and attribute these memories to false remembrances put into southern heads by European Christian missionaries "who are against Islam." They insist that there were European slave traders and refuse to admit to any permanent scars that slaving could have left on the national consciousness.[29] It was such prejudices that lay behind the unspoken communication gap, periodically ruining various much-vaunted north-south peace negotiations.

Territorial Imprecision

As demonstrated above, the present boundaries of the Sudan are the product of non-European foreign conquest, followed by indigenous revolt, followed by European and Egyptian re-conquest, leading to the bizarre diplomatic construct known as "the Anglo-Egyptian condominium." The Sudanese often try to present Mohamed Ahmed al-Mahdi, the great rebel leader against Ottoman Egypt, as the founder of Sudanese nationalism. This is another example of Arab appropriation of cultural symbols pertaining to the country. Even a cursory glance at the history of southern Sudan shows that if the southerners took advantage of the Mahdist rebellion to eliminate Ottoman garrisons in their areas, they later fought bitterly against attempts by the Mahdists to re-occupy the vacated positions and to extend northern control over the south.[30] Thus, the claim by the Sudanese Arabs that the south was one with the north in the fight against Ottoman Egyptian imperialism is right when it is limited to the initial revolt; it is false when that claim is extended to the successor Mahdist state that replaced the Egyptians. The south therefore was re-included in the Sudan only by the British, acting in concert with Egypt and seeking at least officially to preserve future Egyptian interests (and the flow of the Nile) in Cairo's former colony. This also is true of the west, where the Darfur Sultanate, which had proclaimed its independence during the Mahdiyya, was re-occupied by the British only in 1916.[31]

The British themselves were never so sure of where the Sudan started or where it ended. During the colonial period, they administered the south as a separate entity until 1947 and only hurriedly brought it back into "the Sudan" when they started to talk to Cairo about the possibility of independence. The

Egyptians, whether under the old monarchy or later, after the Nasserist revolution, wanted the Sudan kept whole because they sincerely hoped to annex it upon independence, using the old "condominium" claim and their history of control going back to the 1880s. A portion of the negotiations between London and Cairo about Sudan's independence revolved around a rather unethical quid pro quo, in which the Egyptians promised to allow the British continued control of the Suez Canal zone in exchange for not separating north from south when giving the Sudan its independence. The strong feelings of the Sudanese were ignored in favor of the two former co-domini's imperial interests.[32] In the end, the Sudan became independent as a unit (if not as a solid block), its Arab leadership refused to join Egypt, and the British lost the Suez Canal zone (for other reasons) within a year (1956).

Clearly, the Sudan as defined by its present borders is an arbitrary construct. Sudanese territoriality cannot be defined by its pre-colonial history, by culture, by language, or even by its colonial history. As a result of the Sudan's cultural heterogeneity and the ambiguous nature of a post-Ottoman polity, it is a contingent state, that is, a state that was created in error.

The Pattern of Post-Independence Politics

The British Legacy

During the 1940s and early 1950s, the British were faced with an almost exclusively Arab "nationalist" movement. Partly by choice, partly out of weariness, partly for lack of any alternative and because they suddenly were in a hurry, they negotiated independence with these interlocutors, without worrying about what might come next. In other words, the Sudanese Arab intelligentsia acquired, through its own efforts and because of the default/incapacity of the other cultural segments of the country, a monopoly over the right to represent the country as a whole. Although the Sudan was multicultural and only had a 30 percent Arab-identified population, it gained its independence as an Arab country.[33] It applied for membership of the Arab League and was accepted, with a degree of condescension, by the Egyptians, Lebanese, Saudis, and other "true Arabs." The Syrians objected, but were overruled.

The real problem, which has continued to affect the current Sudanese state, was that there were no modern political structures in the Sudan at independence. The nationalist movement had largely been an extension of the traditional *turuq* (sing. *tariqa*: Muslim religious brotherhood), and particularly of the two main ones, the Ansar (Mahdist and anti-Egyptian) and the Khatmiyya (mainstream Sunni and pro-Egyptian).[34] These religious brotherhoods had not created political parties; they had created clans, networks, and proto-nepotist associations. The government was seen as the old Ottoman hukum, a tool for extracting resources from a numbed peasantry. Everyone paid lip service to economic development, but for many, the aim of contending for power was not to implement policy. It was to control the ministry of finance (for dishing out bank loans) or the ministry of external trade (for distributing import licenses), or the ministry of agriculture (for favoring relatives with government-subsidized fertilizers and pesticides). Families, regional clans, and the politicized turuq fought with each other for control of the hukum. There were only two policies on which most politicians concurred: keep the goodies within the golden circle of the best Sudanese Arab families and keep the southerners under control. The first policy led to periodic military coups to arbitrate the constant bickering between the ruling families, who wanted larger shares of the nation's wealth; the second policy led to civil war.[35]

The Functioning of the System

The system was succinctly described by one of Sudan's most popular politicians, Mohamed Ahmed Mahjoub (1908–1976), in his memoirs:

The parties found themselves without any particular aim; all attempts at formulating a cohesive policy were frustrated. Personal and sectarian rivalries became predominant. The parties were based on tribal and sectarian alliances rather than on firm programs. . . . As a result, the generals took power and then stayed in office misruling the country shamefully.[36]

Sadiq al-Mahdi, one of the foremost "democratic" leaders, who, as head of the 'Umma party representing the Ansar Brotherhood, was several times prime minister during the civilian regimes, described the system more vividly:

The main political leaders walk around parliament with baskets for MPs. They pick up parliamentarians and put them in their basket. When the basket is full enough they become Prime Minister. When a certain number of MPs have jumped out of the basket, they cease being Prime Minister.[37]

Sudan's first democratic period was very brief (1956–1958) and ended in a military coup when the two elite clans could not agree on a way to divvy up the spoils of rule. From then on, there ensued a painful political seesaw between military rule (1958–1964 and 1969–1985) and civilian rule (1964–1969 and 1985–1989).

The "classical" Sudanese political system, whether "democratic" or military, was never capable of dealing with the deep-rooted identity problems gnawing at the country's innards. The various regimes behaved as if the Sudan were a given when it was in fact a question mark. They included token members of the minorities in their governments, ruled through cronies who perpetually squabbled, and always counted on foreigners (Egyptian President General Abdul Nasser, the Russians, the Arab League, and the Americans) to bolster the perennially collapsing economy. In a polity which was in fact a power extension of lineages and family systems, corruption was a way of life. The periods of "nationalization" were the worst for the Sudan, and asset stripping increased exponentially during such times.[38] Early experiments at IMF-sponsored structural adjustments in the 1980s mostly meant privatizing the money-making sectors of the economy while letting the non-profit-making social sectors die a slow death, further destabilizing the country through broadening poverty.

As the social services and transportation and communication networks disintegrated, the culturally heterogeneous regions of the country developed a growing alienation from the Arab center. The south was often mentioned as an example of this process, but it was not. The south in fact had been alienated all along, from the Sudan's inception. However, in the west, the black Muslim populations were partly coerced, partly seduced through Islamic solidarity into supporting the Arab north in its war against the south. By the 1980s and the beginning of the second civil war in 1983, this form of "false consciousness" worked less and less well and the economically and socially alienated west rose on its own to fight the Arab center.[39] By the early 1990s, it was the equally disenfranchised Beja who in turn developed their own anti-Arab guerrilla movement along the Eritrean borderlands. Eventually the SPLA decided to broaden its fighting coordinates and started to refer in its literature and communiqués to "the south and other marginalized areas of the country." Cultural heterogeneity finally threatened to unravel the very fabric of the state.

The Southern Question

From the beginning, the south was at the heart of the country's contradictions. The problem stemmed largely from the fact that the dominant Sudanese Arab elite was viscerally incapable of recognizing that there was any problem at all, and when it saw one, it immediately attributed it to evil foreigners.[40] Thus, in 1965, during the Round Table Conference organized in Khartoum to try to negotiate an end to the first civil war in the south, Sayed Ismail al-Azhari, a respected politician and former prime minister, attributed the whole problem to "a carefully prepared diabolical plan which had no other purpose than to develop antagonisms and conflicts between the children of the same land."[41] Missionaries were targeted by such statements, and in early 1964, they were expelled en masse from the country. Such forced attempts at Arabization and Islamization were thoroughly unsuccessful because they were not part of a grassroots campaign, but rather the top-down imposition of a foreign culture on a subjugated people without consideration of the nature of the relationships between dominant and dominated social groups.

The lack of forethought was obvious from the start, as when the southern troops of the Sudan Defense Force mutinied in August 1955 after being told that, with independence, their British officers would be replaced by Sudanese Arab ones.[42] The mutineers ran into the bush when a combined force of British and Sudanese troops tried to disarm them. Thus, the war started in the south even before the country became fully independent.

Independence negotiations only made matters worse. The southerners wanted to obtain some kind of constitutional protection from full Arab domination and demanded a federal system. However, the Constitutional Committee prepared a proposal wherein the Sudan would be a united state (article 1), Arabic would be the official language (article 4), and Islam would be the state religion (article 5). The southern MPs in the Transitional Assembly (twenty-two out of ninety-seven) reiterated their demands for federal status. On 19 December 1955, Mubarak Zaruq, a majority MP, tabled a motion saying that "the Constituent Assembly should take into consideration the demand from the southern MPs aiming at the creation of a federal status." In exchange, Zaruq asked them to vote for the independence motion. Reassured, the southern MPs voted in favor of the motion. In time-honored fashion, a committee was created to discuss federal status. With a membership of forty-three northerners against three southerners, the committee duly declared in December 1956 that federalism would be unworkable. It was the first step along a very long path leading to what Abel Alier, a famous moderate southern politician, would later call "too many agreements dishonored."[43]

By February 1972, due to the interplay of the local geopolitics of the Cold War, both the Arab north and the southern rebels found themselves exhausted and bereft of external support.[44] This forced them into signing a peace agreement sponsored by Ethiopian Emperor Haile Selassie and the Organisation of African Unity (OAU). The main provision of the "Addis Ababa Agreement," as it became known, was the creation of the federal structure that had been refused at independence, with a clearly defined Southern Region to be administered by a People's Regional Assembly and a High Executive Council located in Juba in the deep south. The rebels had fought for independence but, given their dire straits, they were happy to settle for extensive regional autonomy.

There were many difficulties, but the system more or less worked for about nine years. During this period, one major tension was over the control of the Nile waters. In 1977, without consulting southerners, Nimeiry's government began work on the Jonglei canal, charting its completion for the mid-1980s.[45] Located within the western border of Upper Nile, the completed and proposed lines of the canal ran from Jonglei up along the Duk Ridge, past Adok, to the White Nile at Malakal. The Jonglei canal—which was the topic of Garang's Ph.D. dissertation in agricultural economics at Iowa State University—displaced local communities and deprived them of dry-season grazing land for their cattle and other livestock.

Soon, the Chevron Oil Company found oil in the south. President Nimeiry immediately began reorganizing the country's administrative boundaries in order to remove the oil region from the jurisdiction of the Juba government. Many southern MPs protested against this abuse of power. In October 1981, Nimeiry dissolved the southern assembly, eventually creating a new province around the oil wells. The ironically misnamed *al-wahda* (unity) province served only to deepen the Sudan's disunity.

It often has been written that the second, current civil war started when Nimeiry, increasingly ill and religiously obsessed, proclaimed Islamic *shari'a* as the legal basis of all legislation in the Sudan. In truth, the southern army mutiny that started the war occurred in May 1983, whereas the shari'a was proclaimed in September of that year. The real cause of the war was the disbanding of the Juba assembly and the attempt forcibly to reorganize provincial boundaries so as to place oil resources, located in the south, out of the reach of southern administration. The other decisions that led directly to the explosion of the conflict (for example, the decision to transfer to the north the black battalions of the army stationed in the south) were only logical consequences of the momentous re-division decision, which amounted to a unilateral abrogation of the Addis Ababa agreement by Khartoum. Once more, in Alier's words, another agreement had been dishonored. The results were to be momentous, since war now has lasted for more than nineteen years.

The Rise of the Muslim Brotherhood and the System's Partial Transformation

The Sudanese *Harakat al-Ikhwaan al-Muslimin* (Movement of the Muslim Brotherhood) is a direct offshoot of its Egyptian mother organization. It was launched in the 1940s by Sudanese students in Cairo who had become interested in the teachings of Hassan al-Banna.[46] They started returning to the Sudan after World War II, but remained dependent on the help of the Egyptian mother organization until 1953, when an autonomous branch of the movement opened in Khartoum. The brotherhood therefore played almost no role in the political agitation that took place at the time of independence. The main development affecting its place in Sudanese politics occurred in 1964, when Hassan al-Turabi took control of the small radical organization. Well educated in France and Britain, extremely bright, and a master political tactician, Turabi rapidly took over the Sudanese Muslim Brotherhood by eliminating the first "historical" generation of leaders (Rashid at-Taher, Sadiq abd-el-Majid), who had fought the military dictatorship of Marshal Ibrahim Abbud, and resolutely turning the Islamist movement toward a form of differential modernity. Women were recruited, technology was embraced with passion, Islamic dogma was considered more for its tactical potential than for its religious value, and, above all, the new movement—renamed *Jebha al-Mithaq al-Islamiya* (Islamic Charter Front)—quickly turned itself into a countersociety. Young men who showed promise were recruited and nurtured, provided housing and jobs, and even found wives when they wanted to marry. Within a few years, the new party had become a tightly knit club, closer to Freemasonry than to the wild-eyed, fanatical group portrayed in the Western media.

This remarkable organization enabled the brotherhood to survive the persecutions of the early Nimeiry years, when the new military dictator tried to emulate Nasser, his mentor, in crushing Islamist groups. By 1977, politically isolated after he had been forced to eliminate his former supporters in the Sudanese Communist Party in 1971, Nimeiry embraced all of the religious opposition groups in the famous *mussallaha al-wataniya* (National Reconciliation) exercise. Sadiq al-Mahdi of the Ansar, Mohamed Osman al-Mirghani of the Khatmiyya, and Hassan al-Turabi with his Muslim Brotherhood all allied with the regime. In many ways it was a case of the dead weight of political reaction finally crushing any hope of political *aggorniamento*—which the Nimeiry regime had hoped to represent. When he took power in May 1969, Colonel Nimeiry had the support of the modernist and secularist forces. His signing a peace pact with the southern rebels three years later, even if it were largely a product of necessity rather than a deliberate choice, was in any case a ray of hope in an almost completely closed political system. But by 1977, after three coup attempts and a relentless campaign organized by the mosques against the legitimacy of his regime, Nimeiry had to embrace the Muslim Brotherhood.

The mussallaha was several things wrapped into one: it was a new lease on life for a tired military/modernist/secularist regime, but it was a reneging of its founding principles and a capitulation to resolute opposition from the politico-religious forces that had dominated the Sudan since the nineteenth century. It also provided a new opportunity for a number of traders (Khatmiyya-linked) and landowners (Ansar-related) who had had to vacate key positions during the early 1970s. Finally, it provided an open door for the Muslim Brotherhood, the youngest, freshest, and most aggressive politico-religious force in Sudanese society. Since the Brotherhood's social base, initially built up from university circles in the 1960s and 1970s, essentially consisted of professionals (lawyers, doctors, teachers, bankers, and engineers), it resolutely set about colonizing the civil service and the financial economy. Turabi was the most accommodating of the three turuq leaders because he did not want to waste his strength on a frontal clash.[47] He preferred to keep burrowing deeper and deeper into the state machinery and into the financial system in order to maximize the impact of his highly educated but small party. Since the Sudanese economy maintained significant external ties through workers' emigration to the oil-producing Gulf countries and benefited from the resulting massive remittance system, he developed clandestine or semi-clandestine "Islamic" foreign exchange channels. This was largely accomplished through the growth of a network of Islamic banks, especially al-Baraka in London, which was later at the heart of the new parallel economic system that his group operated after the 1989 coup. Turabi also created, with tacit government approval, a whole bevy of mass organizations, such as the *shabab al-binna'* for young men and its female counterpart, *raidat an-nahda*.[48] At times he managed to hijack existing groups, such as the *Da'wa islamiya*, the main Islamic charity and social service organization, which became an Islamist stronghold during the 1980s.

In terms of grand political strategy, a new special slot had just opened, which the *ikhwaan* could now occupy. As the war dragged on, the state became poorer and poorer, weaker and weaker, increasingly losing control of the military. The traditional politico-religious forces that had led the country to this extremity began seriously to fear for the future and approached the rebels for negotiations. In November 1988, Mohamed Osman al-Mirghani, sheikh of the Khatmiyya tariqa and president of its political branch, the Democratic Unionist Party (DUP), traveled to Addis Ababa, where he met SPLM/A leader Garang. He was unsure of the popularity of the effort, but when he returned to Khartoum huge crowds of well-wishers came to welcome him at the airport and carried him home in triumph. For hard-line supporters of Arabic supremacy, the situation had become very serious. Turabi now could step in and ride the limited but very resolute force that continued to regard al-Mirghani's efforts with extreme distaste.[49]

The countdown had begun. During the night of 30 June 1989, three days before a government delegation was due to fly to Addis Ababa for peace talks, the Muslim Brotherhood struck, taking over the government in a daring minority coup and installing the NIF.

The Coup and Its Logic

Shortly after the coup, a government paper summarized the reasons for the military takeover by the NIF:

Sadiq al-Mahdi's government had been on its way to make peace with the rebel movement and the minister of justice had prepared a project to abrogate the September Laws. The government had been going to announce through the minister of justice a set of lawsuits against the main Islamic banks in order to weaken the opposition. After peace, the opposition was to be imprisoned. The rebels cleverly played on the contradictions between the political parties. The "Big Houses" [al-biyutat] had chosen for tactical reasons to grant the rebels advantages they could never have dreamt of.[50]

It is clear that: (a) preventing peace (seen as a loss of power for the Arab elite) was the key reason for the coup; (b) the "September Laws," which symbolized the Islamist stance in Sudanese political life, were seen as a fundamental point, therefore making their abrogation unlikely for the duration of the regime; (c) the Islamic banking system was a core feature of the Front's system; and (d) the biyutat, or the "Great Houses" of the Ansar and Khatmiyya traditional elite, were perceived as traitors to the Arab cause, having sold out to the heathen southern rebels for tactical reasons. The Muslim Brotherhood has maintained tight relations with government and the NIF's successor, the NC, even since Turabi's ouster.

The Features and Policies of the Regime

The NIF/NC regime has succeeded on several fronts.[51] The first is ideological. The Sudanese regime is often seen as Islamist. This conclusion is exaggerated. In fact, the regime used the ideological paraphernalia of radical Islam in order to legitimize the political control of a certain segment of an ethnically heterogeneous polity over ethnically different groups and other segments of its own ethnic group. Understanding this point is crucial to the understanding of the "Islamist" regime in the Sudan.

The regime's co-optation of radical Islamic trappings has rendered its ideological attitude milder than its critics profess. The shari'a, as embodied in the September Laws (which the regime inherited from the Nimeiry dictatorship), is a political marker rather than a guide to action. Bowing to the shari'a is akin to accepting the dictatorship of the proletariat in many of the former communist regimes. It means paying homage to the official doctrine of the ruling group, although nobody (including the ruling group) actually expects those principles to be put into practice. The actual execution of shari'a principles, especially its controversial *hudud* system of criminal penalties, is very rare. When it occurs, it is done in a spirit of ethnic control rather than religious purity.[52] Abdel Salam Sidahmed, a Sudanese analyst, calls this phenomenon "Islamic symbolism."[53] Common people in the Sudan simply call the Muslim Brotherhood *tujjar ad-din* (merchants of religion). The neglect of the actual practice of radical Islam, as exemplified by the Taliban in Afghanistan, has brought the ikhwaan into conflict with true Islamic radicals, such as the members of the Ansar as-Sunna sect.[54] Lack of adherence to strict Muslim law demonstrates that the regime's policy of violent military action in the south, with its practice of indiscriminate killings, is not primarily the expression of religious intolerance, but rather of a need for racial and cultural control.[55] Ugly as the policy is, it so far has proved successful.

The second aspect of the regime is political, because it is a minority regime. In the April 1986 elections, the last free elections in the Sudan, the Muslim Brotherhood won 51 seats out of 264, which made it the third party in the country.[56] It is important to note that out of these fifty-one seats, twenty-three were "graduate" seats. The "graduate" college was a carryover from colonial times that allowed educated people (university graduates, army officers, and civil servants above a certain rank) to vote twice, first in a one-man, one-vote constituency, and a second time for a special seat. The Muslim Brotherhood, due to its professional membership and impeccable electoral discipline and organization, won twenty-three out of the twenty-eight graduate seats. One could win a graduate seat with very few votes. Thus in Bahr-el-Ghazal (where there are very few educated people) Muslim Brotherhood candidate Ali Tamim Fartak got his seat with 158 votes. In comparison, his political comrade Ibrahim Ahmad Omar needed 10,135 votes to win a regular seat in Khartoum. To be elected in even the most hotly contested graduate seats, candidates only needed about 3,000 votes. This meant that the NIF only won around 15 percent of the popular vote. It is doubtful that it would win more today.[57] Yet, even with such a limited plurality, the Muslim Brotherhood continued in 2002 to exert control over the political system, which constitutes an obvious political success.

The regime's third "success" is economic, and complex. The Sudan has for many years had a paradoxical economy. Judging by official economic statistics, the country should have been bankrupt years ago and its population, in the north as well as the south, should have sunk below the worst levels of absolute poverty. Yet, in spite of obviously difficult circumstances, this has not been the case. The reason is what has been called the *murghtarbin* (expatriate) economy.

In the early 1980s, about 10 percent of the adult male population of the Sudan was working abroad, mainly in the oil-rich Gulf countries. The percentage of skilled workers employed abroad is much higher.[58] In 1986, the Bank of Sudan estimated at $1.4 billion the real amount of the remittances from abroad (while the official figure put remittances at less than $400 million). The real figure is probably much higher, and other analysts have credibly put it at around $3 billion per year. This has led to a double process: first, an enormous amount of money is sent abroad again, as these remittances are not invested in the country; second, most of these remittances are made through either informal or Islamic routes rather than through the official banking channels, which have always paid beneficiaries at the fast-depreciating official exchange rate.[59] In addition, other sums are directly invested by the expatriates in their countries of residence or in Europe and North America. This process has led to massive capital flight, estimated at between $15 billion and $21 billion, thus making the Sudan a net exporter of capital rather than an importer. A very large proportion of this considerable floating capital is in the hands of the Islamic banking system or of individual members of the ruling party. Along with substantial revenues from the oil sector, this situation has enabled the regime to survive financially and to spend over $1 million per day on the civil war.[60]

Fourth, the ruling party has cleverly profited from the massive social changes that have occurred due to the factors already mentioned—the war, the considerable population displacements resulting from it, the political failure of the old Arab elite, the massive expatriation of skilled manpower, and the transition from a productive rurally based economy to a speculative international financial economy. Today the Sudan is divided into five population groups. At the top is the Islamist bourgeois elite, with good connections to the outside world, to the Islamic banking circuits, and to the formal economy. This class is largely "Arab" but also comprises some members of the non-Arab Muslim groups (Beja and western blacks) who have been co-opted for political reasons. Then there are the remnants of the traditional Arab bourgeoisie. They survive either indifferently, when they have murghtarbin relatives abroad, or poorly when they do not, but they are politically marginalized and largely kept out of the formal productive sector. Third come the Sudanese Arab masses (peasants and petty traders) who eke out a precarious living either by subsistence agriculture or on the margins of the informal economy. Fourth are the marginalized Muslim populations of the west and east. The final group are the *janubiyin* (southerners), who either live in the army free-fire zones of the south or else survive in extremely dire circumstances as displaced people in the north.

This extraordinarily unequal social system is relatively stable. This result implies only a limited success for the regime, since it carries with it the potential both of grave social troubles in the north (which have only been sporadic so far) and of continued war in the south, west, and east. The regime has nevertheless managed to control a highly fragmented society, which tends to sink into localized isolation rather than to mobilize itself to conquer a central power perceived as distant and at times irrelevant.

The fifth and final "success" reflects the regime's military power. The Sudanese army at times is seen as being "in power," since it carried out the 1989 coup. Whether or not this is true is one of the greatest enigmas, but it seems unlikely. "The army," defined as the social military group that ruled the Sudan between 1958 and 1964 and again between 1969 and 1985, has been deeply modified. Over 3,000 officers were cashiered within a year of the 1989 coup, indicating that the Muslim Brotherhood held only minority support in the traditional officer corps. They were replaced by what the Sudanese popular voice calls the "test tube officers," young men either devoted to the Islamist cause or simply ambitious who were sent to Iraq or to Libya for brief officer-training courses lasting about six months. In addition, the regime made official the tribal militias that existed prior to 1989 and were responsible for most of the exactions committed during the "democratic" regime of Sadiq al-Mahdi, especially during 1988. These militias were expanded and systematized, and their recruitment was extended to the Arab population, many of whom joined more out of sheer poverty than out of enthusiasm for the Islamist cause. Under the name of *difaa esh-shabiyya* (Popular Defense Forces, or PDF) they constituted a second political army side by side with the traditional armed forces. These troops, indoctrinated into the regime's official ideology, often bore the brunt of the worst fighting in the south. They suffered heavy losses but also committed some of the worst atrocities of the war. A mixture of regimental pride, politico-religious ideology, and Arab nationalism has kept them going in spite of very difficult circumstances over a huge and hostile theater of operations.

Conclusion

The Sudan is a huge and heterogeneous country where several cultures co-exist within an ill-defined space. The predatory tradition of Ottoman Egyptian rule fashioned the outlook of a traditional, Arab-identified elite that, out of cultural pride and greed, has kept a stranglehold on the political life of the country until very recently. When the regime's own contradictions finally led it to political bankruptcy in 1989, it was overthrown by a smaller, younger, and more professional segment of its own ethnic group. Far from favoring a new political openness, this new group repackaged the old themes of Arab domination into a more attractive, radical Islamic guise. Since this group was tightly knit, well led, well organized, and capable of taking advantage of the new opportunities introduced by the creation of the Islamic financial system, it managed both to keep the ethnically heterogeneous elements at bay and to establish its domination over the other segments of its own ethnic group. In the process of achieving these aims, it divided the country even more. The Sudan since independence has been either a failed or failing state. During all but eleven of these years, it has been at war with itself. Today, in large parts of the country, it does not provide security and public order, logistical and communications infrastructures, or basic medical and educational services. Its current civil war has claimed 2 million lives. In the course of the war, the state has routinely used terror against its own civilians. Four million Sudanese are internally displaced, and over 2 million are dependent on food aid.

Are there solutions to such a situation? Possibly, but they are not simple. The partition of the Sudanese state seems an obvious prerequisite for peace. Since the days of the slave trade, the animosity that has accumulated between north and south makes reconciliation almost unthinkable. Yet, the southern leadership is undemocratic, inefficient, and deeply divided, and it is unlikely to win self-determination or secession simply by force of arms.

Achieving peace through negotiations is possible, but unlikely. The Sudan's government is resolute in its policies for a variety of reasons that range from ideological to economic to personal.[61] Especially after managing to exploit the country's oil resources, it has fairly strong reasons to believe that it will survive financially and militarily. The country's partition would result in the loss of southern-based oil resources, an unlikely sacrifice. Unless international pressure is stepped up considerably, it is likely that the Sudan will suffer either a long-drawn-out conflict on the Angolan model or else some kind of pseudo-solution, where elements of the southern leadership will be offered sufficiently attractive terms to be co-opted into the system. However, the Sudan since independence has experienced a rather original tradition of civilian *intifada* (uprisings), which managed to overthrow apparently well-entrenched dictatorships. Therefore, a surprise development cannot be ruled out, especially considering the grinding and growing poverty of the northern masses.

Notes

1. USAID, "Sudan—Complex Emergency Situation Report #3 (FY 2002)" (31 January 2002), http://www.reliefweb.int.

2. John Harker et al., "Human Security in Sudan: The Report of a Canadian Assessment Mission," prepared for the Canadian Minister of Foreign Affairs (Ottawa, January 2000), 2.

3, USAID, "Sudan—Complex Emergency Situation Report #1 (FY 2000)" (11 September 2000), http://www.reliefweb.int.

4. World Bank, "Sudan at a Glance" (21 September 2001), http://www.worldbank.org/data/countrydata/aag/sdn_aag.pdf.

5. "He Won!" *The Economist* (6 January 2001), 42; Economist Intelligence Unit (EIU), *Sudan—Country Profile 2000* (London, 2000), 30–31.

6. Ann Mosely Lesch, *The Sudan: Contested National Identities* (Bloomington, 1998), 15, 17; idem., "Sudan: The Torn Country," *Current History*, XCVIII (May 1999), 218.

7. See Douglas Johnston and Gérard Prunier, "The Foundation and Expansion of the Sudan People's Liberation Army," in M. W. Daly and Ahmad Alawad Sikainga (eds.), *Civil War in the Sudan* (London, 1993), 117–141.

8. Douglas Johnston, *Nuer Prophets: A History of Prophecy from the Upper Nile in the Nineteenth and Twentieth Centuries* (Oxford, 1994), 344; Sharon Hutchinson, *Nuer Dilemmas: Coping with Money, War, and the State* (Berkeley, 1996), 6.

9. Khartoum National Unity Radio (in Arabic), 9 June 1991 (1500 GMT), as printed in Foreign Broadcasting Information Service (FBIS), "'Large Numbers' Returning from Ethiopia," FBIS-NES-91-111 (10 June 1991).

10. Hutchinson, *Nuer Dilemmas,* 342.

11. J. Millard Burr and Robert O. Collins, *Requiem for the Sudan: War, Drought, and Disaster Relief on the Nile* (Boulder, 1995), 296.

12. Lam Akol on London BBC World Service, 2 September 1991, as printed by FBIS, "Breakaway Commander Interviewed," FBIS-NES-91-172 (5 September 1991).

13. Jemera Rone, *Civilian Devastation: Abuses by All Parties in the War in Southern Sudan* (New York, June 1994), 92; Norwegian People's Aid estimate, as quoted in Burr and Collins, *Requiem,* 301.

14. US Committee for Refugees (USCR), "USCR Mid-year Update on Sudan Sept. 2001" (24 September 2001), http://www.reliefweb.int.

15. USCR, "Sudan Government bombs civilian targets 113 times this year according to new research by Aid Workers" (7 November 2000), http://www.reliefweb.int; USCR, "Mid-year Update."

16. Harker, "Human Security in Sudan," 4, 7.

17. AFROL News, "Unique Opportunity for Viable Peace Process in Sudan" (30 January 2002), http://www.afrol.com/countries/sudan/sudan_news.html; International Crisis Group, "God, Oil and Country: Changing Logic of War in Sudan" (28 January 2002), http://www.intl-crisis-group.org/projects/showreport.cfm?reportid=534.

18. The classic work of reference on the period is Richard Hill, *Egypt in the Sudan (1820–1881)* (Oxford, 1959).

19. There were quite a few Arab Egyptians (usually Copts) in the Ottoman Sudan Civil Service.

20. The standard history is Peter M. Holt, *The Mahdist State in the Sudan (1881–1898)* (Oxford, 1958).

21. The British had already occupied the Uganda Protectorate, the British East Africa Protectorate (Kenya Colony after 1920), and British Somaliland. The Sudan was

hemmed in to the southwest by Belgian expansion (the Belgians even occupied part of Sudan until 1910), blocked toward Ethiopia by that country's political renewal under Emperor Menelik II, and blocked westwards by French Equatorial Africa.

22. See Robert Mantran (ed.), *Histoire de l'Empire Ottoman* (Paris, 1989); Halil Inalcik and Donald Quataert (eds.), *An Economic and Social History of the Ottoman Empire (1300–1914)* (Cambridge, 1994).

23. See Muhammad Fuad Shukry, *Khedive Ismail and Slavery in the Sudan (1863–1879)* (Cairo, 1937).

24. See Gérard Prunier, "La Traite Soudanaise (1820–1885): Structures et Périodisation," in Serge Daget (ed.), *De la Traite à l'Esclavage* (Paris, 1989), 521–535.

25. On this, see Darrell Bates, *The Fashoda Incident of 1898: Encounter on the Nile* (Oxford, 1984).

26. For indirect rule, see Robert I. Rotberg, *A Political History of Tropical Africa* (New York, 1965), 291–294.

27. For a study of this "unbearable lightness of colonizing," see Francis Deng and Martin Daly, *Bonds of Silk: The Human Factor in the British Administration of the Sudan* (East Lansing, 1989).

28. See Francis Deng, *War of Visions: Conflict of Identities in the Sudan* (Washington, D.C., 1995); Ali Mazrui: "The Multiple Marginality of the Sudan," in Yusuf Fadl Hasan (ed.), *Sudan in Africa* (Khartoum, 1971), 240–255.

29. European slave traders operated in the south during the 1840s and 1850s, but their activities remained a marginal phenomenon when measured against the total Sudanese slave trade.

30. See Robert O. Collins, *The Southern Sudan (1883–1898): A Struggle for Control* (New Haven, 1962).

31. See A. B. Theobald, *'Ali Dinar, Last Sultan of Darfur (1898–1916)* (London, 1965).

32. See Gabriel Warburg, *Historical Discord in the Nile Valley* (London, 1992).

33. Most of the late-colonial British writers (K. D. D. Henderson, J. S. R. Duncan, James Robertson) seem perfectly at ease with this conclusion. It is only in the recently published official documents (and Douglas H. Johnson (ed.), Institute of Commonwealth Studies, British Documents at the End of Empire Project, *Sudan: Part II (1951–1956)* [London, 1998]) that we find discreet worries about the probable Arab domination of the country from missionaries, British administrators in the south, and some southern chiefs.

34. For an enlightening study of the contradictions during the buildup to independence, see Afaf Abdel Majid Abu Hasabu, *Factional Conflict in the Sudanese Nationalist Movement (1918–1948)* (Khartoum, 1985).

35. The whole system has been described in biting detail by Mansour Khalid in two books: one in English, *The Government They Deserve* (London, 1990); and the other, more detailed, in Arabic, *an-nukhba as-sudaniya wa idman al-fashel* (Cairo, 1993), II. A one-time crony of former dictator Gaafar Nimeiry, Khalid was in a good position to study the Sudanese political elite.

36. Mohamed Ahmed Mahjoub, *Democracy on Trial* (London, 1974), 297–298.

37. Sadiq al-Mahdi, "Reflections on Government and Politics in the Sudan: Our Experience in Office," paper read at a Staff Conference of the Political Department of the University of Khartoum, 2 December 1967.

38. "Socialism" was the catchword of the first years (1969–1973) of the Nimeiry system. In practice, it meant confiscation and transfer of assets to the regime's cronies.

39. For a description of this process in the 1980s, see Gérard Prunier, "Ecologie, Structures Ethniques et Conflits Politiques au Dar Fur," in Hervé Bleuchot, et al. (eds.), *Sudan: History, Identity, Ideology* (Oxford, 1991), 85–103.

40. A remarkable Sudanese intellectual of the 1950s could write in all seriousness that there were "no racial or cultural divisions in the Sudan." Mekki Abbas, *The Sudan Question* (New York, 1952), 179.

41. Inaugural Address to the Round Table Conference, Khartoum, 16 March 1965.

42. For a description of British colonial policies in the south and of the process leading to the 1955 mutiny, see Robert O. Collins, *Shadows in the Grass: Britain in the Southern Sudan (1918–1956)* (New Haven, 1983).

43. Abel Alier, *The Southern Sudan: Too Many Agreements Dishonored* (Exeter, 1990).

44. For a description of this process, see Mohamed Omar Beshir, *The Southern Sudan, from Conflict to Peace* (London, 1975); Gérard Prunier, *From Peace to War: The Southern Sudan (1972–1984)* (Hull, 1986), 7–12.

45. Girma Kebbede, "Sudan: The North-South Conflict in Historical Perspective," in Kebbede (ed.), *Sudan's Predicament: Civil War, Displacement and Ecological Degradation* (Ashgate, 1999), 18.

46. The best general introduction to radical Islam is Nazih Ayubi, *Political Islam: Religion and Politics in the Arab World* (London, 1991). On the Sudanese Muslim Brotherhood movement, one can consult Hassan Makki Mohamed, *Harakat al-ikhwaan al-Muslimin fi'l Sudan (1944–1969)* (Khartoum, 1974); Hayder Ibrahim 'Ali, *Azmat al-islam as-siyasi: al-jebha al-qaumiya fi'l Sudan: namudhayan* (Cairo, 1991); Hassan al-Turabi, *al-harakat al-islamiya fi'l Sudan* (Cairo, 1991); Abdel Salam Sidahmed, *Politics and Islam in Contemporary Sudan* (New York, 1996).

47. He was the only one who rose to high government position, eventually becoming attorney general of the Sudan toward the end of the Nimeiry regime.

48. This toleration on the part of Nimeiry came from the fact that he had not understood the new political dynamics of the country and still feared much more the old Ansar and Khatmiyya groups.

49. Beyond the Muslim Brotherhood party faithful, this group included the fundamentalist Muslims, nationalist Army men, some of the new oil-linked bourgeoisie, and some black Muslims who had previously thrown in their lot with the Arabs and who stood to lose if the Christian southerners were given a stake in the state.

50. *as-Sudan al-Hadith* (23 May 1990). The September Laws, enacted by Nimeiry in September 1983, established the Islamic shari'a.

51. There are very few systematic studies of the Sudanese Islamist regime since 1989. For a sympathetic presentation, see Abd-el-Wahab al-Effendi, *Turabi's Revolution* (London, 1991). For a critical view, see Hayder Taha, *al-ikhwaan wa'l asker* (Cairo, 1993). For a more balanced evaluation, see Sidahmed, *Politics and Islam.*

52. It thus is interesting to note that the latest cases of amputation for theft (in February 2001) were meted out to western Sudanese blacks. Just as in the period of Nimeiry's extensive application of hudud penalties, the victims are almost never Arabs.

53. See Sidahmed, *Politics and Islam,* 219–224.

54. Ansar as-Sunna has several times taken the law into its own hands, murdering "impious" people, such as singers, or even opening fire on "false" mosques, killing dozens of people.

55. In the Nuba mountains, mosques are routinely burned or bombed. But there the Muslim population is black African.

56. This was in an election where thirty-seven out of the sixty-eight southern seats could not be contested because of the war.

57. Hence the persistent refusal to organize free elections.

58. It is about 60 to 65 percent of the skilled work force. See Mohamed el-Awal Galal ad-Din, "Sudanese Migration in the Oil Producing Arab countries," in N. O'Neill and J. O'Brien (eds.), *Economy and Class in Sudan* (London, 1988), 291–305.

59. Financial go-betweens remit local currency to the beneficiaries and keep the foreign currency abroad. A small proportion is used for basic imports, but much more is never repatriated. See Richard Brown, *Public Debt and Private Wealth: Debt Capital Flight and IMF in the Sudan* (London, 1992), 210–229.

60. Non-Islamist businessmen have been even more systematically marginalized by the selective use of credit and import licenses. The recent oil boom (since 1999) has reinforced the economic hegemony of the National Congress.

61. In spite of the rather forgiving and easy-going nature of the (northern) Sudanese political culture, the amount of hostility that has accumulated against the present regime would make it economically and even physically dangerous for the Muslim Brotherhood to abandon power, absent very strong guarantees of the safety of its members.

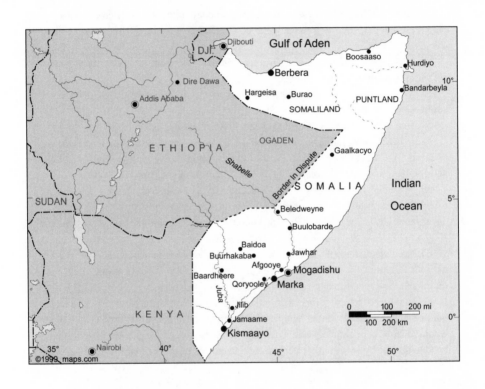

CHAPTER FIVE

Somalia: Can A Collapsed State Reconstitute Itself?

WALTER S. CLARKE
ROBERT GOSENDE

Probably few people around the world took notice on 19 September 2000, when the newly elected interim president of Somalia, Abdiqassim Salad Hasan, addressed the UN Millennium General Assembly in New York. In the fifteen minutes allotted to him on the podium, he requested assistance in rebuilding his country's infrastructure and hoped, by his presence, to highlight the important political changes introduced in Somalia during the previous months. In fact, many people hoped that the new president's appearance in New York would mark an important step in a major state restoration process that began as an initiative by neighboring Djibouti. It also involved artful and low-key diplomatic efforts by the UN, the Organization of African Unity (OAU), the Arab League, and several Horn of Africa neighbors. President Abdiqassim's call for assistance was received politely but with justifiable caution by other representatives present, and all that he took home with him were best wishes and general admonitions to keep working for national reconciliation.

The Abdiqassim government remains highly contested and its survival looks uncertain, with the total territory under its control probably much less than that held by Somalia's fractious warlords. The "Arta group," which established the process through which the new government came into being, is not just another faction. By speaking before the United Nations General Assembly (UNGA), the new government established a level of legitimacy not obtained in any of the previous dozen efforts to restore a government to the collapsed state of Somalia. Somalia's collapse continues to mark the low-water point of post–Cold

War politics in the developing world. Despite President Addiqassim's efforts, Somalia has no meaningful widely recognized national authorities to run a state, perform its functions, control immigration, or maintain security. Somalia is considered by some to be a likely refuge for terrorists in the post–11 September world.

Somalia and the Cold War

Somalia's failure may be only partly related to the end of the Cold War. Over the years, its dictator, Siad Barre, built his harsh regime first on a combination of pseudo-socialism, the army, and his personal police force. At the end, his rule had disintegrated into clan-related isolation, and he was derisively called "the mayor of Mogadishu." During the Cold War, the Soviet Union provided the weapons for Siad's regime, and the world humanitarian community supplied food in sufficient quantities to serve the needs of the people and leave a surplus that the government turned into operational funds. Prior to the dramatic reversal of alliances in the Horn of Africa in 1977, Somalia largely subsisted on foreign aid; by the time the Cold War ended, Siad had lost all important foreign and domestic allies. The collapse of his regime was seemingly inevitable, and when he fell in 1991, and the clans fought to take his place, there was no foreign champion available to help the people of Somalia restore their state. When the world belatedly turned its attentions to Somalia's self-imposed tragedy in mid-1992, its agents lacked the experience, tools, and vision necessary to create the foundations for a viable society. The West's intervention was probably doomed from the outset because no one knew how to or wanted to disarm and jump-start a heavily armed and chaotic society.

Somalia remains a paradox for outsiders, as well as for a great number of Somalis. The former Somali state has fractured into largely self-governing regions, only one of which appears viable. Despite many efforts to resurrect the Somalia of 1960, the shape of what everyone is striving for is problematic. Will the old Somalia emerge under a new form of governance? Will the Somali people accept the dispersion of power to regional or new national political entities? The basic dilemma is that Somalia is a relic of the Cold War, a period in which the great powers treasured stability and influence, propping up fragile states like Somalia through the generous provision of arms and foreign assistance. Those international rules changed radically when the East-West competition for influence evaporated after the end of the Cold War. So did Somalia's internal political dynamics. The corrupt government came under fire; the opposition, largely established along clan lines, was as heavily armed as the government, and political merit was measured only by firepower. The post–Cold War world has not been kinder to Somalia.

When Somalia collapsed in 1991, few people seemed to care. When decisions were made later to intervene to save the starving and destitute, there was confusion about the international role to be played. Armed intervention was necessary to protect the humanitarian process. Instead of using the period of substantial armed intervention to protect those Somalis who wanted to restore normalcy and governance, the interveners further empowered the warlords. The international actions by the Unified Task Force (UNITAF) complicated the political environment for the restoration of some kind of peace, and in fact, very much complicated the implementation of the UN mandate. Fundamental errors of judgment by the U.S. and UN interveners in Somalia in 1992–1993 included the notions that the Mogadishu warlords possessed some kind of legitimacy beyond their clans, that their cooperation could be secured through displays of force and concessions such as non-interference with crimes against fellow Somalis, and that the international involvement in Somalia could be limited and brief. In fact, the warlords of Somalia were, to a man, opposed to the foreign intervention and only used the respite provided by UNITAF and the United Nations Operations in Somalia (UNOSOM I and II) to wring whatever position and profit they could from the international presence. The solicitude of the world community toward the pretensions of Mogadishu's warlords facilitated the short-term interests of the foreign forces by lowering chances for immediate disagreement and confrontation, but the lack of any longer term political strategy on the part of the interveners left the political initiative entirely in the hands of those who had the most to gain from the departure of foreign military forces and the perpetuation of chaos.[1]

The 5 June 1993 ambush in Mogadishu, which killed twenty-four Pakistanis and severely wounded ninety-two others, resulted from the perception of Mohamed Farah Aideed, Mogadishu's most powerful warlord, that the UN presence would be prolonged and that the signs of creeping normalcy as civil society began to reassert itself were inimical to his longer term interests. Aideed's decision to go to war against the United Nations on 5 June 1993 (the so-called "change of mission," according to many critics of UN policies in Somalia) was his own, not the UN's. A warlord needs disorder to prosper, and Aideed chose a previously announced arms inspection as a pretext for war.

In Somalia, the forces of disorder were stronger than the "normal people," who wanted nothing more than an opportunity to live in peace. We examine Somalia's socio-political fabric and then trace the decline and disintegration of the state.

A Seemingly Cohesive Culture

How could a state with a strongly cohesive cultural history, a common language and religion, and a shared history of nationalism in opposition to former
European colonial masters and non-Somali neighbors have collapsed so completely? The Somali people share a strong folk tradition, based on the legend of
a common ancestor. That has provided the dominant culture to vast reaches of
the Horn of Africa for most of the past millennium. Somali speakers currently
are found, from north to south, roughly from Dire Dawa in the northern Ogaden
to the Gulf of Tadjoura in Djibouti and from there to central Kenya, and east to
west from the western Ogaden to Cape Guardafui, the easternmost point of the
African continent. The Somali cultural zone covers something like 400,000
square miles, a little less than the area of the state of Texas, an unusual phenomenon on a continent that numbers some 2,000 languages. Unlike most African countries that came to independence in the 1960s and were required to
forge a national identity out of a multiplicity of ethnic groups, Somalia was a
predominantly single-nationality state, with about 80 percent of the peoples
sharing a common ethnic identity and speaking the same language (with some
dialectical differences). Including the sedentary *sab*, the agriculturally based
peoples who constitute most of the remaining 20 percent of the population, the
Somali world maintains a common religion (Sunni Islam). In pre-colonial times,
a Somali found his/her identity through membership in a discrete kinship group
based on descent.[2] There were well-recognized mechanisms (the *shir*) that provided structures for restoring peace between subclans and families. Somali society, nonetheless, had a history of warfare among clans and among subclans.

Somalia's population at the time of its collapse in 1991 was somewhere
between 8 million and 10 million, of which about one-third were internally
displaced from their home regions. There are five major clan families in Somalia: Hawiye, Darod, Isaq, Dir, and Digil-Mirifle. Each clan family is subdi-
vided into six or more major clans, which are themselves separated into subclans,
lineages, and extended families. According to one Somali scholar, "clanism is
the Somali version of the generic problem of ethnicity or tribalism: it represents primordial cleavages and cultural fragmentation within Somali society."[3]
As we will see below, clanism lies at the root of the country's collapse. Paradoxically, clanism was seen by many Somalis involved in the most recent restoration efforts as providing a foundation for the country's recovery.

Looking back at Somalia's failure to reconstitute itself during the past decade, one might legitimately ask if the Somali nation ever constituted a state.
Somali traditional pastoral culture is based on the rugged life of nomads who
move their herds of camels, cattle, and sheep from place to place in search of

water and pasturage. Somali history indicates that the several clans periodically preyed on each other and especially on the sedentary agricultural groups who live between Somalia's two major rivers, the Juba and the Shabelle. Before the arrival of European colonial military forces in the later part of the nineteenth century, however, Somalia's coastal areas had for several centuries been controlled by Omani and Zanzibari sheikhs.

Rather late in the scramble for Africa, in the 1880s, Somali territory became the object of imperial designs by various European states and Ethiopia. The British somewhat reluctantly seized land in the north, primarily to support their forces in Aden. Somalis on the southern Benadir coast were treated rather more harshly by the Italians, whose occupation appeared focused primarily on diverting the attentions of competing British and Ethiopian empires from their newly obtained holdings in Eritrea. Ethiopia maintained ancient claims to the Ogaden, which were later recognized arbitrarily by Europeans. French imperialism focused on squeezing the Italian and British influences out of Ethiopia. After having been denied the use of port facilities at Aden by the British, France established a port at Obock in 1884, to provide a coaling station for its ships engaged in supporting colonial aims in Madagascar and Indo-China.[4] A French-built narrow-gauge railway between Djibouti and Addis Ababa remains one of the major Ethiopian outlets to the sea. Well before the full penetration of their territories by foreign powers, the lands of the Somali were already condemned to be on the margin of world interests.

Somalia is a cultural nation, but it was never a single coherent territory. Clapham recently observed that "over large areas of Africa, the idea of a 'state' derives only from the imposition of colonial rule. . . ."[5] This is true in most cases. For Somalia, however, the roots of the modern "Somali state" came only at the end of the colonial era, in 1960, when the two products of separate British and Italian colonial administrations voluntarily joined together. The remaining portions of the "Somali nation" remained under Ethiopian, French, and Kenyan sovereignty. Unfortunately, the voluntary independence arrangements joining Italian Somalia and British Somaliland did not result in a happy marriage.

Early Elected Government a Generally Negative Experience

The post-independence civilian government in Somalia proved to be experimental, inefficient, corrupt, and incapable of creating any kind of national political culture. The Somali political system quickly devolved into the dynamics of clan scheming and disputes. The already weak democratic system received a major shock on 15 October 1969, when Abdirashid Ali Shermarke, the country's second president, was assassinated by a bodyguard. Regime change can produce a crisis even in the most developed political systems, but Somalia's feeble democratic structures never recovered. The assassination of its elected president marked the end of an unsuccessful experiment with a Western form of government, and the failure was generally welcomed by most Somalis, fed up as they were with the antics of politicians.

The Somali parliament was scheduled to fulfill its constitutional obligation to elect a successor to slain President Abdirashid Ali Shermarke on the morning of Monday, 21 October 1969. On Sunday, 20 October, the city was rife with rumors that corrupt parliamentarians were energetically bidding up the price of the presidency, with Hagi Musa Bogor, a Mogadishu businessman, leading the pack with the price of 55,000 Somali shillings (then approximately $8,000) as his payment for votes. Rumors also were heard all that week that either the Somali National Police Force, then under the command of General Mohammed Musa Abshir, or the Somali National Army, commanded by General Mohammed Siad Barre, would intervene to stop corrupt parliamentarians from selling off the office of the presidency. In the early hours of Monday, 21 October, Siad Barre and the army intervened. Prime Minister Mohammed Haji Ibrahim Egal and his cabinet were arrested. Somalia's constitution was suspended, the country's eighty-six political parties were banned, and, promising an end to corruption, Siad Barre declared himself chairman of a twenty-five-member Revolutionary Council. During the Barre years, General Abshir generally managed to maintain the integrity of the National Police, and he remains an elder statesman, playing a significant role in efforts to return civil society and governance in Somalia.

Initially, Siad Barre received widespread support from the Somali people. He was decisive, a quality missing from the democratic governments that had preceded him. While becoming increasingly intolerant of any form of political activity or dissent, he opted in 1970 for a highly centralized system on the Eastern European model, declaring that Somalia would henceforth benefit from "scientific socialism" and would become a socialist state. Posing as a compulsive "modernist," he banned all clan-based organizations. He forbade all references to clans and subclans in discussions and in public documents. His repressive regime soon developed substantial internal opposition, and despite his philosophical opposition to ethnic parochialism, Siad Barre increasingly relied upon his own Marehan clan and the Ogadeni clan of his mother to provide the key members of his government and administration.

His quest for a national unifying ideology focused early on a long-standing popular theme: the pan-Somali dream of unifying the Somali "nation" under a single Somali flag. The three colonial powers (Britain, France, and Italy) and Ethiopia had divided up the Horn of Africa in the late 1880s so that artificial borders separated Somalis into five political jurisdictions. British Somaliland and Italian Somalia joined themselves at independence, but this still left significant Somali populations in northwestern Kenya, the Ethiopian Ogaden, and in French Somaliland (now Djibouti). The five-pointed star on the national flag was characterized as the symbol of the "five Somali lands," and it was the goal of all patriotic Somalis to support the needed efforts to rejoin the three "lost" territories to the motherland.

The Decline and Fall of the Somali State

Hoping to bring two of the three "lost" Somali territories under his control in one bold move, Siad saw a special opportunity in 1977. Ethiopia's revolutionary government appeared weakened by a growing rupture with its traditional ally, the United States. The Carter administration had imposed military and economic sanctions to protest the Ethiopian regime's scandalous human rights violations. The small, but strategically important, French Territory of the Afars and Issas (former French Somaliland, soon to be renamed the Republic of Djibouti), was becoming independent in June 1977. The new Djibouti government was expected to be vulnerable because the French had only recently switched administration of the colony from the Afar ethnic group to the majority Somali population. Siad sent armed forces into the Ethiopian Ogaden just one month before Djibouti's independence. Mogadishu-backed partisans struck the first blows of the war in May, cutting the Addis Ababa–Djibouti rail link to the sea in two places. Siad hoped these actions would cripple nascent Djibouti and its ancient enemy, Ethiopia, leaving both states vulnerable to his diplomacy and military forces. At the outset, the Ogaden War was very welcome in Somalia, and Siad's popularity reportedly rose to levels near to those following the 1969 coup.[6]

Aided by the presence of 4,000 French Legionnaires, airmen, and gendarmes, the new Somali-based Djibouti government carefully avoided Siad's embrace, making clear that it had no interest in joining a Mogadishu-led union of the Somali people.[7] The tiny new state bravely and effectively destroyed the concept of "Greater Somalia" by its early actions. Siad Barre's dream of conquering the Ogaden was also thwarted when, early in the conflict, his major foreign sponsor, the Soviet Union, which had massively armed the Somali army during his years in power, decided that newly Marxist Ethiopia offered much more attractive possibilities and promptly abandoned its erstwhile "socialist" ally. The Soviets, with direct support from Cuban military units moved quickly from Angola, initiated one of the largest airlifts of the Cold War to prop up the initially hard-pressed Ethiopian regime.

The Somali army, buoyed by the presence of a significant Ogadeni-supported insurgency group, the Western Somali Liberation Front (WSLF), initially captured most of its primary objectives in the Ogaden, moving forces to the outskirts of Dire Dawa, the central rail head of the Addis-Djibouti railway, and to Gode on the Shabelle river, nearly 350 miles inside Ethiopia. By the middle of September 1977, the Somali National Army (SNA) and irregulars of the Western Somali Liberation Front occupied up to 90 percent of the Ogaden.[8] Somali forces, however, were unable to sustain their dramatic initial victories in the face of a newly supplied Ethiopian government, now firmly backed by Soviet and Cuban advisers who, because of their recent Soviet alliance with Somalia, knew all the strengths, tactics, and weaknesses of the Somali military. By March 1978, Siad had been forced either to remove or to abandon his forces in the Ogaden. Frustrated by the collapse of the Ogaden campaign, Siad ordered the executions of six Issaq generals for alleged "activities against the state."[9]

Siad's debacle in the Ogaden provided the first step in what eventually became Somalia's slide into anarchy and failure. By overextending his forces, Siad simultaneously weakened his military power base and demonstrated the weaknesses of dictatorial rule. Over 1 million Somali refugees fled the Ogaden. Most moved into former British Somaliland. In their turn, the people of Somaliland, predominantly members of the Issaq clan, suffered the greatest economic deprivation from the war; it had been principally their husbands, sons, and fathers who had shed Somali blood in Siad's quixotic effort to conquer Ethiopia, a much larger country with a population four times that of Somalia. Following Siad's defeat in the Ogaden and the execution of the generals, opposition groups began to flourish, first in northern Somalia and later in the central and southern regions of the country.

Following an abortive coup attempt in April 1978 by army officers identified with Mijertein clan elements from the Mudug region northeast of Mogadishu, Siad abandoned any semblance of governing without clan considerations. All but one of the coup plotters were captured and summarily executed. The one survivor fled to Ethiopia, where he established an anti-Siad opposition group, the Somali Salvation Democratic Front (SSDF). Siad's displeasure with the Mijertein led to massive repression in the Mudug area in 1979, when his dreaded "Red Berets" destroyed reservoirs, causing the deaths of thousands of people and livestock and a rapid increase in the number of internally displaced persons (IDPs).

In April 1981, a group of several hundred Issaq expatriates met in London to found the Somali National Movement (SNM). The Issaq is the clan family that provides the majority population of the northern cities of Hargeisa, Burao,

Berbera, and their environs. The SNM had one major goal, ridding Somalia of Siad Barre, and it initiated a military campaign in 1988. Burao and part of Hargeisa, at that time Somalia's northern capital and second largest city, were captured in May 1988 by SNM forces.[10] Siad determined to make the northern provinces pay for their rebellious ways. His counter-attacks in the north eventually led to a siege of Hargeisa, with air and artillery attacks on the surrounded city. By the end of May 1988, some 35,000 civilian non-combatants had been killed in Hargeisa, which the Somali military, under the command of General Said Hersi "Morgan," Siad's son-in-law, leveled with massive artillery fire and aircraft bombardment. The city's ruins were then mined. Large parts of it remain uninhabitable in 2002.

General Morgan was wounded at Hargeisa, and his replacement, Brig. General Ahmed Warsame, continued the slaughter of innocents. When Somali air force pilots rebelled at the senseless slaughter of their fellow citizens, they began to defect with their aircraft to Ethiopia. General Warsame then hired somewhat more dependable mercenary pilots from South Africa and Zimbabwe.[11] In July–August 1988, more than 300,000 Issaq refugees fled into Ethiopia. Another 500,000 Issaqs fled to other parts of Somalia. The Somali regime was clearly desperate, and in Western capitals Siad's hold on power came into question.[12]

Another group that earned the special ire of Siad Barre was the Hawiye, probably the largest clan in Somalia. The Hawiye are divided into several large subclans, whose traditional lands range from Galcaio, the capital of the Central Region, south to the Benadir coast, which includes Mogadishu. Siad Barre's reliance upon his own Marehan clan, his mother's Ogadeni clan, and the Dolbuhante, was much resented by the Hawiye. That group had provided several of Somalia's independence-era leaders, including the first army commander in chief. Siad reserved his most savage repressions for the Hawiye; they were close at hand and, because of their size and their proximity to the capital, were perceived to be the greatest threat to Siad's increasingly brutal rule. Siad's repression of the Hawiye led directly to the formation of a Hawiye opposition movement, the United Somali Congress (USC).

The Somali government's progressive alienation of the major clans in the north and central regions also led to the formation of the Somali Patriotic Movement (SPM), a gathering of former military personnel and unhappy civilian combatants of Ogadeni background. Although the SPM received some SNM financial support, the three major insurgent groups fought intensively but separately against Siad Barre during the final three years of his regime, gradually gaining more strength and territory.

World public opinion turned sharply against Siad when, in early 1989, his Red Berets were turned loose on the capital city. Ostensibly there to eliminate

Issaq subversives, the shock troops rounded up Issaqs, Hawiye, and anyone else believed to harbor ill-will toward the president. On 9 July 1989, Salvatore Colombo, the Roman Catholic bishop of Mogadishu, was killed. Siad blamed religious extremists, but all the evidence pointed toward his own Red Berets, who by this time operated without restraint.

Seemingly oblivious to growing internal unrest in Somalia, the United States sought in 1980 to replace its Horn of Africa Ethiopian ally by offering military assistance to the Siad Barre regime. The quid pro quo allowed the United States to acquire access to partially completed Soviet installations at the port and airfield at Berbera in northern Somalia. There is no doubt that the United States was in part motivated by the hostage-taking in Tehran in 1980 and the subsequent decision to establish a U.S. Rapid Deployment Joint Task Force to be able "to project power" into the Persian Gulf region. But it was a deal with the devil as far as Somalia's opposition was concerned, and many Somalis were still resentful of this act when the United States arrived at the head of an international peace force in 1992.

The Siad regime soon became infamous for its bald manipulation of numbers of refugees and internally displaced persons. As a result, international assistance for the country's immense IDP problem provided a steady source of income to Siad's corrupt regime. In mid-1988, virtually at the last minute, the United States called off Siad's long-scheduled official visit to Washington, D.C. He would have been President Reagan's last official foreign chief of state visitor. U.S. economic assistance was suspended in October 1988. As late as August 1989, the United States continued to use the port of Berbera and downplayed Siad's petulant hints at possibly restoring relations with the Soviet Union.[13] But other things were happening in the world, especially in the Soviet Union, where moderating political forces and economic distress were forcing the state to reconsider its foreign obligations. By early 1990, the U.S. government had put Siad Barre and his downward-spiraling regime on public notice because of its human rights violations and general misconduct.[14] International aid groups sought to reduce their exposure in Somalia, and the United Nations High Commissioner for Refugees (UNHCR) and other relief agencies began to provide humanitarian supplies to refugees and displaced persons from Ethiopia, Kenya, and northern Somalia, thereby avoiding direct coordination with Mogadishu.

In 1989, Siad attempted to deflect some of the international criticism of his military campaigns by releasing political prisoners. But it was too late. His exactions had cost him the support of the Ogadenis and the Dolbuhante. They turned on the now Marehan-dominated Somali National Army. Siad's unpopularity became so great by 1990 that people openly mocked him. When spectators at a soccer match between teams representing the provinces of Jubba and Shabelle decided to leave the stands at mid-time for prayers in the infield, this was seen as an affront to Siad because of his recent repression of religious leaders. The president was present in the stands and his security personnel were ordered to break up the gathering. When spectators threw rocks and bottles in the direction of the presidential box, Siad ordered his Red Berets to fire into the crowd. Sixty-two people were killed and another 200 were badly wounded.[15]

By the time when the Siad regime celebrated its twentieth anniversary in power in November 1989, its future appeared bleak. Foreign embassies were under siege by Somalis in search of visas to flee the country. Siad's government was disintegrating, with defections and arrests thinning its ranks. The Somali National Movement, still a substantial force in northern Somalia, announced that Ahmed Omar Jess, an Ogadeni and former military commander whose troops were involved in leveling Hargeisa, had met with them.[16] In 1990, USC forces were launching raids within sixty miles of the capital. The SPM, refreshed by a continuing flow of Somali army deserters, was successful in central and southern Somalia and threatened the vital port city of Kismayu. As Siad's forces exacted reprisals throughout the country against those suspected of disloyalty, human rights organizations publicized the abuses; Somalia was now a pariah state.

In the end, Siad had no foreign support beyond token donations from Libya and Egypt. The *Economist* reported at the time that "[t]he geopolitics of the cold war briefly made Somalia look important. Now that is over. . . ."[17] Henceforth, Somalia's importance was to be measured only by the misery of its people.

Despite the recent, still uncertain, efforts to form an administration, there has been no national government of any kind in Somalia since Siad's ignominious 21 January 1991 flight from the capital. His departure from Mogadishu was somewhat anti-climactic, as the normal functions of government institutions had already ceased to exist. Violent looting of the capital city had been begun many months earlier, by government forces.[18] Advancing rebel forces followed suit. For the civilian population, there was no water, electricity, or food. Ministries and government offices were abandoned, and no attempt at law and order was possible in the advancing anarchy. At the end of his regime, Siad's forces controlled only the international airport, the radio station and Villa Somalia, the presidential palace.[19] The ambitions of warlords meant that the Somali people were condemned to support senseless civil wars among themselves to determine which aspiring local leader would have the right to sift through the ruins of the failed state.

Civil War and Foreign Intervention

In the fight for Mogadishu that followed Siad's escape from the capital, the physical structures of government were pillaged and eventually taken apart to be sold for scrap. It is generally believed that the fighting in Mogadishu during 1991–1992 between factions of the dominant Hawiye clan led to at least 35,000 deaths among non-combatants. With rare exceptions, there were almost no foreigners present to register the devastation. All foreign embassies, all international agencies, and all but one or two foreign non-governmental organizations departed the capital within a few weeks of the collapse of the Siad Barre regime.

During this period, Somalia intruded briefly on America's focus on the mounting operations to thwart Saddam's invasion of Kuwait. While steaming eastward in the Indian Ocean in route to the Persian Gulf, the USS *Guam* was ordered to reverse course and head toward Mogadishu; on 5 January 1991, a sixty-man Marine covering force was dropped into the American Embassy compound in Mogadishu, and the first sixty-one evacuees were flown out. "Operation Eastern Exit" concluded the following day with 220 people evacuated, including the Soviet ambassador and his staff, some other third country nationals, and the covering force. The evacuees were dropped off in Muscat, Oman, and the *Guam* sailed on to join the war. Only the Italian embassy in Mogadishu remained open for a few more days, in a last-minute effort to arrange a ceasefire in the city.[20]

It was not until UN Secretary-General Boutros Boutros-Ghali decided in January 1992 to send a representative, James Jonah, to Somalia to look into the humanitarian conditions that the world began to recognize the tragic dimensions of Somalia's failure. Timidly, the UN sent military observers in March 1992 and later deployed some international troops whose effectiveness was neutralized by the warlords of Mogadishu.

Boutros-Ghali named a special representative to Somalia in April 1992. Mohamed Sahnoun, a seasoned and highly respected Algerian diplomat, attempted to mediate between the clans. He was able to maintain the traditional peacekeeping requirements of neutrality and impartiality, and his mild-mannered style resonated among the Somalis. Although Sahnoun eschewed military intervention in Somalia, believing that it would inflame Somali nationalism and that diplomacy could prevail, his efforts came to naught because he had nothing beyond his own powers of persuasion to break Somalia's cycle of despair. Sahnoun resigned in October 1992, when the UN's first interjection of peacekeepers into Mogadishu failed to quell fighting in the city.[21] The 500 Pakistani troops that undertook this mission were operating under a Chapter VI mandate that precluded their being able to use force to restore order. They ended up being pinned down at the Mogadishu airport by Aideed's USC forces.

After a few enterprising and very courageous journalists focused on the ravaged state in early 1992, the United States and the world began to take interest.

Media reporting emanating from the small band of intrepid journalists who braved the incivility of southern Somalia's civil war horrified the world's conscience. Worldwide television coverage emphasized the desperate plight of women, children, and the elderly ravaged by drought and starvation while warlords preyed upon relief shipments arriving in the port of Mogadishu. The administration of George H. W. Bush, preoccupied by events in the Balkans and the 1992 electoral campaign, resisted for many months the entreaties of the press and U.S. public opinion to do something about Somalia.

In August 1992, the United States and a small group of allies, working with the UN High Commission for Refugees and the World Food Program, began airlifting food supplies into eight regional airfields in south-central Somalia in a mission dubbed "Operation Provide Relief." While authorizing U.S. participation in this food relief effort, President Bush resisted any suggestion that U.S. troops be sent to Somalia to facilitate relief and restore order. The Bush administration believed that the United States had no national interests at stake in the northeast corner of Africa, and the president had the full support of the U.S. military in this point of view. Somalia was no longer of strategic interest, and the Defense Department did not wish to have its personnel involved in an area where the tactical risks appeared high and the rewards very low.

But Operation Provide Relief soon proved inadequate to the requirements of the mission. Relieving starvation in Somalia could not be achieved by simply avoiding the nation's capital and flying into remote regional dirt strip airfields with no local police or security of any type. Somalia's warlords, always alert to any income-producing gambit, monitored the operations of U.S. and humanitarian agencies. They threatened to take aircrews hostage, while unloading the food cargoes into waiting vehicles and demanding "taxes" of several thousand dollars in cash before the aircraft were allowed to depart. Meanwhile press coverage of Somalia's horrific starvation continued. The public in the United States and Western Europe began to call for a more robust intervention in Somalia.

In November 1992, following his electoral defeat, President Bush requested options from Gen. Colin Powell, chairman of the Joint Chiefs of Staff (JCS). Yet Somalia's plight coincided with the disintegration of Yugoslavia. On 25 November, President Bush chose the most robust of the Pentagon's options for intervention in Somalia: he sent two full infantry divisions with considerable airlift, sealift, engineering, and logistical support to open the locked warehouses of Mogadishu and to clear south-central Somalia's principal roadways for the delivery of humanitarian food shipments.[22]

With little time to set up the operation, the U.S. military decided to use similar tactics to those employed so successfully against Iraq in Operation Desert

Storm—a large and robust force to overwhelm potential opposition and lessen the opportunities for losses in battle. Although the rules of engagement established for the intervening military force were very restrictive, the president made it very clear that the new mission in Somalia, "Operation Restore Hope," would be very different from Operation Provide Relief. He said that the United States needed to "stop these thugs from continuing to rip-off their own people."[23] When the Pentagon set up the rules of engagement, however, UNITAF members were instructed to ignore "Somali-on-Somali" violence.[24]

Despite misgivings about the mission from some quarters in the military, most commanders seemed confident about the tasks to be performed in Somalia. Adm. David Jeremiah, deputy chairman of the Joint Chiefs under Gen. Colin Powell, said, "It will be easy. Somalia has a long coast line, and it is relatively flat and treeless."[25] There is no evidence, however, that any of the 25 November senior decision-makers had ever visited Somalia or met any Somalis. General Powell reached into the retirement rolls of the State Department for Robert Oakley, a former U.S. ambassador to Somalia, to provide political guidance for the U.S. force. It was made clear that humanitarian goals, however critical, were secondary to the U.S. military's desire to keep its operation as short, safe, and simple as possible.

U.S. military planners had scant regard for the skills and ambitions of the restless irregular forces contending for Mogadishu, but they nevertheless wished to avoid confrontations. Pentagon JCS planners, leaving nothing to chance in the labyrinthine UN diplomacy, drafted the relevant UN Security Council Resolutions (UNSC 794 for UNITAF, and UNSC 814 for UNOSOM II), envisioning Operation Restore Hope as a very brief mission. The prevailing military preference was not to become involved in "nation building," and Pentagon planners gave the United Nations the difficult job of rebuilding Somali institutions. Restore Hope was to be as much as possible a purely military operation. All domestic Somali political considerations were to be set aside. Once they were on the ground, the interveners made arrangements with Mogadishu's two major warlords, Mohamed Farah Aideed, champion of the South side of town, and Ali Mahdi Mohamed, leader of the North side, and conceded to them police protection and judicial powers in their respective camps. In exchange, the two factions would agree to store their principal weapons and avoid confrontations with UNITAF until the end of the intervention, when a UN force would take over.

The U.S.-led Unified Task Force intervention in Somalia began on 9 December 1992. President Bush used all of his persuasive skills to pull together a coalition of twenty-one countries to join in the effort. The United States and its allies eventually deployed 37,000 men and women to central Somalia. Department of Defense planners promised a short-lived "humanitarian" operation. Initially, the United States said that troops being sent to Somalia would be home before the inauguration of President Clinton, in late January. However, given the constraints of the small port of Mogadishu and the single-runway Mogadishu airport, it was only possible for the planned two full infantry divisions and their support elements to be in place in Somalia by the end of January 1993. UNITAF completed its relatively narrow list of primary objectives within the first two weeks of the initial deployment. After that point, U.S. commanders of UNITAF were intent upon a quick departure. In their haste to get out, certain delineated mission objectives, such as the minimal restoration of roads and bridges in southern Somalia—necessary for the alleviation of starvation in the most affected parts of the country—were set aside as being too time-consuming. In one poignant demonstration of U.S. servicemen's ever-constant desire to do the right thing, the Navy's Seabee commander pleaded unsuccessfully with the UNITAF commander for permission to take his two battalions out of the Port of Mogadishu for this purpose. The two battalions came and went from Somalia without ever taking their equipment out of the port.

There was no provision whatsoever for the restoration of a single indigenous Somali police force or for the reestablishment of at least minimal incarceration and court functions in the country. No coalition country within UNITAF, other than Australia, had funds for such essential functions.[26] Yet, the need for such functions became quickly apparent, even though the United States steadfastly shunned any kind of policing responsibility or disarmament, saying that such activity would represent "mission creep." When one compares the mission of Operation Restore Hope with what little it attempted, it quickly becomes apparent that UNITAF commanders were engaged more in "mission shrink" than in an effort to contain the mission within the mandate prepared for it.

U.S. military leadership was first and foremost concerned with force protection and keeping to a short schedule, leaving all medium and longer term political considerations to the follow-on UN mission. So, throughout the late winter and spring of 1993, the U.S. military leadership and the Department of Defense undertook all decision-making and management responsibility for U.S. efforts in Somalia. The incoming political leadership, under Secretary of State Warren Christopher and National Security Adviser Anthony Lake, played virtually no role in the urgent decision-making that was necessary during this critical period. It appeared to those in the field in Mogadishu trying to communicate with the Department of State that no one was reading their messages. The new administration was "not focusing on Somalia."[27] Its lack of focus is striking, given that, at that time, Somalia was the only place in the world where American troops were at risk.

On 4 May 1993, U.S. commanders turned over their headquarters to the incoming UN command. By then, the main body of U.S. forces and most of the original UNITAF forces from other coalition countries had long since departed. UN commanders inherited a smaller and much less coherent force but were left with daunting tasks of policing and military disarmament. Meanwhile, the warlords, especially Mohammed Hassan Farah Aideed, the Habr Gidr commander in south Mogadishu, were determined to test the will of the UN and the remaining intervening forces. So, one month and one day after the UNITAF commanders departed, Aideed's forces ambushed Pakistani troops departing from an arms storage site inspection and guarding feeding stations in south Mogadishu. These were premeditated acts of murder perpetrated upon lightly armed Pakistani troops. The Pakistanis were taken completely by surprise. The situation had grown relatively peaceful. They were in the habit of carrying little ammunition with them to the feeding stations. On 5 June, Aideed's forces mingled with the remaining women and children in line at the stations and within two hours twenty-four Pakistanis had been slain. Aideed had delivered a message to the world: he was fed up with humanitarian operations; the foreign presence had interfered with his internal lines of communication and denied his ability to prey upon humanitarian relief workers; he was ready to become Somalia's next dictator.

Admiral Jonathan Howe, the special representative of the UN secretary-general in Mogadishu, has been roundly criticized for his reaction to these killings. He declared Aideed an outlaw and posted a $25,000 reward for his arrest. Aideed responded by posting a $1 million reward for Howe. Whatever the wisdom of Howe's decision concerning the amount of the reward, Aideed provided the UN and the outside world with a momentous and precedent-setting challenge. What was the world going to do about this horrific act—the premeditated murder of twenty-four Pakistani peacekeeping troops—at a time when there were over 90,000 peacekeepers deployed around the globe?

Senior policy-makers in Washington, many of whom had been junior officers, both military and civilian, in Vietnam, regularly alluded to parallels they saw between Vietnam and Somalia during the crisis. When, in August 1993, Maj. Gen. Thomas Montgomery, deputy UN force commander and the senior U.S. military officer in Mogadishu, requested six Bradley fighting vehicles (armored personnel carriers) and six M1A1 Abrams tanks for use in punching through Aideed's .50 caliber-machine-gun-armed converted trucks in case a U.S. helicopter was shot down, the request was refused. One senior Department of Defense official told us that the request reminded him of Vietnam: "Today you want a platoon of armor and next week it will be a corps."[28]

There was, of course, no parallel with Vietnam. In one case the United States was opposing a well-entrenched and well-financed war of national liberation, and in the other, it was trying, unsuccessfully, to deal with fifteen warlords who wanted little more than to run and rob Somalia for themselves. Richard Holbrooke would later coin the term "the Vietmalia complex" to describe what had overtaken some senior decision-makers during the Somali, Rwanda, and Bosnia-Herzegovina crises. This complex continues to confound U.S. decision-making.

The United States remained in Somalia for six more months following the "Blackhawk Down" debacle of 3–4 October 1993—an ill-fated assault on a rebel headquarters in Mogadishu in which eighteen U.S. soldiers and hundreds of Somalis were killed—sending in a much more robust force but limiting it entirely to a mission of static force protection. All of this was done in the most public fashion, with the end date of the mission clearly identified as March 1994. All Aideed and the other warlords had to do, then, was mark their calendars and wait a while in order to wreak havoc again on Somalia's long-suffering population.

Among the several states that failed, in whole or in part, during the post–Cold War decade, none has had quite the impact on the government of the United States and the American people as that of Somalia. At the outset, the desperate failure of Somalia intruded deeply into the sensibilities of the U.S. government and public. Yet, the deaths of the eighteen U.S. Delta Force personnel in the Mogadishu assault at the beginning of October 1993 caused the United States two weeks later to back off from a critical incursion into Haiti. Somalia-influenced sensibilities were the probable cause of the U.S. decision to force a reduction in UN force presence in Rwanda immediately prior to the genocide there in 1994. The U.S. government decided that it would never again chance combat in Africa.

State Failure a Long, Painful Process

It would be comparatively easy to decide that Somalia failed on 12 January 1991. That date effectively marked the end of an exceedingly corrupt regime. But failure in Somalia, as in other afflicted countries, was the result of a long process; state failure is not a single event. One of the most acute signs of failure in Somalia was the lack of hope of returning to anything other than what most Somalis had known for the previous dozen years: tyrannical leadership favoring the few over the interests of the many. Each clan and subclan had geared itself for war. Alliances were made for self-protection. Those clans populous enough to envisage emerging as a national victor in the war process selected their champions to go to war in the name of the clan. The war leaders had no illusions that they were fighting for Somalia; they were fighting for individual and clan power. No one saw his or her warlord as either a statesman or a demo-crat. Each clan provided significant material and massive human support for the civil war because each clan group wanted to ensure that the next Siad Barre, the next dictator, would be under its banner, with all of the perquisites that would flow from possession of the central government.

The role of warlords in modern civil wars may also be examined in eco-nomic terms. Making war is a costly affair. The cash resources available in a country like Somalia, one of the poorest states on the planet, are limited. To obtain arms and munitions, a warlord needs foreign allies. To obtain and main-tain foreign allies, a warlord must find common interests with them: these can be material in the sense that a warlord may promise future access to resources or influence. But in their relations with the fighting men, warlords must come up with either cash or loot. In Somalia, the warlords promised houses, land, possessions, and women.

Mohammed Hassan Farah Aideed was certainly one of the most resolute warlords. He was selected by his subclan, the Hawiye Habr Gidr, because of his military background and resolute personality. Resigning his post as Somali ambassador to India in 1988, Aideed returned to Somalia, where he built a military force manned primarily by destitute Hawiye nomads living in the cen-tral region, which at the time was suffering the harsh effects of a prolonged drought. Galcaio, the capital of that region, was Aideed's hometown. Using weapons mostly captured from the Somalia military, he gathered his horde and marched on the national capital. Once the battles of Mogadishu and central Somalia were won, he established his force in the southern section of the capi-tal city in the homes abandoned by leaders, administrators, and business people associated with the former government. Many of the veterans of his successful campaign married or returned to their families; to replenish his forces, Aideed drew upon the largely landless, homeless, and deprived young herdsmen, who had no families in the city. To ensure their loyalty, the enterprising commander provided them both a cause and periodic rewards of loot and shelter. The young soldiers, or *moryean,* subsisted on raids and "protection" money paid by busi-nessmen. Many were hired by members of the international humanitarian com-munity to provide security. Partially armored vehicles, mostly Toyota landcruisers converted into gun carriers, were turned out by the dozen in Aideed's garages, and these were leased to the moryean to make their protective role more convincing.

On a strategic level, Aideed needed to ensure that no one would return to Mogadishu to reclaim homes and possessions allocated to Aideed's command-ers and loyalists. When the international humanitarian community discovered the desperate situation of the IDP camps in the "triangle of death" (the triangular area bounded by Mogadishu, Baidoa, and Kismayu, then under the control of Aideed and his allies), they found that it was Aideed who had cut off the supply of food to those camps. The penury of the camps' inhabitants, mostly composed of women and children who belonged to Siad Barre's officials, as well as local Rahenwein opponents, was essential to Aideed. It ensured that in their weakened condition they would not be able to return to Mogadishu. Aideed and his allies did not plan on foreign military intervention to provide food to the families of the losers in Mogadishu's civil strife. Closing the warehouses to the humanitarian community and allowing the people in the camps to starve was a serious miscalculation on Aideed's part. The resulting crisis served as the "trigger" that led the international community to decide to intervene in Somalia in 1992.

Aideed was a ferocious military campaigner who gave no quarter to either combatants or civilians. He was feared by enemies and allies alike. Not given to debate or the questioning of his authority, once UNITAF had brought calm to Mogadishu, Aideed insisted that everyone defer to him as "Mr. President." Any visitor to his headquarters building and private residence, located behind a hill of dirt just down the road from the U.S. Liaison Office, was obliged to go through the charade of being met by his "foreign minister" (reportedly recently returned from driving a cab in the Maryland suburbs of Washington, D.C.) before being ushered into his presence. Given such recognition by the local UN administration, UNITAF commanders and officers, and visiting private and official delegations from Germany, Egypt, Italy, Korea, et. al., Aideed was unquestionably a much more important man at the end of the initial international intervention than he was at the outset. In the end, of course, Aideed died, just as he had lived, in battle on 1 August 1996 from wounds sustained in the Medina neighborhood of Mogadishu while leading the fight against Abgal followers of Ali Mahdi. Three days later, his son, Hussein Aideed (a former California resident and Marine Corps reservist), a few days short of his thirty-sixth birthday, was designated his successor. Hussein continues his father's policies; he took the lead in forming a coalition of warlords in opposition to the Abdiqasim government. He also requires that everyone use the title inherited from his father, Mr. President.

Considerations for Intervention in a Failed State

Somalia's starvation was tragic, but it was also a symptom of deeper issues of societal breakdown. At the outset, any military intervention force in a complex humanitarian emergency must make its plans knowing that the injection of a foreign military presence affects the domestic political dynamic, and must determine what positive processes it should support to help the situation return to some form of normalcy. Such interventions should be planned comprehensively to ensure that each participant on the "humanitarian battlefield" is able to exercise his or her specialty efficiently, without diminishing the efforts of others. The military component must understand that its primary function in an armed humanitarian intervention is to support and protect the international care givers and positive national elements. While applying their international mandate impartially, the military actors must understand that they cannot be neutral in the face of violations of international law and human rights.

What were the major failures in the international interventions in Somalia?

1. Inadequate planning for the UNITAF operation. Unrealistically, it was too narrowly focused on a few short-term humanitarian issues, thereby avoiding the more difficult political issues. The Pentagon blatantly passed the difficult issues off to the much weaker and less cohesive UN-led successor force. Much valuable time was lost because UNITAF had no mandate to engage Somali militants. Quite contrary to normal practice at the UN, where resolutions are drafted in the secretariat for the Security Council, the JCS planning staff drafted both of the operational mandates (UNSCR 794 for UNITAF and UNSCR 814 for UNOSOM II) to ensure that the mandates did not get in the way of U.S. command preferences. Although the military component is expected to protect its force, risks cannot be totally avoided.

2. The awkward personnel selected for the operation. In contrast to the hundreds of civil affairs officers deployed in Grenada and Panama prior to Operation Restore Hope and similar numbers in Haiti, Bosnia, Kosovo, etc., there were never more than twenty-four civil affairs officers in Somalia under UNITAF. Civil affairs officers provide continuing liaison with local communities. They explain official policies and can provide feedback to their commanders on the moods of the community. Someone thought that Restore Hope could be a purely military operation—quick in, quick out, without anyone's feet getting wet.

3. The political techniques utilized by the civilian side of the operation. The initial efforts to reconcile Aideed and his primary nemesis, Ali Mahdi, involved awarding them police and judicial powers in their enclaves. These large concessions may have bought some relative and temporary security for the UNITAF operation, but it presented UNOSOM II, holding a broad mandate to deal with all the factions, with a virtually insurmountable obstacle. The various Addis Ababa–based national reconciliation conferences (in January and March 1993 and in October 1993, after the disastrous Olympic Hotel raid in Mogadishu early that month) shared a common miscalculation: that only people with guns could bring the country together. The Mogadishu faction leaders were permitted both to develop the agendas and to decide who else would attend the conferences. In fact, late in 2002, the warlords perceive no interest in changing Somalia's collapsed state status.

4. Disregard for impartiality. From the early days of UNITAF to the end of UNOSOM II, the military forces failed to maintain impartiality in carrying out their mandates. Both UNITAF and the U.S. Liaison Office in Mogadishu were extremely attentive to the concerns of Aideed, to the point of meeting with him or his senior associates virtually every day. No other warlord received such attention, although there was an effort to keep Ali Mahdi Mohamed, the major north Mogadishu leader, "in the loop." Oakley openly shunned Morgan, Siad Barre's son-in-law and "the Butcher" of Hargeisa. Most of the other warlords in Mogadishu and the area were given scant attention. Omar Jess, one of Morgan's field commanders at Hargeisa, who became reconciled with Aideed, was invited to each of the national reconciliation conferences held under UNITAF and UNOSOM auspices. During their stays in Mogadishu in 1993, the authors were repeatedly asked—even by Aideed's own fellow Habr Gidr clan members—why the United States had selected Mohamed Farah Aideed to be Somalia's next president.[29] Warlord reconciliation was clearly a device to provide a "soft landing" for the initial intervening forces. It made unlikely the chances for the long-term success of the UNOSOM II operation.

5. Disarmament is not a bridge too far. The common wisdom was that the intervening forces would have suffered greater losses if disarmament were attempted. However, it is doubtful that the moryean would have remained loyal to the warlords had they seen clearly that they would have had to fight a superior force. Somalis try to survive to fight another day, somewhere else. Also, the moryean were young mercenaries. They fought for money, and the warlords lost their sources of ready cash when the intervening forces arrived. It is by no means clear that the intervening forces suffered fewer casualties by making concessions to the warlords and putting them in charge of the reconciliation conferences.

6. Failure to utilize traditional Somali reconciliation methods. While the ultimate responsibility for restoration of their state was always the responsibility of the Somali people, in 1992, an outside military force was almost certainly necessary, to act as catalyst to neutralize the hold of warlords on local communities and to permit the traditional problem-solving mechanisms of Somali culture to flourish. The shir, or *guurti*, as is it is known variously in Somalia, consists of meetings of elders to carry on political or economic matters of particular interest to the community. All members in such convocations are equal, and their decisions are binding on all involved.[30] Such meetings were not theoretical in the Somalia situation in 1992. The principles of the shir were later employed with comparative success at the Borama Conference in "Somaliland" in March–May 1993, and in Kismayu throughout most of 1993. At no point in the various processes attempted in Mogadishu and elsewhere during the 1990s were the Somalis to be "saved" by anyone other than themselves. For outsiders, the key was to be able to protect normal Somalis from warlords while they fashioned their reconciliation processes.

Had there been a long-term political strategy for the UNITAF operation, the planners would have focused on Somali cultural traditions and political techniques to facilitate reopening civil society. Problem-solving at the national level in a segmentary lineage society is a difficult, though not impossible, matter. It is a subject well studied in anthropological literature on Somalia.[31] Fundamental to all such plans is the need to establish a political dynamic that would seize political initiative from warlords and other miscreants and place it in the hands of traditional and positive elements in society. In Somalia, there were four significant groups that would have cooperated in such an endeavor: (1) Somali women, who, overwhelmingly and courageously, demonstrated by their actions a commitment to peace and civil society; (2) traditional elders and other local leaders, who resented the actions of the warlords and would have provided the basis for the restoration of local government legitimacy; (3) downtrodden agriculturalists and other southern minorities who saw no difference between the stranglehold of Siad's army and secret police on their communities and that of the warlords; and (4) tradesmen, intellectuals and other urban elites who wanted to throw the nomadic militiamen and moryean out of their homes and businesses. International political doctrine is unclear or nonexistent in these areas, but it should favor victims rather than their oppressors.

7. *Holding "national reconciliation conferences" outside the country.* Isolation from the common people of Somalia was a serious error. The favored conference sites, Addis Ababa and Nairobi, were expensive and privileged private deals between warlords and their henchmen. Under UN leadership, the people of Somalia should have been invited to choose their representatives to be sent to a national conference (shir) within Somalia itself. For many reasons, it would have been better to hold such a national conference outside the principal cities or towns. By early 1993, most major Somali urban or semi-urban areas were incapable of supporting a large meeting. Actions by the intervening force would have been required to establish a secure conference village. By holding the conference in Somalia, it would have been possible to include many more people in the deliberations and to provide for many more observers. A national shir would have been expensive, but even if it lasted for a year, it would have cost the intervening forces and the UN a great deal less than the bounty hunt and war. In the end, Somali civil society needed a number of years

to come up with a partial solution in which no foreign military support played a role.

It is important to remember that in 1992–1993, in Somalia, no warlord could have maintained his power without powerful support from his own ethnic group. By establishing a conference in Somalia outside the main Hawiye cultural zone, there would have been strong pressure on Aideed to join internationally sanctioned moves toward a return to civil society. In the end, this was the formula essentially taken by the Somalis themselves. Had the United States and UN employed these techniques in 1993–1994, Somalia might have been spared an extra six or seven years of suffering.

The European Commission's Efforts to Restore Local and Regional Structures

With the cooperation of the government of Kenya, the European Commission (EC) sponsored two seminars in 1996 in which a selected group of thirty eminent and respected Somalis from within Somalia and from the Somali diaspora were invited to examine various forms of decentralized government and to give their views on their applicability to Somalia. Assisting in the seminars were representatives of the EC and various resource persons from academic centers. Of the four models reviewed, the decentralized unitary state and the federal model were selected as the most likely to succeed in a future Somali state. Both models were to be driven by institutionalized power-sharing. At the second session the majority of the Somali representatives favored the decentralized unitary state model, with some looking at such consociational practices as a rotating presidency to encourage better collaboration between Somalis. The participants were nonetheless concerned about the development and allocation of state resources.[32] Such matters as health, education, and veterinary controls could easily be handled at the regional level, but whether police and other security issues should be national or regional responsibilities could not be resolved. Diplomacy and foreign assistance would be a national charge, but there was little enthusiasm for a national army.

Participants believed that Somalia could move from its chaotic state into the desired decentralized state in a series of steps that would begin with the selection of regional representatives to a transitional electoral body. These representatives would include both traditional and elected leaders. The representatives would then appoint or elect someone to lead the executive. Duly designated transitional assembly committees would examine the various components of a constitution incorporating the requirements for a decentralized state. The immediate goals for a new government would be security, including the demobilization of militias, economic development, the establishment of law and order, and capacity building.

The conferences in Kenya were not welcomed by the warlords in Somalia. Hussein Aideed's faction protested that they were held without his sanction. The Aideed group stated that it would attend such meetings only if it "was invited as the government, while treating others as opposition."[33]

The Arta Initiative

A wide-ranging and significant Somali national reconciliation conference, the thirteenth such initiative since January 1991, was first proposed in March 1998 at a meeting of the Intergovernmental Authority on Development (IGAD), a regional body composed of the states of the Horn of Africa. At this meeting, the chair, Hassan Gouled Aptidon, then president of Djibouti, stated that the only way to save Somalia was to move the process out of the hands of faction leaders and warlords.[34] President Gouled had, for many years, been searching for some way to bring his fellow Somalis in Somalia to peace. In March 1999, Ismail Omar Guelleh, the newly elected president of Djibouti, took over the IGAD chair, and carrying on his uncle's quest, persuaded the Ethiopian government to let him endeavor to bring peace to Somalia.

Although Djibouti's government is composed almost entirely of ethnic Somalis, it provided a neutral site to receive delegations from throughout Somalia. Given the fact that there was no site in Somalia that could be protected against the certain objections of the warlords, Djibouti offered the advantages of protection, relative ease of access to Somalis wishing to join the process, and credibility among Somali clans. The Djibouti government had never sided with one group or another in the Somali civil war. The goal of the conference organizers was to seek the widest possible participation from Somali civil society, both within Somalia and in the substantial Somali diaspora. Warlords were informed that they would be welcomed to the national reconciliation meeting, but would not be accorded any higher status than normal Somalis. Active diplomacy eventually led to support for the Djibouti initiative from the UN Secretary-General, the Arab League, the Organization of African Unity, and IGAD. In February 2000, UN Secretary-General Kofi Annan loaned David Stephen, a UN civil servant with long experience working in Somalia, to the reconciliation project.

There was, and remains, opposition to the Djibouti initiative and the subsequent formation of a government—from the former British Somaliland, which "retrieved" its sovereignty from the south in 1991, and from the northeast area of Somalia, which declared its autonomy as "Puntland" in 1989. The unilateral declaration of Somaliland's independence has yet to receive significant diplomatic recognition; Puntland has never asserted independence, but it calls for a "federal Somalia," which would protect it from Mogadishu.[35]

In March 2000, a technical committee composed of eight exiled Somali intellectuals was invited to sit down with Djibouti officials to set up the peace conference. There was considerable reluctance among cooperating academics and NGOs to organize the conference along clan lines, but it was eventually agreed that clans and subclans were the only useful organizational units acceptable to all Somalis. On 2 May 2000, the national peace conference was convened in Arta, a hilltop town located about forty miles west of Djibouti city. More than 2,000 delegates, elders, and observers representing all Somali clans and subclans were present. The conference immediately broke down over issues of representation. After an intensive period of negotiation, in which the relative size and significance of clan and subclan groups were finally agreed upon (larger clans with proportionally more delegates, smaller with fewer delegates), the conference reconvened on 14 May. An all-Somali conference committee was formed on 15 May to guide the remainder of the conference. The subsequent three weeks were spent in comparative calm as the pre-planned first, "healing and reconciliation" phase took place. On 16 May, the second phase, drawing up a national charter, began. Exactly one month later, on 16 June, a "transitional national charter" (TNC) was approved by the conference.

Some factional leaders and warlords attended the Arta conference. Among them were Ali Mahdi Mohamed, hotelier and leader of north Mogadishu and Mohamed Farah Aideed's major opponent in the 1991–1992 civil war in the capital; Hassan Mohamed Nur, leader of the Ethiopia-supported Rahanwein Resistance Army (RRA); Mohamed Abshir, former police chief and rival to Abdullahi Yusuf, who was later deposed as leader of Puntland; Abdulrahman "Tur," the first president of Somaliland, 1991–1993; and most dramatically, General Morgan. One Arta observer expressed the feeling of most delegates to the presence of warlords: "Better to have them inside the tent than outside throwing stones."[36] Morgan's presence probably was the reason for the brief attendance after 9 July of his chief rival in southern Somalia, Omar Jess, now a close ally of Hussein Aideed. Hussein visited Djibouti but not Arta during the conference; he departed in fury when he learned that he would not be accorded special standing at the conference. It should be noted that the younger Aideed ran into some hard times in early 2001, as members of his faction raided and destroyed his home in Mogadishu because they had not been paid or received any loot. Somaliland's President Mohamed Ibrahim Egal spurned the conference, arresting some people who wished to attend. Puntland's then-leader, Abdullahi Yusuf, remained an aggressive opponent of the Djibouti initiative and its results. During the Arta conference, he decreed that all Puntlanders who attended the conference would be permanently barred from returning home. But Abdullahi Yusuf was chased out of Bosasso in August 2001, after attempting illegally to extend his mandate as president.[37]

On 9 August 2000, the national peace conference nearly broke down a second time, this time over the composition of the planned 225-member National Transition Assembly (NTA) and whether it or the general delegates would elect the interim president. After the direct intervention of President Guelleh, who persuaded the restless delegates to work through the weekend, and more hard work by Somali elders, it was decided to follow the charter; NTA members would be elected on a clan basis, and the NTA would elect the president, who would serve in an interim capacity for three years until true national elections could be held. Demonstrating the special trust and respect accorded to him as host and facilitator of the conference, Guelleh was asked to appoint the extra twenty deputies from influential conference participants who might otherwise not be selected, thus expanding the NTA to 245 members. The NTA quickly was perceived as the primary mechanism for power-sharing among the four major clans, the Darod, Digil-Mirifle, Dir, and Hawiye, and dozens of significant subclans. Siad's rule and the civil war had devastated virtually every other social structure and institution. Tens of thousands of Somalis had gone into exile, and a number of NTA delegates also held U.S., Canadian, or European citizenship. The NTA was inaugurated on 13 August 2000. The membership includes twenty-five women, "a significant gesture," according to observers, provided as a reward for their courage and perseverance during the civil war.

There were three candidates for the transitional presidency. All were members of the dominant Hawiye clan, and each had also served, at one time or another, as a senior official under former dictator Siad Barre. They were Abdullahi Ahmed Adow, former ambassador to the United States; Abdiqassim Salad Hassan, former deputy prime minister and interior minister; and Ali Mahdi Mohamed, the north Mogadishu leader. Victory went to Abdiqassim, who was judged the more effective negotiator. As a member of the same Habr Gidr subclan as the Aideeds, it was hoped that his selection would facilitate the further decline of Hussein Aideed, the young warlord. In the national assembly, under the temporary leadership of Mohamed Abshir, the *doyen* of Somalia's political community, Abdiqassim was elected president on 25 August 2000 and was sworn in two days later in Djibouti. In 2002, the new government's hold on parts of Mogadishu and a corridor down the Benadir coast toward Kismayu remained shaky. Later in the year, many of these same persons and factions met in Kenya to try, once again, to bring sustainable peace to Somalia.

Lessons Learned

The limited success of the Somali national reconciliation process was due to a number of factors present in most examples of state collapse.

—*The post–Cold War peacekeeping paradigm is simply inadequate.* There is no such thing as a humanitarian surgical strike; all military interventions are, by definition, political interventions, and unless there are clearly understood political guidelines and goals, such interventions are unlikely to succeed.[38]

—*War fatigue was not taken into consideration by the intervening forces.* War fatigue was already apparent in the 1993 period; Somali women were actively engaged in the search for ways to get the moryean off the streets. From their perspective, the key was education and shelter, but Mohamed Farah Aideed's incursion upset the process. Why were the warlords permitted to foil that process for so long? The U.S. forces simply watched Aideed's forces rebuild after significant losses sustained during the 1993 combats. The quick departure of U.S. special forces after the 1993 debacle was also a mistake.

—*External support.* The UN has projected up to $100 million to help in the rehabilitation of Somalia's administration. This will depend on contributions from a largely skeptical international community. But until the Abdiqassim government can demonstrate broader backing, it will not receive the kind of assistance it needs.

It has been conventional wisdom for years that the number one problem faced by Somali society was excessive "clanism." The new system depends on finding a balance among the clans, and the results look fairly democratic in scope. It is possible that the clan competition for power and resources that tore the country apart after the downfall of Siad Barre may simply be more compelling and permanent than anything that broad power-sharing might be able to produce.

For the Transitional National Government (TNG) to succeed, it needs to maintain its multiclan framework and to demonstrate that it offers a credible and stable governance alternative to warlord rule. The TNG must be able to withstand attack from jealous warlords. Because the TNG cannot expect any direct foreign military or police intervention to neutralize the force of warlord arms, the transitional government must adopt a strategy to expand its influence through artful suasion and by building formal and informal alliances. The process of restoring Somalia to some form of rational administration will require patience and imagination.

The TNG should accept some power-sharing in the redevelopment of common services at the port of Mogadishu. It would be wise for the TNG to accept the fact of Somaliland's independence and to work out some mutual political recognition with that northern territory. Paradoxically, time may very well be on the side of the TNG. Despite the setback to the reviving economy caused by the forced closure of the Barakat bank in 2002, there are many other signs of growing business confidence in the future of the country. Most Somalis want nothing more than a normal life, free of intimidation and with economic opportunity. If the TNG can demonstrate that government can be a benign force committed to these goals, it may succeed.

It took a long time for Somalia to collapse; its decade-long struggle to redefine itself demonstrates that state failure can be a chronic malady for which there are no clear medical remedies.

Notes

1. The period of the U.S.-led UNITAF was from 9 December 1992 until 4 May 1993, when it was replaced by a UN-led force commanded by Turkish Lieutenant General Cevic Bir, with U.S. Major General Thomas Montgomery as deputy UN commander and U.S. force commander. After the departure of the UNITAF force, the remaining U.S. forces under General Montgomery's command consisted of a 1,200-man rapid reaction force and approximately 2,000 logistical support troops. The U.S. component departed in March 1994, and the remaining UNOSOM II forces were removed under U.S. military cover in early March 1995.

2. Lee V. Cassanelli, *The Shaping of Somali Society: Reconstructing the History of a Pastoral People, 1600–1900* (Philadelphia, 1982), 19.

3. Hussein M. Adam, "Somalia: A Terrible Beauty Being Born?" in I. William Zartman (ed.), *Collapsed States: The Disintegration and Restoration of Legitimate Authority* (Boulder, 1995), 70.

4. See Said S. Samatar and David D. Laitin, *Somalia: Nation in Search of a State* (Boulder, 1987), 48–68.

5. Christopher Clapham, "Failed States and Non-States in the Modern International Order," Purdue University Conference on Failed States (Florence, April 2000), 4, www.ippu.purdue.edu/info/gsp/FSIS-CONF3/papers/claphaam.html.

6. Alice Bettis Hashim, *The Fallen State: Dissonance, Dictatorship and Death in Somalia* (Lanham, MD, 1997), 102.

7. Walter Clarke, "The 'Esayi Dream: A Footnote to the Ogaden War," *Northeast African Studies,* XIII (East Lansing, 1991), 29–38, discusses Djibouti's interesting moves to resist Siad and to profit from the war.

8. Helen Chapin Metz (ed.), *Somalia: A Country Study* (Washington, D.C., 1993, 4th ed.), 184–186.

9. Ibid., 189.

10. Ibid., 48–52.

11. Hashim, *The Fallen State,* 113.

12. Jane Perlez, "Over 300,000 Somalis, Fleeing Civil War, Cross into Ethiopia," *New York Times* (13 August 1988), 1, 4.

13. Linda Feldman, "Weak U.S.-Backed Somali Regime Looks Again to Soviets," *Christian Science Monitor* (22 August 1989). By this time, most U.S. officials were ready to write off Siad, but certain influential conservative groups remained skeptical about the cool attitude adopted by the George H. W. Bush administration. See the Heritage Foundation, "Preserving American Security Ties to Somalia," *Backgrounder* (26 December 1989), 13.

14. Neil Henry, "Deaths of Civilians and a U.S. Turnabout Put Pressure on Somali Leader," *International Herald Tribune* (20 February 1990).

15. "Somalie: massacre sur un stade: soixante-deux morts en présence du président," *Le Monde* (11 July 1990), 5.

16. "Somalia: Realignment in the North?" *Africa Confidential* (29 July 1989), 4. Jess later established his own militia in the Juba area.

17. "Somalia: The Mayor of Mogadishu," *The Economist* (29 September 1990), 51.

18. Peter Biles, "Somalia: What Will Happen to Siad's Children," *BBC Focus on Africa* (March 1991), 6.

19. "Somalia: In the Throes of Agony," *The Indian Ocean News Letter*, CDLXI (12 January 1991), 1–2.

20. Ibid.

21. See Mohamed Sahnoun, *Somalia: The Missed Opportunities* (Washington, D.C., 1994), 89.

22. Alberto Coll, "The Problem of Doing Good: Somalia as a Case Study in Humanitarian Intervention," *Carnegie Council Case Study on Ethics and International Affairs*, XVIII (1997), 5. It is interesting that Coll describes in some detail the process that led to the U.S. intervention without revealing that he was one of the principal Pentagon players in that process. Coll was assistant secretary of defense for special operations and low-intensity conflict (SOLIC) in the last two years of the George H. W. Bush administration.

23. George H. W. Bush, "Humanitarian Mission to Somalia: Address to the Nation, Washington, D.C., December 4, 1992," *U.S. Department of State Dispatch* (7 December 1992), 865–866.

24. The Rules of Engagement for Somalia are provided as an annex to U.S. Army Field Manual, *Peace Operations, FM 100-23* (Headquarters, Department of the Army, December 1994).

25. Statement made in a planning meeting at the Pentagon prior to Operation Restore Hope, November 1992, according to a participant.

26. See Lieutenant Colonel Michael J. Kelly, *Restoring and Maintaining Order in Complex Peace Operations: The Search for a Legal Framework* (The Hague, 1999), I, 311. Kelly was the legal adviser to the Australian contingent. Under Australian protection, a group of local elders were empowered to try one of Aideed's most bloody henchmen. The man was found guilty, and following an appeal, was executed.

27. Statement by Susan Rice (National Security Council adviser on Africa during the first four years of the Clinton administration) at the conference "Learning from

Operation Restore Hope: Somalia Revisited," held at Princeton University, 21–22 April 1995.

28. Conversation with Robert Gosende (Washington, D.C., June 1993).

29. Gosende arrived in Mogadishu in December 1992 as Special Envoy Oakley's public affairs officer; in March 1993, he replaced Oakley as special envoy. Clarke arrived in early March 1993 as Gosende's deputy, and left at the end of June.

30. Margaret Castagno, *Historical Dictionary of Somalia* (Metuchen, N.J., 1975), 142.

31. See Erika Pozzo, "Customary Law of Somals and Other African Peoples," in Hussein M. Adam and Charles L. Geshekter (eds.), *Proceedings of the First International Congress of Somali Studies* (Atlanta, 1992), 277–288.

32. Karin von Hippel (ed.), "Decentralized Political Structures for Somalia" (16–18 November 1996, Lake Nakuru, Kenya), 4.

33. "Somali Faction Refuses to Take Part in Ongoing Peace Talks," *Agence France Presse* (19 November 1996).

34. "Somalia: IRIN Guide to the Somali National Peace Conference" (Geneva, 30 June 2000).

35. For a more detailed discussion of the Puntland initiative from the perspective of an interested scholar, see Martin Doornbos, "Somalia: Alternative Scenarios for Political Reconstruction," *African Affairs*, CI (2002), 93–107.

36. UN Office of Coordination of Humanitarian Affairs (OCHA), "Somalia: IRIN Focus on the Djibouti Peace Conference" (Geneva, 23 August 2000).

37. "Fighting in Puntland," UN Integrated Regional Information Network (Nairobi, 6 August 2001).

38. Walter S. Clarke, "Failed Visions and Uncertain Mandates in Somalia," in Walter Clarke and Jeffrey Herbst (eds.), *Learning from Somalia: Lessons of Armed Humanitarian Intervention* (Boulder, 1997), 5.

PART TWO

Dangerously Weak

Caribbean Sea

Ríohacha
Santa Marta
Barranquilla
Cartagena
Valledupar
COSTA
RICA
San José
Caracas
10°
PANAMA
Panama
Magangué
Montería
Cúcuta
VENEZUELA
Bucaramanga
Pacific
Medellín
Tunja
5°
Manizales
Ocean
Pereira
Ibagué
Bogotá
Buenaventura
Palmira
COLOMBIA
Cali
Neiva
Popayán
Pasto
0°
Quito
ECUADOR
BRAZIL
0   100   200 mi
PERU
0   100 200 km
80°
75°
70°
65°

©1999 maps.com

CHAPTER SIX

Colombia: Lawlessness, Drug Trafficking, and Carving Up the State

HARVEY F. KLINE

A strong Colombian state has never existed for the great majority of its people. At first, since little was expected of the state, few people thought that it had "failed," although some people—especially poor ones—no doubt did, when they lacked protection. Indeed, government decision-makers consciously avoided constructing a strong army or national police force, which led to a tradition of private justice and a violent national history. Then the final element was added: Colombia became the leading drug-producing nation in the world. The accompanying money and firearms further weakened the state and strengthened private protection arrangements.

By the 1990s, levels of violence reached the point that many Colombians believed that the state had "failed." Soon thereafter, when Colombia's violence and drug industry spilled over into neighboring countries, the international community became aware of the government's failure. By the end of 2001, many Colombian urban dwellers had also reached that conclusion, because they lived in constant fear of attack and were afraid to leave urban centers even for short trips to the countryside. Nearly everyone agreed that the Colombian state had failed—but in truth it had not. It had never succeeded. It had always been weak.[1]

Decisions Made (or Not Made) in the First 138
Years of National History (1820–1958)

Colombia began as a weak state. Nothing was done for most of the first 138 years of independence to change that sense of insufficiency.

Spanish and Portuguese colonies in the new world imported a governmental system that appeared to be centralized, but that functioned poorly. In theory, political authority in the Iberian colonial fragment came from the king. The Council of the Indies issued rules for the colony, which were carried out by viceroys, *audiencias*, and *cabildos*, none of whom were selected democratically. What on paper was an efficient, centralized bureaucracy, in practice functioned under the policy, "I obey, but do not comply." This phrase, Phelan argued, reflected a centralization of authority among the viceroys and governors that was more apparent than real.[2]

Studying what today is Ecuador, Phelan found that the coastal areas were never subjugated as intensively as the sierra. In fact, many coastal areas remained unconquered until the nineteenth and twentieth centuries. Nor was the administration particularly centralized. Many administrative decisions were actually made in the Indies by several competing agencies; local conditions and local interest groups played significant roles.[3]

There are no comparable studies of colonial Nueva Granada (as Colombia was called until 1852); the Spanish crown might have had substantial authority in Bogotá (as it did in Quito), but that did not mean that it had authority in Medellín (any more than it did in Esmeraldas). Bushnell argues, in effect making the same point that Rotberg makes in the opening chapter of this book, that states are not created equal. "This political disunity was to some extent inevitable. Certainly no part of Spanish America had so many natural obstacles to unity—so many obstacles to transportation and communication per square kilometer—as New Granada, with a population scattered in isolated clusters in various Andean ranges, not to mention other settlements along the coast."[4]

In Nueva Granada, the process of independence was regional, with Cartagena and Bogotá often going separate ways. If the fall of the Spanish crown led to the lack of a legitimate political regime, it also led to a more decentralized and weak state bureaucracy. *Patrias chicas* ("little fatherlands"—vast territories dominated by a local family) became stronger, as did individual large landholdings. Landowners held power within their territories, in effect existing as private governments.

Three key clusters of decisions in the first years of the independent history of Colombia produced a weak political regime.[5] Although no specific individuals can be given credit or assigned blame for these decisions, the decisions were the seeds from which the failing state was to germinate.

The Legal System

The first decisions had to do with the nature of rule enforcement—the legal system. The decision not to construct a strong law enforcement branch of government, since it might be a threat to civilian government (1830 to the present), and the decision to allow private groups to take the place of official law enforcement (from the landowners of the nineteenth century to the paramilitary groups, assisted by the military, who were enlisted to fight the guerrillas in the period from the late 1960s to the late 1990s) were critical.

The government never attempted to construct a police force of a size sufficient to enforce its decisions. Nor were the national armed forces or the police allowed to have much power. As former president Alfonso López Michelsen pointed out in 1991, private landowners in the nineteenth century made the rules for the areas of their landholdings, chose some of their employees to enforce them, and imprisoned workers who misbehaved. López argued that the country had made a trade-off. Unlike other Latin American countries, violence did not originate from the government, but rather from the lack of government.[6] These decisions eventually resulted in powerful "self-defense" or "paramilitary" groups.

Although it is questionable whether a strong national police force was feasible in nineteenth century Colombia, the basic reasons for keeping the police weak included the Colombian leaders' fear of the institutions of a strong state, especially powerful armed forces and police. Many other Latin American countries had seen such institutions end elective governments. In addition, Colombian leaders, primarily from the upper economic groups, did not want to raise the taxes necessary for a strong military and national police. Better to let those who needed a police force (the large landowners) do it themselves and pay a sort of "user's' fee." The decision not to construct a national police force left effective power in local hands, instead of delegating it to some distant national government.

The federalist period of nineteenth century Colombia (1853–1886) was one of even less central authority. During this period, law enforcement rights and duties reverted to the states.

The Use of Violence in Politics

A second set of decisions had to do with the use of violence in politics, often in the name of party (from 1838 until at least 1965). This violence intensified when religion became part of the partisan conflict, even though nearly all parties were Catholic (as of 1853 and continuing until 1965). The consequences of using violence were made potentially less serious for individuals at certain times when partisan violence was amnestied (most recently in 1953 and 1958). It was also decided that, given the relatively closed nature of the political regime during the National Front (1958–1974), even Marxist guerrilla violence was justified (late 1950s to the present) and might be amnestied.

As a result, political competition in Colombia was never limited to peaceful means. There were eight civil wars during the nineteenth century, six of which pitted all (or a section) of the Liberal party against the Conservative party. In the course of these civil wars, the peasant masses "participated" in national politics, but only dimly knew of the national political system. This participation did not mean that the masses had influence on the policies of the elites. In the main, it stemmed from their affiliations with a large landowner, who instructed them when and against whom to fight. In those civil wars, thousands of poor *campesinos* died.

This tradition continued into the twentieth century, with a short period of partisan violence in 1932 and then *La Violencia* (1946–1965). Zambrano Pantoja interprets this historical trend:

> The *real people*, that is to say, the majority of the population, learned politics through the use of arms before they did through the exercise of the suffrage. First, one learned to fight, and later, to vote. This caused the exercise of politics to be conceptualized as a conflict before it was conceptualized as a place of concord, in this way applying the generalized idea that *war is the continuation of politics by other means*.[7]

The frequency and intensity of violence in the nineteenth century had effects that lasted at least until the end of La Violencia. The numerous civil wars, with the widespread participation of the campesinos, led to a strict and intense partisan socialization of the masses. Many campesino families had "martyrs," family members who had been killed, disabled, or raped by members of the other political party. Although the original party identification of campesinos came from their *patrones,* at some point this identification developed a life of its own. Santa said that Colombians began to be born "with party identifications attached to their umbilical cords."[8] As a result, other cleavages (such as social class and regionalism) became secondary to the primary party one. Third parties were notably unsuccessful until the early 1990s.

Violence became the normal way to handle conflict. As a Colombian sociologist said to the author in an interview, "We have no ways to channel conflicts. Probably because of the traditional, oligarchic set up of the Liberal and Conservative parties, we never developed peaceful ways to resolve conflict. If we have disagreements we only think of violence as the way to solve them."[9]

The Elite Political Game

The final set of decisions had to do with rules for elite behavior within Colombian democracy. While the members of each party were allowed and even encouraged to take up arms against the members of the other, the party leaders generally got along well with each other. They came from the same economic groups, belonged to the same exclusive social clubs, and at times entered into governing coalitions—most notably in the National Front.

There were twelve occasions between 1854 and 1949 when one political party at the elite level entered into a coalition with all or part of the other political party. These elite coalitions tended to take place when presidents assumed dictatorial powers, when party hegemonies shifted, and, especially in the twentieth century, when elite-instigated violence cascaded out of control.[10]

The longest, most formal coalition was the National Front (1958–1974). In a consociational agreement first proposed by leaders of the Liberal and Conservative parties but later approved in a national referendum and as a constitutional amendment, power was shared equally.[11] The presidency alternated between the two parties (no other was legal), while all legislative bodies were divided equally, as were executive cabinets at all levels, governors, mayors, and non-civil-service bureaucrats.

One might have expected the Colombian state finally to develop in a more modern way under the National Front, since the old party hatreds had ostensibly been discarded. However, as Leal Buitrago argues, during the years of the National Front Colombia lost that opportunity:

> . . . Bureaucratization and clientelism substituted for sectarianism as the source of reproduction of the political parties. But in spite of the profundity of this change, the long-lasting political weakness of the state was not significantly altered. The bureaucratization of the dual party system and the transformation of clientelism into the axis of the political system prevented the widening and modernization of the state from significantly increasing the extent of the state.[12]

Rather than building a state that would have been better prepared to deal with current and future problems, Colombian policy-makers "played" what Geddes has called the "politician's dilemma." Like Salvador Allende in Chile in the early 1970s, they had to choose between their need for political survival (clientelism) and longer term interests in regime stability (building the state).[13] They chose survival.

New Challenges Arising in the 1960s–1980s

Although the Colombian government had but tenuous control over the great majority of the national territory, three "new" groups emerged during and after the National Front, providing novel challenges to the government and setting up *de facto* governments in parts of the country. In rough chronological order, the groups were guerrilla groups, paramilitary squads, and drug dealers. While the analysis below suggests that they are separate groups, in fact they are somewhat interconnected. Coalitions were in constant flux, and the only constant theme seems to have been "the enemy of my enemy is my friend."

Guerrilla Groups

The influence of Marxist revolutionary groups in the countryside goes back to the final years of La Violencia. In the years since the National Front, there have been four major guerrilla organizations in Colombia.

The first such group to emerge, toward the end of La Violencia in 1962, was the pro-Castro Ejército de Liberación Nacional (ELN, Army of National Liberation). The ELN arose after a group of Colombian scholarship students went to Cuba at the height of the Cuban missile crisis in 1962. Some of the group asked for and obtained military training and began a series of discussions about a "foco" strategy for Colombia. This strategy called for a guerrilla group to start from a small area, develop militarily, and govern in a way that favored the interest of the common people. The ELN was officially born on 4 July 1964, and was initially comprised primarily of university students.[14]

In 1966, the communist-dominated Fuerzas Armadas Revoluciónarias de Colombia (FARC, Armed Forces of the Colombian Revolution) was founded, although communist-oriented peasant defense groups pre-dated it by more than fifteen years. As early as 1949, the Communist Party urged the proletariat and others to defend themselves.

After 1974, a pro-Chinese (Beijing) Ejército Popular de Liberación (EPL, People's Liberation Army) adopted the "prolonged people's war" strategy but was soon close to extinction.[15] It accepted a peace proposal in 1989, but reappeared in the 1990s. The Movimiento 19 de abril (M-19, 19th of April Movement), claiming to be the armed branch of Gustavo Rojas Pinilla's party, Alianza Nacional Popular (ANAPO, National Popular Alliance), appeared in January 1974. The name was chosen because of the allegation that the National Front government had stolen the presidential election of 19 April 1970 from Rojas. While the party engaged in violence for nineteen years, in 1989 the M-19 accepted a peace proposal and became a legal political party.

Paramilitary Groups

Private justice began early in Colombian history; the country has been rife with paramilitary groups since its inception. They appeared in a different form in the twentieth century, during La Violencia. The first self-defense groups to organize then were the "peasant self-defense" groups in Tolima, with a concentration of about 1,000 families. In the 1950s, similar groups appeared in other places. Ironically, the FARC developed out of one such group.

After the end of La Violencia, paramilitary groups were backed legally by Decree 3398 of President Guillermo León Valencia (passed in 1965) and Law 48 under President Carlos Lleras Restrepo (issued in 1968). The basic clause said that the government could use any citizen in activities to reestablish normalcy. In this way, the weak state could enlist the help of private groups to battle the guerrillas. The national army might arm and train the private individuals, and close ties developed between many paramilitary groups and the military.

In the 1970s, with the growth of the FARC and its hostility toward the civilian population (especially ranchers and large farmers, who could pay protection money), those with traditional political affiliations adopted a "self-defense" structure to repel the guerrilla attacks. Many of those self-defense groups arose in response to the constant demands of the guerrillas because it was clear that the government could not protect honor, life, and property throughout the national territory.[16]

For example, a medium-sized farmer in Urabá described the problems that led to the formation of paramilitary groups: "Here the communists and the guerrillas want to throw us out. But we're not going to let them screw us. Journalist, everything I'm saying is true. But don't print my name." Off the record, banana growers affirmed that the government had never worried about their zone. Before the formation of the paramilitary groups, the region's work inspectors and judges could not work because the machine guns of the FARC and the EPL would not let them. There were also armed unions. According to the banana growers, they might as well have declared independence from Colombia.[17]

During the presidency of Virgilio Barco (1986–1990), paramilitary groups experienced a dramatic change. Earlier, such groups were comprised of individuals who produced legal agricultural products. However, as the drug lords became wealthy, they bought more land. While at first they bought land to become "gentleman farmers," later the land was used to grow coca. Soon, drug money began supporting paramilitary squads.

Two other important things occurred by the end of the Barco presidency. First, the number of deaths attributed to paramilitary group activity exceeded those from guerrilla activities. Second, although the connection between the Colombian military and the paramilitary groups had officially ended, that relationship in fact continued to exist.

Drug Dealers

Drug-organized crime—and its accompanying money and firearms—brought a final ingredient to the deadly Colombian concoction. Drug trafficking, and even the organized crime that accompanied it, at first was not considered a threat to the Colombian government. It was not that different from other illicit economic activities, such as smuggling, that had previously existed. However, it became a threat when drug groups became so powerful that any politician, judge, or journalist opposing them could be bought or killed.

The country's role in the international drug market developed very rapidly. One reason for this rise was the major drive against drugs launched by Mexico in 1975, at the urging of the U.S. government. This led to Colombia becoming "the epicenter of marijuana production in the hemisphere . . . ." Colombia came to provide 70 percent of U.S. marijuana imports.[18]

Marijuana provided start-up cash for drug entrepreneurs. Some drug leaders from Medellín used money from marijuana to shift production and export to the new drug of choice in the United States, cocaine—which had the other virtue of having a higher value per volume. Coca, the raw material for cocaine, was grown principally in Peru and Bolivia and shipped to Colombia as coca paste. The cocaine refining industry became centered in Colombia, according to Thoumi, because drug dealers realized that, compared to its neighbors, the country was less likely to arrest or prosecute drug traffickers.[19]

Drug smuggling changed when two Medellín dealers decided to switch from individuals carrying small amounts of drugs ("mules") to the lower costs and higher volume offered by using airplanes. Cocaine sales to the United States grew appreciably. In 1970, U.S. Customs seized only 100 kilos of cocaine; by 1982 this figure was 45 metric tons.[20]

The emergence of the drug trade should also be seen in the context of other events in Colombian society. After the 1950s, peasants were forced off their land. Many of them went into "misery belts" around the major cities; others colonized the more remote parts of the country. Of the latter, Colombian political scientists Orjuela and Barrera point out:

> There communities with very weak social cohesion were set up, in locations with only a scarce presence of state institutions. Those areas were especially ideal for the flourishing of a parallel economy based on the cultivation and trafficking of cocaine and marijuana. There the drug dealers filled the space left by the state; they constituted for thousands of Colombians a social security system that provided the income through assuring transportation and the prices that no one guaranteed to the [other] small peasant producers.[21]

Hence the weak state that existed in Colombia made it possible for drugs to become rooted in the countryside. This, in turn, made the Colombian state even weaker, as drug dealers established private governments in parts of the country. As their illicit wealth increased, they armed themselves and collaborated with both paramilitary groups and guerrilla groups, which made the state weaker yet.

In the same way, the lack of opportunities in the legitimate economic realm encouraged Colombians to seek opportunities in the illicit one. In a study of the impact of drug trafficking in Antioquia, Arango Jaramillo studied twenty drug dealers. Of these, 70 percent came from campesino backgrounds. Only two had university educations, while eleven had only primary school educations.[22] Although there is no way to know if this breakdown is representative of the country as a whole, it does raise an important possibility. The drug trade not only filled the political space unoccupied by the government, it also afforded economic opportunities that were unavailable in the legitimate economy.

The response of the weak Colombian government to the drug trade was tentative and experimental. The Alfonso López Michelsen administration (1974–1978) reacted to the drug trade by opening a *ventanilla siniestra* ("left-handed" or "sinister" window) in the Banco de la República, at which anyone could exchange dollars for pesos, with no questions asked. In effect this provided a legal way for illicit narco-dollars to enter the economy. Other dollars entered through the long-flourishing black market, leading to the unusual situation that the black-market rate for dollars was *below* the official rate. Many other drug dollars were placed in banks and investments in other countries. While at the beginning of the 1970s the dollars that entered Colombia through this window were equal to 20 percent of the legal exports, at the beginning of the following decade they constituted 48 percent.[23]

A new economic group, whose importance is hard to estimate, grew up around the illicit drug industry. Although later the cartels of Medellín and Cali became internationally known, as early as December 1981 the Colombian drug industry held a secret national convention at which 223 drug-gang bosses created a death squad called "Death to Kidnappers" (Muerte a Secuestradores, MAS). The *mafiosi* pledged U.S.$7.5 million to the squad, whose goal was to kill all kidnappers and to end the guerrilla practice of kidnapping people, including the "honest, hard working drug gang bosses," for ransom.[24]

The drug dealers' connection with a paramilitary group is far from the only interrelationship among the various armed actors. The government also had relationships with the paramilitary groups until the Barco years. In addition, guerrilla groups developed relationships with drug dealers, first by protecting their fields and factories, later by "taxing" them, and in some cases by entering the drug enterprise directly. Finally, there seems to be little doubt that drug groups entered into politics, not only in the National Congress but by influencing the presidency, even before the years of Ernesto Samper.

The Additional Weakening of the State in the Past Sixteen Years

Since 1986, Colombian presidents have employed three different approaches to the weak state and to escalating violence. The first mode came when two presidents (Virgilio Barco, 1986–1990, and César Gaviria, 1990–1994) developed policies to increase the power of the Colombian government and to lessen political violence. The second mode was when President Ernesto Samper (1994–1998) became too concerned with protecting his own presidency from charges of drug connections to do much about rising political violence, especially from paramilitary groups that were growing in numbers and weaponry. The third mode was when President Andrés Pastrana (1998–2002) centered his presidency on negotiations with the FARC and the ELN, albeit with little success. At the end of these sixteen years the Colombian state was failing more than before and levels of violence continued to increase.

Between 1986 and 1994, the Barco and Gaviria governments negotiated with guerrilla groups and conducted indirect negotiations and plea-bargaining with drug leaders and members of paramilitary groups. Barco's government failed to change the constitution through the traditional amendment process. During Gaviria's government, a referendum called for a constituent assembly, which proclaimed a new constitution on 4 July 1991. This constitution attempted to open up the political system so that guerrilla activities would not be needed, and to create a more efficient judicial system so that lawbreakers would be punished.

That these policies did not lead to lower levels of violence is shown in tables 6-1 and 6-2.[25] Table 6-1 demonstrates that all indicators of violence were higher in the Barco years than the Betancur ones. This clearly shows the effect of the combination of a rise in guerrilla violence; the appearance of death squads, with tacit approval if not active support of the Colombian armed forces; and the "drug wars." While some responsibility lies within the Barco administration, every leader governs in a context that has been created by both his immediate and his distant predecessors. The situation Barco faced originated in the entire history of violence—the Colombian political model.

Table 6-2 shows that, with one possible exception, human rights violations were more numerous in the Gaviria years than in the Barco ones. The possible exception is in "presumed political assassinations," although if one adds that category to "political assassinations," the Barco administration averaged 2,216.3

Table 6-1. *Average Number of Human Rights Violations in Colombia, 1983*

Presi-dent	Assassi-nations	Disap-pearances	Deaths in combat	Kidnap-pings	Total murders	Percent political violence
Betancur	788.25	126	286.5	233	12,264.5	9.55
Barco	2,093.5	168.25	839.25	760	21,524.5	15.35
Gaviria[a]	1,829	180	1,364	1,550	28,284	15.33
Average	1,484	150.77	651.88	613.56	18,160	12.54

Source: Author's calculations from Inter-American Commission on Human Rights, *Second Report on the Situation of Human Rights in Colombia* (Washington, D.C., 1993), 123, 183.
    a. One year only.

while the average during the Gaviria years was 2,189.4. With a slight bit of rounding, that means that twenty-seven fewer people were killed for "political" and "presumed political" reasons each year during the Gaviria years.

Homicide rates in Colombia, meanwhile, reached astronomical levels. Homicide became the leading cause of death. The homicide rate in the early 1990s (77.5 per 100,000 inhabitants) was not only the highest in the world, but it was three times higher than that of the country with the second highest homicide rate, Brazil (24.6 per 100,000), and over nine times higher than that of the United States (8.0 per 100,000).[26] By the mid-1990s Colombia had the second highest homicide rate in the world, surpassed only by South Africa.

Other sources conclude that "political homicides," which encompass "presumably" political ones, deaths in battles with guerrilla groups, and "clearly" political homicides, varied between 11 and 18 percent of the total homicides between 1988 and 1990.[27] If one added the 1,500 deaths from the drug war in 1989–1990, political homicides would make up 24.6 percent of homicides in 1990, clearly the worst of recent years. Camacho concluded that 75 to 80 percent of the violence in Cali was "private," that is, having to do not with political issues, but rather with private settling of accounts on such matters as debt, property, sexual and marital issues, robberies, bar room brawls, and family violence.[28]

The Recent Presidencies

Two men have been president since the abortive state-building presidencies: Ernesto Samper (1994—1998) and Andrés Pastrana (1998—2002). The first spent most of his presidency trying to remain in power after it was alleged that he had received drug money during his electoral campaign. There are some indications that efforts to build the state in other ways suffered because of this

Table 6-2.   *Comparison of Human Rights Violations in the Barco
and Gaviria Years*

Average number per year

Violation	Barco (1988–1990)	Gaviria (1991–1994)
Political assassinations	576.3	860.2
Presumed political assassinations	1,685.0	1,185.0
Social cleansing	285.3	342.0
Deaths in combat	1,020.5	1,317.8
Obscure assassinations	3,824.3	5,159.5
Disappearances	162.5	187.8
Wounded	866.5	1,284.8
Tortures	30.0	166.5
Arrests (political)	912.5	1,102.0
Death threats	120.5	225.8

Source: Author's calculations from *Justicia y Paz.*

primary concern.[29] Pastrana's presidency featured negotiations with the two major guerrilla groups, but these were ultimately unsuccessful.

During the Samper presidency, drugs continued to be exported from Colombia in roughly the same amounts as before, while new leaders and new cartels appeared. While key leaders of the Cali group were in jail and narcoterrorism seemed to be a thing of the past, one report suggested that the imprisoned Cali leaders, the Rodríguez Orejuela brothers, were plotting the deaths of Samper, the national prosecutor, the U.S. ambassador, and others.[30]

Drug monies seemed, even more than before, to have completely infiltrated the Colombian political system. The lower house of the National Congress considered the accusation that Samper had received as much as U.S.$6 million from the Cali drug leaders during the 1994 campaign. Although the legislature refused to impeach Samper, many (including the U.S. government) considered him guilty, and inadequately judged by a congress composed of members who had also received drug money.

Guerrilla groups continued to be active in ambushes, bombings, and kidnappings. In August 1996, guerrillas captured sixty members of the army in the Amazon jungle region, stating that they would be released only when the Colombian government agreed to remove all troops from the area. The Samper government acquiesced in late November 1996. In May 1997 journalist Jorge Enrique Botero interviewed FARC leader Alfonso Cano and concluded that the guerrilla group had no interest in demobilization or disarmament, unless the government agreed to a social and economic program "of a communist party in power."[31]

During the Pastrana presidency, although negotiations with the leaders of the FARC were begun, kidnapping by guerrilla groups increased, including "miraculous fishing" (*pescas milagrosas*, a method of stopping vehicles on rural highways and kidnapping the passengers). Other incidents included ELN kidnappings of passengers on an airplane flight in April 1999, and churchgoers in Cali the following month. Overall, during the four years of the Pastrana presidency, there were on average nine kidnappings a day.[32]

Paramilitary groups continued to flourish, even when their leaders, such as Fidel Castaño, were killed. His brother Carlos replaced him. According to Human Rights Watch, Castaño's group killed 300 noncombatants between July and December 1996.[33]

In 1997, there were indications that, for the first time, paramilitary groups were going to organize on a national level. The Autodefensas Unidas de Colombia (AUC, United Self-Defense Groups of Colombia) was founded on 18 April 1997, with one of its goals to achieve the same status as guerrilla groups. The AUC thus became the latest actor in the Colombian riddle.

Finally, the U.S. government refused to certify, in both 1996 and 1997, that the Colombian government was cooperating in anti-drug activities. This "decertification" affected legal Colombian exports, as well as the amount of resources the country received for its anti-drug activities.

The Samper government was both preoccupied and weaker. As the U.S. Department of State concluded in early 1998, the controversy over drug money "significantly diminished the president's moral authority and political ability to govern." As a result, "the control of the central government over the national territory [was] increasingly challenged by longstanding and widespread internal armed conflict and rampant violence—both criminal and political." The report suggested that guerrillas had a significant degree of influence in 57 percent of the nation's municipalities, while human rights violations by the government continued.[34]

The situation changed little under the Pastrana government. The government's major policy—the negotiation of guerrilla truces—proved unsuccessful. In the early months of the presidency, an agreement was reached with the FARC, under which the guerrilla group would control a "demilitarized zone" of 16,266 square miles (roughly the size of Switzerland) in the Amazon jungle in the southern part of the country in return for peace negotiations. Although, allegedly, the FARC used this territory for coca growing, troop training, and a safe refuge for sympathizers, no progress was made in negotiations. Finally, on 20 February 2002, President Pastrana formally ended the negotiations. National army troops began reoccupying the demilitarized zone immediately, and in the following weeks violence increased.

Peace talks with the ELN were also unsuccessful. The stumbling block was the ELN's goal to establish a demilitarized zone, similar to the FARC's. Local residents—no doubt assisted by Castaño and the AUC—resisted and prevented compromise.

In December 2000, the Bogotá newspaper *El Tiempo* reported that 3,289 civilians had been assassinated by guerrilla and paramilitary groups since 1 January 1999. Guerrilla groups accounted for 51 percent of the assassinations.[35] In March 2002 another Bogotá newspaper, *El Espectador*, reported that 338 Colombians had died in the guerrilla conflict in the first sixty-six days of the year.[36] Additional information from the Colombian government suggests few changes in the level of violence. The number of individuals kidnapped increased during the 1990s. Common criminals perpetrated the most kidnappings, 4,946; the FARC, 3,943; the ELN, 3,307; other groups, 2,219; the EPL, 1,307; and paramilitary groups, 193.[37]

Data from the Colombian Ministry of Defense indicate that there was no clear trend in the levels of violence during the first full year of the Pastrana government. While levels of hostage taking, terrorism, and looting were lower than in the previous two years, there was a dramatic increase in "attacks on people," both by guerrilla and paramilitary groups.[38] Amnesty International, in its report on the year 2000, indicated that in Colombia

—More than 4,000 people were victims of "political homicides";

—300 people disappeared;

—300,000 people were displaced by the violence;

—1,500 people were kidnapped by guerrillas and paramilitaries; and

—Torture continued as a "generalized practice."[39]

The Pastrana years showed no decline in the level of violence.

In the 2002 national elections, Colombians overwhelmingly chose Álvaro Uribe as president. Uribe's campaign seemingly made him out to be the exact opposite of Pastrana—there were to be no more negotiations with the guerrilla groups, and the armed forces were to be strengthened. In the first months of his presidency, Uribe took steps to keep his campaign promises. Most notably, he started to set up a body of some 200,000 "peasant-soldiers." These troops were to assist the regular army in its activities against the guerrillas. Some critics wondered, however, whether the peasant-soldiers would turn out to be just a new version of an old Colombian phenomenon: paramilitary irregulars.

The Failure of the Colombian State

Colombian scholars, in writings and interviews, mention variations of three arguments when discussing the failure of the state and the violence in their homeland. First, the government has failed at state building because Colombia has historically been a weak state. The second reason for failure is that drugs have brought vast amounts of money to the country. The third problem is modernization. I name these three arguments the "Sins of the Fathers," "Modernization," and "Money Talks." The three are not mutually exclusive and can be interwoven.

The Sins of the Fathers

The first argument is somewhat tautological: no recent administration has been able to impose control over the national territory because such authority never existed previously. As noted above, Colombia has historically avoided constructing a large police force that would allow the national government to enforce its decisions throughout the country. Former President López believed that the paramilitary groups were the logical extension of the pattern set by the large landowners of the previous century. It should also be remembered that the Colombian government, during the presidencies of Guillermo León Valencia and Carlos Lleras Restrepo, called for all private citizens to assist the military in its struggle against the guerrillas.

Into that institutional vacuum, new actors entered to perform the functions that the state might have performed but never did. Because of the power of these non-state actors (guerrillas, drug dealers, and paramilitary squads), González asked whether Colombia was "not witnessing today the onset of a greater collapse of the institutions of the state . . . ?"[40]

Colombia lacked a strong state before the new problems arose in the 1960s–1980s. The state might have been slightly stronger at the end of the Gaviria government, especially because of a reform of the National Police. However, in 2002 the state was still not strong enough to meet its challenges.

Added to this weakness is the country's long history of violence. It is difficult to map a direct link between the earlier partisan and the current violence, but some studies suggest a connection. Pizarro, for example, shows how the FARC developed in areas where there was a "persistence of the forms of the earlier political violence, especially the 'political banditry,' which survived until at least 1965."[41] Salazar's research shows that young people in Medellín who participated in drug and common criminal violence in the 1980s came from families who were forced to remain in Medellín by the partisan violence of the 1950s and 1960s.[42]

One should be very careful with automatic explanations such as "the culture of violence" or "violence causes violence." But Colombians were taught to be violent before they learned to vote.[43]

Modernization

Chronologically, the first complication in the transition from the traditional dysfunctional system to the current one, which functions even less well, was the process of modernization. In the past fifty years, Colombia has changed from an illiterate rural country to a more literate urban one. Sánchez points out that at the end of World War II, "Almost three fourths of the population was comprised of peasants; more than half was illiterate; and 3 percent of the land-owners monopolized half the land."[44]

This modernization caused several kinds of difficulties. The first is simply having people in closer contact with each other than before. As a Colombian historian stated, "Urbanization brought many problems of conflict from the countryside to the cities. People are closer together in the cities, have more conflicts, and use violence in those conflicts."[45]

A second complication of modernization is the lessening of the influence of the Roman Catholic Church. The Church was part of the problem from the nineteenth century until the end of La Violencia; Colombia suffered under bad government when the power of the Church was at its apogee. Nevertheless, the Church tried to teach a moral code, such as "Thou shalt not kill." With urban-ization, however, the power of the Roman Catholic Church decreased in Colombia.

Finally, modernization means mass media, and that means more informa-tion about the violence that is taking place. Although the Colombian govern-ment has tried to restrict publicity about violence, at times it is impossible to avoid knowing about the most recent guerrilla attack, the latest car bomb, the massacres of the paramilitary groups, the hijacking of buses, and the murder of soccer players.

Money Talks

The third complication in attempting to establish a strong government has to do with the vast amount of money that flowed into Colombia with the drug trade. Thoumi states: "Several authors have tackled the difficult task of esti-mating the size of the Colombian illegal PSAD industry's income. . . . Al-though subject to great uncertainty, it is estimated that Colombian industry profits have fluctuated between U.S.$2 and $5 billion per year."[46]

There is no doubt that a considerable amount of the wealth earned by *narcotraficantes* was returned to Colombia through arms shipments. The de-mand for arms rose, as organized crime (drugs, guerrillas, and death squads) sought additional weapons and private citizens needed defensive equipment to protect themselves. While there are no figures for the total number of small arms in Colombia, over 30,000 were sold legally each year between 1991 and 1993.[47]

The effect of drug wealth has been seen throughout Colombia. Paramilitary groups, formerly composed of private farmers and ranchers who produced legal products, became dominated by the narcotraficantes. One of the major reasons that the Colombian governments failed in their negotiations is that the guerrilla groups have such wealth from coca and poppies that there is little that the government can offer to them. Reports indicate that guerrilla groups, paramilitary squads, and drug dealers are better armed than the government.[48]

While the law-breaking groups seem to have unlimited funds, that is surely not the case of the Colombian government. Over the past decade, higher percentages of the government's budget have been devoted to the armed forces and the police. An analysis of the government's budget between 1980 and 1990 shows that expenditures on social matters (education, health, housing, and social security) fell from 41 to 34 percent of the budget, although that meant a relatively constant 7.5 percent of the gross domestic product.[49]

Conclusion: The Failing State in Colombia

In general, there was more violence during the period of the Gaviria government than the Barco one, and more in the Barco years than in the Betancur period. Further, it appears that violence increased during the Samper and Pastrana years. What is one to infer? One explanation is that the violent momentum, begun even before the Betancur administration, continued into the Barco and Gaviria years and accelerated during the Samper and Pastrana years. Another explanation is that the reforms under Gaviria (especially the establishment of the Office of the General Prosecutor, the end of narcoterrorism, and the partial demobilization of the death squads) simply have not yet had time to take effect.

A third explanation of this escalating violence is that a more profound state breakdown occurred in Colombia during the Gaviria years and thereafter. In his study of the period of La Violencia, Oquist argued:

> Intense partisan rivalry led to an extreme decrease in state power, which was manifested by: (1) the breakdown of the nation's political institutions; (2) the loss of legitimacy of the state for significant parts of the population; (3) contradictions within the armed apparatus of the state; and (4) the physical absence of the state in certain areas of the country.[50]

A similar process has occurred in Colombia since the 1980s. It would be preferable to conceive La Violencia of the 1940s–1960s and the violence of the

1980s–2000s as low points in the effectiveness of the Colombian national government, which at no point in its history has applied its laws successfully throughout the entire country.

No one, to my knowledge, has attempted a precise measurement of state effectiveness in Colombia. Yet it seems intuitive that the preoccupation of the government with the violence coming from guerrilla groups, drug dealers, and death squads has left it neither the time nor the financial resources to control "common" crime.[51]

Hence the description of the current "partial collapse" of the Colombian state seems well captured by Orjuela and Barrera:

> ... [Colombia's] geographic marginality, the scarce social and transportation infrastructure, the difficulties of police control, administrative corruption, party incapacity—all are conditions which are favorable to the cultivation and processing of the coca leaf. The space left by the state is filled by the drug dealers, the armed opposition groups, the civil movements and the vigilante groups, whether they are called "self-defense" or "paramilitary" ones. . . . We find ourselves, then, facing a fragmented state that has lost the monopoly on the legitimate use of force; a state that has lost its capacity to represent and integrate new social forces, and, therefore, the possibility to channel social tensions and regulate conflicts.[52]

Violence in Colombia has increased, and the control of the central government in Bogotá decreased during the Samper and Pastrana years, making even worse the "partial collapse of the state."

The general feeling of Colombians was captured by the leading newsmagazine, *Semana*, which described the terrifying nature of life in their country:

> For foreigners who arrive in this country for the first time, the first thing that surprises them is the blatant way in which Colombians run red lights after 10 at night, or the mania that they have of always looking over their shoulders to make sure no one is following them. For Colombians, used to living in insecurity for many years, these things seem normal.
>
> What does surprise everyone is knowing that in many towns people sleep with their shoes on in case the guerrillas or paramilitaries arrive and they have to run away—when they don't sleep in the woods to avoid that. Or that it has become more common for people, when they go to weddings or on one of those short trips that they still make outside the city, to bring a kidnapping kit—comfortable shoes, a warm coat, a toothbrush,

and a good book—just in case. Or that psychiatrists see more people everyday who arrive with an attack of nerves. "It is a fear without hope of changing it. As if we were living eternally in purgatory, wishing for a miracle in order to arrive to heaven but always suspended there," says psychiatrist Luis Carlos Restrepo. . . .[53]

The same edition of *Semana* also reported that guerrillas had blown up 644 power poles in the previous two years. Should peace come to Colombia, repairing the country's infrastructure will no doubt be easier than repairing the psyches of its people.

Where should Colombia be placed in comparison to other countries at risk? Should Colombia be termed a failed state? Central government has ceded de facto authority and physical control over large portions of the country to guerrilla and paramilitary groups. Insecurity is omnipresent, with the country leading the world in both murders and kidnappings. Corruption is endemic. Narcotics trafficking is corrosive and all consuming. But the central government controls and provides other political goods in the capital and in other major cities, per capita GDP levels are comparatively high, infant mortality levels remain low, education and literacy rates are strong, and the international legitimacy of Colombia is positive.

Colombia is failing. With the exception of ethnic, religious, linguistic, or cultural divisions, the country arguably exhibits all of the traits of the generic weaknesses typified by violence, disorder, and loss of territory. However, it has not "failed," since the Colombian state still delivers political goods to a majority of its people.

Notes

1. This chapter is based on more than thirty years of research on and residence in Colombia. Information about the Barco and Gaviria presidencies can be found in Harvey F. Kline, *State Building and Conflict Resolution in Colombia, 1986–1994* (Tuscaloosa, 1999). The information about the Samper and Pastrana presidencies comes from a forthcoming book on the subject.

2. John Leddy Phelan, "Authority and Flexibility in the Spanish Bureaucracy," *Administrative Science Quarterly* (1960), 51.

3. Ibid., 22.

4. David Bushnell, *The Making of Modern Colombia: A Nation Inspite of Itself* (Berkeley, 1993), 12.

5. The historical circumstances leading to these "decisions" are described in Harvey F. Kline, *Colombia: Democracy under Assault* (Boulder, 1995), 30–34.

6. Alfonso López Michelsen, "Del orígen de la violencia en Colombia," *El Tiempo* (Bogotá) (14 July 1991).

7. Fabio Zambrano Pantoja, "Contradicciones del sistema político colombiano," *Análisis Conflicto Social y Violencia en Colombia* (1988), 23, emphasis in the original.

8. Eduardo Santa, *Sociología Política de Colombia* (Bogotá, 1964), 44–48.

9. Confidential interview, Colombian sociologist, Bogotá, 24 May 1994.

10. Harvey F. Kline, "The National Front: Historical Perspective and Overview," in R. Albert Berry, Ronald G. Hellman, and Mauricio Solaún (eds.), *Politics of Compromise: Coalition Government in Colombia* (New Brunswick, 1980), 68–69.

11. The term was first used by Arend Lijphart, "Consociational Democracy," *World Politics,* XXI (1969), 207–225, and was skillfully applied to the Colombian case by Jonathan Hartlyn, *The Politics of Coalition Rule in Colombia* (Cambridge, 1988).

12. Francisco Leal Buitrago, "Defensa y Seguridad Nacional en Colombia, 1958–1993," in Leal Buitrago and Juan Gabriel Tokatian, *Orden Mundial y Seguridad: Nuevos Desafíos para Colombia y América Latina* (Bogotá, 1994), 132.

13. Barbara Geddes, *Politician's Dilemma: Building State Capacity in Latin America* (Berkeley, 1994), 18.

14. Eduardo Pizarro, "Revolutionary Guerrilla Groups in Colombia," in Charles Berquist, Ricardo Peñaranda, and Gonzalo Sánchez (eds.), *Violence in Colombia: The Contemporary Crisis in Historical Perspective* (Wilmington, 1992), 177.

15. Ibid., 179.

16. *Semana* (17 May 1988), 26.

17. Ibid.

18. Bruce Bagley, "Colombia and the War on Drugs," *Foreign Affairs*, LXVII (1988), 73–74.

19. Franciso Thoumi, *Political Economy and Illegal Drugs in Colombia* (Boulder, 1995), 172–176.

20. Bagley, "Colombia and the War on Drugs," 75–76.

21. Luis Javier Orjuela and Cristina Barrera, "Narcotráfico y Política en la Decada de los Ochenta: Entre la Represión y el Diálogo," in Carlos G. Arrieta, Luis J. Orjuela, Eduardo Sarmiento, and Juan G. Tokatlian, *Narcotráfico en Colombia: Dimensiones Políticas, Económicas, Jurídicas e Internacionales* (Bogotá, 1989), 209.

22. Ibid.

23. Ibid., 215.

24. *Latin America Weekly Report* (8 January 1982).

25. In trying to evaluate the level of violence (and by implication, government control of the country) one problem is the reliability of data. Time-series data allow us to reach certain conclusions in our comparisons of the Barco and Gaviria administrations. However, we should always be cautious and open to conflicting interpretations. For the purposes of this chapter, I have used data from the Inter-American Commission on Human Rights and the Roman Catholic Church's Intercongregational Commission of Justice and Peace. The important point is not whether their data are more reliable; rather, it is a question of trends.

26. Armando Montenegro Trujillo, "Justicia y Desarrollo," Bogotá, Departamento Nacional de Planeación (20 April 1994).

27. "Justicia y violencia," *Coyuntura Social*, VI (1992), 49.

28. Alvaro Camacho, "Public and Private Dimensions of Urban Violence in Colombia," in Berquist, Peñaranda, and Sánchez, *Violence in Colombia*, 241–242.

29. Interview, former Samper government official, November 1999.

30. *El Tiempo* (19 May 1997).

31. *Semana* (26 May 1997), 16.

32. *El Espectador* (23 August 2002).

33. Joshua Hammer, "Colombia: 'Head Cutters' at War," *Newsweek* (2 June 1997), 42.

34. U.S. Department of State, *Colombia Country Report on Human Rights Practice for 1997,* Bureau of Democracy, Human Rights, and Labor (30 January 1998).

35. *El Tiempo* (10 December 2000).

36. *El Espectador* (8 March 2002).

37. Colombian Ministry of Defense, at http://www.mindefensa.gov.co/ ini_frames.asp?cod_modulo=5.

38. Ibid.

39. *El Tiempo* (31 May 2001).

40. Fernán E. González González, "¿Hacia un 'nuevo colapso parcial del Estado'? Precariedad del Estado y Violencia en Colombia," *Análisis Conflicto Social y Violencia en Colombia* (1988), 8, 11–12.

41. Eduardo Pizarro, "Revolutionary Guerrilla Groups in Colombia," in Berquist, Peñaranda, and Sánchez, *Violence in Colombia,* 174.

42. Alfonso Salazar J., *No Nacimos Pa'Semilla* (Bogotá, 1990), passim.

43. As pointed out by one sociologist, two new structures for mobility developed in Colombia: one from the violent groups—guerrillas, paramilitary squads, and drug dealers—and the other from groups trying to defend other citizens from those lawbreakers. Alvaro Camacho's research on Cali found that there were 4,500 private policemen registered with local authorities, while the local police force had 2,800 men. Alvaro Camacho, "Public and Private Dimensions of Urban Violence in Colombia," in Berquist, Peñaranda, and Sánchez, *Violence in Colombia*, 241–242. This begs two questions: How many "private policemen" were there in Cali who had not registered with the local authorities? How many people in Colombia are employed by private security agencies?

44. Gonzalo Sánchez, "The Violence: An Interpretive Synthesis," in Berquist, Peñaranda, and Sánchez, *Violence in Colombia,* 77.

45. Confidential Interview, Colombian historian, Bogotá, 25 May 1994.

46. Thoumi, *Political Economy,* 199.

47. Andres Jose Soto Velasco, "El Control de las Armas Ligeras," in Buitrago and Tokatian, *Orden Mundial y Seguridad*, 124, 126.

48. Confidential Interview, Colombian sociologist, Bogotá, 19 July 1991.

49. "Gasto Social," *Coyuntura Social*, VI (1992), 13.

50. Paul Oquist, *Violence, Conflict, and Politics in Colombia* (New York, 1980), 177.

51. The new head of the National Police recognized this reality in 2000 and promised to give more resources for the protection of citizens from the growing crime problem.

52. Orjuela and Barrera, "Narcotráfico y Política en la Decada de los Ochenta," 212–213.

53. "Muertos de miedo," *Semana* (15 January 2001).

CHAPTER SEVEN

Indonesia:
The Erosion of State Capacity

MICHAEL MALLEY

Introduction

The Indonesian state has not failed, but since 1997 indications have grown that its failings are more serious than previously estimated. Indonesian politicians and pundits, as well as foreign observers, frequently warn that the country is likely to disintegrate. Accepting the doomsayers' main contentions—namely, that the central government has been weakened and that a range of mostly regional challenges have strengthened—I contend that the country's conditions are less dire than popularly believed. When placed in the comparative, analytical framework Rotberg outlines in the introduction, Indonesia appears vulnerable and weak, but hardly failing, let alone failed or collapsed.

The major threats to the Indonesian state arise from the unresolved political and economic impact of the 1997–1998 economic crisis. That crisis created conditions that favored the breakdown of a three-decade-old authoritarian regime, but not the quick construction of a democratic one.[1]

In addition to Robert Rotberg and the other participants in the Failed States workshop who provided helpful comments on earlier drafts of this chapter, I would like to thank Donald Emmerson for his written comments and Gerry van Klinken for an illuminating discussion regarding the sources of communal conflict in Maluku and Kalimantan as well as the sources of state failure more broadly. All errors of fact and interpretation, of course, remain mine alone.

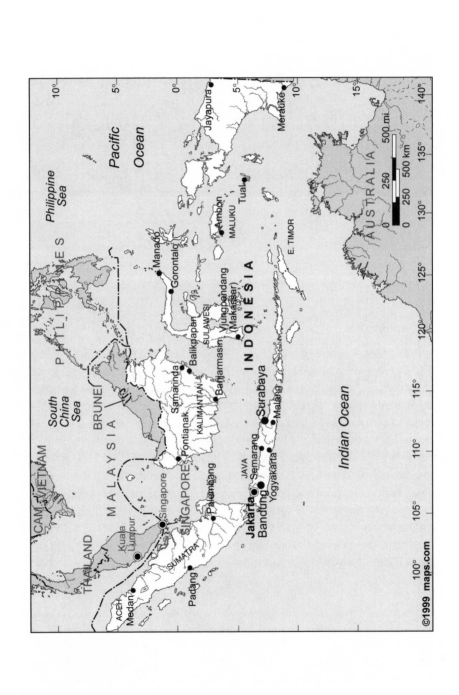

Elections in 1999 produced a deeply divided legislature whose leaders spent most of their time fighting for political survival, often by collaborating with elements of the old regime rather than rooting them out. In 2001, legislators removed the country's first democratically elected president and replaced him with his vice president. These power struggles left Indonesia's leaders little time to make policies that would resolve the challenges that they had inherited from the previous regime. Most pressing are the massive public debt, a result mainly of a state-led bailout of financial institutions made insolvent by the economic crisis; demands for increased autonomy or even independence from areas that were politically subordinated, economically exploited, or militarily brutalized in previous decades; and rising social disorder, particularly inter-communal violence that has displaced more than 1 million people from their homes.[2]

At least three other factors moderate the impact of these challenges. One is that the state's territorial claims are unchallenged, outside the rebel-held regions in two provinces. Instead, elites in most regions continue to seek autonomy within the state of Indonesia, and national political and military leaders have responded to those demands with negotiation rather than coercion. Consequently, the probability of a general civil war or widespread violence remains low. A second factor is the relatively good socio-economic conditions in which the majority of Indonesians live, despite the continuing impact of the 1997–1998 economic crisis. Although that event drove a large proportion of Indonesians below the poverty line, economic growth resumed in late 1999, inflation has remained low, and few of the socio-economic conditions that signal state failure elsewhere, such as rising infant mortality, are found in Indonesia. Finally, international support for Indonesia's territorial integrity as well as political and economic reform remains high. In contrast to the 1950s, when the United States aided independence-minded rebels, today's rebels cannot count on the support of any foreign government.[3] Instead, foreign governments and international lenders place a high priority on Indonesia's political unity and economic recovery. Even as foreign countries pushed for East Timor's independence, they stressed their opposition to further secessionist movements, and although the International Monetary Fund recently withheld promised loans for nearly a year, its representatives continued to engage Indonesian officials in a dialogue about necessary reforms.

Indonesia is not bound to fail. But whether the Indonesian state grows stonger or weaker depends largely on the consolidation of a stable national government that is able to devote less attention to ensuring its own survival and more attention to resolving economic and regional challenges and reforming the institutions through which it deals with its citizens. If such a government does not emerge, the debt burden will continue to grow, regional grievances will go unresolved, and the state's capacity to provide basic public goods will affect people far beyond the regions that are engaged in today's separatist and communal conflicts.

From Economic Crisis to Political Transition

In May 1999, Indonesia held its most free and fair legislative elections since 1955. Five months later, it held the first contested presidential election since its founders declared independence in 1945. Yet, international attention was drawn not to the country's remarkable democratic transition, but to the possibility of its disintegration. Midway between the legislative and presidential elections, the United Nations supervised a referendum in which nearly 80 percent of East Timorese voted for independence. And while foreign eyes were focused on that tiny territory's fate, separatist movements in two much larger provinces revived and strengthened. Rapidly, bloody ethnic and religious conflicts in several other provinces resulted in thousands of deaths and created hundreds of thousands of refugees. In countless regions local officials and activists demanded greater political and fiscal autonomy from Jakarta. These pressures, like those for democratization, exploited the dramatic decline in the national government's power and authority that followed the onset of economic crisis in 1997.

The Political Impact of the Economic Crisis

The economic crisis that occurred in many countries in East and Southeast Asia during 1997–1998 had a devastating impact on Indonesia and set the stage for its ongoing political transition. In 1998, gross domestic product (GDP) contracted by about 14 percent, while inflation rose to 80 percent. During the previous decade, growth had averaged about 7 percent annually, and government policy had kept inflation below 10 percent. In addition, the country's currency suffered a massive devaluation. From a pre-crisis level of 2,400 per U.S. dollar, the rupiah swung wildly between 8,000 and 17,000 before settling into a wide band between 7,000 and 9,000 during late 1998 and 1999. This result, too, must be measured against prior conditions. For more than a decade before the crisis, Indonesia's financial authorities had managed the currency's value to achieve a consistent annual depreciation of about 3 to 4 percent.[4]

The crisis tested more than the government's economic management skills. Since President Soeharto took power in 1966, he had promised to bring development, not democracy. In fact, he and his fellow army officers spoke proudly of their success in 1965–1967 in "annihilating" what had been the world's third largest communist movement; more than half a million suspected leftists were killed, and many more interned for a decade or more.[5] Those killings laid the foundation for an explicit policy of depoliticization as a prerequisite for economic development. His doctrine of the "floating mass" held that the bulk of the population should be allowed to "float" above politics except for perfunctory participation in quinquennial general elections. He and his lieutenants created a regime party (Golkar), based on the bureaucracy and supported by the army, and compelled all other parties to merge into two (the larger, Islamic-oriented Development Unity Party, and the smaller Indonesian Democracy Party, a fusion of Christian and nationalist parties). For three decades, these policies prevented opposition groups from organizing significantly against his rule. In early 1997, just months before the onset of economic crisis, Soeharto secured his party's largest margin of victory ever (74 percent), and, in March 1998, he stage-managed his uncontested indirect election to a seventh consecutive five-year term as president.

Because the regime claimed legitimacy on the basis of its ability to deliver economic development rather than the promotion of popular participation, the 1997 economic crisis posed a direct challenge not just to its skill in making economic policy, but to its right to rule.[6] In previous crises, Soeharto had demonstrated his ability to take tough measures. In the mid-1970s, the state-owned oil company went spectacularly bankrupt, accumulating debts of more than $10 billion while world oil prices were at historic highs. Rather than protect close associates who had run the company and others who had benefited from its largesse, he appointed professional managers and limited the extent to which the company would be treated as a cash cow for political and patronage purposes. In short, he placed state interests in oil revenue ahead of private gains.[7]

In the mid-1980s, as oil prices and therefore government revenues plummeted, he again made difficult economic policy changes. Rather than continue to protect and subsidize the import-substituting heavy industries whose development his government had funded with oil revenues, he adopted a radical set of policies to promote labor-intensive, export-oriented industries. This required that the ports become more efficient. Rather than attempt to reform the corrupt customs service, which had provided lucrative sources of income for favored officials, he replaced it with a private Swiss company (SGS). And, recognizing that one of the chief reasons for promoting exports was to create a new, taxable industrial base, not simply to earn foreign exchange, he adopted sweeping tax reforms that enabled the government to increase its collection of value-added and income taxes as the economy grew during the late 1980s and 1990s.[8]

Soeharto's response to the 1997–1998 crisis remains difficult to explain. Between July and October 1997, he took actions reminiscent of previous crises. In August and September, technocrats announced policy adjustments, such as widening the band in which the currency was permitted to fluctuate, cutting public spending, and canceling high-profile projects. Since most of these projects were linked to Soeharto's children or cronies, he appeared yet again to be willing to put the country's economic health ahead of his associates' private economic interests. In October, his government approached the IMF for assistance and quickly announced additional reforms that would eliminate privileges that his children and cronies had enjoyed. Yet, in November, the tide began to turn. Soeharto reinstated many of the previously canceled projects, and one of his sons announced that he would sue the central bank governor and the finance minister. They had closed his bank along with several others that had become insolvent. As Soeharto's commitment to reform appeared to weaken, investors looked hopefully to the announcement of the new state budget in January 1998 for a signal that the government remained committed to reform. Instead, they were shown a budget in which core assumptions about economic growth, exchange rates, and revenue reflected the government's unwillingness to acknowledge the extent of the crisis and make appropriate responses. Within a month, the rupiah fell from about 5,000 per dollar to nearly 14,000 per dollar.[9]

Three reasons are commonly offered to explain Soeharto's inability to take strong measures in the late 1990s. One is that he found it politically difficult to accept IMF conditionality, particularly after he was photographed signing a memorandum of understanding as IMF Managing Director Michel Camdessus stood imperiously, arms folded, looking down on him. In previous crises, Indonesia had dealt with the large World Bank mission in Jakarta, and aid had not been explicitly or publicly conditioned on specific reforms.[10] Mutual agreements were reached and reforms implemented over time, which leads to the second reason. Previous crises had not required sudden changes. Soeharto himself may not have understood that, however bitter the IMF's medicine, it had to be swallowed quickly before bad debts snowballed and the costs of bailing out the financial sector overwhelmed the economy. Finally, there is the issue of Soeharto's children. In previous crises, they had been too young to have important interests. By 1997, however, their interests were enormous and it was clear that they had not made their money in the rapidly growing, highly competitive production of export manufactures, but in the decreasing number of highly protected economic sectors, such as transportation, telecommunications, and agricultural processing.

Regime Breakdown and Transition

Most Indonesians placed the blame squarely on Soeharto's desire to protect his family's economic interests.[11] For two months after Soeharto was reelected to his seventh five-year term as president in March 1998, public protests against his rule took place on university campuses across the country. By the end of April, security forces could no longer contain them, and hundreds of thousands of members of the public joined in. Some protests turned violent in early May, after Soeharto raised fuel prices, but he nonchalantly left the country for a meeting in Cairo. While he was there, security forces killed several student protesters and the capital suffered three days of rioting in which hundreds of people died. Only at this point did a cross-section of the regime's opponents among the political elite begin to organize, and to call on Soeharto to resign. Upon hearing of the riots, Soeharto told an Indonesian audience in Cairo that if the public no longer wanted him, then, borrowing a phrase from his native Javanese, he would "leave the kingship and assume the position of a sage."[12] A week later, after returning home, he did resign, and his vice president, Bacharuddin Jusuf Habibie, assumed the presidency.

Despite public animosity toward him, Soeharto made little attempt to negotiate his exit from office or shape the terms of the political transition. For several days, he tried unsuccessfully to mollify his opponents by offering to hold fresh elections or revamp his cabinet, but when protesters and political elites alike rejected these proposals, he simply resigned. Although public protests against Soeharto had been large and widespread, the protesters had not developed an organizational core with which the government could negotiate, or even a program for change over which others could bargain. This situation left Habibie, who had been vice president for only two months, and a legislature whose members Soeharto had screened prior to their election in 1997, substantially in control of the country's political transition.

The major public demands had been for "total reform" and an end to "corruption, collusion, and nepotism." Habibie responded by declaring an eighteen-month timetable for political reform that included the writing of new laws on political parties and elections, followed by fresh legislative elections in mid-1999, and, finally, a presidential election before the end of 1999. In November, the country's highest constitutional body, the People's Consultative Assembly (MPR), convened in special session to set a date for new elections, as Habibie wanted. Despite being stacked with Soeharto appointees, the Assembly also adopted a motion that directed the government to "combat corruption, collusion, and nepotism," and specifically named Soeharto as one of its intended targets. In addition, the Assembly reduced the military's share of appointive seats in the House of Representatives to 38 from 75 out of 500. Two months later, the House adopted laws that permitted political parties to be formed freely and created an inclusive electoral commission to oversee the planned election. Student groups continued to demand radical changes, including Habibie's resignation and the appointment of a "presidium" of neutral leaders, but more senior social and political figures worked feverishly to create political parties to compete in the promised general election.

Although widely heralded as free and fair, the legislative elections held in May 1999 failed to produce a majority party or even an obvious majority coalition. Out of the forty-eight parties that contested the election, five won nearly 91 percent of the votes. A secular nationalist party (PDI-P) won 34 percent, the old regime's party (Golkar) took 22 percent, a rural Muslim party (PKB) won 13 percent, the Islamic party permitted under the old regime (PPP) won 11 percent, and a new, predominantly urban, Islamic party (PAN) earned 7 percent. These shares were diluted further by the armed forces' appointive seats in the House of Representatives.[13]

The political impact of this ambiguous election outcome became increasingly evident as the October presidential election approached. The president and vice president are chosen by the People's Consultative Assembly, which includes the 500 House members as well as 200 appointees, 135 of whom are chosen by provincial legislatures (five from each province) and sixty-five of whom represent a range of social groups and are chosen by the electoral commission. Faced with the need, for the first time ever, to devise a means of nominating and electing a president, legislators resorted to horse trading. The leader of the smallest Islamic party acquired the chairmanship of the Assembly, while the head of the old regime's party took control of the House. Then, rather than put the popular leader of the first-place party into the presidency, the parties relegated her to the vice presidency and awarded the top job to the head of the rural Islamic party. In exchange, the new president, Abdurrahman Wahid, selected a cabinet in which all major parties and the armed forces were represented.

The most obvious result of all these compromises was the weakness of the democratically elected central government. After a brief honeymoon, nearly the entire legislature turned against Wahid.[14] Members of the House of Representatives accused him of failing to respond effectively to the persistent economic crisis and sources of regional instability, of engaging in corruption, and generally of providing weak leadership. They established separate committees to investigate his alleged involvement in two financial scandals and his firing of two ministers, one from the vice president's party and another from the old regime's party. These pressures forced him to divert scarce political capital from the pursuit of policy objectives to the defense of his own power.

Members of the Assembly threatened to oust Wahid at their annual session in 2000, but settled for a deal in which he revamped his cabinet and turned over substantial responsibility for running the government to his vice president,

Megawati Sukarnoputri, and one of her key allies, a retired army general. However, these moves failed to satisfy Wahid's rivals, and during 2001 his relations with legislators and Megawati worsened. The House censured him twice, and the Assembly removed him from power at a special session in July. This allowed Megawati, also the leader of the country's largest party (PDI-P), to ascend to the presidency in 2001. But as the country's new vice president, the Assembly then elected Hamzah Haz, head of the PPP, who had led a coalition of Islamic-oriented parties that opposed her bid for the presidency in 1999 on the grounds that women were unfit to lead a predominantly Muslim country.

Megawati's election brought stability to national politics, but little progress toward resolving the country's major problems. Her government is widely regarded as ineffective, but she is expected to remain in office until elections are held in 2004 and is favored to win reelection to the presidency then.[15] The apparent paradox of persistent problems and increased political stability reflects two prominent characteristics of the political system that have emerged since Soeharto's resignation in 1998. One is the government's unique quasi-parliamentary structure, which requires the president to maintain broad support in the legislature.[16] This is an easier task for Megawati, whose Indonesian Democracy Party-Struggle holds the greatest number of seats, than it was for Wahid, whose National Awakening Party is fourth in number of seats. The other is the need to form coalitions among parties, since the country's electoral system almost guarantees that no one party will secure a majority. With just 31 percent of the seats in the House and 27 percent in the Assembly, Megawati's party cannot govern alone. However, deep personal differences among party leaders, and ideological ones among the parties, inhibit the formation of stable coalitions. As a result, Megawati finds it difficult to translate her more stable political position into more effective policies, but her opponents find it even more difficult to assemble a coalition capable of dislodging her.

From Democratization to Disintegration?

The peaceful transition, within eighteen months, from an authoritarian government that had been in place for more than three decades to a democratically elected one would normally be a cause for some celebration. Yet, at each stage in the transition, foreign observers focused more closely on the prospect that the country might fall apart—that it might follow the path that Yugoslavia had blazed in the mid-1990s.[17] Foreigners were not alone in expressing these concerns; Indonesian analysts and politicians have done so frequently. Former President Wahid himself warned the People's Consultative Assembly in August 2000 that a "wave of disintegration is threatening the existence of the unitary state and national unity." After succeeding him, Megawati declared that "national unity will be the first priority of my Cabinet."[18]

Observers in 2002 point to at least four different sets of issues as indications that Indonesia faces a serious prospect of disintegration. One is the country's brewing fiscal and economic crisis, which threatens the government's capacity to deliver public goods, ranging from health and education to public order. The three other sets of issues concern challenges that a weak central government finds difficult to manage. Most prominent are the separatist movements in staunchly Muslim Aceh at the far western end of the country and predominantly Protestant Papua (formerly Irian Jaya) at the far eastern end, as well as the already successful case of heavily Roman Catholic East Timor, which achieved independence in 1999. In addition, there are communal conflicts, principally the bloody struggle that began in early 1999 between Christians and Muslims in the northern Maluku archipelago and has since claimed more than 6,000 lives and displaced more than 500,000 people. Other ethnic and religious conflicts have resulted in hundreds of deaths and displaced tens of thousands. Finally, there is a broad range of regional demands for enhanced political and fiscal autonomy from Jakarta.

Potential Fiscal and Economic Crisis

The economic crisis of 1997–1998, and Soeharto's response to it, created serious economic management challenges for his successors, but the rapid rotation of presidents—from Soeharto to Habibie to Wahid to Megawati in just over three years—has prevented the government from addressing them in a coherent way. Moreover, in the absence of sustained coordinated action, the magnitude and complexity of Indonesia's economic policy challenges have grown. By the time Megawati took office in July 2001, public debt amounted to about $150 billion, approximately equal to the country's annual economic output, and debt service payments accounted for more than 40 percent of routine government spending.[19] About half of the debt is owed to foreign creditors. Effective management under Megawati, which depends on the legislature's cooperation, could bring the debt under control and create conditions more conducive to economic growth. Failure to do this, however, carries a serious prospect of default and slow or negative growth.

The government's major problems stem from efforts to bail out the country's banks, which the economic crisis drove into bankruptcy. By the end of 1998, about 70 percent of all bank loans were classified as "non-performing," and the country's major, and most minor, commercial banks were insolvent. To prevent a collapse of the financial sector, the government issued a comprehensive deposit guarantee, which required it to devise a means of rebuilding the banking sector. In 1998, with input from the IMF, the government devised a two-part strategy. One element was recapitalization of the banks, which the government accomplished over the next two years by injecting equity into banks in the form of various types of bonds. The other was the establishment of the Indonesian Bank Restructuring Agency (IBRA) under the ministry of finance, to which banks could transfer their non-performing loans. The agency received very broad authority. It could close, consolidate, or sell banks; restructure their debts; and even manage or sell the assets of the banks' creditors. Since then, it has done each of these acts.[20]

The government's response to the financial crisis affects, and complicates, all areas of economic policy. By rescuing the financial sector, the government acquired enormous debt (at least $60 billion at recent exchange rates), control over more than 70 percent of all bank assets, and ownership of many of the country's largest corporations.[21] Debt repayment increases pressure to cut spending and raise income. Since fuel subsidies accounted for 4 percent of GDP in 2001, and primarily benefited middle- and upper-class people able to afford fuel purchases, they have become the main target of efforts to reduce spending. (Although Indonesia is an oil exporter, it imports lower grade petroleum from the Middle East to refine into gasoline, diesel, and kerosene for the local market.) Revenue can be increased in several ways, by raising taxes, broadening the tax base, increasing the collection rate, or selling assets acquired by IBRA. Higher revenues can also be collected if the economy were to grow, which would swell the tax base as well as raise the value of the government's shares in state-owned and IBRA-controlled companies.

Under Wahid, little progress was made on any of these fronts, though the economy did grow steadily during his first year in office. Fuel subsidies were cut for domestic industry and foreign shipping, but not for consumers, which led to a large black market in retail-priced fuel. No significant progress was made on tax reform, and IBRA was unable to sell a large amount of assets under its control. However, the blame cannot be put entirely on Wahid. The House of Representatives contributed to these failures by intervening repeatedly in IBRA asset sales and passing a labor law that required businesses to pay laid-off workers 75 percent of their wages for six months.

Despite these problems, Indonesia's economy appeared, on the surface at least, to be doing well until early 2001. After contracting nearly 14 percent in 1998, its economy grew slightly in 1999, and the rate of growth accelerated to 4.8 percent in 2000 as a result of domestic and foreign demand. Non-oil exports grew by 23 percent in 2000 and returned to their pre-crisis levels (measured in U.S. dollars). The ratios of Indonesia's rate of export growth to those of Thailand and Malaysia have stayed nearly the same over the crisis period 1997–2000.[22] For the most part, these economic growth figures are reflected in the welfare of Indonesian citizens. Between mid-1997 and 1998, the poverty rate doubled as the economy contracted sharply, but since growth resumed in mid-1999, poverty rates have returned to their pre-crisis levels. A recent study has shown that neither children's health nor school attendance has deteriorated since 1997.[23]

Below the surface, the picture is grimmer. Indonesia's economy remains smaller than prior to 1997, and consequently its people live a more precarious existence than they did previously. In 2000, a draft World Bank study estimated that "around *half* of all Indonesians now face a greater than 50-50 chance of becoming poor."[24] In order for per capita income to regain its pre-crisis level, the economy would need to grow at 4 percent annually until 2005.[25] This goal seemed within reach until the power struggle between Wahid and the legislature halted progress on economic reform. By early 2001, this struggle had led to a slowdown in investment, industrial output, and imports; a rise in interest and inflation rates; and a dramatic weakening of the rupiah.[26]

Increased political stability under Megawati has not been enough to stimulate a general improvement in economic conditions. Economic growth has been too slow to raise per capita income significantly. In 2001, economic output increased by 3.3 percent, and it was growing at a similar rate in 2002. Worryingly, increases in private and government consumption were the main engines of growth, while exports and investment declined. In the first half of 2002, the amount of domestic investment that the government approved fell by 72 percent compared to the same period in 2001, while foreign investment approvals fell by 42 percent.[27] Net foreign investment is actually declining: according to estimates by Standard & Poors MMS International, Indonesia received $38 billion in foreign direct investment during 1994–1997, but $50 billion has been withdrawn from the country since.[28]

The lack of investment indicates that even current low growth rates may not be sustainable and reflects investors' underlying skepticism about the government's commitment to undertake economic reform and establish the rule of law. Megawati's failure to tackle corruption has riled voters and deterred business investment. Public opinion surveys repeatedly have found widespread dissatisfaction with the government's failure to curb corruption. A survey conducted by the country's leading newspaper in mid-2002 found that 85 percent of voters were "very disappointed" with President Megawati's efforts to stamp out "corruption, collusion, and nepotism," and only one-fifth were satisfied with the government's law enforcement efforts in general, down from one-half during her government's first three months in office.[29]

Corruption appears to be getting worse, with strongly negative implications for the country's economic outlook.[30] On Transparency International's annual corruption index, Indonesia fell from 85th out of 91 countries in 2000 to 96 out of 102 countries in 2002. The governor of Indonesia's central bank remains in office despite his conviction for helping Golkar, ahead of the 1999 election, siphon $80 million out of a bank that the government had taken over during the 1998 financial crisis. The customs service, whose corruption led Soeharto in 1985 to outsource much of its work to a Swiss firm, has recovered its legal and illicit roles. Economists at the University of Indonesia found that undervaluation of imports had cost the state treasury more than $1.2 billion in lost duties during 2000, and the trade and industry minister has complained that facing "the practice of smuggling is actually scarier than confronting the WTO . . . and free markets."[31]

Corruption in the courts is particularly serious. In one of the more remarkable cases in 2002, a Jakarta court declared a Canadian-owned insurance firm "bankrupt," even though it was in good financial health, as Indonesian insurance industry regulators recognized. Only after intense foreign pressure did the Supreme Court intervene and overturn the decision. Another court in Jakarta overturned a ruling by an international arbitration panel that had ordered the state-owned oil company to compensate its American partner for pulling out of a joint venture, even though the arbitration ruling had been upheld by courts in Singapore, Hong Kong, and the United States. In July, a special United Nations rapporteur, sent to assess the country's legal system, confessed, "I didn't realize that the situation could be as bad as what I've seen." During his visit, an Indonesian group released a report based on a year-long study of the courts system that detailed how judicial decisions are sold.[32]

The longer Indonesia's government delays in addressing these issues, the longer sustained economic recovery will be delayed and the more likely that slowly changing indicators of state weakness, such as rising infant mortality rates and declining life expectancies, will appear.

Separatist Issues

As president, Soeharto confronted persistent armed separatist movements in the provinces of Aceh, Irian Jaya, and East Timor, but none of these movements forged ties with anti-regime protesters in 1998 or played a significant role in shaping the terms of the political transition.[33] This profile changed, however, once Soeharto had been forced from office and the military was shown to be divided and unwilling to defend him. From mid-1998 onward, leaders of each separatist movement aggressively moved to resume their struggles, doubting that the change of power in Jakarta would resolve their grievances. Pro-independence rumblings in other provinces, particularly oil-rich Riau, contributed to a sense among Jakarta's political elite that secessionists might destroy the state before the elite could install a democratic regime.

EAST TIMOR.   When the Dutch East Indies achieved independence in 1949 as the new Republic of Indonesia, East Timor remained under Portuguese rule as it had been for three centuries. The people of East Timor did not participate in nationalist and anti-colonial movements against the Dutch and never came to imagine themselves as part of a broader Indonesian nation. Likewise, prior to Portugal's precipitous decision in 1974 to decolonize the territory, few Indonesians imagined East Timor as properly a part of their country. However, fearful that leftist movements in the territory would gain power and turn it into a "Southeast Asian Cuba," the staunchly anti-communist regime in Jakarta invaded that half of the island in 1975. By the 1980s, it had crushed the East Timorese resistance, but in the process at least 50,000 people were killed and a similar number died of war-induced famine and disease, equivalent to perhaps one-sixth of the territory's population.[34] In 1976, Indonesia organized a "representative council" of East Timorese who requested Indonesia to accept the territory as its newest province. Despite widespread East Timorese collaboration with Indonesian rule, the United Nations continued to consider the territory as separate from Indonesia. And in the minds of most East Timorese, it remained a nation separate from Indonesia.

During the 1990s, a new generation of East Timorese revitalized opposition to Indonesian rule. This generation resented Indonesia's rule for many reasons other than the brutality of its military during the 1970s. Most important were a lack of economic opportunities and continued repression. Indonesian bureaucrats filled many of the region's most important political posts, and migrants from Sulawesi and other islands dominated the marketplaces that the Indonesian government constructed. In 1995, violence between merchants from East Timor and Sulawesi led several thousand immigrants to flee back to Sulawesi and Java. After Soeharto resigned the presidency in 1998, East Timorese began to speak more openly of independence, and many more Indonesian migrants left the territory.

For Soeharto and the army, East Timor was a symbol of national pride, but for Habibie it was a liability. A generation of army officers had acquired battle experience and earned promotions during operations there, and civilian officials had spent heavily to bring economic development to a remote, impoverished place that the Portuguese had neglected. Recognizing widespread East Timorese support for independence would have required the military and politicians to admit that their successes had actually been failures. However, heavy investment in the territory's roads and schools had not won Indonesia much support, and the poor province required constant subsidies. Moreover, Indonesia's poor human rights record in East Timor was a continual irritant in Jakarta's relations with its major donors. With little personal stake in East Timor, Habibie and his advisers were not inclined to bear these burdens, and in May 1999 his government reached agreement with the United Nations to allow a UN-supervised referendum on the future status of East Timor.

Although the ballot was conducted peacefully at the end of August, horrific violence followed in September. After nearly 80 percent of East Timorese voted in favor of independence, pro-Indonesia militias, which the Indonesian army organized and equipped, killed several hundred East Timorese and drove about one-third of the tiny territory's 850,000 people out of their homes and across the border into Indonesian West Timor.[35] Despite the Indonesian military's clear opposition to East Timorese independence, Indonesia's People's Consultative Assembly voted later that year to rescind its claim of sovereignty over East Timor.

In October, amid the chaos, the United Nations established a transitional administration to govern the territory. It held legislative elections in August 2001, held a presidential election in April 2002, and granted independence to the new state in May 2002. During this time, Indonesia permitted many of the refugees on its part of Timor island to return to East Timor, and by the middle of 2002 only a few tens of thousands remained. President Megawati even attended East Timor's independence celebration, though her visit lasted only four hours and took place under the watchful eyes of a 2,000-member Indonesian military task force that included six warships stationed near East Timor's capital, Dili.

ACEH.   Unlike East Timor, Aceh occupies a prominent place in the creation of Indonesian nationalism. The Netherlands waged war in that region for four decades before achieving control of it in 1913, later than any other part of its East Indian colony. During the Indonesian revolution against Dutch rule in the late 1940s, Aceh became a major source of funds and supplies to revolutionary forces. The Japanese occupation during World War II eliminated Dutch control over Aceh, and a social revolution after the war almost completely removed the elite on whom Dutch rule had depended, thereby deterring the Dutch from even attempting to reassert their control.[36]

Aceh differs crucially from East Timor in another respect. In recent decades it has been a major source of revenue for the Indonesian state, whose second largest natural gas field lies off the Acehnese coast. Since the 1970s, the national government and multinational corporations have built a sprawling industrial complex that liquefies most of the gas for export to northeast Asian markets, and supplies the rest to local factories. The offshore field can produce 1.6 billion cubic feet of gas per day, with output valued at about $100 million per month. The loss of Aceh would be costly psychologically as well as financially.

Since East Timor's separation from Indonesia in 1999, Aceh's separatist movement has posed the most serious threat to Indonesian unity.[37] Although it has not gained access to the revenues that natural gas production generates, it is better organized and armed than the movement in Papua. Two main groups are leading the movement for Acehnese independence. The Free Aceh Movement (GAM) has about 10,000 members, though fewer than 2,000 are armed. Its titular head is Hasan di Tiro, who has lived abroad since the 1950s. He founded the movement in 1976 and declared Aceh's independence on 4 December of that year. Jakarta easily suppressed the movement in the late 1970s, but GAM regrouped during the 1980s and launched a rebellion in 1989. By 1993, the Indonesian military had quelled that insurgency, but its brutal tactics strengthened anti-Jakarta sentiment. As many as 5,000 people are believed to have died during the crackdown, and the uncovering of mass graves in 1998 refueled public animosity toward Indonesian troops and sparked fresh violence.

In the more open political climate since 1998, another group has emerged. Under the leadership of university students in Banda Aceh, the provincial capital, the Aceh Referendum Information Center (SIRA) was established in February 1999. It loosely unites a broad range of non-governmental organizations behind a demand that Jakarta permit the province to hold a referendum on independence. On 8 November 1999, just two weeks after Abdurrahman Wahid was elected president, SIRA organized a public demonstration in Banda Aceh that is commonly estimated to have attracted nearly 1 million people out of the total provincial population of just over 4 million.

The two groups have a common set of grievances, which the majority of Acehnese appear to share. One is the sense that governments in Jakarta have not adequately recognized the uniqueness of Acehnese society and cannot be trusted to do so. Besides resisting colonial rule longer than any other part of Indonesia, it is known to Acehnese and other Indonesians alike as a particularly Islamic society. In the 1950s, Acehnese joined an armed movement to make Indonesia an Islamic state. Although they failed to achieve that goal, they did win the status of "special region" rather than a mere province. However, national governments gradually took back the rights attached to this status—mainly local control over religious and educational affairs. Another goal arises from Jakarta's exploitation of the region's economic resources, especially its natural gas. That grievance fueled GAM's revival in the late 1980s. Third, Acehnese resent Jakarta for the widespread human rights abuses that occurred in the military's anti-insurgency campaign during Soeharto's last decade in power. Although the number of people killed was few in comparison to East Timor, the impact of army operations was widespread and indiscriminate, which encouraged a broad range of Acehnese to view themselves as not just economically exploited but also brutalized and vulnerable to renewed army brutality.

The rapid strengthening of the Acehnese separatist movement in the wake of Soeharto's resignation caught Indonesian political and military leaders by surprise, and their weakness since then has yielded an uncoordinated, often contradictory approach to resolving the conflict. Civilian politicians, especially Wahid, favored efforts to accommodate Acehnese interests, but military and police leaders have sought to undermine talks or agreements between the government and GAM representatives and to promote a military resolution of the conflict. In the absence of a clear policy, negotiations have stumbled and fighting has intensified.

In May 2000, the Wahid government and Acehnese rebels signed an agreement in Geneva for a "humanitarian pause" during which aid could be distributed to tens of thousands of people displaced by the fighting. In September, both parties agreed to extend the pause until mid-January 2001. Throughout this period, however, hundreds of people continued to be killed, mainly in army and police attacks on civilians suspected of aiding the rebels. As the new year approached, army officers lobbied for a more forceful approach, while legislative leaders pressed the government to negotiate with a broad range of Acehnese groups, not just GAM.

As Wahid's power ebbed in early 2001, prospects for a peaceful resolution of the conflict in Aceh also diminished. In March, attacks by the armed Free Aceh Movement forced ExxonMobil to halt production of the province's major resource, natural gas, which disrupted exports to Japan and South Korea and caused some factories in Aceh to shut down. The next month, Wahid issued a presidential instruction that outlined a six-point "comprehensive solution" to the conflict. Initially, only the single point concerning military action was implemented, and the number of people killed in the conflict rose from 256 in the four months preceding the instruction to 539 over the following four months.[38]

In an effort to undermine Acehnese support for independence, the House in July 2001 passed a law granting Aceh's provincial government a large share of revenues from natural gas exports, as well as rights to impose Islamic law (*not* a key demand of any major Acehnese group), to hold direct elections for local executives, and to form its own police force. However, the new law won few supporters in Aceh and failed to reduce the violence there. Just days after it was passed, the police arrested five GAM representatives with whom the government had been negotiating and charged them with subversion, though most were released by the end of the year. The military bolstered its presence enough to enable ExxonMobil to resume production in July, but violence remained common and the government's control tenuous. On 20 December, GAM attacked a convoy of buses carrying local ExxonMobil staff, killing one worker, and claimed responsibility for causing an air force transport jet to crash and burn on the same day. Red Cross workers conservatively estimated that 1,500 people, mostly civilians, were killed in Aceh during 2001.

Megawati's government has pursued a combination of military and diplomatic efforts that have put the rebels on the defensive without bringing the conflict closer to an end. In January, government troops managed to kill GAM's top military commander. In February, Megawati issued an order that called for the "annihilation of the separatist movement" and established a special regional army command for Aceh. In May, under increasing military pressure, GAM negotiators in Geneva acceded to Jakarta's demand that they accept the new provincial autonomy law as the framework for further discussions. However, GAM viewed the law as the starting point for future talks, while Jakarta saw it as the end point, and fighting between the two sides continued. By the middle of the year, several hundred people had been killed and the government seemed increasingly inclined to declare a state of emergency in the province and to permit the military to intensify its war against GAM. In late August, the government told the rebels to accept the provincial autonomy law and resume negotiations by early December or face harsher military action.

Despite the efforts of international mediators, including the Henry Dunant Centre in Switzerland, which has facilitated the sporadic talks between Indonesia and GAM, and retired American Gen. Anthony Zinni, who has traveled to Aceh and took part in the May 2002 negotiations, the conflict shows little sign of abating. After four years of growing conflict, many people on both sides have developed economic stakes in its continuation. Armed forces on both sides of the conflict routinely extort money from businesses and commercial traffic on the province's main highway. The "marijuana trade, illegal mining and logging and protection rackets all flourish" in Aceh's "largely lawless environment," and local bureaucrats and politicians who remain loyal to Jakarta are enjoying access to dramatically increased amounts of revenue that the national government transfers to the province under the terms of the new special autonomy law. Many officials allegedly profit from rampant smuggling through the duty-free port of Sabang on an island near the provincial capital.[39] The deep involvement of political and military elites in the underground economy is so serious that, according to the head of the International Crisis Group's Jakarta office, "the war in Aceh is about money." In her view, the Indonesian government should "not be talking about a military solution" but about "ending corruption . . . and making the conflict less profitable for all parties concerned."[40]

PAPUA.   Since the onset of Indonesia's political transition, the level of violence in Papua has been far lower than in Aceh or East Timor. While the death toll in Aceh approached 1,000 in 2000 and surpassed that figure in 2001, the number of deaths in Papua probably was less than 200 in 2000–2001. This reflects the province's more forbidding terrain rather than less serious grievances against Jakarta. The province has slightly more than 2 million people spread over 422,000 square kilometers, an area nearly eight times larger than Aceh, including tropical rain forests and snow-capped peaks. Moreover, as a result of migration from other parts of Indonesia, indigenous Papuans account for only about two-thirds of the province's population and immigrants dominate most of the leading economic sectors.

Like the Acehnese, Papuans resent Jakarta's control over the exploitation of their natural resources, particularly as symbolized by the enormous Freeport copper and gold mine, which processes more than 200,000 metric tons of copper ore each day and 3 million ounces of gold annually. Disposal of processed ore has turned 230 square kilometers of delta into an environmental wasteland. In recent years, company revenues have reached nearly $2 billion dollars per year, but only since 1996 has it pledged to spend even 1 percent of that money on community development.[41] Papuans also resent the transfer of their land to Jakarta-based timber barons and to hundreds of thousands of government-sponsored migrants, mostly from Java. Human rights abuses at the hands of the Indonesian security forces and the dominant role of non-indigenous Indonesians in the local bureaucracy further stoke anti-Indonesian sentiment. Other Papuan complaints mirror those of the East Timorese. Unlike the Acehnese, who can claim an important role in the Indonesian revolution against Dutch rule in the late 1940s, Papuans claim that they were excluded from talks about their own future in the 1940s, when the Netherlands was able to keep control of the territory, and again in the 1960s, when Indonesia gained control.

In Papua, as in Aceh, a longstanding rebel movement has been joined by a more recent civilian organization to press for independence from Indonesia. The Free Papua Organization (OPM) was founded in 1965, shortly after the United Nations transferred the territory from Dutch to Indonesian control in 1962–1963. The OPM declared the formation of a Government of West Papua in 1971, two years after Soeharto staged an "Act of Free Choice," in which his government organized about 1,000 tribal elders to ratify union with Indonesia.

In the late 1970s and early 1980s, the rebels and Indonesian troops engaged in periods of intense military conflict. In contrast to Aceh, which produced an active rebellion in the early 1990s and endured a harsh military crackdown, violence in Papua was limited during the late 1980s and 1990s.

Since 1998, hundreds of public figures in Papua have cooperated to build an increasingly well-organized independence movement. In contrast to Aceh, this movement is dominated by civilian groups that espouse a nonviolent strategy. There is no guerrilla army committed to violent forms of struggle. In mid-1998, they established the Forum for the Reconciliation of Irian Jaya Society, which called on the government to open discussions about the territory's political status, but allowed that the outcome could be less than full independence. In February 1999, President Habibie was persuaded to hold a National Dialogue with 100 Papuan leaders, but their blunt demand for independence soured further chances for dialogue and led to a crackdown on independence supporters. In February 2000, about 500 Papuans attended a four-day meeting at which they elected a thirty-one-member Papuan Presidium Council to prepare a transitional government. In May and June, with funds from Indonesia's government, they held a week-long Papuan People's Congress, at which 2,700 registered participants established a 501-person legislature to complement the executive council. In addition, a loosely organized militia, known as the Papuan Task Force, has sprung up across the province and has about 15,000 members. Although some elements have ties to members of the council and enforce law and order in the absence of Indonesian control, most are organized along tribal lines and some engage in criminal activity. One of its main units is controlled by the son of the council's president.[42]

As in the case of Aceh, the national government has pursued a range of uncoordinated policies that have combined to intensify anti-Indonesian sentiment in the province and increase, albeit more gradually, the level of violence. During his first year in office, Wahid adopted a conciliatory approach. He released Papuan activists whom Habibie's government had jailed, permitted Papuans to fly their flag so long as it was not raised higher than the Indonesian flag, and agreed to rename the province "Papua." When the 2000 congress adopted a resolution that declared Papua to have been sovereign since 1961, however, the government's approach toward Papua hardened. The national assembly refused to change the territory's official name to Papua. Toward the end of 2000, as the anniversary of the original congress's declaration of independence approached, the government sent more troops to the province, forbade the flying of the Papuan flag, and arrested the leaders of the civilian separatist movement for publicly advocating support for Papuan independence. Sporadic attacks on Indonesian police and military posts, presumably by members of the OPM, sparked indiscriminate reprisals against Papuan civilians.[43]

Under Megawati, policy either remains uncoordinated or intentionally combines a velvet glove with a mailed fist.[44] The contrast came sharply into view in late 2001. In October, after months of debate and vigorous lobbying by a range of Papuan elites, the House of Representatives passed a law that granted Papua "special autonomy." In addition to revenue-sharing provisions more favorable than those granted to other provinces, Jakarta made political concessions that it did not make to Aceh, whose leaders lobbied much less aggressively. Most importantly, it restricted the positions of governor and vice governor to native Papuans and established a provincial upper house—which no other province has or ever has had—whose membership is also limited to native Papuans.

Just one month after this law was passed, the leader of the Papuan Presidium Council and de facto head of the province's independence movement was assassinated after leaving the provincial headquarters of the army's special forces, where he had attended a ceremony to mark a national holiday. A police investigation subsequently resulted in the indictment of several special forces officers, who were scheduled to be tried in a military court in late 2002. The murder turned public opinion strongly against the government's autonomy plan, and Megawati was compelled to cancel a visit to Papua during which she had intended to celebrate Christmas with the region's largely Christian population and ceremonially hand over the new law, which took effect in 2002.

Although Papua has avoided the widespread violence that has occurred in the other regions discussed in this chapter, many Papuans fear they are increasingly likely to be attacked. The army's top commander in the region since early 2001 is Mahidin Simbolon, who served several tours of duty in East Timor and served as chief of staff of the army command that included that territory during 1999, when army-trained militias wreaked havoc there. The region's leading human rights group believes that militias, including Laskar Jihad (Jihad Militia) units, are being trained to foment similar violence in Papua.[45] In July 2002, news of a secret police operation to create a "zone of peace" and to keep the province within Indonesia by cracking down on separatists, even though the province is largely peaceful, fueled Papuans' fears of violence. It also eroded their faith in the central government's promises of autonomy, since the special autonomy law required the police to coordinate its activities with the provincial governor and legislature, which its regional commander apparently had not done.[46]

Despite the lower level of violence in Papua than in Aceh, and the more difficult terrain in which separatist activists must operate, several factors raise the likelihood that its bid for independence will succeed. One is the questionable legal grounds on which the territory became part of Indonesia. Another is the province's land border with Papua New Guinea, which affords rebels an opportunity to organize outside Indonesian territory. Its location and cultural similarities have also gained it the sympathy of many countries in the South Pacific Forum, which includes other predominantly Melanesian nations. Moreover, its location promises to keep the territory's struggle on Australia's political agenda. Canberra has steadfastly opposed Papuan independence, fearful not only of angering Indonesia, but also of inviting the creation of yet another poor, politically unstable neighbor. However, precisely because developments in Papua have the potential to affect Australian security, the government's view may change as conditions in Papua evolve.

Communal Conflicts

Another source of violence since Soeharto's fall is what Indonesians typically call "horizontal conflict" between communities within the country, in contrast to the vertically oriented conflicts between separatist groups and Jakarta. Although intercommunal violence occurred during the Soeharto era, it did not achieve the same scale as it has since. The Norwegian Refugee Committee, which maintains a database of internally displaced people throughout the world, estimates that the number of IDPs in Indonesia jumped from less than 20,000 at the end of 1997 to about 600,000 at the start of 2000 and to more than 1.4 million by June 2002.[47] The main cause of this dramatic increase was not the separatist movements in Aceh and Papua, but intercommunal conflicts in parts of Maluku, Kalimantan, and Sulawesi.

The conditions that preceded and accompanied each conflict are complex and in many ways similar. The main elements seem to include conflicts between indigenous and immigrant groups that tend to profess different religions and compete for access to economic resources. Yet, similar conditions can be found across the country, while bloody conflicts are isolated. Ongoing research suggests that one of the chief determinants is whether local elites actively seek to mobilize supporters along communal lines to attack another group defined in terms of its cultural identity as threatening to their own identity and material interests. Another is whether the local political and security apparatus remains neutral when such conflicts occur, or takes sides. What remains unclear is whether elites in other regions are less motivated to act in this manner or conditions do not favor such strategies, and why army and police units might be more capable of acting neutrally in one location but not another. Rather than analyze each case in detail, I focus on the bloodiest conflict and summarize the other two.

MALUKU.   Nowhere in Indonesia have more people died and been displaced during the country's ongoing political transition than the Maluku islands. Since it began in early 1999, the conflict there has claimed more than
6,000 lives and driven more than 500,000 people from their homes.[48] Initially,
fighting was concentrated on the island of Ambon, particularly in Ambon City,
the capital of Maluku province. Traditionally, Christian Ambonese comprised
a majority of the island's inhabitants and dominated the provincial bureaucracy. Over time, Muslim immigrants evened the balance, and in the 1990s
President Soeharto broke with tradition and twice appointed a Muslim as governor of Maluku. Muslims gradually displaced Christians in the bureaucracy,
threatening networks of patronage that reached deep into local society.

Although tensions were running high prior to Soeharto's fall, the local government and security forces were ill equipped to deal with serious unrest. One
researcher found that when the conflict began, Ambon's city police station could
accommodate only twenty detainees, its fire department had only two fire engines and had access to almost no hydrants, and "the provincial government's
disaster relief coordination service, tasked with simply counting victims, did
not even have a motorcycle, let alone a motorcar" to serve a city of more than
300,000 people.[49]

During the second half of 1999, a separate set of local conflicts resulted in
fighting among Christians and Muslims in the northern Maluku islands after
Jakarta decided to remove them from Ambon's control and create a province of
North Maluku. This touched off a struggle between the Muslim Makian and the
predominantly Christian Kao, who had competing land claims. The Makian
linked their demand for the creation of their own subdistrict (*kecamatan*) to a
provincial-level struggle between two royal families for dominance within the
new province. In October, the Kao destroyed a number of Makian villages and
drove the Makian to neighboring Ternate and Tidore islands. In response, Muslims drove Christians out of the city of Ternate.

A turning point occurred during the last week of 1999, when Kao villagers
attacked a Muslim subdistrict, killing more than 500 people and turning more
than 10,000 into refugees. This incident received widespread attention in Indonesia and motivated the formation of Muslim militias elsewhere in the country
to protect Muslims in Maluku. In early January, more than 100,000 people
marched in Jakarta to demand a holy war on behalf of Maluku's Muslim communities. Leading politicians, including Amien Rais, the chairman of the
People's Consultative Assembly, addressed the rally. Within weeks, militias
began to arrive in Maluku, but they did not make a significant impact until mid-
year when members of the well organized Laskar Jihad arrived.[50] In April, the
Laskar Jihad announced publicly that it was training at least 2,000 members at

a base near Jakarta and intended to send as many as 7,000 members to defend Muslims in Maluku. The organization's leaders even met with Wahid in April to inform him of their plans.[51] Although he angrily dismissed them, he was unable to prevent them from sending their forces to Maluku in May.

The arrival of Laskar Jihad forces led to a dramatic worsening of the conflict during the remainder of 2000. It stirred the government and the military to take actions that seemed by mid-2001 to have sharply limited the potential for further violence. Following its arrival, the Laskar Jihad established control over local militias and gained access to sophisticated weaponry, mainly through collaboration with sympathetic army troops. Then it launched a devastating attack on a Christian village located between two Muslim villages in Halmahera. While the attack was intended as a response to the Christian attack the previous December, it also illustrated its strategy of clearing Christians from predominantly Muslim areas.

Less than two months after the Laskar Jihad began to arrive, Wahid declared a state of "civil emergency" in Maluku and North Maluku. In addition, he replaced the Christian regional military commander with a Hindu and increased the number of troops in the region. By the end of the year, nineteen battalions were stationed in the islands.[52] These changes had little effect until early 2001, when a joint battalion of elite marine, air force, and army troops directly under the national headquarters' command began to crack down on militia groups in Maluku. Ostensibly, their goal was to retrieve hundreds of automatic weapons that Muslim militias had seized from an army post in June 2000. However, the outcry from the Laskar Jihad suggested that the group itself was one of the military's main targets. Its leaders and other Muslims in Maluku bitterly accused the battalion of siding with Christians and murdering Muslims, and in November 2001 the government withdrew the battalion and replaced it with members of the army's special forces.[53]

The joint battalion's other main targets were members of army and police units who had been swept up in the conflict. Many of them had deserted, joined local militias, or collaborated with local people of the same faith. As one close observer noted, "evidence on the ground pointed to a security apparatus in serious disarray," which he attributed to conflicting chains of command, and the inadequacy of the military budget, which compelled soldiers and officers alike to seek alternative sources of income and build close relations with local society.[54] Even the regional police commander forthrightly acknowledged that thousands of members of his force needed to be replaced since they were "no longer able to carry out their tasks in a neutral manner."[55]

The Indonesian army may not be the only force that suffers from disciplinary problems. At the beginning of 2001, Ja'far Umar Thalib, the leader of Laskar

Jihad, reached an agreement with Muslim leaders in Maluku to implement *shari'a* in the region, even though Indonesian law does not permit it. Then they set up more than 100 posts to stamp out immoral behavior, such as prostitution and the consumption of alcohol and illicit drugs. However, in March one of Ja'far's own lieutenants was caught in a sting. He admitted to adultery, and under Ja'far's orders members of the militia carried out the sentence that the shari'a requires: stoning to death. Indonesian police temporarily detained Ja'far when he returned to Java, but the government did not charge or try him.[56]

Since the middle of 2001, North Maluku has been largely peaceful, and the level of violence in Maluku has declined markedly. In both provinces, the conflict has segregated Christians and Muslims and reduced the opportunities for conflict between them, especially in North Maluku, where Christians have always been a small minority. The joint battalion's aggressive tactics in Maluku province, where Laskar Jihad concentrated its forces, also helped to reduce the level of violence.[57] Encouraged by this condition and the apparent success of similar peace talks on Central Sulawesi, two senior government ministers organized negotiations among thirty-five Christian and thirty-five Muslim leaders from Maluku, and, in February 2002, the parties reached an eleven-point agreement that included the disarmament of all warring groups.

The agreement did not immediately bring peace to the region, because hard line groups opposed its terms and the government lacked the capacity to enforce them. Both problems are reflected in the actions of the Laskar Jihad and the government's response. The militia group did not participate in the peace negotiations, and afterward immediately rejected one of the agreement's main points—that outside forces should leave the region. In April, the government increased pressure on all groups to surrender their weapons. This led to a number of violent incidents that included the burning of the governor's office. Later that month, Ja'far Umar Thalib, the chief of Laskar Jihad, delivered a fiery sermon in which he allegedly called on his followers to attack the enemy and kill members of former president Soekarno's family (which would include the current president, his daughter). Two days later, well-armed and organized Muslim groups attacked a Christian village, and civilian, police, and military authorities accused each other of failing to prevent the assault. Though authorities in Maluku remained too weak to challenge Ja'far and the Laskar Jihad, those on Java were stronger and bolder; in early May, police arrested Ja'far when he arrived in Java. Although they charged him with provoking violence in Maluku and threatening to kill the president, the vice president and other Muslim political party leaders quickly made high-profile visits to Ja'far's jail cell. Over the next few months, Maluku suffered further bombings, and repeated postponements allowed Ja'far to avoid trial.

KALIMANTAN.   Violence between indigenous, mostly Christian and animist Dayaks and Muslim immigrants from the island of Madura, near Java, has occurred several times in the provinces of West and Central Kalimantan, but in contrast to the violence in Maluku, it has not been continual and has claimed fewer victims. In early 1997, about 500 people were killed, and about 25,000 driven from their homes in West Kalimantan when Dayaks attacked Madurese. Two years later, with the help of indigenous Malays, who are mainly Muslim, Dayaks again attacked Madurese. This time the death toll reached only about 200, but another 30,000 Madurese were displaced.[58] In early 2001, Dayaks in the main cities of Central Kalimantan repeated the exercise, managing to kill about 400 people and forcing more than 50,000 to flee their homes.[59] No further outbreaks of violence have occurred since then.

As in Maluku, indigenous groups resented the loss of economic resources and opportunities to immigrants, but in Kalimantan they competed more for access to land and forest resources than for positions in the civil service and control over government spending. In heavily forested but sparsely populated Kalimantan, Soeharto had seen tremendous opportunities; he parceled out logging concessions to well-connected officials and businessmen and encouraged migration from heavily populated Java and Madura to reduce population pressure. Dayaks, who lacked official land titles, found themselves gradually pushed off land that they considered their own. Much like Papuans and Timorese, they also found themselves regarded as primitive, and unfit to hold important positions in local government, and consequently deprived of access to the new sources of wealth that government development programs created.

Communal conflicts occurred in Kalimantan prior to 1997, but they did not involve large-scale destruction and loss of life. People in West Kalimantan commonly cite about a dozen incidents of Dayak-Madurese clashes over two decades preceding the recent bloodletting. And in Central Kalimantan, the national government was forced to fly thousands of troops to the provincial capital in 1993 to quell demonstrations against a rubber-stamp legislature that had elected a well-connected bureaucrat from Java as governor rather than a leading Dayak politician.[60]

The sharpest contrast between earlier and more recent conflicts lies in the capacity of the security forces to quell or forestall widespread violence. Of the most recent incidents, the first and last are most striking. In early 1997, Soeharto was still in office and the economic crisis that precipitated his fall had not yet begun. Yet his regime was weakening and no longer able to control society in West Kalimantan as it had previously. Perhaps more shocking, however, was the response of the military under Wahid to violence in Central Kalimantan. Police and army units were unable to coordinate their efforts and stood aside as the fighting went on, while the navy sent ships to evacuate tens of thousands of Madurese and take them back to Java and Madura.

SULAWESI.   As in Kalimantan and Maluku, conflict in the district of Poso, in Central Sulawesi, generally pits Muslims against Christians. And as in those other places, it seems attributable to a combination of intense economic and political competition, elite manipulation of religious differences that mirrored economic ones, and ill-prepared and unreliable security forces.[61] Though the conflict there has received less attention than Maluku and Kalimantan, it provides the first evidence that localized conflicts may become directly linked.

Indonesians have begun to number the episodes of violence in Poso as they would book chapters. "Poso I" took place at the end of 1998, amid a failed bid by a Christian politician to win election as district head and take the place of a Muslim official. On 24 December, which by coincidence was both Christmas Eve for Christians and the first day of Ramadan for Muslims, a brawl broke out between drunken youths of the two faiths. Local officials then moved to enforce a ban on the sale of alcohol during the Muslim fasting month, but conflicts erupted as Christian shopkeepers attempted to protect their stores against zealous groups of Muslim youths who wanted to destroy stocks of alcoholic drinks, not just ban their sale. The failed candidate for district head later encouraged Christian gangs to attack Muslims. Although a peace was negotiated among local religious and community leaders, no one was arrested. Widespread uncontrolled fighting erupted in April and May 2000 for reasons that remain unclear. Known as "Poso II" and "Poso III," these episodes involved a wave of Muslim attacks on Christians followed by a wave of Christian reprisals that together resulted in perhaps 300 deaths and more than 70,000 displaced persons. During Poso II, local Muslim leaders successfully pressed provincial leaders to withdraw the police, which enabled them to attack Christians at will.

As the Laskar Jihad presence grew, a fifth round of fighting broke out in November and 15,000 people fled their homes. But this time, Indonesia's national government took firm action to stem the violence and promote a peaceful resolution of the conflict. Changed external conditions in the wake of 11 September seem chiefly responsible for Jakarta's decision to replace its hands-off approach with a more active one. The United States, increasingly concerned about the spread of militant Islam and aware of speculation about links between Laskar Jihad and al Qaeda, pressed Jakarta to resolve the conflict. Top government ministers visited the region, and in December, the government hosted a peace conference that brought Christian and Muslim leaders together for several days and yielded a ten-point agreement. However, the government has been unable to commit enough troops to the region to disarm militias or investigate violent incidents, and, in mid-2002, a series of attacks threatened to scuttle the peace agreement. The government sponsored brief, ineffective talks between the parties in August and proposed further meetings later in the year.[62]

Autonomist Pressures

Demands for regional autonomy have been far more common than those for independence. Though less attractive fodder for observers who seek to dramatize the potential for national disintegration, the widespread nature of autonomist pressure suggests that the state faces deep-rooted pressure to reform its basic institutional ties between the central and regional governments. Advocates of enhanced regional autonomy have made three major types of demands: for local control over the appointment of local officials, for a larger share of the revenues that the national government derives from their region, and for enhanced politico-administrative status.

During 1998, demands for the removal and replacement of regional chief executives stirred more people to protest publicly than did any other issue, largely because of their association with Soeharto. However, Habibie, Soeharto's successor, removed no governors and just ten district executives from office that year.[63] Coincidentally, though, a large proportion of regional chief executives' terms expired just before and shortly after Soeharto's resignation. Thus, even though public protests forced very few from office prematurely, an opportunity existed for regional reformers to challenge Jakarta's traditional control over the appointment of such officials.

Between mid-1997 and the end of 1998, the terms of three-quarters of all governors expired, and during 1998–1999 about two-thirds of all district executives' terms expired. The earlier and more condensed period of gubernatorial appointments occurred during a time when Soeharto and Habibie, though weak, were able to resist their less organized opponents. Only one of the new governors was neither a bureaucrat nor a military officer, and the military's share of governorships declined only modestly, from about 53 percent to 44 percent. Despite widespread allegations of bribery and corruption, and violent public protests at the inauguration of some governors, only two governors subsequently have been forced to leave office, including one in the uniquely troubled province of Aceh.

The later and more prolonged period during which district officials' terms expired created much greater opportunities for change. Between the beginning of 1998 and September 2000, military officers won just 15 percent of these posts, compared to more than 50 percent during the previous fifteen years. However, the chief beneficiaries of the military's declining fortunes have been civil servants; over the same period, their share rose from less than half to about three-quarters, while just 12 percent of all new district executives were neither officers nor bureaucrats.[64] The lack of new faces at the district level, and the ability of key supporters of the old regime to maintain their grip on regional power led to violence similar to that which occurred in 1998. By mid-2001, riots and other forms of violence had accompanied the election or inauguration of at least eight district executives.

In addition to reducing Jakarta's control over regional political appointments, regional governments sought to reduce their striking dependence on the national government for budgetary resources. Under Soeharto, district as well as provincial governments typically relied on transfers from the national government for more than 80 percent of their income. Within weeks after Soeharto resigned, provincial governors whom he had appointed began to lobby Jakarta to obtain a larger share of the income from national government revenues collected in their provinces. These demands came not just from governors of regions rich in natural resources, such as East Kalimantan and Irian Jaya, but from those that depended heavily on industry and commerce, such as West Java. Just weeks after he had been inaugurated amid massive opposition, the governor of East Kalimantan traveled to Jakarta to make the case for his province to retain 75 percent of the revenues from the production of oil, natural gas, and timber. He was joined by the governors of West Java and Irian Jaya, whose appointments Soeharto had approved not long before he resigned. The governor of West Java later said he hoped that the province could collect a tax on the export of textiles, "so that we don't just collect the pollution."[65]

In response to these pressures, in April 1999 Habibie's government passed a pair of landmark laws to decentralize political authority and fiscal resources to district governments. Habibie and his civilian advisers recognized that the highly centralized system developed during the Soeharto years had become untenable. At the provincial and district levels, branch offices of national government ministries and regional army commands sharply limited the power of local governments. In late 1998, without consulting regional politicians or interest groups, a small team of bureaucrats hurriedly drafted new laws on regional government and center-region fiscal relations. The incumbent House of Representatives, elected in 1997 during the last Soeharto-era election, passed the laws less than two months before the historic election of 1999, in which most members lost their seats.

The first law grants district-level governments (of which there are approximately 350) authority over a wide range of matters, reserving only defense, foreign affairs, justice, religion, and monetary policy exclusively for the national government. The act explicitly awards local legislatures the right to elect district heads without interference from Jakarta. The second law provides a fiscal base on which districts can exercise their new political authority. This law commits the national government to share a specific proportion of its general revenues with district governments, and grants natural resource–producing regions the right to retain a specific proportion of revenues derived from the production of those resources.

Both laws took effect in January 2001 and have become sources of debate and concern. Inadequate preparation and inconsistent implementation have caused confusion among national and regional officials and contributed to political conflict among national, provincial, and local officials. Wahid, though sympathetic to the interests of the regions, struggled merely to survive and failed to issue the regulations needed to implement the new laws. In contrast, Megawati is inclined to revise the new laws in ways that strengthen central authority over regional affairs, but she failed in mid-2002 to obtain legislative support. Despite innumerable problems in implementing the laws, they appear to have achieved the principal aim of their drafters: to stem radical demands for autonomy by providing a framework in which the center and regions can negotiate a looser relationship without tearing the country apart.

Demands for increased political autonomy have included efforts by local elites to divide existing districts and provinces into smaller ones in which they can ascend to the top positions and gain control over local resources. To many Indonesians, a surge in this sort of demand at the same time as separatist movements were growing stronger and communal conflicts were intensifying seemed to heighten the prospect of national disintegration. The national government under Habibie responded to these demands by creating nearly three dozen new districts in provinces outside Java, a process that continued through 2002. By mid-year, the number of district level jurisdictions had grown by about 100, or one-third, and applications for the creation of seventy-six more were pending approval of the House of Representatives.[66] In addition, the national government has created four new provinces, chiefly for small ethnic groups whose elites felt marginalized from political power in their original provinces.

Conclusion

Advocates of the disintegration thesis correctly diagnose Indonesia's general problem—a dramatic weakening of the national government—and are able to identify many of the crises that afflict the country. However, they overestimate the importance of those individual crises for the Indonesian state as a whole and underestimate the significance of the national government's responses to regional pressures, as well as the potential for the government to take more effective action in the future.

Take the violent crises first. During the last four years, Indonesian authority has receded significantly in Aceh, Papua, and much of Maluku, and disappeared from East Timor. However, there are two key points to note about these crises. One is that none has enveloped a neighboring province. This is true in two senses. Warring parties have not shifted their operations out of the regions in which they initiated conflict, and refugees from these conflicts have not replicated their struggles in the places to which they have fled. To be sure, conflict in Central Kalimantan took place along lines similar to those it followed in neighboring West Kalimantan, but conflict in one province did not "spread" to or "cause" conflict in the other. Instead, each had similar underlying social, economic, and political conditions that have been conducive to similar conflicts. In the case of the Maluku islands, it can be argued that flows of refugees from one part of that archipelago to another have tended to reproduce conflict patterns, but the same cannot be said about flows of refugees out of Maluku to other regions, or about flows of refugees out of Aceh, Kalimantan, Poso, East Timor, or Papua. Certainly, large concentrations of refugees have sparked conflict with the communities in the area around their camps, but this hardly amounts to "spreading" or reproducing the initial communal or separatist conflicts from which they fled.

The second point is that there have been only two cases of widespread violence during the post-Soeharto era that were not preceded by similar conflicts while Soeharto was president, namely in Maluku and Poso. In each of the other cases, large-scale conflicts had occurred that warned of the potential for future violence. Indeed, precedents for contemporary conflicts in Aceh and Papua can be found in the period before Soeharto came to power.

Together, these two observations suggest that the potential for violent conflicts to emerge suddenly, or spread contagiously from one region to another, is more limited than most observers imply. It also means that opportunities exist for interested and capable actors to mediate and contain conflicts before they reach the intensity of those described in this chapter.

Consider the instances of non-violent regional pressures on Jakarta. The ongoing political transition has been good for regional political elites. As elections of district heads show, local elites have expanded their control of this key position, largely at the expense of the military. And whenever these elites have sought greater autonomy, Jakarta has been inclined to recognize their demands and negotiate the surrender of some rights and resources. Moreover, the House of Representatives has been willing to write the terms of these deals into law. In no case has the military used force to suppress demands for greater political and fiscal autonomy, even though it violently opposes demands for independence and actively undermines government efforts to negotiate with rebels.

In sum, Indonesia's national government is weak and confronts a broad array of challenges. It may yet be forced to accept the autonomy of another province or two, and this outcome would be more painful psychologically and financially than East Timor's departure. However, the most serious challenges to its authority are limited in scope and number. In the vast majority of regions, groups seek to reduce, not repudiate, its authority. Wisely, the national government under Habibie and Wahid sought to renegotiate center-region relations rather than sustain a highly centralized system of rule that the national government could no longer afford to enforce. Unwisely, neither government took effective steps to resolve the country's debt burden or to improve its economic management in general, and neither was able to reform the methods of the military or the police.

If Indonesia's new president and legislature use their resources to resolve these problems, the result is likely to be a more decentralized, possibly somewhat smaller polity, not another Yugoslavia. If they simply perpetuate the struggles for power that have marked the past four years, without addressing the challenges outlined above, economic troubles are likely to undermine the government's fiscal capacity, which will limit its ability to reform state institutions. That, in turn, will diminish the state's significance to more of its citizens. Under such a scenario, Indonesia would no longer be a weak and vulnerable state, but a failing one.

Notes

1. This point is argued more fully in Michael Malley, "Beyond Democratic Elections: Indonesia Embarks on a Protracted Transition," *Democratization*, VII (2000), 153–180.

2. The Norwegian Refugee Council, Global IDP Database (28 August 2002), located at www.db.idpproject.org.

3. Audrey R. Kahin and George McT. Kahin, *Subversion as Foreign Policy: The Secret Eisenhower and Dulles Debacle in Indonesia* (New York, 1995).

4. These developments are chronicled and analyzed in the "Survey of Recent Developments" that appears in each issue of the *Bulletin of Indonesian Economic Studies*, the leading source of academic research on the Indonesian economy.

5. Robert B. Cribb, "Problems in the Historiography of the Killings in Indonesia," in idem. (ed.), *The Indonesian Killings of 1965-1966: Studies from Java and Bali* (Clayton, Victoria, 1990), 1–44; Robert B. Cribb, "How Many Deaths? Problems in the Statistics of Massacre in Indonesia (1965–1966) and East Timor (1975–1980)," in Ingrid Wessel and Georgia Wimhöfer (eds.), *Violence in Indonesia* (Hamburg, 2001), 82–98.

6. R. William Liddle described this as "performance legitimation," in his "Soeharto's Indonesia: Personal Rule and Political Institutions," *Pacific Affairs*, LVIII (1985), 68–90.

7. John Bresnan, *Managing Indonesia: The Modern Political Economy* (New York, 1993), 164–193.

8. On Indonesian economic policies during the Soeharto era, see Hal Hill, *The Indonesian Economy since 1966: Southeast Asia's Emerging Giant* (Cambridge, 1996). On tax reform, see Malcolm Gillis, "Comprehensive Tax Reform: The Indonesian Experience, 1981–1988," in idem. (ed.), *Tax Reform in Developing Countries* (Durham, 1989), 79–114.

9. Andrew MacIntyre, "Political Institutions and the Economic Crisis in Thailand and Indonesia," in T. J. Pempel (ed.), *The Politics of the Asian Economic Crisis* (Ithaca, 1999), 153–161.

10. Jeffrey A. Winters, *Power in Motion: Capital Mobility and the Indonesian State* (Ithaca, 1996), 148.

11. On this period, see Donald K. Emmerson, "Part IV: The Fall of Suharto and After," in Donald K. Emmerson (ed.), *Indonesia beyond Suharto: Polity, Economy, Society, Transition*, (Armonk, NY, 1999), 295–361; R. William Liddle, "Indonesia's Democratic Opening," *Government and Opposition*, XXXIV (1999), 94–116; Malley, "Beyond Democratic Elections;" Rizal Sukma, "Indonesia: A Year of Politics and Sadness," in *Southeast Asian Affairs 1998* (Singapore, 1998), 105–123.

12. Emmerson, *Indonesia beyond Suharto*, 299.

13. PDIP-P is Partai Demokrasi Indonesia-Perjuangan (Indonesian Democracy Party-Struggle); Golkar is Partai Golongan Karya (Functional Groups Party); PKB is Partai Kebangkitan Bangsa (National Awakening Party); PPP is Partai Persatuan Pembangunan (Development Unity Party); PAN is Partai Amanat Nasional (National Mandate Party).

14. Arief Budiman, "Indonesia: The Trials of President Wahid," in Anthony Smith and Daljit Singh (eds.), *Southeast Asian Affairs 2001* (Singapore, 2001), 145–158.

15. Michael S. Malley, "Indonesia in 2001: Restoring Stability in Jakarta," *Asian Survey*, XLII (January/February 2002), 124–132.

16. In August 2002, the Assembly adopted a constitutional amendment that, among many other things, makes the president directly elected and thereby brings the form of government much closer to a presidential one.

17. For views that a breakup was likely, see John R. Bolton, "Indonesia: Asia's Yugoslavia?" *Far Eastern Economic Review* (1 April 1998); "Indonesia: Balkans of the East?" *Time* (7 June 1999); Anthony Spaeth, "Is Indonesia Starting to Break Up?" *Time* (3 August 1998); "An Asian Balkans?" *The Economist* (13 November 1999); Michael Richardson, "Southeast Asians Fear a Breakup of Indonesia," *International Herald Tribune* (16 November 1999); David Rohde, "Indonesia Unraveling?" *Foreign Affairs*, LXXX (2001), 110–124. Compare the less apocalyptic views in Anne Booth, "Will Indonesia Break Up?" *Inside Indonesia,* LIX (1999); Robert Cribb, "Not the Next Yugoslavia: Prospects for the Disintegration of Indonesia," *Australian Journal of International Affairs*, LIII (1999); Donald K. Emmerson, "Will Indonesia Survive?" *Foreign*

Affairs, LXXIX (2000), 95–106; Michael van Langenberg, "End of the Jakartan Empire?" *Inside Indonesia*, LXI (2000); Michael Malley, "Indonesia: Violence and Reform beyond Jakarta," in Anthony Smith and Daljit Singh (eds.), *Southeast Asian Affairs 2001* (Singapore, 2001), 159–174.

18. For the Wahid quotation, see "Soal Belum Selesainya Seluruh Persoalan, Presiden Mohon Maaf," *Kompas* (8 August 2000); for Megawati's statement, see Lindsay Murdoch, "Megawati's Cabinet Passes Crucial Test," *Sydney Morning Herald* (10 August 2001).

19. On Indonesia's public debt, see International Crisis Group, "Bad Debt: The Politics of Financial Reform in Indonesia," Report No. 15 (Brussels, 13 March 2001).

20. In addition to the regular coverage of IBRA's creation and operation in the *Bulletin of Indonesian Economic Studies*, see "Indonesia Begins to Rebuild Its Financial Sector," *Tokyo-Mitsubishi Review*, IV (1999).

21. For the figure of $60 billion, see Howard Dick, "Survey of Recent Developments," *Bulletin of Indonesian Economic Studies*, XXXVII (2001), 22. For the figure of 70 percent, see Mari Pangestu and Miranda Swaray Goeltom, "Survey of Recent Developments," *Bulletin of Indonesian Economic Studies*, XXXVII (2001), 167.

22. Dick, "Survey."

23. Emmanuel Skoufias, Asep Suryahadi, and Sudarno Sumarto, "Changes in Household Welfare, Poverty and Inequality during the Crisis," *Bulletin of Indonesian Economic Studies*, XXXVI (2000).

24. On child welfare, see Lisa A. Cameron, "The Impact of the Indonesian Financial Crisis on Children: An Analysis Using the 100 Village Data," *Bulletin of Indonesian Economic Studies*, XXXVII (2001). For the World Bank study, see "Poverty Reduction in Indonesia: Constructing a New Strategy," Discussion Draft (Jakarta, October 2000), ii.

25. Dick, "Survey," 39.

26. Pangestu and Goeltom, "Survey," 141–171.

27. *Kompas* (5 August 2002).

28. Michael Shari, "Indonesia," *Business Week* (20 May 2002, international ed.).

29. *Kompas* (22 July 2002). Similar results were obtained in polls conducted by a leading social science research institute. See E. Shobirin Nadj, Rahadi T. Wiratama, and Wildan Pramudya A., "Pendapat Publik Tentang Kinerja Pemerintahan Megawati" (Jakarta, 2002), available at http://www.lp3es.or.id/program/polling1/kinerja1.htm; and E. Shobirin Nadj, Rahadi T. Wiratama, and Wildan Pramudya A., "Pendapat Publik Tentang Problem Internal Dan Masa Depan Partai Politik Di Indonesia" (Jakarta, 2002), available at http://www.lp3es.or.id/program/polling2/internal1.htm.

30. Prema-chandra Athukorala, "Survey of Recent Developments," *Bulletin of Indonesian Economic Studies*, XXXVIII (August 2002), 143–145.

31. Quoted in *Tempo Interaktif* (27 February 2002), http://www.tempo.co.id/news/2002/2/27/1,1,45,id.html.

32. *Jakarta Post* (22 and 23 July 2002).

33. Additional historical background on each of these conflicts can be found in Michael Malley, "Regions: Centralization and Resistance," in Emmerson, *Indonesia beyond Suharto*, 71–105.

34. Cribb, "How Many Deaths?" 90–94.

35. For details, see the report by James Dunn, special rapporteur of the United Nations Transitional Administration in East Timor, "Crimes against Humanity in East Timor, January to October 1999: Their Nature and Causes" (14 February 2001).

36. Tim Kell, *The Roots of the Acehnese Rebellion, 1989–1992* (Ithaca, 1995), 8–10.

37. International Crisis Group, "Aceh: Why Military Force Won't Bring Lasting Peace (Brussels, 12 June 2001); Human Rights Watch, "Indonesia: The War in Aceh" (New York, August 2001).

38. Reports by human rights groups, cited in "Aceh: Running out of Hope," *Van Zorge Report*, III (1 October 2001), 15.

39. John McBeth, "Profiting from Conflict," *Far Eastern Economic Review* (25 July 2002).

40. Sidney Jones, "The Key Step for Peace Is Ending Corruption," *International Herald Tribune* (23 July 2002).

41. Michael Shari and Sheri Prasso, "Freeport-McMoRan: A Pit of Trouble," *Business Week* (International Edition) (31 July 2000).

42. *Far Eastern Economic Review* (16 November 2000).

43. Historical background is summarized and these attacks are detailed in the Human Rights Watch report, "Violence and Political Impasse in Papua" (2001); on the People's Congress, see also *Van Zorge Report* (5 June 2000). Recent academic studies of Papuan nationalism include Peter King, "Morning Star Rising: Indonesia Raya and the New Papuan Nationalism," *Indonesia*, LXXIII (April 2002); Octavius Mote and Danilyn Rutherford, "From Irian Jaya to Papua: The Limits of Primordialism in Indonesia's Troubled East," *Indonesia*, LXXII (October 2001); David Webster, "'Already Sovereign as a People': A Foundational Moment in West Papuan Nationalism," *Pacific Affairs*, LXXIV (Winter 2001–2002), 507–528.

44. Peter King, "Indonesia's Hidden Treasure," *Australian Financial Review* (16 November 2001).

45. *Sydney Morning Herald* (22 January 2002).

46. *South China Morning Post* (30 July 2002).

47. The Norwegian Refugee Council, Global IDP Database (see note 2 above).

48. For extensive coverage of conflict in Maluku, see the International Crisis Group report "Overcoming Murder and Chaos in Maluku" (Brussels, 19 December 2000); Gerry van Klinken, "The Maluku Wars: Bringing Society Back In," *Indonesia*, LXXI (April 2001); and "War in the Malukus," *Van Zorge Report* (18 July 2000).

49. Van Klinken, "The Maluku Wars," 9.

50. For background on this organization, see Greg Fealy, "Inside the Laskar Jihad," *Inside Indonesia* (2001); Sadanand Dhume, "Islam's Holy Warriors," *Far Eastern Economic Review* (26 April 2001).

51. *Kompas* (7 April 2000).

52. *Suara Pembaruan* (29 December 2000).

53. *Kompas* (23 January, 19 June 2001). See also the Laskar Jihad website for reports and commentary, at http://www.laskarjihad.or.id.

54. Van Klinken, "The Maluku Wars," 8.

55. *Kompas* (12 July 2001).

56. *Kompas* (17 May 2001).

57. International Crisis Group, "Indonesia: The Search for Peace in Maluku" (8 February 2002); Christopher R. Duncan, "The Aftermath of Civil War," *Inside Indonesia,* LXIX (January–March 2002).

58. John McBeth and Margot Cohen, "Dayak Destruction: New Ethnic Violence Erupts in Kalimantan," *Far Eastern Economic Review* (1 April 1999); Human Rights Watch, *Communal Violence in West Kalimantan* (New York, 1997).

59. *Jakarta Post* (8 March 2001).

60. Malley, "Regions," 89–93.

61. For detailed accounts of the violence in 1998 and 2000, see John McBeth and Oren Murphy, "Bloodbath," *Far Eastern Economic Review* (6 July 2000); Rohde, "Indonesia Unraveling?" For accounts by an anthropologist who knows the region well, see Lorraine V. Aragon, "Communal Violence in Poso, Central Sulawesi: Where People Eat Fish and Fish Eat People," *Indonesia*, LXXII (October 2001), and "Waiting for Peace in Poso," *Inside Indonesia*, LXX (April–June 2002).

62. *Kompas* (28 August 2002).

63. *Media Indonesia* (30 December 1998).

64. These figures are estimates, based on a sample of six provinces that include about one-quarter of all districts in the country, and are current through September 2000. See Michael Malley, "Subnational Politics and Electoral Institutions in Indonesia's Democratic Transition, 1998–2000," presented at the annual meeting of the American Political Science Association, Washington, D.C. (August 30–September 3, 2000).

65. *Kompas* (10 September 1998); *Bali Post* (10 September 1998); *Serambi Indonesia* (13 September 1998); *Suara Pembaruan* (18 September 1998); *Pikiran Rakyat* (29 October 1998).

66. *Suara Pembaruan* (6 July 2002).

CHAPTER EIGHT

Sri Lanka:
A Fragmented State

ERIN K. JENNE

States can be classified using a simple continuum of health. Most liberal democracies, for example, are successful by almost any measure. In contrast, states such as Somalia and Sierra Leone are demonstrably failed in almost every way. Still other states do not fall readily into either category. North Korea and Iraq enjoy a monopoly of legitimate force within their borders, but do not provide their citizens with the basic services expected of modern states. These states are not yet racked by revolution or unrest but remain vulnerable to such pressures, due to their increasing dysfunction; their illness may be likened to a cancer growing from within. Another set of states, including Indonesia and the Philippines, can and *do* provide their citizens with basic social services, but are beset by a chronic pattern of national insurgencies and domestic strife. Such states are effectively fragmented, but continue to provide their citizens with public services while attempting to contain internal insurrections. Their illness can be likened to a cancer advancing from the extremities.

Both weak and fragmented states exhibit *symptoms* of state failure. Weak states remain territorially intact, but fail to provide basic services to their citizens. Conversely, fragmented states provide services to their citizenries, but have lost—or are losing—coercive control over significant portions of their territory. Collapsing these two dimensions into a single measure of state failure risks placing weak states, such as North Korea, in the same category as fragmented states, such as Indonesia. Such problematic classifications should lead one to question the analytic and practical usefulness of *unidimensional* mea-

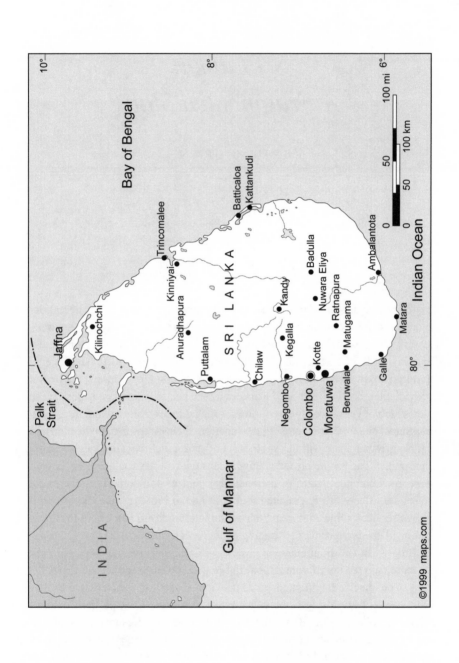

Palk
Strait

Jaffna

Kilinochchi

INDIA

Gulf of Mannar

Bay of Bengal

Trincomalee

Kinniyai

Anuradhapura

S R I   L A N K A

Puttalam

Chilaw

Kegalla

Kandy

Negombo

Colombo

Kotte

Moratuwa

Beruwala

Matugama

Ratnapura

Nuwara Eliya

Badulla

Batticaloa

Kattankudi

Ambalantota

Matara

Galle

Indian Ocean

10°

8°

6°

80°

0   50   100 km
0   50   100 mi

©1999 maps.com

sures of state failure, particularly when these tools are used to prescribe intervention policies.

This chapter introduces a two-dimensional measure of state failure, which is
useful for two reasons. First, it can be used to diagnose tough cases that are
successful on one measure of statehood but failed on the other. Second, a two-
dimensional model yields a spatial map that may be used to trace a state's medical
history, with the understanding that there is no one-to-one correlation between
the territorial and governmental dimensions of state health. This, in turn, may
assist in constructing more effective interventions that are tailored to the needs
and experiences of each ailing state.

The tough case of Sri Lanka will be used to test the usefulness of a two-
dimensional measure of state health. On the basis of Sri Lanka's high government functionality and low territorial control, I label Sri Lanka a fragmented
state. Its government is functional by most measures. The country holds regular, free elections and boasts broad civic freedoms. Although Sri Lanka's
economy has slowed considerably, due to decades of civil war, its annual growth
has averaged 4.6 percent.[1] Its per capita GDP is generally low, but the government provides food subsidies, free health services, free education, and subsidized public transportation to all of its citizens.[2] For these reasons, Sri Lanka
has long been viewed as a harbinger of economic and social progress among
developing countries of the region.

On the negative side of the balance sheet, Sri Lanka has effectively lost the
monopoly of coercive force over significant portions of its territory. For almost
two decades, the government has been embroiled in a military campaign against
the Liberation Tigers of Tamil Eelam (LTTE), a group of insurgents that has
used guerrilla warfare to obtain a separate homeland state (Tamil Eelam) in the
north and east for Sri Lankan Tamils.[3] The Tamil movement was originally
directed against Sri Lanka's discriminatory education and language laws, which
had been enacted by successive post-war governments as a means of appealing
to the majority Sinhalese.[4] By the 1980s, however, these protests had morphed
into a well-organized insurgency led by the militant LTTE. The insurgency has
been variously aided by the Indian central and Tamil Nadu governments, contributions from the expatriate Tamil community, and—more recently—
proceeds from drug- and weapons-trafficking as well as extortion, racketeering, abductions, and bribery in LTTE-held regions.

The introductory chapter in this volume defines failed states as states that
(1) have lost control over their borders; (2) cannot protect their citizens from
organized violence (and sometimes even prey upon their citizens); (3) cannot
prevent the growth of organized crime; (4) have weak or failed institutions;
(5) fail to provide adequate health care, education, or other social services; and

Figure 8-1.   *Typology of State Health*

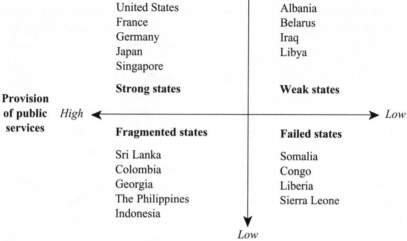

Territorial control

High

Canada	North Korea
United States	Albania
France	Belarus
Germany	Iraq
Japan	Libya
Singapore	

Strong states   **Weak states**

Provision
of public   *High*
services

Fragmented states   **Failed states**

Sri Lanka	Somalia
Colombia	Congo
Georgia	Liberia
The Philippines	Sierra Leone
Indonesia	

Low

(6) have lost legitimacy in the eyes of their populations. As noted earlier, however, states often do not suffer from these symptoms in equal proportion. Some states *do* in fact have stable institutions, provide social services and political goods to their populations, and enjoy legitimacy in the eyes of most of their citizens. Despite these positive indicators, however, they may have lost control over portions of state territory where they also do not enjoy popular legitimacy. "Weakness" does not adequately capture the condition of such states, since their political and economic institutions remain strong and robust. This analytical quandary demonstrates the need for a *two-dimensional* definition of state failure. Thus, the indicators of state failure may be divided into two qualitatively different dimensions of state health: (1) a monopoly of legitimate force over state territory, and (2) the provision of public goods to state citizens (see figure 8-1).[5]

States with high scores on the provision of public services but low scores on the territorial dimension are called *fragmented states*—this is an analytical category additional to the unidimensional classifications of weak, failed, and collapsed. Fragmented states retain the capacity for coping with problems of territorial control due to their sustained government capacity. However, this category is not a stable equilibrium, since a government forced to battle with powerful substate actors is likely to undermine its functionality on the other dimension. If this problem is not dealt with adequately, fragmented states could eventually fall into the category of failed or even collapsed states. Assistance from the international community may therefore become necessary to avert such an outcome.[6]

The Sri Lankan state meets only the territorial component of failure: the government has lost a monopoly of legitimate control over significant portions of territory in the north and the east now controlled by the LTTE. However, the state retains a functioning government and provides reliable public services to most of its citizens. It also boasts a robust economy, as well as free and fair elections. Sri Lanka is therefore a fragmented state. On the basis of this diagnosis, I suggest that the Sri Lankan state should be assisted by (1) facilitating a settlement between the LTTE and the government; and (2), offering inducements for substantive cooperation between the Tamil and Sinhala communities on the ground.

Sri Lanka's fragmentation was initiated by the *exclusion* of one communal group (the Tamil minority) from the economic, social, and political benefits enjoyed by the Sinhala majority. Long-standing anti-Tamil policies galvanized the minority to mobilize around grievances of collective discrimination in the 1970s. Sporadic ethnic protests and riots gradually developed into an organized insurrection once the minority began to receive substantial military aid from India and Tamil Nadu. In the following two decades, sustained warfare and the LTTE's institutional incentives combined to widen and deepen the country's ethnic divide.[7]

Sri Lanka's Path to Fragmentation

The island now known as Sri Lanka has been a multi-ethnic society from its earliest recorded history. The Sinhala claim to have been among the earliest colonizers of the country, settling in the dry north and central regions around 500 B.C.E. Over the next 1,500 years, they developed a great civilization, known for hydraulic engineering and irrigation canals as well as its reverence for, and protection of, Buddhist institutions. It is not known precisely when ethnic Tamils arrived in the country, although they are said to have appeared sometime in the third century B.C.E. Most evidence suggests that the two communities lived together in harmony during the first few centuries of Sinhala-Tamil coexistence.

In the following several hundred years, the Tamils and Sinhalese periodically engaged in struggles over the small island country. Tamil adventurers from southern India briefly usurped the Sinhala throne in the second century B.C.E. In the fifth and sixth centuries C.E., increasingly assertive Hindu empires in southern India fed Sinhala fears of assimilation, thereby rekindling ethnic tensions. Pressure from Tamil invaders eventually forced the Sinhalese to retreat south, where they established the center of their civilization in Kandy. This last stronghold was finally ceded to the British in 1815. Legends of historical Tamil-Sinhala struggles are documented in the *Mahavamsa*, a text that chronicles the rise and fall of successive Buddhist kingdoms, written by Buddhist monks in sixth century C.E. This text has become central to contemporary Sinhala identity.[8]

Beginning in the 1500s, Sri Lanka came under the influence, first, of the Portuguese, and then, of the Dutch. The European powers were intent on establishing trading posts on the island, while converting its inhabitants to Christianity. Sri Lanka's colonial rulers succeeded in substantially weakening the country's Buddhist-Sinhala institutions. In doing so, they politicized religious and ethnic differences. The Portuguese, in particular, were almost fanatical in their attempts to force educational and religious change on Sri Lanka. They discriminated against non-Catholic religions and in favor of Christian converts— those who converted to Catholicism were given privileged positions in maritime trade, for example. The Portuguese also destroyed Buddhist (as well as Hindu) temples and gave the temple lands over to Roman Catholic orders. The Buddhist monks—demoted from their position of religious and political dominance—were forced to flee inland to Kandy.

Compared with that of their colonial predecessors, British influence in Sri Lanka was relatively benign. Having overthrown the Dutch in 1796, British colonizers proceeded to replace Sri Lanka's hierarchical political institutions with more liberal government structures. They usurped the power of local chiefs and assumed control over provincial administration; they also further reduced the privileged status of Buddhism, placing it on equal footing with that of other religions. In the 1820s, in an effort to consolidate control over the island, the British invested heavily in road construction and began to experiment with the cultivation of commercial crops, which later gave rise to Sri Lanka's plantation system. As self-consciously "enlightened" rulers, the British also implemented political reforms; they dramatically extended the franchise under the constitutions of 1931 and 1946, preparing the country for independence in 1948. In these and other ways, the British facilitated the development of a modern Sri Lankan state.

They also succeeded in heightening ethnic tensions in Sri Lanka. By stripping the powerful Sinhala Buddhist clergy of their privileges, for example, the British unwittingly laid the groundwork for a blacklash against Tamil Hindus by disgruntled Buddhist monks.[9] The Buddhist clergy would play a key role in passing anti-Tamil legislation after Sri Lanka achieved independence. Anti-minority sentiment in the post-independence period was also fueled by the fact that the British had favored ethnic Tamils as functionaries in the colonial government. Indeed, under British colonial rule Tamils were over-represented in universities and the civil service and held a disproportionate share of the wealth.[10]

The British agricultural system further exacerbated Sri Lanka's ethnic divide. When plantations first appeared in the 1830s, a peasant farmer enjoyed a much higher social status than did a landless plantation laborer. Moreover, the low wages paid to plantation workers failed to draw Sinhala peasants from their own plots. In order to meet the growing demand for labor, low-wage migrant workers were therefore imported from southern India. An inexhaustible supply of Indian Tamils effectively solved the labor shortage. However, this stopgap measure would prove very costly to Sri Lanka in the long term, due to a growing rivalry between native Sri Lankans and the new arrivals. Tensions intensified in the early twentieth century, when the gradual "pauperization" of peasant farmers drove them into competition with Tamil laborers for jobs on the now-thriving plantations.[11] In spite of these problems, the British administrators continued to import Indian laborers to work their plantations.

The Portuguese, Dutch, and British colonial policies had the overall effect of strengthening ethnic consciousness in Sri Lanka. As a result, ethnicity was one of the most salient political issues in post-independence Sri Lanka. Voters consistently rewarded politicians who played on ethnic chauvinism.

The Post-Independence Era

In the immediate post-independence period, Sri Lanka (then Ceylon) was hailed as a rising star in Asia. It had emerged relatively unscathed from World War II—despite attacks by the Japanese—and had been a functioning democracy since the constitutional reforms of 1931. Sri Lanka boasted an educated workforce and a high rate of literacy—compared to other states in the region— as well as an internationally competitive export economy based on tea, rubber, coconuts, and other commercial crops. Moreover, Sri Lanka had undergone a peaceful transition to self-rule and was widely considered a model of stability for the region.[12] So what went wrong? Why, despite initially favorable indicators, did Sri Lanka become embroiled in a violent civil war?

Its political institutions—together with ethnic divisions inherited from the colonial period—led to Sri Lanka's ultimate fragmentation. Under the Westminster parliamentary model, the party that wins the most votes in national elections forms the government. Since the majority of Sri Lanka's population is ethnic Sinhalese, no political party could hope to rule without the support of this crucial constituency.

By the time of independence in 1948, Sri Lanka's political elites had already learned the power of ethnic politics. Sinhala-Tamil competition over jobs had intensified greatly during the Depression of the 1930s. In response to this conflict, the (Sinhala-dominated) trade unions promulgated a "Ceylonization" principle, which held that Sinhala workers should be given preference in hiring practices. This nationalist stance greatly increased the popularity of Marxist parties. Not to be outdone, the nation's new leaders pushed through a slate of anti-Indian legislation as a means of "demolishing a potentially powerful prop of left-wing groups."[13]

In an effort to retain its popularity while fending off challengers, the new Sri Lankan government greatly undermined the goal of ethnic integration set forth in the country's constitution. Immediately following independence, the United National Party (UNP) government began to push a nationalist agenda through parliament. The Ceylon Citizenship Act of 1948, the India-Pakistan Residents Act of 1949, and the Ceylon Parliamentary Elections Act of 1949 had the combined effect of depriving recent Indian immigrants of their political rights.[14] The new government had thus "ethnically outbid" leftist politicians who were pedaling anti-immigration policies to dislocated Sinhala laborers and peasants. The new legislation effectively rendered plantation Tamils stateless. As a consequence of these laws, approximately half of the immigrant population was forcibly repatriated to southern India by the early 1970s.

Sri Lanka's experience proves the old adage that democratically elected leaders routinely sacrifice long-term gains for short-term benefits (i.e., reelection). To retain its popularity in the post-independence period, the UNP government doled out generous welfare payments to Sinhala peasants at the expense of much-needed investment in the manufacturing sector. This policy perpetuated inefficient subsistence farming, drained government coffers, and encouraged dependency among Sri Lankan citizens. Future governments would find it difficult to correct these inefficiencies, as voters routinely punished efforts to reduce welfare payments in the interest of long-term development.

Such generous benefits could not be sustained. By the 1950s, the state treasury was sorely strained, and efforts to rein in spending provoked a wave of civil disobedience.[15] In the context of a sluggish economy and increased competition over jobs, voters became increasingly dissatisfied with the government. In order to bolster popular support, political elites turned to ethnicity as a means of garnering the votes of the crucial Sinhala constituency. The government targeted the indigenous Tamil minority.

The Sri Lanka Freedom Party (SLFP) came to power in 1956 on a platform of Buddhist nationalism, vowing to make Sinhala the sole official language of Sri Lanka. Prime Minister Solomon West Ridgeway D. Bandaranaike fulfilled this promise by introducing the Official Language Act of 1956, which made Sinhala the official language of Sri Lanka and discriminated against the use of English and Tamil in the public sphere. After Bandaranaike was assassinated in 1959, his wife, Sirimavo, assumed power and continued his anti-Tamil policies. Slowly, these policies began to produce their desired effect. From 1956 to 1970, government employment of ethnic Tamils dropped from 40 to 1 percent in the armed forces, from 30 to 5 percent in the administrative service, and from 50 to 5 percent in the clerical service.[16] Anti-Tamil discrimination was then extended to the educational sphere. In 1972, the populist United Front (UF) successfully introduced legislation to restrict the number of Tamils in higher education. This law drastically reduced Tamil enrollment in Sri Lanka's traditional universities, and new, generally inferior, institutions were established in the north for minority students. Wealthy Tamil families responded to these pressures by sending their children to universities abroad. Together, these laws had the effect of marginalizing the Tamil minority in Sri Lankan society.

Anti-Tamil sentiment in the Sinhala majority thus combined with Sri Lanka's majoritarian institutions to create incentives for successive governments to champion discriminatory policies. These policies proved reliable vote-getters among the Sinhalese, whose support was necessary for gaining and maintaining political power. As a consequence, the Sri Lankan state eventually lost its multiethnic character. By the early 1970s, the government was catering solely to Sinhala interests, at the expense of minority protection. The armed forces and civil service were completely in the hands of ethnic Sinhalese. Meanwhile, ethnic Tamils endured effective political and social exclusion, with Tamil quotas in university enrollment, and Buddhism and Sinhala privileged over minority religion and language in public life.

In response to signs of growing ethnic divisiveness, the Sri Lankan government began to dismantle some of this anti-minority legislation in the late 1970s. These actions came too late.[17] Long dissatisfied with their marginalized position in Sri Lankan society, ethnic Tamils had begun to demand autonomy more loudly and more violently. At the same time, Tamil militants were gradually amassing the resources to challenge the Sri Lankan state.[18] They attacked in 1983, and the civil war began.

External Factors

One factor contributing to Sri Lanka's fragmentation is a sizable Tamil population just twenty-nine miles from Sri Lanka's coastline. The Sinhala "minority complex" is largely driven by the close proximity of the South Indian state of Tamil Nadu—home to 60 million Tamils. The Sinhalese have long feared an invasion of Indian Tamils, which could render the Sinhalese an ethnic minority in Sri Lanka and diminish their political and economic advantages. From the ancient period chronicled by the *Mahavamsa* to the present day, the Tamil threat from the north has featured prominently in Sinhala history. This complex only intensified when the British withdrew their forces in the 1940s, leaving the Sinhalese in a position of vulnerability vis-à-vis the Tamils in India and their ethnic brethren in the north of Sri Lanka. Indeed, Tamil Nadu has a long history of political and military involvement in Sri Lankan politics. Seen in this light, the Sinhala perception of a Tamil threat becomes far more explicable.

This threat is still very real. India and Tamil Nadu have played key roles in the development of the contemporary Tamil insurgency. For years, Tamil rebels obtained refuge in Tamil Nadu when they were weak or when government forces were in pursuit. In the 1970s and 1980s, Tamil Nadu provided financial assistance to the LTTE, as well as arms, safe homes, and training camps for Tiger insurgents.[19] These activities received the tacit approval of the Indian government, which disapproved of Sri Lanka's westward tilt and feared antagonizing Tamil Nadu's nationalist leaders. Indeed, it was India's intelligence service (RAW) that trained the Tigers in their infancy, ensuring their safe haven and transit. India also refused Sri Lanka's repeated requests for a joint patrol of the Palk Strait to halt LTTE arms smuggling. With cross-border assistance, the LTTE thus developed a vast weapons procurement network that provided it with regular shipments of landmines, grenades, and mortars, and other conventional arms. In the 1990s, the Tamil Tigers had made the transition from a rag-tag group of insurgents to a formidable fighting force. By 1995, they boasted a small air force, mobile radar, anti-aircraft missiles, and a large supply of volunteers to carry out suicide missions against civilian and military targets in Sri Lanka.[20] The LTTE even acquired a fleet of vessels to carry out smuggling operations, making it the only insurgency group in the world with its own navy.[21]

The Indian government withdrew its support for the Tiger movement following the Indo–Sri Lankan Peace Accord in 1987. Moreover, popular support for the Tiger cause in India—even in Tamil Nadu—dried up in the wake of the Tigers' assassination of Indian Prime Minister Rajiv Gandhi in 1991. The LTTE therefore had to cast a wider net. In early 1996, it was estimated that 80 to 90 percent of LTTE resources came from farther abroad.[22] A well-connected and affluent community of expatriate Sri Lankan Tamils helped to bankroll LTTE operations; the organization also earned remittances from gasoline stations, restaurants, and shops that it owned and operated around the world. By the late 1990s, the LTTE received the bulk of its revenue from investing, freight shipping, human trafficking, munitions smuggling, money laundering, extortion, and (probably) drug running—thought to be the most profitable of its operations. As of 1997, the LTTE operated a fleet of at least ten freighters to support these activities. All of these ships were equipped with the latest radar and Immarsat communication technology and were registered in Panama, Honduras, or Liberia, all of which have notoriously lenient open registries.[23] Having developed a truly global network of support, the small guerrilla movement has actually *grown* in strength since the beginning of the war.

In the absence of external patronage, the Tamils could not have marshaled the resources to challenge the state so effectively, nor would the Tamil-Sinhala divide have been so politicized in the first place. If the British colonial government had not played favorites, anti-Tamil sentiment might not have been so salient at the time of Sri Lanka's independence. Finally, if the new democracy had been federalist rather than majoritarian, the Tamil minority might have been coopted into the state rather than systematically excluded.[24] These factors have combined to widen and deepen state fragmentation.[25]

Institutionalizing the Divide

Sri Lanka's ethnic divide will not be easily mended, even if the two sides manage to conclude a peace settlement. This is because the war economy in the north and east creates strong incentives for LTTE militants to perpetuate the two-decade-long conflict.[26] For years, the Tigers received generous remittances from wealthy expatriates to continue their military operations. Moreover, taxes on the movement of goods and services, trafficking, extortion, racketeering, and theft have become integral parts of the economy in LTTE-dominated regions and continue to serve as important sources of income for the Tigers. The influx of humanitarian aid has only exacerbated the problem, creating "economies of dependency" for displaced people and lining the pockets of corrupt officials.

Predictably, the LTTE resisted meaningful dialogue with the government for over a decade. During the 1990s, LTTE leader Velupillai Prabhakaran repeatedly reneged on offers to negotiate with the government, often by demanding unrealistic preconditions for entering into talks. Nor could the government conclude a peace settlement with more tractable Tamil leaders: the Tigers consistently "spoiled" talks from which they were excluded, using terror and intimidation to prevent moderate Tamil organizations from concluding pacts with the government. In 1995, for example, the Tigers assassinated the leader of rival People's Liberation Organization of Tamil Eelam (PLOTE) after he had agreed to disarm and negotiate peacefully with the government.[27]

Another factor that mitigates against peace is the fact that an entire generation of young people has been raised in a climate of violence and corruption.
These youngsters lack the education, skills, and mentality to integrate into the
normal labor force.[28] To make matters worse, the Tigers have made prodigious
use of child soldiers to carry out their missions, which include suicide bombings. In 1998, the government reported capturing 29 LTTE fighters on the battlefield—of these, fully 25 were below the age of 18 and at least one was only 13
years old.[29] Tiger recruitment of children has continued apace, even since the
February 2002 cease-fire. Reports from Batticaloa District indicate that the LTTE
has taken advantage of the cease-fire to move about the district, visiting schools
and families to forcibly conscript young boys and girls; indeed, many families
have considered moving out of the area to protect their children.[30] The LTTE
will not be able to maintain its strategic strength—which entails retaining its
existing cadres while recruiting new ones—without continuously demonstrating their militant commitment to Tamil Eelam. These institutional constraints
lower the odds of establishing a permanent peace.[31]

The ethnic divide is only likely to intensify if LTTE control over these regions is institutionalized under a "confederal" arrangement, which has been
proposed as a means of preserving the Sri Lankan state. Since the LTTE signed
the Memorandum of Understanding with the government in 2002, the army,
police and Special Task Force units in eastern Sri Lanka have largely confined
themselves to their camps. The LTTE has made full use of this retrenchment by
smuggling in weapons and ammunition along the southeastern coast of the island, bypassing the army blockade off the Mullaitivu Coast entirely; the Tigers
have assigned twenty-four-hour surveillance of all government camps in the
east in order to track any army movements.[32] The LTTE has also intensified its
extortion efforts throughout the east, reportedly in sums of up to $1,000; teach-
ers and government officials, meanwhile, have been asked to pay 12 percent of
their salary, as opposed to 5 percent previously. There has also been an increase in the numbers of abductions for ransom.[33] In the event that an LTTE-
dominated government is established for the region, there is little doubt that
it would be a military autocracy.[34] Moreover, despite suggestions that the
LTTE has abandoned its goal of a separate Tamil state in favor of "internal self-
determination," analysts familiar with LTTE politics posit that Tiger leaders
view an autonomous government in Tamil regions as a halfway house on the
road toward full Tamil independence.[35]

The above factors have interacted to deepen and politicize Sri Lanka's ethnic divide. It should be clear that averting state failure in Sri Lanka will neces-
sitate reforming the country's unitary political system to include a minority

voice. In addition, it will be necessary to resolve Sri Lanka's regional security dilemma, which continuously fuels the Tamil-Sinhala conflict. Last but not least, resolution of ethnic tensions in Sri Lanka will require addressing the LTTE's institutional incentives to continue hostilities, as well as extortion, theft, bribery, and weapons-smuggling operations. Until this latter issue is addressed in a substantive manner, no amount of mediation—either direct or indirect—can heal Sri Lanka's divide.

Averting State Failure in Sri Lanka

Following several failed attempts to negotiate with the LTTE in the mid-1990s, President Chandrika Kumaratunga's government concluded that the best means of resolving the crisis was to undercut LTTE strength and legitimacy. With this in mind, the administration implemented a two-pronged strategy. The government first introduced devolution legislation in parliament to appeal to Tamil interests, and thereby undermine popular support for the LTTE. At the same time, the government escalated its military campaign against the Tigers in an effort to diminish the LTTE's strategic leverage. This dual-track policy was thought to be the best means of forcing the Tigers to the bargaining table.

This plan, unfortunately, was built on faulty premises. To begin with, it was questionable whether the government could ever bring the LTTE to heel. In 1997, the government launched a major military campaign against the Tigers (Operation Jayasikuru, or "Victory Assured") aimed at opening a land route to the Jaffna Peninsula, the Tigers' stronghold. Set for completion in six months, the mission was cancelled after eighteen months, due to heavy government losses. This debacle demonstrated the unlikelihood of government victory on the battlefield.[36] Military victory remained hard to attain for three main reasons: (1) troop morale in the armed forces was very low, leading to serious recruitment and desertion problems; (2) the army was constrained in battle by civilian leaders who were answerable for their actions in democratic elections, whereas the LTTE had no such constraints and could fight a dirtier war; and (3), the army's conventional military tactics were ill suited for guerrilla warfare, giving the Tigers a significant strategic advantage. Unsurprisingly, the 1997 operation damaged the government side far more than it did the LTTE.

The other prong in President Kumaratunga's strategy—unilateral devolution—suffered from the same flaws as the more recent proposal for ethnic confederation. Problematically, both plans would transfer power to the provinces *without the condition of disarmament*; this would legitimize LTTE control over political institutions in the north and east without placing conditions on LTTE stewardship. Unilateral devolution would thus give the Tigers the best of both worlds by institutionalizing the LTTE dominance in Tamil areas while allowing the Tigers to remain mobilized militarily. This result, in turn, would enhance rather than diminish the LTTE and create the conditions for establishing a separate Tamil state—developments that would make the Tigers even *less* amenable to peaceful co-existence within a multi-ethnic state.

Ethnic partition would take the devolution solution one step further, by creating new states or state-like entities from the territory of an existing state.[37] Due to the controversial nature of this approach, it is generally considered a remedy of last resort. Proponents of ethnic partition argue that the only realistic solution to entrenched civil conflict is to separate the warring groups into two or more new states, by means of population transfers if necessary. After years of relentless blood-letting between the Tigers and the armed forces, Sri Lanka's voters were keen in 2001 to try a more radical approach. The elections accordingly brought a new government to power on a promise of peace. Pursuant to a hoped-for peace agreement between the government and the LTTE, Prime Minister Ranil Wickremesinghe and the Tigers agreed to a permanent ceasefire in 2002 under a Norwegian-brokered Memorandum of Understanding. The deal, widely viewed as a breakthrough, calls for negotiating a *de facto* internal state partition.

The biggest problem with this plan is that it would do nothing to resolve the regional ethnic security dilemma that gave rise to the Tamil-Sinhala conflict in the first place. It merely raises the stakes of war by transforming an internal dispute into a quasi-interstate conflict. Second, partition would produce incentives to "cleanse" ethnically the regions through population expulsions and the prevention of refugee return.[38] It would also create a security dilemma for new subminorities, who, fearing reprisals, may either flee the region or strike preemptively, generating further conflict at the local level. Finally, confederal arrangements are inherently unstable, either resulting in full partition or reverting back to a unitary state. A full partition, moreover, is probably infeasible in Sri Lanka, since the Sinhala majority is fiercely opposed to a divided Sri Lankan state, which would only feed the Sinhala minority complex.

Another means of achieving real peace in Sri Lanka would be to interdict arms shipments to the LTTE. Some have argued that today's civil conflicts are both worsened and perpetuated by the post–Cold War boom in light arms trade. Since the end of the Cold War, cash-strapped former Soviet republics and other former East bloc countries have attempted to sell off their arms stockpiles through covert deliveries to guerrilla organizations and other nonstate actors. According to this thesis, the increased availability of light arms permits paramilitaries to arm themselves with much greater ease, thus intensifying security dilemmas in divided or weak states and accelerating state failure. Divided states therefore cannot be strengthened without better regulation of international arms flows.

There are a few problems with this argument. First, light arms were available even before the end of the war. During the Cold War, the U.S.S.R., the United States, and their respective allies armed and funded numerous governments and other organizations to fight their proxy wars all around the world. Indeed, the conflicts in many of today's failed and failing states—including Angola, Sierra Leone, Colombia, Somalia, the Sudan, as well as fragmented Sri Lanka—began well *before* the end of the Cold War; their wars were prosecuted with arms obtained through a variety of legal and illegal channels. In some cases, weapons sold to belligerents in one war were later resold to another organization for use in a different war. Most famously, the United States sold weapons to Iraq during the 1980s that were later turned against the United States during the Gulf War. The Soviet arms pipeline to Afghanistan in the 1980s was later diverted to feed conflicts in South and Central Asia, and many of the leftover weapons from the Afghan War ultimately ended up in Pakistani arms bazaars. Given the singular failure to control the arms trade in a tight bipolar system, it is hard to imagine how international arms control may be better achieved in a loose unipolar world, particularly one in which the world's only great power has focused most of its attention on its own narrowly defined foreign policy goals.

Indeed, a supply-side remedy to civil war is likely to suffer from the same problems as the United States' ineffectual "war on drugs," where the destruction of coca fields in Colombia merely led to *increased* production of coca in other countries, such as Peru and Bolivia. Critics of the war on drugs call this the "balloon effect," where the contraction of drug production in one area merely produces an equivalent bulge of production in another, without affecting the overall supply. In the same way, destruction of one weapons procurement network is likely to give rise to another to take its place. This will occur so long as the *demand* for weapons is still there. For these reasons, any effective remedy to Sri Lanka's fragmentation must adopt a demand-side approach in order to treat the *causes* of conflict rather than its symptoms.

External Solutions

At its best, external intervention is an effective remedy for state fragmentation. The problem is that the "correct" form is often difficult to achieve. To be effective, outside assistance must be (1) credible, (2) powerful, and (3) impartial. If the third party is weak or has little vested interest in resolving the state's divisions, its intervention will carry little weight in the calculations of the war-

ring parties. Conversely, if the third party is viewed as strong and has sufficiently vested interest in the conflict to be a credible player, it is unlikely to be
impartial. In this case, intervention may actually intensify an internal security
dilemma, thus worsening the conflict. Unhappily, Sri Lanka has been the recipient of both types of intervention.

India's intervention in 1987 was an example of the last type. The Indian
government was both powerful and highly motivated to retain its hegemonic
position in South Asia. Unfortunately, India was incapable of brokering a solution to Sri Lanka's conflict in an impartial manner. As part of an agreement
between the Indian and Sri Lankan governments, India sent troops to Sri Lanka
in order to restore peace and disarm the rebels. Although the Tamils were originally welcoming of the Indian Peace Keeping Force (IPKF), ethnic Tamil support turned to opposition once the IPKF began to attack the LTTE, using counter-
terrorist tactics to recapture the Jaffna Peninsula. India's peacekeeping effort
thus served to radicalize the Tamil community, which rallied around the LTTE
against both the Indian and Sri Lankan forces. To complicate matters further,
the growing size of the occupying force began to fuel anti-Indian sentiment
among ethnic Sinhalese, leading the Sri Lankan government to funnel aid co-
vertly to the Tamil rebels in a bid to dislodge the IPKF from the country. After
a number of military embarrassments, India finally withdrew its troops in 1990.[39]

Although intended to resolve the conflict, India's intervention thus exacerbated Sri Lanka's ethnic divide. This case demonstrates that when a third party
is strong and its threats credible, its intervention is unlikely to be perceived as
impartial by both sides of the conflict. The IPKF's efforts to rout the guerrilla
movement inadvertently radicalized the Tamil community, thereby strengthening the Tigers' power base. The Sinhalese, meanwhile, viewed the IPKF as a
foreign agent for Tamil separatism, which further provoked Sinhala nationalism. As with the U.S. intervention in Vietnam, direct military intervention in
Sri Lanka intensified recriminations and galvanized support for hard-line nationalists on both sides, adding fuel to the flames.

The United Nations has been seen as another logical candidate for negotiating and enforcing peace in Sri Lanka. In contrast to India, the UN is not invested in the outcome of the conflict. Hence, a UN peacekeeping mission would
be less likely to encounter strong resistance from either side; its decisions are
also more likely to be accepted as just arbitration of Tamil-Sinhala differences.
In practice, however, the UN tends to favor the government side in civil conflicts.[40] If the UN were to follow such a policy in Sri Lanka, it would surely lose
the support of the Tamil minority on the ground. Further, UN involvement
would almost certainly be opposed by Sinhala nationalists, for whom an externally imposed peacekeeping force represents an unacceptable violation of Sri
Lankan sovereignty. A second problem is that the UN, unlike India, is a collec-

tive of sovereign states. Since member states can withdraw from UN operations at any time, its commitments are inherently unstable. As a consequence, a UN involvement may lack the credibility necessary for resolving Sri Lanka's ethnic security dilemma, a central cause of the conflict.

The Norwegian negotiators have suffered many of the same disadvantages. Until 2002, Norway's dogged efforts to broker a peace deal in Sri Lanka had borne little fruit. In 1999, the government and the LTTE invited Norwegian negotiators to mediate the conflict, which they began to do in secret. For three years, the Norwegians failed to secure a cease-fire between the LTTE and government representatives.[41] In 2002, however, Norway finally triumphed. Its Memorandum of Understanding led to a permanent cease-fire and laid the basis for subsequent peace talks. However, it is unclear how much of the credit for this victory rightfully belongs to the Norwegian mediators. Prime Minister Wickremesinghe came to power on a campaign promise of peace; moreover, the LTTE and Wickremesinghe's UNP are believed to have agreed to a cease-fire in secret before the elections. If that is true, Norway's involvement *in and of itself* mattered little in bringing the two parties to the bargaining table. Norway's failure to induce a mediated solution up to this point is probably a function of the fact that it had been unable to impose significant costs on either side for declining to negotiate. Truly efficacious mediators must be able to sanction parties that negotiate in bad faith. If the mediator is able to offer important inducements for negotiating in good faith, the effectiveness of intervention will increase.[42]

The discussion above illustrates the Catch 22 of external solutions to violent civil conflict. To be successful, outside mediation must be backed by a significant and credible threat to intervene, either politically or economically. An effective intervener is therefore strong and has a vested interest in resolving the conflict. In the case of Sri Lanka, India fits the bill nicely. However, as evidenced by the disastrous IPKF intervention, third parties sufficiently invested in resolving a conflict are also likely to be seen as partial by one or both sides. This could undermine the mediator's credibility as a disinterested arbiter, a perception that may serve to exacerbate the conflict. In other words, truly disinterested third party mediators are unlikely to be sufficiently invested to be effective.

The Civic Solution

A more creative remedy involves developing civic associations on the substate level. Posner argues that voluntary civic organizations yield "social capital," a resource vital to the functioning of state institutions.[43] It follows that the more people voluntarily associate with one another—in the form of political organizations, sports clubs, labor unions, or religious groups—the more they value cooperating with an ever-widening group of people. Civic institutions thus serve as incubators for social norms of trust and reciprocity. These norms increase the value of cooperation over defection and promote the creation of governments that provide public goods such as law enforcement, mass education, and national defense. Posner posits that in the case of state failure, civic associations can assist in reconstructing the state and, in extreme cases, can even substitute for the state.

Posner himself notes, however, that this remedy cannot be used to resolve *violent* state breakdown or fragmentation, as in the case of Sri Lanka. He states that where state failure is associated with violent civil war, the necessary preconditions for developing trust and reciprocity in society are absent. However, if it turns out that Sri Lanka's conflict cannot be resolved through elite channels, a civic approach may be worth exploring. Perhaps the construction of a non-ethnic Sri Lankan identity or the facilitation of inter-ethnic cooperation at the grassroots level may help resolve Sri Lanka's divisiveness. De Silva, for example, argues that educational reform may help rebuild the Sri Lankan state. He posits that substantive concessions to the Tamil minority in the realm of education may serve as a crucial trust-building measure on the part of the Sinhalese. At the same time, multi-cultural education programs may be used to promote ethnic tolerance in Sri Lankan society.[44] The hope is that ethnic accommodation on the mass level will eventually push Tamil and Sinhala leaders to conclude a peace deal in accordance with the wishes of their respective ethnic constituencies.

Unfortunately, civic remedies alone will not mend the Sri Lankan state. The Tigers have proved unwilling to abandon secessionism in return for marginal increases in minority enrollment at the university level. Nor will a public campaign of multi-culturalism reverse the damage wrought by decades of minority discrimination and twenty years of war. However, the underlying logic of this approach is sound. Meaningful dialogue and cooperation between the Tamil and Sinhala communities *is* crucial to the consolidation of a multi-ethnic Sri Lanka. However, in order to heal the Sri Lankan state, it will first be necessary to address Sri Lanka's ethnic security dilemma, LTTE incentives to continue the conflict, and electoral incentives to discriminate against Tamils.

A Composite Solution

Genuinely failed and collapsed states such as Sierra Leone and Somalia enjoy little control over the territory within their borders; this creates significant negative externalities for their neighbors. Such states also lack a functional government that may be assisted in resolving the problem of state breakdown. Direct external intervention may therefore be required to resuscitate failed states. Fragmented states, on the other hand, still possess a functional government that may be assisted in reasserting control over state territory. Indirect assistance may accomplish this task better than direct intervention, which—as seen from the Indian intervention—may paradoxically actually fan the flames of communal strife and exacerbate state instability.

This chapter argues that Sri Lanka's fragmentation is a function of the following variables: a regional security dilemma posed by an external Tamil homeland, a majoritarian political system that reifies Sri Lanka's ethnic divide, and incentives for the LTTE to continue the separatist conflict. These factors interact to perpetuate state fragmentation. External assistance to Tamil guerrillas feeds Sinhala fears of subjugation, which in turn strengthens the position of Sinhala nationalists in parliament. Meanwhile, expatriate assistance strengthens the Tigers' bargaining hand against the government, encouraging the LTTE to adopt an even more intransigent stance toward the Sri Lankan state.

Institutional incentives for the LTTE to continue the hostilities pose the third major obstacle to resolving Sri Lanka's divisions. Although the Tigers are not representative of the Tamil community as a whole, no genuine peace can be negotiated without support from the LTTE. Moderate Tamil representatives cannot make overtures toward the government without being targeted by the Tigers, who actively "spoil" all such negotiations.[45] Clearly, LTTE incentives to perpetuate the conflict must be addressed before any peace settlement can be reached.

"In-group policing" may be one way to achieve this goal.[46] That is, ethnic Tamils could be recruited into the military and law enforcement agencies, particularly in the northern and eastern administrative provinces. It should be noted in this context that the Sri Lankan government has already tried to increase minority enrollment in the armed forces. In May 1999, the army launched a massive recruitment of ethnic Tamils, but the response was disappointing, due to LTTE intimidation of ordinary Tamils. If the government hopes to overcome this obstacle, it must be prepared to guarantee protection to minority recruits *as well as* their families. Moreover, the Sri Lankan army might be more successful in its recruitment efforts if Tamil recruits could be guaranteed positions in future political institutions of the north and east. Such offers could be guaranteed by outside organizations—the United Nations or the South Asian Forum—which could monitor and enforce these agreements by imposing economic sanctions on the government and/or local authorities if they reneged on their promises. Ultimately, these recruits could serve as the foundation for in-group policing of Tamil regions in a reconstituted Sri Lankan state.

In-group policing could help resolve Sri Lanka's fragmentation in two ways. First, government cooptation of ethnic Tamils may serve to de-ethnicize the conflict, making it appear more resolvable to both sides. Second, offering Tamils a stake in a reconstituted state could provide the basis for integrating Tamil militants into future political structures of Tamil regions, providing incentives for the LTTE to end the insurgency without losing face. This result, in turn, would diminish the Tamil "threat" in the eyes of the Sinhalese, since coopted Tamils would be disinclined to ally with their co-ethnics across the Palk Strait against a government in which they now had a stake. Indeed, cooptation is a tried and true method of turning real or perceived enemies into staunch allies. This solution could be supplemented by a joint Indo–Sri Lankan naval block- ade of Sri Lanka's northeastern coastline. An effective naval blockade would temper Tiger militancy by restricting access to arms and other supplies from abroad. It would undermine the LTTE's bargaining leverage vis-à-vis the state, creating incentives for the Tigers to cut a deal with the government before their bargaining power was diminished further.

The final impediment to resolving Sri Lanka's fragmentation is its majoritarian political system, which has excluded the Tamil minority from po- litical power. So long as the state's political structures remain unaltered, the Tamil community is unlikely to submit itself to a state in which Tamils and their interests are systematically marginalized. Moreover, it is doubtful that the rebels would agree to a settlement in the absence of credible guarantees of minority protection, particularly given the harsh reprisals they are likely to face in the absence of such guarantees. One solution would be to alter the Sri Lankan constitution so that minority support is *required* to govern. This may be accom- plished through political arrangements that institutionalize inter-communal power-sharing. For example, voters could be allowed to rank-order political parties in order of preference; majority parties would then be required to obtain a prescribed minimum level of support from the Tamil minority in order to form a government.

Although consociational structures are prone to inefficiencies related to func- tional redundancy (see, for example, Belgium and Switzerland), while others fail to guarantee inter-ethnic cooperation (consider the breakdown of consocia- tional structures in Lebanon), other power-sharing arrangements are less prob- lematic. These include a minority veto over language or education laws and the requirement that ethnic Tamils be represented in the governing coalition as the heads of key ministries. Outside organizations could promote inter-ethnic co- operation on the ground by making international assistance conditional upon the formation and maintenance of truly multi-ethnic governing coalitions. For example, the United Nations, ASEAN, or the World Bank could offer financial aid to multi-ethnic political and civic associations as a means of encouraging inter-ethnic cooperation at the grassroots level. Such aid could serve as downpayments on the reconstruction and consolidation of a truly multi-ethnic Sri Lankan state. In sum, carrots may overall be more effective than sticks in inducing stable inter-ethnic cooperation in Sri Lanka.

The above proposals—in-group policing for Tamil regions, cooptation of ethnic Tamils into state institutions, reforming Sri Lanka's majoritarian political structures, and providing international aid to Sinhala-Tamil associations—are all based on the principle of assisting the governments of fragmented states in bridging their own divides. Here, the challenge lies in helping governments to reassert territorial control in a way that coopts opponents of this process and promotes inter-communal harmony on the ground. This goal is best accomplished through indirect rather than direct intervention, which should only be undertaken in cases of genuine state failure.

Conclusion

This chapter argues that resolving Sri Lanka's fragmentation is best accomplished *indirectly,* by assisting the government to reassert control over its borders while simultaneously promoting inter-ethnic cooperation on the ground. To be effective, this plan must address the specific causes of Sri Lanka's persistent divisiveness: (1) the regional ethnic security dilemma, (2) Sri Lanka's majoritarian political system, and (3) LTTE incentives to continue the armed conflict or (if a settlement is reached) to engage in racketeering, bribery, abductions, smuggling, extortion, and the intimidation of political opponents in the north and east. I argue that coopting ethnic Tamils into state institutions in Tamil regions may help combat the first and third problems. A massive Indo–Sri Lankan naval blockade of the northeastern coastline would put a chokehold on LTTE revenue derived from smuggling operations and other organized crime, while restricting the Tigers' ability to procure illegal arms. Doing so would undercut the LTTE's military leverage against the government, creating greater incentives for the Tigers to negotiate a peace settlement in order to lock in diminishing gains. Third, the cooptation of Tamil militants into the future political institutions of the north would give the rebels a stake in the system, creating disincentives for them to ally with their ethnic brethren in India against the Sri Lankan government. Such policies may go a considerable distance toward eliminating the ethnic security dilemma in Sri Lanka. Finally, any peace agreement between the LTTE and the government should be conditional upon the observance of civic freedoms and minority rights in Tamil regions. This mandate can be enforced by establishing an international monitoring group that generates periodic reports on the rights and freedoms enjoyed by people living in these areas.

Consolidation of a multi-ethnic Sri Lankan state will require meaningful and lasting inter-ethnic power-sharing. Inter-ethnic cooperation on the ground can help construct a truly civic state from the bottom up. To this end, inducements for Tamil-Sinhala cooperation by outside actors may be combined with institutional guarantees of Tamil protection, such as a minority veto in parliament or a constitutional amendment requiring Tamil representation in the governing coalition and in key ministries. International organizations can facilitate this process by offering financial aid to multi-ethnic political and civic organizations at every level of government. These proposals are consistent with the principle of indirect assistance, which is the best means of healing deeply divided states. It should be clear that Sri Lanka's fragmentation cannot be resolved without substantial Tamil cooptation into state institutions. To delay in this process risks undermining the government's ability to function, which, in turn, risks Sri Lanka's slippage into the category of failed states.

This analysis yields general lessons for conflict mediation. Truly failed or failing states often call for direct intervention as a means of controlling the negative externalities of low territorial control in the absence of effective governing institutions. As the Sri Lankan case demonstrates, however, direct military intervention is usually a poor response to the problem of divided states. This is because armed interveners are unlikely to be perceived as impartial by the warring parties. As a consequence, overt intervention in divided states may actually exacerbate the inter-group security dilemma, fanning the flames of sectarian conflict. Due to the strength of their political institutions and an often highly charged ethnic divide, fragmented states instead call for more indirect forms of intervention.

Specifically, such policies should aim to enhance the value of ethnic coalitions over that of ethnic strife. International organizations and bodies such as the Council of Europe, the European Union, the United Nations, the World Bank, and the International Monetary Fund are well positioned to alter the decision calculus of warring parties by making loans, grants, and membership in valued international organizations contingent upon the observance of sustained inter-ethnic cooperation. By increasing the value of the peace dividend and educating the people on the ground concerning the opportunity costs of foregoing these benefits, international organizations may go a considerable distance toward making the leadership on both sides of the divide truly accountable to the people that they claim to represent.

Notes

1. Donald R. Snodgrass, *Ceylon: An Export Economy in Transition* (Homewood, Ill., 1966); Henry J. Bruton, Gamini Abeysekera, Nimal Sanderate, and Zainal Aznam Yusof, *Sri Lanka and Malaysia: The Political Economy of Poverty, Equity, and Growth* (New York, 1992); World Bank, *World Development Indicators* (Washington, D.C., 1998), as cited in Donald R. Snodgrass, "Economic Development of Sri Lanka," in Robert I. Rotberg (ed.), *Creating Peace in Sri Lanka: Civil War and Reconciliation* (Washington, D.C., 1999), 90.

2. V. Nithiyanandam, "Ethnic Politics and Third World Development: Some Lessons from Sri Lanka's Experience," *Third World Quarterly*, I (April 2000), 2, fn. 2.

3. The Sri Lankan Tamils make up approximately 13 percent of Sri Lanka's population.

4. Although there are almost no visible markers between the two communities, they speak different languages and the Sinhalese are Buddhist, whereas the Tamils are primarily Hindu (some are Muslim).

5. *Provision of public services* may be indexed and plotted on a single dimension. This index may include the delivery of health services throughout the state, the provision of basic education to the entire citizenry, basic nourishment of the poor, regular payments to the police and armed forces, adequate law enforcement; and the provision of public infrastructure, including public sanitation, electricity, heat, and water, as well as transportation and communication services. The dimension of *territorial control*, drawn from Max Weber's classic definition of the state, may be expressed as a continuum that indexes the capacity to limit organized violence upon state territory, the ability to defend state borders, control of movement of people and goods across state borders, the ability to collect taxes throughout the state, and basic security for all citizens across state territory. See Max Weber, *From Max Weber: Essays in Sociology,* H. H. Guth and C. W. Mills (eds.) (London, 1970), 78. By combining the two measures of statehood, we obtain four ideal types of state health, as pictured in figure 8-1.

6. The war, spanning almost two decades, represents a substantial drain on state resources. Over the course of the nineteen-year conflict, more than 60,000 people have been killed and over 800,000 displaced; U.S. Department of State, *Sri Lanka Country Report on Human Rights Practices for 1998,* Bureau of Democracy, Human Rights, and Labor (26 February 1999). Tens of thousands of citizens, otherwise employed in the normal economy, have been drafted into the army, navy, air force, and police in an effort to end the insurgency. The war has also hurt Sri Lanka's tourist industry and diverted millions of dollars to countries with greater domestic stability. By one estimate, the opportunity costs of the war amounted to US$ 12 billion by 1994. Saman Kelegama, "Economic Costs of Conflict in Sri Lanka," in Rotberg, *Creating Peace in Sri Lanka,* 77. Moreover, the costs of fighting the insurgency have increased over time. As a percentage of overall government expenditure, defense outlays increased from 3.1 percent in 1982 to 21.6 percent in 1996.

7. Albert O. Hirschman, *Exit, Voice and Loyalty* (Cambridge, MA, 1970).

8. See especially K. M. de Silva, *A History of Sri Lanka* (Delhi, 1981). Also see Library of Congress, *Sri Lanka—A Country Study* (Washington, D.C., 1988); Chandra Richard De Silva, *Sri Lanka: A History* (Delhi, 1997), 1–16.

9. In the pre-colonial era, the Sri Lankan state was essentially merged with Buddhist institutions. The clergy enjoyed financial support from state coffers, and located their temples close to the royal palace for greater control over the state institutions. Although the strength of the Buddhist clergy had already been undermined by Portuguese and then Dutch missionary efforts, it was not until the British assumed power that the Buddhist clergy lost their institutional privileges in Sri Lankan politics. This set the stage for successive waves of Buddhist revivalism, starting in the late nineteenth century, largely as a reaction to British influence in Sri Lanka.

10. David Little, "Religion and Ethnicity," in Rotberg, *Creating Peace in Sri Lanka*, 45–48.

11. Nithiyanandam, "Ethnic Politics," 4–7.

12. Snodgrass, "Economic Development of Sri Lanka," 89.

13. K. M. de Silva, *Managing Ethnic Tensions in Multi-Ethnic Societies: Sri Lanka 1880–1985* (Lanham, MD, 1986), 155, as cited by Nithiyanandam, "Ethnic Politics," 7.

14. Ibid.

15. Snodgrass, "Economic Development of Sri Lanka," 94.

16. Amita Shastri, "Government Policy and Ethnic Crisis in Sri Lanka," in Michael E. Brown and Sumit Ganguly (eds.), *Government Policies and Ethnic Relations in Asia and the Pacific* (Cambridge, 1997), 146, as cited by Rotberg, "Sri Lanka's Civil War," in *Creating Peace in Sri Lanka*, 6.

17. Little, "Religion and Ethnicity," 48–50.

18. See Sumantra Bose, *States, Nations, Sovereignty: Sri Lanka, India and the Tamil Eelam Movement* (New Delhi, 1994), for a discussion of how Sri Lanka's assimilationist policies profoundly alienated its Tamil minority, gradually fueling the development of a *de facto* sovereign Tamil nation.

19. Chris Smith, "South Asia's Enduring War," in Rotberg, *Creating Peace in Sri Lanka*, 17–18.

20. Reuters News Service (20 and 23 August 1995).

21. Ibid.

22. Correspondence with Douglas Ranmuthugala, senior analyst with the Australian Federal Police's International Operations Support Team, Canberra, September 1998, as cited in Peter Chalk, "Liberation Tigers of Tamil Eelam's (LTTE) International Organization and Operations—A Preliminary Analysis," Commentary No. 77, Canadian Intelligence Service Publication (17 March 2000), http://www.fas.org/irp/world/para/docs/com77e.htm.

23. Ibid.

24. Sri Lanka's majoritarian political system—put in place at the time of independence—was finally amended in 1978, at which time it was replaced with a proportional representation (PR) system. This change, together with a system of regional govern-

ment gradually implemented throughout the 1980s, was intended to resolve the Sinhala-Tamil conflict. However, not only were these measures "too little, too late," but Sri Lanka simultaneously replaced its British-type parliamentary system with a presidential system, in which the president is elected by the people and is vested with significant powers. Since 1978, Sri Lanka's president has been the head of state, the head of government, the head of the cabinet, and the commander-in-chief of the armed forces. As such, the president is not directly answerable to the legislature, is immune from legal proceedings in both official and private capacities, and has the power to dissolve parliament, make high judicial appointments, and rule by emergency decree. The "devolution" of power to the regions therefore served primarily as window dressing for what remained a highly unitary state, in which the Tamil minority had no effective voice. For the history and make-up of Sri Lanka's political system, see George E. Delury (ed.), *World Encyclopedia of Political Systems and Parties* (Washington, D.C, 1999), 1034–1040.

25. For an in-depth discussion of how these factors have interacted to produce a distinct Tamil national identity—in opposition to a more inclusive Sri Lankan identity—see A. Jeyaratnam Wilson, *Sri Lankan Tamil Nationalism* (London, 2000).

26. Marie-Joelle Zahar, "Fanatics, Brigands, Mercenaries . . . and Politicians: Militia Decision-Making and Civil Conflict Resolution," unpub. Ph.D. dissertation (McGill University, 2000). In her work, Zahar uses the cases of Lebanon and Bosnia to show convincingly how protracted civil conflicts create institutional incentives for fighting factions to avoid peace settlements.

27. Mizan Khan, "Sri Lankan Tamils in Sri Lanka," MAR project files (13 April 1995; updated 27 June 1999).

28. Darini Rajasingham-Senanayake, "The Dangers of Devolution: The Hidden Economies of Armed Conflict," in Rotberg, *Creating Peace in Sri Lanka*, 60–61.

29. U.S. Department of State, *Sri Lanka Country Report for 1998*, 10.

30. Frances Harrison, "Tiger Rebels 'Dragoon Tamil Teenagers,'" *BBC World: South Asia* (1 February 2002).

31. Interview, K. Sritharan, spokesperson for the University Teachers for Human Rights (Jaffna) [UTHR(J)], (Cambridge, MA, 17 April 2002).

32. UTHR(J), "LTTE Bypasses Operation Waruna Kirana: Tigers Use Ceasefire to Bring in Arms Supplies through Southeast Coast," http://www.island.lk/2002/04/21/defenc01.html.

33. Harrison, "Tiger Rebels."

34. In the context of discussions over an interim government, all other Tamil political parties, civic associations, churches, and the people themselves have been pressured into voicing full support for the LTTE. These groups have also declined to demand a place in the interim government, claiming that the Tigers fully represent the interests of the Tamil people. If they are not even accorded a place at the negotiating table, it is unlikely that these groups would be allowed a greater participatory role in any future administration.

35. Interview, K. Sritharan.

36. Neil DeVotta, "Control Democracy, Institutional Decay, and the Quest for Eelam: Explaining Ethnic Conflict in Sri Lanka," *Pacific Affairs*, LXXIII (2000), 6–8.

37. *Partition* is another solution that has recently gained popularity in academic and policy circles. For examples of this argument, see Chaim Kaufmann, "Possible and Impossible Solutions to Ethnic Civil Wars," *International Security*, XX (1996); idem, "When all Else Fails," *International Security*, XXIII (1998); John Mearsheimer and Stephen Van Evera, "When Peace Means War," *New Republic* (18 December 1995), 16–21. One of the problems with this approach is that it does nothing to resolve the security dilemma that caused the ethnic war—it merely raises the stakes of combat by transforming an internal war into an international conflict. At the same time, partition legitimizes ethnic cleansing under the euphemistic term "population transfers," a policy that resulted in the death of roughly 300,000 ethnic Germans under the Benes Decrees of post–World War II Czechoslovakia. For an excellent critique of this approach, see Nicholas Sambanis, "Partition as a Solution to Ethnic War: An Empirical Critique of the Theoretical Literature, *World Politics*, LII (2000), 437–483.

38. Rajasingham-Senanayake, "The Dangers of Devolution," 66–67.

39. Smith, "South Asia's Enduring War," 19–25.

40. DeVotta, "Control Democracy," 8.

41. "LTTE Dashes Oslo Peace Bid," *The Times of India*, online (9 April 2001), http://www.timesofindia.com/.

42. Shimali Senanayake, "Sri Lankan Cease-Fire Offers Hope," *Washington Post* (22 February 2002).

43. Daniel Posner, "Civil Society and the Reconstruction of Failed States," in Robert I. Rotberg (ed.), *When States Fail: Causes and Consequences* (Princeton, 2003, forthcoming).

44. Chandra R. De Silva, "Education Ameliorating Political Violence," in Rotberg, *Creating Peace in Sri Lanka*, 109–117.

45. See Steve Stedman, "Spoiler Problems in the Peace Process," *International Security*, XXII (1997), 5–53.

46. For a game-theoretic account for how in-group policing may serve as a useful mechanism for resolving ethnic conflicts, see James D. Fearon and David D. Laitin, "Explaining Interethnic Cooperation," *American Political Science Review*, XC (1996), 715–735.

CHAPTER NINE

Tajikistan:
Regionalism and Weakness

NASRIN DADMEHR

Tajikistan is a weak, recently failed state. Given what Tajikistan has endured since its independence in 1991, its failure is not surprising. The end of the Cold War and the disintegration of the Soviet Union "imposed" independence on this poorest country of the old Russian empire. The economic consequences of independence and the struggle over reforming the political system brought an avalanche of problems that culminated in a bloody civil war. The dramatic consequences of this five-year war were enough to push Tajikistan into failure.

Throughout the civil war (May 1992–June 1997), despite an official government in Dushanbe, the Tajikistani capital, there was no state authority in many parts of the country. During this period, the government was virtually absent from citizens' social lives. It was even more absent from their economic lives; salaries were paid rarely. For many, drug smuggling gradually became the main source of income. The state lost its meaning in Tajikistan during the war.

However, the 1997 peace agreement between the government and the opposition forces slowed the descent into permanent failure. With the help of the opposition, the Tajikistani government developed an administrative presence in the country, although some regions, especially in the east, remained totally beyond government power, and even beyond the opposition's control. International aid for post-war reconstruction helped the economy to show some positive signals of growth; normalcy returned after 1997. Peace saved Tajikistan

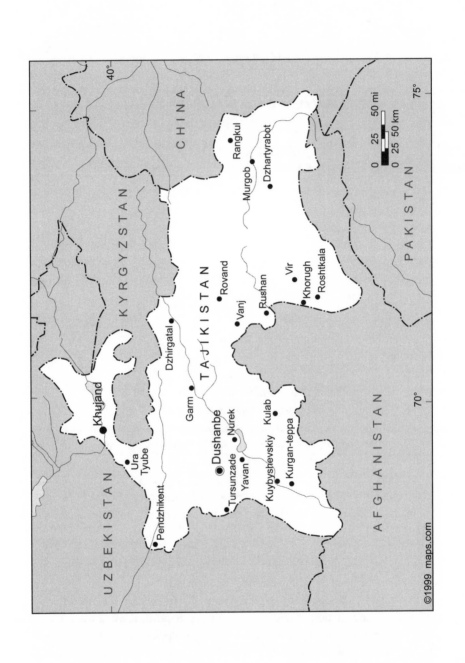

from collapse and gave new hope for reconstructing a state based on respect for citizens' rights and interests.

Nevertheless, despite the peace agreement's positive impact on the country, Tajikistan remains fragile, and new and old problems raise serious doubts about its stability. The enormous damage to agricultural and industrial activities caused by the war, the lack of a policy to manage the budget in accordance with the most important needs of the people, and periodic drought, are obstacles to economic development.

This chapter examines the causes of state weakness in pre- and post-independence Tajikistan and the role of the civil war. It analyzes the Tajikistani government's failure during the war, as well as the impact of peace. It focuses on the necessity of preventing state failure in Tajikistan and on what can be done to maintain stability and peace in this strategic Central Asian country.

Soviet Elements of State Weakness

In their sovietisation of Central Asia, which then included the Turkestani governorship of Imperial Russia, the Khanate of Khiva, and the Emirate of Bukhara, the Bolsheviks divided the region into different territories, mainly based on the theory of "one language = one ethnic group, one ethnic group = one territory."[1] This new ethnic administration sought to split Central Asia, and to prevent local ethnic groups from rallying around a larger cause, such as pan-Turkism or pan-Islamism. The strong resistance of the Basmachis—armed Muslim rebels—to the Bolsheviks strengthened the latter's resolve to splinter the region into different territories and ethnicities.[2]

Central Asia was divided into new Soviet socialist republics largely along ethnic lines. Nevertheless, the Tajiks, despite having their own language and a culture belonging to the Iranian family, were denied the right to their own republic. In 1924, they were granted an autonomous republic in the Uzbek SSR.[3] Yet, Tajik intellectuals and politicians continued to demand the right to an independent state. This struggle continued until the Soviet Socialist Republic of Tajikistan (SSRT) was established in 1929.[4]

The creation of the SSRT was a victory for the Tajiks, but was also accompanied by a major failure. Samarkand and Bukhara, the two capitals of Tajik culture, remained within Uzbekistan, forcing the Tajiks to forge a new identity without their historic cultural centers. These losses were a fundamental blow to the Tajiks' nation-building process and deeply affected their political life.[5] Tajik intellectuals, mostly centered in these two cities, remained in Uzbekistan; thus, in the Bolsheviks' view, the new Tajikistan, mostly populated by mountain dwellers, had to be formed with the help of non-Tajiks. Given this fact, the

Russian government, and later the Uzbek regime, assumed important roles in the management of the country. This process undermined the Tajikistani sense of national sovereignty.

State-Building

The treatment that the Tajiks received from the Bolsheviks was not only limited to delaying their own republic. The territory that they were granted was also problematic. Indeed, "Tajiks [were] given an impossible piece of territory with a disparate population and [were] forced to make a nation out of it."[6] The country, 93 percent mountainous, of which over 50 percent is uninhabitable, was divided into four different regions (provinces), with little possibility of contact among them. The regions are: Sogod in the north, formerly Leninabad, with Khujand as its center; Dushanbe and thirteen districts in the center; Gorno-Badakshan (known as Pamir), in the east; and Khatlon in the southwest. This last region was formed in 1992 from the two regions of Kulab and Kurgan-teppa, in order to add power to Kulab, the native region of the new government's officials, and to diminish the power of Kurgan-teppa, a region with a strong tendency to support the Islamic opposition.

"Political power in the republic came to rest on the dominance of a number of regional groups, while the project of promoting a Tajikistani national consciousness to help bind the republic together failed to penetrate into many regions."[7] The control of political power became a serious issue of rivalry among different regions. The elite of Khujand held power from the 1950s until the outbreak of the civil war in 1992. In such a context, regionalism replaced nationalism.

Regionalism not only affected nation-building, it undermined national sovereignty in Tajikistan. The political preeminence of the Khujandis, tied as they were culturally, politically, and economically to Uzbekistan, opened the door to the pervasive influence of its bigger neighbor. That influence endured until the end of the Soviet period and became an important element in undermining stability in Tajikistan after independence.

Economic Policy and Tajikistani Sovereignty

Despite the fact that Tajikistan showed some important economic growth in other areas in the first decade after World War II, Moscow compelled Tajikistan to concentrate on cotton production. Because of a lack of skilled workers and technicians, Russians staffed many high-level positions; the economy relied on them rather than on Tajiks. In general, in industrial fields, between 60 and 80 percent of the technicians came from outside Tajikistan.

Soviet economic policy disturbed Tajikistan, like many other republics within the U.S.S.R., by relocating a part of the local population from one region to another in order to bring the available labor supply closer to factories or agricultural centers. Tajikistan suffered one of the highest rates of population relocation in the U.S.S.R. The process of relocation began in the 1920s and was repeated in the 1950s, 1960s, and 1970s. The forced relocations resulted in the creation of new social groups based on region of origin, an element that deepened a sense of regionalism and played a significant role during the civil war.

Independence and Civil War

Soviet President Mikhail Gorbachev's accession to power in 1985 opened the door to expressions of discontent by Tajiks. Soon, cultural and political dissidents began to appear on the political stage of Tajikistan. The Popular Movement of Rastokhiz (Rebirth), the Democrat Party of Tajikistan, and the Islamic Rebirth Party emerged as the most important factions. At first, the groups' demands were nationalistic and centered on cultural questions, especially the language question. These new intellectual groups demanded that Tajiki replace Russian as the state language. Their efforts finally resulted in a 1989 law that recognized Tajiki as the national language and Russian as the language of inter-ethnic communication.

During the same period, social tensions arose in Tajikistan, mostly between Tajiks and ethnic minorities. These tensions were caused by social demands and poverty, and turned violent. The most important and bloody of these riots occurred in early 1990; twenty-one people lost their lives. The main issue was the shortage of housing.[8]

Following the events of 1990, and during a state of emergency, the government held parliamentary elections for Tajikistan's Supreme Soviet (legislature). Opposition groups were not allowed to participate in these elections, so the communist deputies took almost all of the seats in the new conservative parliament. Opposition groups continued to demand change, and under this pressure, parliament founded a fifty-five-member commission to formulate a new constitution. The commission never presented a draft.

The abortive coup against Gorbachev in Moscow in 1991 was fatal for the communist leaders of Tajikistan, who had supported the authors of the coup. Profiting from the communists' weak position, new Tajikistani political groups called for an end to communist power and the organization of free elections.

However, the turn of events in Moscow suddenly meant that Tajikistan, like many other Soviet republics, would receive unrequested independence.

Independence had dramatic economic consequences for Tajikistan; it was suddenly separated from half of its customary revenue. Independence also broke the old political order; the Tajikistani communists, still in power, lost Russian communist support. This shift gave hope to new political groups seeking to end communism's monopoly on power. The Democratic Party of Tajikistan, the Islamic Rebirth Party, Rastokhiz, and several other national and regional groups continued their efforts to demand the recognition of their cultural identities and their ability to share power. In May 1992, backed by popular support and two months of non-stop demonstrations, they succeeded in imposing a coalition government on the communists.

To contest the coalition government, the communists armed their supporters and battled against the pro-opposition population. Soon, armed opposition groups formed, and an all-out war ensued. It endured until the capture of Dushanbe by the pro-communists and the establishment of a new communist government in December 1993.

The new government was shaped almost exclusively by the communists of the Kulab, a region in the south, in alliance with the communists of Khujand in the north. This lack of inclusiveness led the non-communist Tajikistanis and those from other regions to reject the legitimacy of the regime. Although one year later this new government legitimized itself by staging elections, it remained weak, especially given the continuation of the war and its extension to the southern and eastern parts of the country. Opposition groups, especially Islamists who had escaped the war in Afghanistan and had received support from the then Tajik Islamic government of that country, attacked the southern part of Tajikistan. Soon, they arrived near Dushanbe. Facing threats from the Islamists and from the Taliban in Kabul, and under pressure from the Russian government to end the war, the Tajikistani government agreed to negotiate peace with the United Tajik Opposition (UTO).[9]

Peace negotiations began in April 1994. Yet, it took more than three years to achieve the 1997 agreement. Under it, UTO leaders came back from exile to Tajikistan and the Commission on National Reconciliation began to implement the accords of the agreement. The more important accords concerned a change of the parliamentary system from one chamber to two, the legalization of religious parties, the organization of new presidential and parliamentary elections, the integration of paramilitary forces into the official armed forces, and the formation of a coalition government. This process ended in early 2000, and the UN, after the first post-war presidential and parliamentary elections had been held in 1999, declared peace to be officially established in Tajikistan.

Though the arrival of peace had positive impacts on different aspects of Tajikistani society, the five-year war had deeply affected it. The political, social, and economic order, already weak, had broken down almost completely during the war. Anarchy and the fragmentation of Tajikistan into different autonomous regions made rebuilding the country difficult.

Lack of State Legitimacy

Elections

Tajikistan's first presidential election took place shortly after independence in 1991, during a state of emergency, and brought to power the candidate of the hard-line faction of the Communist Party. This election, during which the communists applied methods of terror and manipulation, held no legitimacy for the opposition or the people and soon led the country into a major political crisis, and later into civil war.

A second presidential election, held in November 1994, served to legalize the winners of the civil war, who had obtained power through violence and bloodshed, including the death of about 60,000 Tajiks.[10] The election was held without an opposition candidate, and Emomali Rakhmonov, the sole candidate and the new head of the Tajikistani communists, was elected president.

A third presidential election, the first after the peace agreement, took place in 1999, when many opposition groups had returned from exile and hoped to participate freely. Yet, this poll was no fairer than the previous ones. The government managed, by terror and manipulation, to eliminate the other candidates from the candidacy list, and thus the president was again the sole candidate. President Rakhmonov won with almost 97 percent of the votes. Based on the same system, the People's Democratic Party of Tajikistan, founded by the president, gained a majority in legislative elections.[11]

Elections are one of the main components of state legitimacy. However, in the absence of a valid and trusted election process, citizens may reject the elected leaders and turn to alternative choices. This has been the case in Tajikistan. The non-democratic nature of the elections produced governments concerned with maintaining their power and monopoly of national wealth rather than with ensuring the interest of the citizens. Tajikistanis have thus turned to alternatives such as regional and religious leaders, warlords, international organizations, and non-governmental organizations that seem to be more able or more willing to respond to their interests than the "official" regime. The presence of these alternative forces, in turn, reduces the legitimacy of the regime and further complicates attempts to build the country's integrity.

Weak Constitution

The lack of a respectable constitution able to function above political divergences and address major issues is another problem that reduces a regime's credibility and leaves citizens with little recourse. Since its creation in 1929, Tajikistan has had five different constitutions. Like other Soviet republics, the first four Tajikistani constitutions were copies of the Soviet Union's constitutions.[12] After independence, the new regime kept the last Soviet one. A new constitution was adopted only after the start of the civil war and the capture of power by the communists. Essentially, it was a tool for strengthening the power of the victors of war. This new Tajikistani constitution was also very similar to the Russian one of 1993. However, in order to erect further barriers against the Islamic opposition, it was even more secular than the original Soviet version and gave more power to the president.

As the constitution in Tajikistan is simply a copy of another nation's constitution—a nation with a different social and political culture—it already contains elements that could contribute to state failure. A constitution should reflect the real needs of a given society. In the case of countries like Tajikistan, where this main element is neglected, the society has no real reference point to solve its major problems. Thus, violence and self-protection replace the rule of law, and lead the state to failure.

History as the Source of Legitimacy

Given its lack of true legitimacy, the Tajikistani government, the victor of the civil war, tried to assert its position by presenting itself as the rightful descendent of powerful historic leaders. While the post-independence communist regime of Tajikistan sharply rejected all opposition demands to replace communist values with nationalistic ones, the new communist government later realized the value of nationalism in supporting its claims to legitimacy. Since the beginning of the peace negotiations, the Tajikistani government cultivated an extremely nationalistic policy and conducted a campaign of propaganda about the Samanid, the only Tajik dynasty of Central Asia. This campaign sought to draw a parallel between that dynasty and the Kulabi regime in Dushanbe in order to gain the support of the citizens on a national level.[13]

It is important to note that the nationalistic propaganda of the Tajikistani regime had another goal: to respond to the aggressive and anti-Tajikistani nationalistic policy of the neighboring Uzbek state. The Tajikistani government wanted to target those who denied the integrity of the Tajiks as a nation and thus the necessity of a Tajikistani state. Uzbekistan's aggressive policy against the national rights of Tajiks, as well as the destructive impact of war, have, paradoxically, developed a Tajikistani sense of nationalism. It stood ready to support any "Tajik" government, even one propped up by Moscow. This neo-nationalism is one of the rare issues on which the Kulabi government and the UTO agreed.

Power Structure and Parallel Forces

Dependency of Government on One Group

Soon after the creation of Tajikistan, its political structure took on a regional color, with leaders from Khujand on top. Such regionalism continued to play a role after independence, especially during the civil war: the pro-communists were mostly from Khujand and Kulab, the Islamists from Garm and Kurgan-teppa, and the democrats derived support from Badakhshan.

In December 1993, the first phase of the war ended with the triumph of the pro-communist Kulabis. They took power and refused to pass it to the Khujandis, who, considering their traditional leadership role, had expected to return to power.[14]

Although this change put an end to the dominant role of the Khujandis in Tajikistani politics, it did not end regionalism in Tajikistan. Rather, it simply transferred power from one region to another. Since then, power has remained mostly in the hands of the Kulabis. Other regions, with few exceptions, have been excluded from participating in the national government. The most important governmental or economic positions have been given to Kulabis. Along the same lines, development projects have been aimed mostly at improving Kulab, and many state resources helped to enrich this region. To emphasize its regional origins, the regime even conducted "national" celebrations, such as Independence Day, in the Kulabi dialect. The emphasis on Kulab angered the other regions and impeded the development of a truly national Tajikistani society.

This emphasis on the regional nature of power significantly diminished the regime's credibility for Tajikistanis from other areas, particularly Khujandis, Pamiris, and Garmis, who view themselves as being ignored and denied by the ruling regime. The Khujandis, former allies of the regime, were rejected both by the government and the UTO, and thus have been completely absent from the prevailing power structure since 2002. In return, they openly expressed their lack of interest in the central government. Pamir turned not only spiritually but economically toward the Aga Khan, the leader of the Ismaili movement.[15] Garm, too, operated semi-independently of the central government and was a region managed almost totally by Islamic forces or independent war-lords. The major institutions of power remained in the hands of the Kulabis in 2002.

Warlords

One of the results of the civil war in Tajikistan, as in many other post-conflict countries, was the emergence of powerful regional warlords. These warlords were active on both sides of the power struggle—the government as well as the opposition. In addition to politically oriented warlords, there were independent ones who did not support any political faction. The appearance of these new elements totally changed the political balance of power in Tajikistan, and no political or economic calculation is possible without taking them into consideration.

As of 2002, the warlords had armed forces and one or more regions under their control. They established their own laws in their regions and became a source of leverage for the local people. The Islamic warlords applied s*hari'a,* the Qur'anic law; some warlords applied a kind of social justice in their region to fulfill the need for the rule of law despite the central government's neglect. These warlords usually had strong popular support among the population under their control; the local people felt more secure under the warlords' protection and preferred them to the corrupt representatives of the national government.

The warlords' main goal was to gain control of local sources of wealth. Cotton, aluminum, and drug revenues framed the conflict between the com-manders of the government and the opposition, or even among the armed forces of each camp. For example, in January 1997, the struggle to take control of Tajikistan's aluminum income turned into a bloody war between the govern-ment and Mahmud Khudoyberdiev, one of the most powerful pro-government warlords.[16] Khudoyberdiev, a Soviet-era officer who fought for the commu-nists during the civil war, attacked the city of Tursunzode, the center of alumi-num production, and succeeded in establishing control over it and its immense income. In August 1997, however, presidential guards, helped by the forces of another commander, after a three-day battle took control of the city; Khudoyberdiev sought refuge in Uzbekistan, and Sohrob, another warlord from the presidential camp, took control of the smelter.

The commanders of small units preyed on the rural population. In many regions, rural producers paid these commanders a part of their profits as a *"laissez-passer"* to the markets. As a result, consumers, most of whom were very poor, had to pay much higher prices, when they could afford to buy goods at all. This process, in turn, deepened the economic crisis and added hunger to the problems of modern Tajikistan.

Warlords also sought to occupy governmental positions related to power and/or wealth, such as the control of armed forces, customs, an so forth. A notable example occurred in the spring of 1999, when Mirzo Ziyayov, one of the main Islamist commanders, jeopardized the entire peace process. Supported by the UTO, he demanded the ministry of defense for himself, but the government refused to give him that position. He threatened to go to war. With most of the Islamic armed forces under his control and close ties to both the Tajik mujahadeen in Afghanistan and the Islamic Uzbeks, Ziyayov was able to push the entire region into a deep political crisis. Even Islamic leaders had no ability to control him. After months of difficult negotiations, the government, though refusing to give him the ministry of defense, created a new ministry for him, the "ministry for emergency situations and civil defense." Ziyayov's presence in the government soon proved its worth when, in the summer of 1999, Uzbek Islamic forces attacked Uzbekistan via Kyrgyzstan; he played a major role in putting down that insurgency.

It is no surprise that in a country where political differences and questions of power are resolved through violence, those who fight will demand their share of the national pie. In such a situation, the government and the opposition have no choice but to rely on commanders and warlords to retain their power. Yet, this double-edged sword leads the government to lose credibility nationally.

In 2002, after the end of the war and the establishment of peace in Tajikistan, the power of the warlords was reduced in some regions, while the development of drug smuggling added to the number who wanted to take the control of whole regions, and roads vital to their trade.

Lack of State Control over Violence

Easy access to small arms has been another consequence of the war in Tajikistan. The impact of this phenomenon on Tajikistani society has produced a marked growth in murder, kidnapping, and extortion. Assassinations and kidnapping are not limited to political groups. Rather, they are used to extort money or wreak personal vengeance. In some cases members of international organizations have been the targets of these operations. In late 1997, Rizvan Sadirov, a rebel commander, kidnapped a French employee of the Red Cross in order to free his men from government prisons. The event took on an international dimension and tragically ended in the death of the French employee. The state lost its monopoly over violence.

Ironically, the establishment of the peace process and the end of the civil war did not stop or lessen this phenomenon of lawlessness. Murder rates grew considerably; murder became the most common way to solve political and economic disputes. Since 1999, the government has tried to prohibit carrying arms in public places, but given the proliferation of armed groups throughout the country, the process of disarmament has been extremely difficult.

The UN and NGOs' State Functions

The UN appeared on the political stage of Tajikistan more than two years after the outbreak of the civil war and after the Kulabi regime's rise to power. In December 1994, the UN Mission of Observers in Tajikistan (UNMOT), entered the country for a period of six months, but its mission was renewed many times. It ended in 2000 after the first post-war presidential and legislative elections.[17]

Although the UN's involvement in Tajikistan was an engagement at the surface level, it mediated relatively successfully between the contending parties.[18] Many other UN organizations, such as the UN High Commissioner for Refugees (UNHCR), the UN Development Program (UNDP), the UN Development Fund for Women (UNIFEM), the UN Office for Project Services (UNOPS), and the World Food Program (WFP), also became engaged in the humanitarian and developmental activities of Tajikistan. A significant number of international NGOs, such as Médecins sans Frontières, the Open Society Foundation, Save the Children, and the Aga Khan Foundation, also became active in Tajikistan. In 2002, these organizations continued to fulfill many societal functions that normally belong to the state. As a result, a part of the population, especially in the war-torn regions, has become economically and socially dependent on international organizations and NGOs, and the activities of these organizations have become vital for people's survival and the country's stability. This dependence on international aid demonstrates the Tajikistani government's weakness.

External Forces and Internal Instability

Tajikistan's geopolitical situation is another element that negatively affects its stability and national sovereignty. Sharing borders with the Commonwealth of Independent States (CIS), Afghanistan, and Uzbekistan has created major external threats to Tajikistan's stability.

Tajikistan's common border with the CIS has encouraged Russia to maintain a strong military presence. Russia has long stationed approximately 10,000 men along the Tajikistan-Afghanistan border. This military presence has grown since the end of the Tajikistani civil war. In 1999, the Tajikistani government granted Russia permission to establish a permanent military base.

Russia explained its presence in Tajikistan by citing the Taliban's role in Afghanistan and the possibility of attacks on Central Asian countries.[19] Russia claimed to fear the emergence of a new Islamic Uzbek armed group.[20] Russia also wanted to fight drug smuggling from Afghanistan. (There is evidence that the Russian military itself has been engaged in the region's drug trade.) By exaggerating threats to Russian security, Russia hoped to extend its control over the region.

Nevertheless, the Russian presence has become a major ingredient of Tajikistan's stability. Without such a presence, Uzbekistan could follow a more aggressive policy toward Tajikistan, and, as demonstrated during the Tajikistani civil war; might even deploy armed forces in order to regain control.[21] Additionally, the strong influence of Russia pushed the Kulabi regime to accept peace negotiations with the UTO and an end to the civil war.

Russia has become the guarantor of Tajikistan's integrity. Although Russia's presence indeed highlights the inability of the Tajikistani regime to govern independently and to ensure the national interests of Tajikistanis. It also weakens the process of nation-building in Tajikistan and, in the long term, may bring new conflicts to the country.

Adding to Tajikistan's stability in 2001 and 2002 has been the stationing on its soil of U.S. troops and additional Russian soldiers. The willingness of the government of Tajikistan to join the new war against terror and fully to assist the United States and its allies in repulsing al Qaeda- and Taliban-inspired militarism has also helped to halt any further failure of the Tajikistani state. Given the nature of the previous internal and external threats to the survival of Tajikistan and successive Tajikistani governments, the war against terror arrived opportunely. Considering Tajikistan's ethnic affinity for Afghanistan's Northern Alliance, and the buffering regional role that Tajikistan (and neighboring Central Asian states) plays in the containment of Afghan-inspired terror, the once vulnerable state has taken advantage of changed regional circumstances to bolster itself against inherent tendencies to fragility. A central question is whether this unexpected high level of foreign support can encourage lasting improvements in the way Tajikistan delivers political goods to its own citizens, and thus ameliorate the state's inherited leadership frailties.

The State and Socio-Economic Development

Tajikistan is rural; almost 72 percent of Tajikistanis do not live in towns or cities. The country is landlocked, and, although less than 10 percent of its land is fully arable, its economy is mainly based on agriculture. Cotton constitutes 50 percent of all production. Aluminum, lead, and electrical power are industrial products, all for export.

During the Soviet period, the economy of Tajikistan depended heavily on subsidies from Moscow. In 1991, as a result of independence, the country suddenly lost almost half of its revenue, and the massive departure of the Russians, who were active in industry, reduced the country's productivity.

Economic hardship was most severe during the five-year civil war. The peace agreement signed in 1997 stopped this free fall. Inflation decreased to 11.5 percent in 2001, and Tajikistan's economic growth rates, while modest, are favorable in comparison to other CIS countries.[22] Per capita GDP remains low, at $1,140.[23] The war and the damages it caused to agricultural and irrigation systems resulted in a further loss of productivity. As a consequence, prices rose dramatically, and Tajikistan's GDP declined by 40–45 percent. Inflation increased 7,400 percent in 1992, and 2,000 percent in 1995. Unemployment affected almost one-fifth of the labor force.

The demilitarization of society and the integration of former combatants into the official army were post-conflict developments. The process was hard and long, and neither the government nor the opposition helped much. The slowness of the process and resulting personal financial problems caused many former combatants to return to their rebel lives and join local commanders who, having their own sources of income (mostly illegal), were able to provide for them. In spite of these difficulties, the demilitarization process ended officially in September 2000.

Another significant impact of the peace negotiations was the return of most refugees to the country. According to the UNHCR, there were more than 100,000 refugees in neighboring countries in 1992, including 60,000 in Afghanistan. About 600,000 people were also internally displaced in Tajikistan.[24] By March 1993, 70 percent of these internally displaced persons had returned to their villages, and following the peace agreement, all the refugees from Afghanistan and more than half from the CIS countries came back home. Even though the return of the refugees was followed by major problems, such as lack of security and lack of access to homes or jobs, their return remained a positive aspect of the peace process.

Despite these positive economic and social signals, Tajikistan's situation in 2002 remained far from stable. The state still fell well short of accomplishing its major socio-economic functions in most sectors. The economic situation, which had showed some signs of development, again began to deteriorate.

The UNDP ranked Tajikistan 103 out of 162 countries in its 2001 Human Development Index, a comprehensive examination of development indicators.[25]

According to the UNDP, 85 percent of the population lived below the poverty line, and hunger and malnutrition were rife. The drought during 1998–2001, which directly affected 2 million Tajikistanis, one-third of the population, added to this problem. The insecurity that began during the civil war has produced high rates of murder and rape. The UNDP reported that the number of rapes in 1997 was 375 percent higher than in 1996. The corruption of the police and the lack of a functioning judicial system highlighted the inability of governmental institutions to protect citizens. Corruption, which has its roots in the last decade of the Soviet period, was a major obstacle to development; it reduced the capacity of the government to feed its people and remained a principal cause of the people's poverty.[26]

Education is another sector that has shown significant decline. Because of economic problems, access to education has become more and more difficult. During the civil war, many schools were destroyed, and, since then, there has been a shortage of teachers, textbooks, and transportation facilities for students. Given the impoverished situation of educated people, higher education has lost its attraction, and corruption has damaged the image of the universities.

Health care and the environment are also critical sectors. Social expenditures fell from 17 percent of GDP in the Soviet period to 3.7 percent in 1996, due to the passage from the Soviet to a market economy. Furthermore, the consequences of war and the fact that the majority of doctors have left the country have added to the decline of the health system. Because of the lack of an adequate health care system, many diseases, such as diphtheria and typhoid fever, have become more prevalent. A major part of the population, especially in rural areas, relied on international organizations, particularly Médecins sans Frontières, for health care.[27]

Environmental problems have also increased significantly. Drinking water is highly polluted. Soil contamination, soil erosion, deforestation, and depletion of fisheries are other examples of environmental degradation.[28]

Conclusion

Tajikistani society has been depressed since independence, and more particularly, since the civil war. The government's failure to accomplish its main tasks and the extreme consequences of the war have thrown the country into a semi-anarchical state. Political rights, economic development, and social life have lost their meaning for citizens who hardly expect their government to fulfill its primary duties.

Nonetheless, it is difficult to call Tajikistan a failed state. Although during the civil war it was a failed state, it recovered after the peace process. In this second phase, it was more accurately a vulnerable post-failed state that had survived the war. But the still omnipresent inheritances of the war, the power-oriented nature of the regime, increasing poverty and corruption, and new forms of violence, make very difficult the process of development and reconstruction. They threaten the stability of peace and may drive the country toward complete failure. The political deterioration of Afghanistan and Uzbekistan, Tajikistan's neighbors, has only accelerated this process. Although Russia's military presence may seem to be an efficient method of preserving regional stability, the record of the Russian army in Chechnya is hardly conducive to optimism and, in the long term, may hinder Tajikistan's desire to strengthen its independence.

Too many risk-inducing elements are still present. It would take little for the country to explode into a new violent crisis. Such a crisis, given the position of Tajikistan between Afghanistan and Central Asia, ties the crisis of one region to difficulties in another. Tajikistan is a key country for regional security; a total failure of Tajikistan would accelerate the development of the political and economic crisis in Central Asia.

A retreat from failure depends on the international community, which needs to support the fragile process of recovery from civil war. It could assist the economic development of the country, and more importantly, convince the government to respect the political rights of the people and protect their social well-being.

Notes

1. Between 1918 and 1936, this region was organized and reorganized many times. From 1918 to 1920 it was organized as three autonomous Soviet socialist republics (Turkestan, Kyrgyzstan, and Turkmenistan) as part of the Russian Federation, with two people's republics (Bukhara and Khwarazm). In 1924, it contained two Soviet socialist republics (Uzbekistan and Turkmenistan), three autonomous Soviet socialist republics (one of them Tajikistan, which was attached to Uzbekistan), and two autonomous regions attached to Russia. In 1929, Tajikistan became a Soviet socialist republic, and thus "independent." The region found its final shape in 1936, when it was divided into five Soviet socialist republics (Kazakhstan, Uzbekistan, Kyrgyzstan, Tajikistan, and Turkmenistan), one autonomous republic (Karakalpak, attached to Uzbekistan), and one autonomous region (Gorno-Badakshan, attached to Tajikistan).

2. "Basmachi" means "bandits" in Russian and is the name given by the Bolsheviks to the armed Muslim groups that revolted against the advancing Soviet powers in the region. The movement began in 1918 and lasted until 1923, though it continued at a low level until the end of the 1920s. See Olivier Roy, *The New Central Asia: The Creation of Nations* (London, 2000).

3. This was partly because of the attraction of some Tajik intellectuals to pan-Turkism and their interest in being part of a Turkic republic.

4. According to another version, Moscow decided to make the Soviet Socialist Republic of Tajikistan a Persian-speaking republic "as a means of influencing the large area of Persian cultural influence from Iran to India." See Barnett R. Rubin, "Russian Hegemony and State Breakdown in the Periphery: Causes and Consequences of the Civil War in Tajikistan," in Barnett R. Rubin and Jack Snyder (eds.), *Post-Soviet Disorder: Conflict and State Building* (New York, 1998), 128–161.

5. See Rahim Masov (trans. Iraj Bashiri), *The History of a National Catastrophe* (Minneapolis, 1996). This book expresses Tajik nationalists' views and sets out the basis of the nationalist policy of the Tajikistani regime.

6. William O. Beeman, "The Struggle for Identity in Post-Soviet Tajikistan," *Middle East Review of International Affairs (MERIA)*, III (1999).

7. Neil J. Melvin, "Conflict and the State in the Caucasus and Central Asia," *Perspectives on Central Asia*, II (1998), http://www.cpss.org/casianw/perca0698.txt.

8. For a detailed account of this riot, see Helskini Watch, *Conflict in the Soviet Union Tadzhikistan* (New York, 1991).

9. The United Tajik Opposition was formed in exile in 1994 by the Islamic Rebirth Party, the Democratic Party of Tajikistan, and other small groups in order to take part in the peace negotiations. The UTO was dominated by the Islamists. Its activity ended in October 1999, when important divergences appeared among its different members shortly before the presidential election in November of the same year.

10. The number of those who were killed during the civil war varies (according to different sources) between 50,000 and 100,000. The UNDP estimates 60,000. UNDP, *Tajikistan Human Development Report 1996* (New York, 1996), 12.

11. International organizations and observers commented unfavorably on each of these elections. See the joint statement of observer missions of the United Nations and the Organization for Security and Cooperation in Europe, Interfax (28 February 2000).

12. The Tajikistani constitutions of 1929 and 1931were copied from the 1918 constitution of the Soviet Union. The Tajikistani constitutions of 1937 and 1978 were copied from the 1936 and 1977 constitutions of the Soviet Union, respectively.

13. The Samanid Empire dominated the region, including parts of present-day Central Asia and Iran, between 819 and 992. Today, the image of the Tajik president is paired everywhere with the image of Ahmad Samanid, the founder of the Samanid dynasty. In September 1999, the Tajik government celebrated for ten days the 1,000th anniversary of this dynasty and changed the name of the Tajik currency from "ruble" to "somoni."

14. Russia has been behind the Kulabis' decision to maintain power, in order to reduce the influence of Uzbekistan in the region.

15. Aga Khan IV is the spiritual head of the Ismaili Movement, a branch of Shi'ism that claims almost all of the population of Pamir.

16. Khudoyberdiev belongs ethnically to the Uzbek minority of Tajikistan.

17. UNMOT was replaced by a new mission, UNTOP (the UN-Tajikistan Office of Peace Building).

18. UNMOT had only between twenty and forty military observers. Its main tasks were to monitor the cease-fire and implement the accords of the peace agreement. See UN Information Department, *Tajikistan—UNMOT* (29 July 1997).

19. For the impacts of Taliban military advances on the political situation of Tajikistan, see Nasrin Dadmehr, "Tadjikistan 1999–2000, la paix menacée par les Taliban et la famine," *Le Courrier des pays de l'Est*, MX (2000), 135–144.

20. During the summers of 1999 and 2000, the Islamic Movement of Uzbek (IMU), which demanded that the Uzbek regime should support Islam, attacked Central Asia. Uzbek policy is repressive of Islam and has been criticized repeatedly by human rights organizations. See Human Rights Watch, *Crackdown in Ferghana* (1998), http://www.hrw.org/reports98/Uzbekistan.

21. Muriel Atkin, "Thwarted Democracy in Tajikistan," in Karen Dawish and Bruce Parrott (eds.), *Conflict, Cleavage, and Change in Central Asia and the Caucasus* (Cambridge, MA, 1997), 277–311.

22. Economist Intelligence Unit, "Country Outlook: Tajikistan" (2002).

23. CIA Factbook, "Tajikistan" (2002), http://www.cia.gov/cia/publications/factbook/geos/ti.html.

24. Francis Deng, "Profiles in Displacement: Tajikistan" (New York, 25 July 1995), http://www.un.org/documents/ga/docs/51/plenary.

25. UNDP, *Human Development Report* (2001), http://www.undp.ru/eng/News/hdr2001/HDR2001overview.pdf.

26. UNDP, *Tajikistan Human Development Report* (1999), www.undp.tj/Tajikistan/index.htm.

27. Ibid.

28. CIA Factbook, "Tajikistan."

PART THREE

Safely Weak

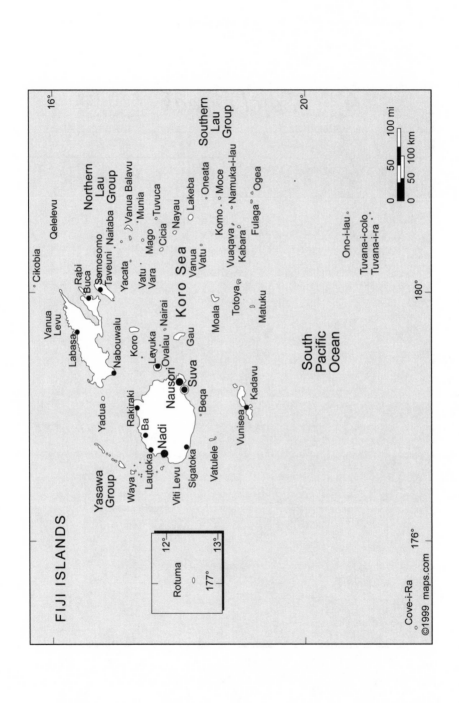

FIJI ISLANDS

Yasawa
Group

Vanua
Levu

Rabi
Buca

° Cikobia

Qelelevu

16°

Northern
Lau
Group

Labasa

Nabouwalu

Semosomo
Taveuni Naitaba

Yacata °

Vanua Balavu

Koro

Leyuka

Yadua °

Rakiraki

Waya

Ba

Lautoka

Nadi

Viti Levu

Sigatoka

Vatulele

Ovalau ° Nairai
Nausori
Suva

Beqa

Vunisea

Kadavu

Vatu ·
Vara

Mago

Munia

Cicia ° Tuvuca

° Nayau

Vanua °
Vatu °

Lakeba

Komo ° Moce

Oneata

Southern
Lau
Group

20°

Vuaqava ,° Namuka-i-lau
Kabara °

Fulaga ° Ogea

Ono-i-lau °

Tuvana-i-colo °
Tuvana-i-ra °

Koro Sea

Moala ♡

Totoya ◎

Matuku

South
Pacific
Ocean

180°

Rotuma

12°

13°

177°

176°

Cove-i-Ra

©1999 maps.com

0   50   100 mi

0   50   100 km

CHAPTER TEN

Fiji:
Divided and Weak

STEPHANIE LAWSON

Introduction

The notion of a "failed" or "failing" state is a broad one, encompassing various degrees or aspects of failure within it. These range from failure to sustain a reasonably stable environment for the people within its borders to those few, rare cases of genuinely collapsed states where no legitimate governmental authority is in effective control of the central apparatus of the state.[1] Fiji belongs on the less extreme end of this spectrum. Indeed, in comparison with many of the other case studies examined in this volume, it must be regarded as having remained, even throughout periods of political crisis, a reasonably well-functioning state. Nonetheless, the country has experienced serious problems in maintaining a stable regime structure and constitutional democratic government since 1987. If one thinks of a continuum along which states are classified from strong to weak to failed and finally collapsed, as Rotberg's introduction suggests, then Fiji lies within the weak state range. And given recent events, it must be regarded as vulnerable to more serious failure in terms of its capacity to provide a secure social, political, and economic environment.

Some of the research for this study was carried out while the author was a visitor with the Department of International Relations, Research School of Pacific and Asian Studies, Australian National University, Canberra, in November 2000 and in March 2001, and with the Department of History and Politics, University of the South Pacific, Suva, Fiji, in April 2001. I am grateful to both for the use of their facilities.

In its short history as an independent state, Fiji has experienced three coups against civilian governments. After the first two, both of which took place in 1987, following seventeen years of relatively stable post-colonial rule, Fiji struggled for a decade to re-establish a democratic constitutional order in a multi-ethnic society in which various communal interests were often assumed to be in conflict. A new, broad-based constitution was promulgated in 1997, and elections held in 1999. They produced, for the first time, a prime minister of Indian descent. But in May 2000, a failed local businessman, George Speight, and a small number of accomplices, took the government hostage at gunpoint. Fiji, it seemed, was simply incapable of sustaining democratic constitutional rule.

As with a number of other failed or failing states, the inability of different ethnic groups to live together under a stable and inclusive democratic system appears to be a significant factor, if not the principal cause, of vulnerability to failure. It should be noted that in both 1987 and 2000 the coup leaders justified their actions principally on the grounds that the interests of indigenous Fijians were under threat from a government controlled by Fiji Indians. Apart from constituting a danger to indigenous rights and interests, Fiji Indians have also long been regarded by Fijian nationalists as an "immigrant race" whose claims to equal political rights lack the legitimacy bestowed by indigenousness. The ascendancy of these attitudes in the wake of the 1987 coups led to the introduction of a constitution in 1990. It effectively enshrined a system of political apartheid.

The establishment of a government of Fijians, by Fijians, and for Fijians led to a situation in which the country was regarded as something of an international pariah. Excluded from the British Commonwealth and condemned in many quarters as an illegitimate, racist regime, the "sovereign Democratic Republic of Fiji," as it was styled under the 1990 constitution, suffered a degree of ignominy that stood in marked contrast to the relatively high regard that it had enjoyed throughout most of its first seventeen years of independent status. It now joined the ranks of many other ex-colonial states in which elected governments had failed to survive the ambitions of a "man on horseback."[2]

From the early 1990s, however, what seemed to be a remarkable shift in political thinking took place. Sitiveni Rabuka, the army officer who had led the 1987 coups and went on to become an elected civilian prime minister under the 1990 constitution, set in train a review of the constitution that changed Fiji's political direction once again. The constitution promulgated in 1997 returned Fiji to a much more open system of government; elections held in May 1999 produced, for the first time, a prime minister of Indian ancestry. But as with the 1970 constitution (abrogated in 1987), indigenous rights and special interests were well protected.

For a year following the elections, Fiji seemed to be on the way to consolidating itself as a successful multi-ethnic state in what can only be described as the most extraordinary political turnaround since 1987. Although a chauvinistic form of Fijian nationalism remained a force in politics, the processes leading to the promulgation of the new constitution and the election of a multi-ethnic government appeared to demonstrate a commitment among a significant number of indigenous Fijians to inclusive, democratic rule. On the international scene, the return of broad-based constitutional government meant that Fiji was welcomed back into the Commonwealth, foreign relations generally were "normalized," and Fiji could once again take a place in international society as a state that measured up to recognized standards of basic political rights for all its citizens.

But on 19 May 2000, Fiji again experienced a radical breakdown of constitutional government. In the immediate aftermath, the prospects of a return to democratic constitutional government in the near future seemed limited. However, in March 2001 the Fiji Court of Appeal upheld an earlier ruling by the High Court in November 2000 that the 1997 constitution remained valid. The Court of Appeal further ruled that parliament had not been dissolved in May 2000 following military intervention, but effectively had been prorogued.[3] In a series of interesting maneuvers of doubtful legality, the interim administration put in place by the army in the wake of the coup nevertheless continued in office. But it was obliged to call fresh elections, and these were held in August 2001.[4] In a poll characterized by increased ethnic polarization, the leader of the interim government was returned to power via the electoral process.

Although the 1997 constitution was reactivated by the courts and fresh elections held, Fiji's constitutional democracy must still in 2002 be regarded as fragile, with the country highly vulnerable to failure at the regime level. Fiji has yet to survive a genuine succession of government for a full and uninterrupted term of office, and one in which Fijian Indians as well as indigenous Fijians have a meaningful share of power. Although Fiji as a state is not a failure, it has so far failed to live up to certain criteria of successful statehood in terms of maintaining basic political security and stability.

States, Statehood, and the State System

The multitude of factors giving rise to the problems of developing world/ex-colonial states, which include many of the small island states of the South Pacific, have been explored not only in the recent failed states literature, but in the "strong state/weak state" literature as well.[5] At a general level, a failed state is "utterly incapable of sustaining itself as a member of the international community." The prime characteristics of the internal conditions giving rise to this failure are civil strife, government breakdown, and economic privation.[6] In considering internal factors, Stohl and Lopez elaborate the concept of a "weak state" that has little to do with weakness vis-à-vis other states but concerns contenders for power within the state. Thus, citing Buzan, they say that the distinguishing feature of weak states is "their high level of concern with domestically generated threats to security of the government."[7] Langford identifies a cluster of internal problems, including "civil strife, political corruption, economic collapse, societal degradation, domestic collapse, human rights abuse, crumbling state infrastructure, and governmental failure."[8] The case of Fiji reflects many of these problems. It must therefore be regarded as a weak state that is vulnerable to further significant problems in maintaining a stable regime structure.

Nicholson focuses more critical attention on the naïve assumption that "if only people were ruled over by members of their own nation, all would be well." He points to the large number of flourishing multinational states on the one hand, and on the other, to the still current, and indeed often excessive, veneration for the concept of nation and therefore of the nation-state, concluding that "nation is a poor basis for state."[9] As we shall see, these observations are especially pertinent to the case of Fiji, where straightforward ethnic tensions between indigenous Fijians and Fiji Indians often have played a less significant role than divisions among Fijians themselves. The fact that much of the failed states and weak states literature focuses on the former colonial world suggests that there are special problems rooted in the colonial experience.

The Colonial State in Fiji

Fiji comprises some 320 islands spread over an area of 650,000 square kilometers in the Southwest Pacific. In terms of population, Fiji's pre-colonial settlement was carried out by different groups at different times, from around 1500 BC to the nineteenth century. This means that the collective entity now known as "indigenous Fijians" has never been homogeneous in socio-political terms, and at the time of European contact "Fiji" (or "Viti") existed as a general name for a quite disparate collection of socio-political entities. The most widely commented on division, and one that has carried the most political salience in the colonial and post-colonial periods, is that between the eastern regions and the western and central regions. This is usually attributed to the differences between the "Polynesian" and the "Melanesian" styles of socio-political organization that characterize these regions, respectively. Another factor is that while the eastern regions are much smaller in terms of population, eastern leaders have historically wielded much more political power.[10]

European settlement began in the early nineteenth century with the development of trade and the arrival of Christian missionaries. Following a period of troubles involving settlers in the islands from the mid-nineteenth century, a prominent chief from the eastern region, Rata Seru Cakobau, asked the British government to encompass the islands within the fold of the British empire. In late 1874, Cakobau and eleven other high chiefs signed an unconditional deed of cession to the British crown.

The formal basis of Fiji's future statehood was thus established with the gathering of the various communities throughout the islands under the mantle of a single colonial authority, recognized under international law if not by all the inhabitants. Indeed, the legitimacy of the act of cession and the colonial government's authority was by no means accepted by all groups in Fiji. Virtually none in the central and western regions had been involved in, or had agreed to, the cession of the whole island group. Attempts to impose colonial rule in these areas therefore met with resistance and only after the deployment of indigenous forces from the east, under British leadership, were these regions "pacified." A feature of the colonial state was in fact its reliance on "loyal" eastern Fijians. Sir Arthur Gordon, Fiji's first substantive governor, was acquainted with the principles of indirect rule and established a system of control through existing chiefs for reasons of both efficacy and economy. Fijian leaders in the central and western regions, however, were not regarded as suitable, so the administration was composed largely of compliant easterners. This pattern of preferential selection persisted throughout the colonial period and into independence, and is reflected in the fact that most of the highest political offices are held by easterners of chiefly status, or those with close connections to them.

The introduction of indentured laborers from India resulted from two major policy considerations. The first concerned preservation of the "Fijian way of life," or at least those aspects that were compatible with both colonial rule and Christian teaching. This was also part of the reasoning behind the bolstering of chiefly status through indirect rule. In addition, the colonial government ended the alienation of native land to Europeans. For ordinary or "commoner" Fijians, protective measures ensured that village life could continue largely undisturbed. These measures included a ban on the extensive use of indigenous labor for plantations. They were later to include a ban on Indians entering Fijian villages, even if invited by local Fijians.

Fiji needed a revenue base which could sustain the colony economically while protecting Fijians from commercial exploitation. Since Fiji's immediate economic future depended on the development of plantations, which required a substantial supply of cheap labor, one solution lay in importing it from a subcontinent teeming with potential workers. Thus Fiji became another destination for the "helots of empire" in a system of slavery by another name—the infamous indenture system.[11] Indian laborers first arrived in 1879 and continued to do so until the system was abolished in 1916. During this period, about 60,000 laborers came to Fiji, and 40,000 chose to remain as free settlers. Most Fiji Indians are descended from this group.

The establishment of a legislative council early in the twentieth century stimulated political activity. Political representation was, from the start, organized on a strictly communal basis in terms of both racially designated seats and racially defined electorates—another feature of the colonial system that has persisted into the present period, although it has undergone many modifications.

Another key issue concerned land. Although Gordon prevented further alienation of land to white settlers, some of the best agricultural land remained in their hands. It was on these tracts, as well as other leased areas, that plantations were established. Gordon also oversaw the start of a process that led to a uniform Fijian land tenure system.[12] That system has been the source of much contention in the present period, since the livelihood of many Fiji Indians remains tied to the land. It has been something of a problem for rural Fijians, too. Some have ready access to arable land but others have very little. The Native Lands Trust Board has also been at the center of a number of corruption scandals. These are issues that underlay the political strife of 2000, and indeed tension during much of the period since independence.

Closely linked to land is the "doctrine of Fijian paramountcy." Stated simply, it holds that the rights and interests of indigenous Fijians with respect to land and customary practices are inalienable. The paramountcy doctrine developed as an orthodoxy from Gordon's time. It reflected not only his concern to protect local interests, but also the concerns of the leading chiefs who sought to preserve their status. That orthodoxy, originally constructed in opposition to perceived threats by white settlers, soon became a rallying cry in opposition to Indian claims for greater political equality.

The military as an institution also impinges on Fiji's current plight.[13] Before colonization, a small force known as the "Royal Army" had been deployed by Cakobau and his British supporters in attempts to control the central and western regions. When Gordon arrived, he used it to subjugate uncooperative areas. The force, renamed the Armed Native Constabulary and consisting exclusively of indigenous Fijians, with recruits coming predominantly from the east, was used for further operations against striking Indian workers in the early 1920s. Fijian soldiers went on to serve in both world wars and the Malayan emergency. During World War II, there had been calls for Indians to enlist, but differing pay rates from those offered to whites prompted most to refuse. During this period, the military evolved into a regular standing army, and became firmly consolidated as a Fijian institution. At the time of the May 1987 coup, 98 percent of the Royal Fiji Military Forces were indigenous Fijians.

The institutions and practices of the colonial regime produced a state that at independence reflected a legacy of the classic "divide and rule" strategy:

—a system of indirect rule that led to the development of an entirely separate system of administration for indigenous Fijians, and in which one segment of the indigenous community was dominant;

—the introduction of many thousands of Indian indentured laborers to support a plantation economy with little regard for how they might be accommodated in the future, especially with respect to access to farming land;

—a racially based system of representation in the legislature that led inevitably to the development of ethnically based parties appealing to communal interests;

—the establishment of a military force composed almost entirely of one ethnic group; and

—the entrenchment of a doctrine of indigenous paramountcy that, however well-intended when first enunciated, laid the foundations for a highly chauvinistic form of Fijian nationalism as it came to be articulated in opposition to Fiji Indian claims.

Fiji's colonial experience therefore gave rise to an independent state characterized by an entrenched "plural society syndrome," in which virtually all political activity was cast in ethnic or racial terms.[14] This result scarcely created the conditions in which democratic constitutional politics was likely to flourish.

The Failure of Constitutionalism in Independent Fiji

Racial politics remained institutionalized under the 1970 constitution of independent Fiji, although there was greater parity of representation. The House of Representatives' electoral system provided for equal numbers of indigenous Fijians and Fiji Indians. It also made provision for the separate representation of whites, part-whites, and "others" in a group known as "general electors." This group, which maintained a close political relationship with indigenous Fijians, remained grossly over-represented until 1990, giving an electoral advantage to the main Fijian party, the Alliance, which governed continuously from 1970 to 1987.

The party system, which had taken shape in the colonial period, was more or less divided along communal lines. As suggested above, this was almost inevitable under a communal system of representation. The National Federation Party

(NFP), formed in the 1960s, was supported largely by Fiji Indians, although membership was technically open to anyone. The Alliance was generally recognized as the indigenous Fijian party, although it incorporated a small Indian Alliance and a General Elector's Alliance. So while both parties were officially multiracial, and sometimes attracted votes from across the communal divide, the general pattern of electioneering and voting followed a communal pattern. Other minor parties reflected certain patterns of dissent, especially among Fijians. The Western United Front, for example, was formed in the 1980s as a vehicle for western and central dissatisfaction over a range of issues, many of which related to eastern dominance. It found some common cause with the NFP, and at one stage entered into a coalition with it. The Fijian Nationalist Party, as its name suggests, attracted the more chauvinistic elements among indigenous Fijians in claiming "Fiji for the Fijians." But it also reflected discontent with the chiefly elite of the Alliance, especially Ratu Sir Kamisese Mara, the prime minister and paramount chief of Lau in the eastern island group.

The party system took a new direction from the mid-1980s with the formation of the Fiji Labour Party. Labour was based initially on the multiracial Fiji Trade Union Congress (FTUC) whose secretary, Mahendra Chaudhry, figured prominently in the party's foundation. Timoci Bavadra, president of the Fiji Public Service Association (FPSA) and an indigenous Fijian, was appointed its first leader. Of the existing major parties, the NFP was riven by internal dissent, even though the ruling Alliance was ripe for challenge. The Alliance leadership appeared aloof and complacent and senior figures in the party were subject to allegations of corruption.

For the 1987 elections, Labour joined in a coalition with the NFP, but as the dominant partner. Their joint rallying cry was that it was time for Fiji to move away from racially based politics and focus instead on social and economic development for the population at large. For its part, many Alliance politicians, although claiming to support multiracial politics, resorted to rhetoric claiming that Fijian interests would face a serious threat under a coalition government. Fijians were urged to remain united behind traditional chiefs in the face of threats to their very existence as a distinct people.

The elections resulted in a narrow but unambiguous win for the coalition. However, the period immediately after the installation of the new government, with Bavadra sworn in as prime minister, was marked by intermittent demonstrations of Fijian nationalist dissent, some orchestrated by defeated Alliance politicians (who boycotted the opening of parliament in protest at their defeat). These events led to the formation of the Taukei movement, committed to overthrowing the new government.[15] Although Taukei nationalism obviously attracted some Fijians, and threats of violence led to law and order concerns, it seemed by the end of the first month that nationalist activity was waning, as fewer people were being drawn to Taukei rallies.

Notwithstanding the behavior of disgruntled defeated politicians and chauvinistic displays of Fijian nationalism, the events of May 1987, when the third-ranking officer of the Royal Fiji Military Forces took the government hostage at gunpoint on the floor of the parliament, came as a surprise to many observers both within Fiji and abroad. For whatever troubles the country had experienced over the years, the resolution of political differences had never before been carried out at gunpoint. But previous experience had not included the transfer of power from the ruling party to the opposition, an event that provided the ultimate test of democratic constitutional processes.[16] Coup-leader Rabuka's major justification was framed in terms of the paramountcy of indigenous Fijian rights and the claim that they were under threat from the new government. Although specific Fijian rights and interests were entrenched under the 1970 constitution, and could not be altered without the consent of the Great Council of Chiefs (who were hardly likely to sign away such rights and interests), this protection was completely ignored.

The 1987 coup created severe difficulties for Fiji on a number of fronts. The economy suffered a significant drop in tourist revenue (its second biggest foreign currency earner after sugar exports), as well as the suspension of aid programs. This prompted a move within Fiji to establish a civilian government, and by September the governor-general announced a proposal for an interim government made up of parliamentarians from both the Alliance and the deposed government. But just as the final agreement on this was reached, Rabuka intervened again on the grounds that it compromised the "objectives" of the May coup, namely the entrenchment of Fijian political supremacy. Rabuka then abrogated the 1970 constitution and declared Fiji a republic. This led to a fresh round of international protests, renewed threats to aid and trade programs, and the exclusion of Fiji from the Commonwealth.

Fiji's immediate political future was set on a course that led, in 1990, to the promulgation of a constitution in which Fiji Indians were relegated to a position of little effective political power. Of the seventy seats in the reconstituted House of Representatives, Fijians were awarded thirty-seven; Fiji Indians, twenty-seven; and others, six. Moreover, all seats were to be elected communally. In other words, whereas the 1970 constitution provided for cross-voting in a number of "national" seats, thereby encouraging some measure of multiracial electoral behavior, the 1990 constitution entrenched an even stronger system of racially based politics.

If its architects believed that this system would contribute not only to Fijian domination but to Fijian unity, they were very much mistaken. Rather, the new provisions simply fuelled political disunity among Fijians. The electoral provisions not only discriminated against Fiji Indians, but also tipped the balance toward rural rather than urban Fijian voters, and eastern versus central and western Fijians. In addition, the political alliance among eastern Fijians was no longer as solid as it had appeared to be in previous years, and serious rivalries had emerged there as well. Various new Fijian political parties formed and factions proliferated. Moreover, the period of Fijian paramountcy in parliament was marked by one corruption scandal after another. Rabuka, having resigned from the military in order to pursue a civilian career in politics, presided over much of this period as the elected prime minister. His party, the Soqosoqo ni Vakavulewa ni Taukei (SVT), had been sponsored by the Great Council of Chiefs, but with Fijian disunity becoming a hallmark of post-coup politics, he was unable to govern except through an unstable coalition. Another irony of this period is that in the 1992 elections, Rabuka defeated a Fijian rival "with the aid of some of the Indian leaders he had overthrown at gunpoint."[17]

The architects of the 1990 constitution had provided for its review within seven years. Although many observers may have harbored a justifiable scepticism as to whether this review would ever take place, a Constitutional Review Committee (CRC) was appointed in 1995. A combination of pressures induced Rabuka and his government colleagues to initiate the review. At home, the government was beset by contradictions—having to play to an ethno-nationalist constituency while trying to manage a national economy largely dependent on the skills and capital of non-indigenous people. Indian protests against the 1990 constitution also received continued support from Australia, New Zealand, Britain, and the United States, which remained Fiji's most important aid donors and trading partners. In addition, economic problems had been exacerbated by high rates of emigration by skilled Fiji Indians and by declining foreign investment.[18] Fijian leaders also found it difficult to retain institutions founded on the explicit denial of political equality. Doing so profoundly undermined Fiji's international respectability. "[R]ejoining the British Commonwealth and so indirectly reviving Fiji's historical association with the British monarchy . . . was widely upheld as restoring the country's lost international legitimacy and enhancing the prospects for an expansion in overseas investment."[19]

In September 1996, the CRC produced a 700-page report that recommended radical changes to the constitution.[20] It was based on a wide consultative process; the commissioners heard submissions from every region.[21] Under its terms of reference, the commission had been asked to recommend constitutional arrangements that would promote racial harmony as well as the economic and social advancement of all communities, while ensuring appropriate protection of indigenous Fijians and "full regard for the rights, interests and concerns of all other ethnic groups."[22]

The report made some pertinent observations on the communal aspects of Fiji's political system and the adaptability of the Westminster system. The commissioners' views were contrary to the insistence of many Fijian nationalists that full parliamentary democracy was a "foreign flower," unsuitable for transplanting in alien soil:

> In Fiji's ethnically mixed society, communal seats have provided assured representation for each community. The cost has been the serious obstacles placed in the way of multi-ethnic government under the Westminster parliamentary system that Fiji inherited. The fault, we believe, does not lie in the Westminster system itself. It has shown robustness in adapting to new political climates. . . . The problems lie in trying to combine the Westminster system with exclusively or mainly communal representation.[23]

The report also spelled out the full implications of a communal system, including the fact that those hoping to be elected would inevitably appeal to communal interests. It addressed the issue of Fijian unity and, on the basis of the political record of the past few years, concluded not only that permanent Fijian unity was unrealistic, but that efforts to pursue it had come at a high cost to Fijians themselves.[24] The key recommendations of the commission were:

1. The primary goal of Fiji's constitutional arrangements should be to encourage the emergence of multiracial governments.

2. The constitution should continue to be based on the Westminster system of parliamentary government.

3. Power-sharing should be achieved through the voluntary cooperation of political parties or increased support for a genuinely multi-ethnic party.

4. The people of Fiji should move gradually but decisively away from the communal system of representation. They should adopt electoral arrangements that encourage parties to seek the support of other communities as well as their own.

5. Backbench members of all parties should have the opportunity to take part in sector standing committees that monitor every aspect of government's responsibilities.

6. The constitution should

(a) recognize the important role of the Bose Levu Vakaturaga [Great Council of Chiefs];

(b) protect individual human rights and the rights of groups, including rights to and in land;

(c) require social justice and affirmative action programs for Fijian and Rotuman communities as well as for other disadvantaged communities and groups.[25]

7. The constitution should be based on the principle that the interests of all communities must be recognized and protected. It should explicitly recognize the protective function of the principle that the interests of the indigenous Fijians are paramount, on the understanding that it does not involve the relegation of the interests of other communities.[26]

From a firm nationalist position, rearticulated from time to time since 1992 (although also interspersed with calls for reconciliation, multiculturalism, and equal rights), Rabuka decided to back the report's broad vision. Although its specific recommendations were modified by a Joint Parliamentary Select Committee, the reformist character of the report was reflected in the final product. Rabuka himself shed tears of humility as he tabled the report in parliament and confessed:

> Ten years ago I was convinced that there was no other way to safeguard the national security interests of Fiji. Today I can say with the same strength of conviction that I believe there is only one way. We must stand together [and] commit ourselves towards a united future.[27]

The 1997 constitution recognized "that the descendants of all those who chose to make their homes in these islands form our multicultural society"; affirmed "the contributions of all communities to the well-being of that society, and the rich variety of their faiths, traditions, languages and cultures"; and announced "pride in our common citizenship and in the development of our economy and political institutions."[28] These and other similar statements of principle, as well as provisions for the separation of religion and state and the equal status of the English, Fijian, and Hindi languages, reflected a strong commitment to the ideals of an inclusive multiculturalism within a framework of democratic constitutionalism. A key recommendation of the report relating to seats in the House of Representatives, however, was only partially embraced. A relatively large number of communal seats were retained: twenty-five for Fijians, nineteen for Indians and four for others. But twenty-five common roll seats were introduced with no racial qualifications for either candidates or voters.

It was on this basis that Fiji's political parties reorganized their electoral strategies for the first set of general elections to take place under the new constitution, in May 1999. Rabuka remained leader of the SVT. Its next most important rival for indigenous Fijian votes was the Fijian Association Party (FAP). The Fijian Nationalist Party, led by Sakeasi Butadroka since it was formed in the 1980s, once again contested the elections under its "Fiji for the Fijians" platform. The Party of National Unity (PANU) represented a western-based Fijian constituency. Another new Fijian party, the Christian Democrats (*Veitokani ni Lewenivanua Vakaristo*), was "dedicated to chiefly tradition and Methodist values but, above all, to ousting Rabuka from power."[29]

The election was not contested as a "Fijian versus Indian" battle. On the contrary, one side consisted of a coalition of Rabuka's SVT; the NFP, still under its long-time leader, Jai Ram Reddy, and still supported almost exclusively by Fiji Indians; and a party representing general electors, the United Generals Party (UGP). The other main grouping, styled the "People's Coalition," consisted of Labour, which now also had a predominantly Fiji Indian support base, PANU, and the FAP.[30] In short, neither of the two main opposing coalition groups was mono-ethnic, even though their constituent parts were rooted largely in particular communities.

The SVT won only eight seats to the FAP's eleven, PANU's four, and the Christian Democrats' three. Fiji Indian voters were also divided, but the split was basically between two parties only: Labour and the NFP. The latter failed to pick up a single seat. Labour won thirty-seven out of the seventy-one seats and could have governed in its own right. This was a spectacular result for Labour, and although the bulk of its support was from among Fiji Indians, some Fijian votes in the open seats almost certainly helped.

The new coalition government, with Chaudhry as prime minister, the leader of PANU as deputy prime minister, and eleven cabinet posts held by indigenous Fijians out of a total of seventeen took office without incident. Indeed President Ratu Sir Kamisese Mara, suspected by some as having played a hand in the 1987 coup after showing himself to be a poor loser at the polls, now urged full support for the new government.[31] Mara himself was alienated from Rabuka and the SVT—another example of the political divisions among indigenous Fijians. It is certainly plausible that the playing out of chiefly rivalries in the contemporary political context, and conversely, the use of chiefly stature as a passport to political prominence, were important factors behind the fragmentation of indigenous Fijian votes among rival parties.[32] Following the elections there was a great deal of dissent among nationalists, with some calling for the immediate overthrow of the new government, but disunity in their own ranks was as much the reason for Labour's outstanding electoral success as was anything else.

Fragmented though indigenous Fijian politics were, Chaudhry could not fail to be acutely aware of how dangerous Fijian nationalism could be. He knew that every effort would have to be made to allay the fears and sentiments aroused by nationalist claims. He became the second Fiji Indian ever to address the Great Council of Chiefs, and his speech there, in the wake of his appointment as prime minister, promised to protect and advance indigenous interests as well as to consult with chiefs. Norton reported that although many Fijians may have continued to feel that a Fijian should lead Fiji, "the predominant view was acceptance in anticipation of action on the electoral promises."[33]

The new government had many difficult tasks ahead, nationalist sentiments being only one problem area. The economy needed urgent attention and, as a Labour leader committed to alleviating poverty and unemployment, Chaudhry attempted to make it an issue for all sectors. One of the most contentious issues, however, concerned the renewal of Fiji Indian farmers' leases on agricultural land, with many Fijians taking a hard line against renewals or even adequate compensation for displaced families. Again, this problem was often portrayed simply as "Fijian versus Indian," with Chaudhry accused of favoring Fiji Indians over indigenous Fijians.[34] A media report a month before Speight's coup said: "Chaudhry's assurances that none of his policies are intended to harm Fijian interests in any way are falling on ears tuned to be deaf to them. His problem with the land lease issue is a massive one that will make or break his government."[35]

These problems were exacerbated by disunity within the coalition, largely revolving around a leadership row and possible split within Labour's main coalition party, the FAP. Ratu Tu'uakitau Cokonauto, the leader of the dissenting faction in the FAP, claimed that Chaudhry was only using the FAP as "an ornament to give the government a Fijian face" and asked, "What Fijian with dignity will allow himself to be used as a chattel to legitimise a government that is overtly anti-Fijian."[36] This attitude was hardly helpful to the cause of government unity. Much attention has also been focused on Chaudhry's personal style, which was frequently described as abrasive and confrontational. In a retrospective analysis, one report says that "with a style that antagonised not only indigenous Fijians, but increasingly his own Labour supporters, [Chaudhry] lay the ground that indigenous Fijian politicians and people with business and other interests threatened by Chaudhry's style of socialism found easy to undermine."[37]

When the government was taken hostage at gunpoint on 19 May 2000, news headlines again focused on "ethnic tensions" as the principal cause behind the takeover. And Speight, as Rabuka before him, could only plausibly justify his actions by reference to a higher cause, namely, the protection of Fijian rights under threat from an "Indian government." But Speight's record made him unconvincing as a selfless hero of Fijian interests. Various reports described him as a bankrupt businessman, not only wanted in Australia for fraud, but more recently sacked by the government as chair of Fiji Hardwoods and due to face extortion charges in a Fijian court.[38] And while he certainly held a trump at the time, in the form of weapons trained at the heads of his hostages, Speight was subsequently shown to have little personal backing among Fiji's most prominent indigenous Fijian leaders. He failed initially to receive backing from the Great Council of Chiefs, which met in emergency session a few days after the coup. If he had expected immediate support from the military, he was disappointed there, too.[39] But media images of some indigenous Fijians demonstrating vigorously in support of Speight's actions, as well as the spectacle of others rioting and looting Indian businesses in the capital as news of the coup spread, gave at least superficial support to his claim that he had widespread indigenous support.[40]

Within a week, the Great Council of Chiefs had acceded to some of Speight's principal demands, including the replacement of the elected government by an interim administration. But Speight now wanted more. His demands included the resignation of President Mara, a permanent immunity from prosecution, abrogation of the 1997 constitution, the restoration of complete Fijian political control, and an interim administration headed by himself, with his own nominees in key positions.[41] Hostages remained imprisoned in the parliamentary compound. In the midst of continuing civil disorder and with the political situation in apparent stalemate, the military stepped in. By the end of the second week of the coup, Commodore Frank Bainimarama, head of Fiji's military forces, imposed martial law.[42] Although Speight was never really in a position to control events, his stated objectives appeared to have been met. Bainimarama revoked the constitution and confirmed the elected government's dismissal. Mara stepped aside as president, while Speight's request for amnesty was endorsed.[43] The hostages were finally released on 13 July 2000.

Subsequent developments saw a new interim civilian government, formed under the supervision of the military and supported by the Great Council of Chiefs. Laisenia Qarase, a man sympathetic to nationalist views, became interim prime minister. While an indeterminate number of indigenous Fijians no doubt supported his administration, it had virtually no legitimacy among the Fiji Indian community. After assuming power, a widespread program of affirmative action aimed at ensuring "progress and development" by indigenous Fijians was announced. Opponents described some of the proposals as nothing short of "ethnic cleansing," especially since the new policies were likely to mean the displacement of significant numbers of Fiji Indian cane growers and their families. Such actions also seem to confirm that the coup really was about ethnic issues or, more specifically, the re-establishment of Fijian ascendancy. Critics nonetheless argued that the coup had little to do with indigenous rights as such, but rather aimed to "restore the power of some defeated politicians, failed businessmen and a corrupt elite that was losing special privileges."[44]

Another aspect of these developments is that past affirmative action regimes had produced little in the way of tangible benefits for most ordinary Fijians. Tupeni Baba, one of the ousted Labour leaders, points out that previous schemes led to mismanagement, corruption, cronyism, and bankruptcy, as well as to the near-collapse of the Bank of Fiji—under the strain of bad debts as well as huge financial losses by the Fiji Development Fund and provincial councils.[45] In terms of domestic order in the weeks and months following the coup, reports of orchestrated destruction, arson, looting, and the terrorizing of Fiji Indians and their homes, especially in rural areas, were common.[46] On the other hand, Speight and twenty associates were charged with treason, a charge to which Speight eventually pleaded guilty. He was given the mandatory death sentence but, not unexpectedly, that was immediately commuted to life imprisonment. It would be surprising if he were not granted a pardon at some stage. The present political leadership of Fiji effectively owes its position to Speight.

International condemnation of the events of 19 May was widespread. Statements from Australia and New Zealand, the European Union (EU), India, and the United States, as well as the Commonwealth, indicated unequivocal support for the elected government and the constitution and unreserved condemnation of Speight's actions. EU envoys sought talks with Mara in the early stages (when he was still president) and warned that an accord due to be signed in Fiji between the EU and former African, Caribbean, and Pacific island colonies was at risk.[47] While unions in Fiji prepared to engage in strike action, the International Confederation of Trade Unions joined in the international condemnation, its secretary declaring that it would take determined action to ensure the restoration of legitimate government.[48]

Five days after the coup, Speight warned against international intervention in the situation, saying that "we are capable of resolving it ourselves" and that "Fijians would accept economic hardship and sanctions for enhanced indigenous rights."[49] With few other options at their disposal, hardship in the form of suspension of aid and defense links, and possibly trade and other sanctions, were indeed threatened by Alexander Downer, the Australian foreign minister. He also warned of the impending suspension of Fiji from the Commonwealth, as well as the cancellation of the Fijian leg of the Olympic torch route.[50] In New Zealand, the Council of Trade Unions pointed out that replacing the constitution with a racially based one was reminiscent of apartheid South Africa, and that Fiji's future participation in international sport would be placed in doubt.[51]

Throughout its tenure as the interim administration and following its formal election in 2000, the Qarase government showed no signs of backing away from a nationalist position, despite much talk of "reconciliation and under-standing" between communities. In Qarase's terms, this phrase meant that Fiji Indians must reconcile themselves to a subordinate status vis-à-vis the para-mountcy of Fijian political control. This was evident in Qarase's speech to the first meeting of a new constitution commission that he set up before the court ruled on the continuing validity of the 1997 constitution. Addressing the as-sembled members, he said that only one perspective could guide them: "And that is our national and collective interests, as a nation, to frame a constitution that would best suit our country with its multi-ethnic and multi-cultural society, but also, taking into account the interest and aspirations of indigenous Fijian and Rotuman communities." He went on to suggest that in 1997, reservations expressed by the Great Council of Chiefs and some provincial councils were not taken fully into account by the government at the time (although the consti-tution was endorsed unanimously by the former body).[52]

Qarase's speech also made much of "determining the common will of the people" and of a commitment to "returning Fiji to constitutional democracy." But at the same time he said that the constitutional protection of Fijian rights and interests was not enough—Fijians must also control government. The con-tradictions embedded in Qarase's speech were clear. And if a new constitution had been drawn up under Qarase's administration, it would almost certainly once again have enshrined a system of political apartheid. The reinstatement of the 1997 constitution, however, was clearly no guarantee of a stable, demo-cratic future. Any government formed under its provisions that can be por-trayed by nationalists as compromising indigenous rights will be subject to the threat of serious destabilization, if not outright intervention, regardless of its parliamentary majority.

Fiji as a Failing State?

Fiji has failed to sustain constitutional democratic government, based on an inclusive notion of legitimate citizenship for all communities in the country, since it became independent. Although Fiji enjoyed a seventeen-year period of uninterrupted parliamentary rule from 1970 to 1987, constitutional structures have not survived a change of government from one dominated almost exclu-sively by indigenous Fijians to one in which Fiji Indians have a meaningful share of political power. When changes of government have initially occurred, civil strife, deliberately orchestrated and encouraged by nationalists and de-feated politicians, has led to serious law and order problems. In 1987, the threat to domestic security was given as a justification for military intervention. In May 2000, civil strife in the form of rioting, looting, and destruction of property, as well as the terrorizing of Fiji Indians followed directly in the wake of Speight's coup. The military once again intervened as an agent in its own right, rather than at the command of a lawful civil authority. These factors are among those generally associated with failed states.

Given the now well-established precedents for military intervention, regime vulnerability in Fiji is a real problem. As I argued in an earlier analysis of the 1987 coups and their longer term implications for democracy in Fiji, a democratic constitutional framework survived the period 1970–1987 at an overt but superficial level. Once the Alliance government, dominated by conservative chiefly figures and supported by traditionalist Fijian conceptions of legitimacy, lost office to Bavadra's coalition, the vulnerability of the constitutional regime was quickly revealed.[53] Similarly, the failure of those who took power after Speight's initial intervention to restore the existing constitutional regime, having opted instead to support the stated objectives of Speight's coup, shows that significant sections of Fiji's indigenous political (and military) leadership are unable to play by the constitutional rules that they themselves had a significant part in shaping, but that turned out not to guarantee them political power.

I have argued that the undemocratic regime instituted after 1987 carried within it the seeds of its own destruction. It rested on a myth of Fijian homogeneity underscored by traditionalist conceptions of legitimate chiefly authority that were increasingly difficult to sustain.[54] Fijian unity under traditional chiefly authority was, in the end, demonstrably unsustainable, as events in the post-1987 period have shown so clearly. A 2001 report quotes one chief, Ratu Ilisoni Qio Ravoka of Varata, as saying that deliberations in the Great Council of Chiefs were marked by "personal differences, backstabbing, *vanua* jealousy, and traditional power struggle."[55] It is unlikely that the immediate future will be significantly different. Indeed, although Qarase's United Fijian Party (officially named the Soqosoqo Duavata ni Lewenivanua, or SDL) won more seats than any other "Fijian" party, seven seats went to other indigenous-based parties, including five to the extremist nationalist Matanitu Vanua (MV).

As for the notion that Fijians can only prosper if ruled by other Fijians, the history of social and economic development among indigenous Fijians in independent Fiji, not to mention the fracturing of indigenous Fijian politics along so many different cleavages, shows how false is such an assumption. Qarase's own speech highlighted the extent to which Fijians are perceived to be lagging behind other communities. Yet, for almost the whole of the independence period, Fiji has been ruled by Fijian-dominated governments ostensibly committed to the paramountcy of indigenous interests and the implementation of affirmative action programs of one kind or another. These programs, however, have been based on a simplistic, and indeed false, dichotomy between disadvantaged Fijians and more fortunate or privileged others, and have served mainly to benefit a select few at the expense not only of Fiji Indians, but of many other Fijians as well. Given these factors, as well as the second-class status that the great bulk of Fiji's other citizens have had forced on them due to such policies, "nation" has proved to be a poor basis for political legitimacy in Fiji. Yet, this is the path that the interim government, the Great Council of Chiefs, and the military were committed to until the Court of Appeal's ruling upholding the 1997 constitution. Even though this constitution has survived, the Qarase government is nonetheless committed to nationalist policies that can only strengthen the divisions within Fiji's polity.

Fiji is now a weakened state where constitutional rule has been severely compromised by nationalist politicians and other opportunists seeking to advance their interests at the expense of both ordinary Fijians and Fiji Indians. But it cannot be regarded as a state that is prone to significant failure, certainly not when compared with a number of other strife-torn places, like Somalia, the Congo, and the components of former Yugoslavia. But like those places, the principal threats to security, order, and justice under a constitutional regime come not from an external source but from an essential weakness within. Much of the failed state and weak state literature has, rightly, focused on precisely this internal weakness. In the case of Fiji, the essential weakness seems to be related directly to the ethnic composition of Fiji's population. But as in so many other cases of so-called "ethnic conflict," there is a great deal more to the story than that. In the final analysis, the problems in Fiji are as much about intra-Fijian political rivalries and sheer opportunism in taking advantage of the ethnic factor.

Notes

1. See I. William Zartman, "Introduction: Posing the Problem of State Collapse," in I. William Zartman (ed.), *Collapsed States: The Disintegration and Restoration of Legitimate Authority* (Boulder, 1995), 1. Here, Zartman argues that state collapse is much deeper than "mere rebellion, coup or riot." He says that it "refers to a situation where the structure, authority (legitimate power), law, and political order have fallen apart and must be reconstituted in some form, old or new."

2. See Samuel E. Finer, *The Man on Horseback: The Role of the Military in Politics* (London, 1962).

3. *Republic of Fiji Islands and Attorney General v. Prasad,* Summary of Court of Appeal Judgement of March 1, 2001. Document at http://www. fijilive.net/extras/ Co...peal_Ruling/march2001/01/lzl3.htm.

4. See Robert Keith-Reid, "What Next?" *Pacific Magazine* (April 2001, South edn.), 19–21.

5. See especially Joel Migdal, *Strong Societies and Weak States: State-Society Relations and State Capabilities in the Third World* (Princeton, 1988).

6. Gerald B. Helman and Steven R. Ratner, "Saving Failed States," *Foreign Policy,* LXXXIX (1992–1993), 3.

7. Michael Stohl and George Lopez, "Westphalia, the End of the Cold War and the New World Order: Old Roots to a 'New' Problem," paper read to the conference on "Failed States and International Security: Causes, Prospects and Consequences," Purdue University, West Lafayette (February 25–27, 1998), www.ippu.purdue.edu/info/gsp/FSIS_CONF/stohl_paper.html.

8. Tonya Langford, "Things Fall Apart: State Failure and the Politics of Intervention," *International Studies Review,* I (1999), 61.

9. Michael Nicholson, "Failing States, Failing Systems," paper read to the conference on "Failed States and International Security: Causes, Prospects and Consequences," Purdue University, West Lafayette (February 25–27, 1998), www.ippu.purdue.edu/info/gsp/FSIS_CONF/mnpaper.html.

10. For a detailed discussion, including some of the controversies surrounding the use of "Polynesian" and "Melanesian" to describe socio-political structures, see Stephanie Lawson, *The Failure of Democratic Politics in Fiji* (Oxford, 1991). For a discussion of political factors associated with the divisions in the wake of the 1987 coup, including imbalances between electorates favoring easterners, see Stephanie Lawson, *Tradition versus Democracy in the South Pacific: Fiji, Tonga and Western Samoa* (Cambridge, 1996), 67–69. Note, also, that the combined population of the central and western divisions, together with the Suva urban area, constitutes almost 80 percent of the total population of Fiji. (See http://www.library.uu.nl.wesp/populstat/Oceania/fijip.htm.) Most Fiji Indians also live in these areas.

11. See Hugh Tinker, *A New System of Slavery: The Export of Indian Labour Overseas 1830–1920* (London, 1974).

12. See Peter France, *The Charter of the Land* (Melbourne, 1969); R. Gerard Ward, "Land, Law and Custom: Diverging Realities in Fiji," in Ward and Elizabeth Kingdon (eds.), *Land, Custom and Practice in the South Pacific* (Cambridge, 1995).

13. For more details see Stephanie Lawson, "The Military versus Democracy in Fiji," in R. J. May and Viberto Selochan (eds.), *The Military and Democracy in Asia and the Pacific* (London, 1998), 141–142.

14. The idea of the "plural society syndrome" is developed more fully in Lawson, *The Failure of Democratic Politics in Fiji,* 35–40.

15. "*Taukei*" translates more or less as "owners of the land." It is often used in contrast with *vulagi,* which means "foreigner" or "stranger," and is often applied to Fijian Indians by nationalist Fijians.

16. This is the key argument of Lawson, *The Failure of Democratic Politics,* and one echoed subsequently by Constitutional Review Commission (CRC) commissioner and academic Brij V. Lal in "A Time to Change: The Fiji General Elections of 1999" (Canberra, 1999), 3, at http://rspas.anu.edu.au/ccp/election.htm.

17. Robert Norton, "Reconciling Ethnicity and Nation: Contending Discourses in Fiji's Constitutional Reform," *Contemporary Pacific,* XII (2000), 85.

18. Ibid., 90. Norton also notes that Indian emigration since 1987 swung the demographic balance in favor of indigenous Fijians (now around 51 percent Fijian to an Indian total of 44 percent) and that this gave Fijian leaders more confidence in proposing reforms.

19. Jon Fraenkel, "The Triumph of the Non-Idealist Intellectuals? An Investigation of Fiji's 1999 Election Results," *Australian Journal of Politics and History,* XLVI (2000), 88.

20. Paul Reeves, Tomasi Rayalu Vakatora, and Brij Vilash Lal, *The Fiji Islands: Towards a United Future,* published as *Report of the Fiji Constitution Review Commission,* Parliament of Fiji, Parliamentary Paper no. 34 (1996).

21. Ibid. Appendix C details the public hearings, while Appendix D lists approximately 230 individual submissions and approximately 550 group submissions.

22. Ibid., 4.

23. Ibid., 11.

24. Ibid., 14–15.

25. Rotuma is a small island to the north of the Fiji islands, incorporated at independence. Rotumans are usually distinguished from Fijians and have always had their own political representatives, although these have generally been counted among indigenous Fijians.

26. Reeves et al., *The Fiji Islands,* 22–23.

27. Quoted in Sandra Tarte, "Melanesia in Review: Issues and Events, 1997 (Fiji)," in *Contemporary Pacific,* X (1998), 426.

28. Constitution of the Republic of the Fiji Islands, as contained in the Act to Alter the Constitution of the Sovereign Democratic Republic of Fiji, signed by K. K. T. Mara, President (15 July 1997), wysiwyg://19/http://www.fijiconstitution.com/constitution/act.shtm.

29. Fraenkel, "The Triumph of the Non-Idealist Intellectuals?" 93.

30. Interestingly, the Fijian Association Party at one stage joined with the NFP and the General Electors Party to field a joint candidate in municipal elections in 1996—thus demonstrating just how fluid allegiances can be. See Sandra Tarte, "Melanesia in Review: Issues and Events, 1996 (Fiji)," in *Contemporary Pacific,* IX (1997), 460.

31. See "Chaudhry Succeeds Rabuka as Fiji's PM as Labour Party Triumphs," *Pacific Magazine* (July/August 1999).

32. Fraenkel, "The Triumph of the Non-Idealist Intellectuals?" 94.

33. Norton, "Reconciling Ethnicity and Nation," 115.

34. For more detail on the land issues and the implications for the May 2000 coup, including Speight's involvement in Fiji Hardwoods and the management of Fiji's valuable mahogany plantations, see Sandra Tarte, "Fiji in Review, 2000," *Contemporary Pacific,* XIII (2001).

35. "The Region," *Pacific Magazine* (April 2000), 27.

36. Ibid.

37. "The Region," *Pacific Magazine* (September 2000), 30.

38. "Coup 'Stems from Personal Grudges,'" *Daily Telegraph* (London, 22 May 2000), 12.

39. Nonetheless, the military and the police stood by while the initial looting and rioting went on after the coup. According to Tarte, an announcement from military headquarters said that while the military did not support the coup and would continue to recognize the elected government, it claimed to be awaiting instructions from the Ministry of Home Affairs, which, in turn, claimed to be awaiting instructions from the new "interim home affairs minister" named by Speight. Some order returned when President Mara declared a state of emergency. The army then deployed two battalions to assist police, but not within the parliamentary compound where the hostages were being held. See Tarte, "Fiji in Review, 2000."

40. In a single day, 167 Fiji Indian–owned shops in the capital, Suva, were looted and burnt, at an estimated cost of 22 million Australian dollars. See *Sun-Herald* (Sydney, 21 May 2000), 7.

41. "Fiji Tribal Chiefs Give In to Gunmen Holding PM," *Daily Telegraph* (26 May 2000), 15.

42. "Miracle on Main Street as Army Takes Over," *Australian* (31 May 2000), 7.

43. "Complex Way of Doing Business," *Australian* (31 May 2000), 6. See also Fiji Constitution Revocation Decree 2000, Interim Military Government Decree No. 1, gazetted 29 May 2000, *Fiji Islands Government Gazette,* I (29 May 2000).

44. "Moves to Restore Order in Fiji," *Pacific News Bulletin* (August 2000), 7.

45. "Fiji's Grappling Questions," *Pacific News Bulletin* (August 2000), 2.

46. See, for example, "Reign of Terror Spreads to Villages," *Sydney Morning Herald* (25 May 2000), 12.

47. "Treaty in Jeopardy, Say Europeans," *Sydney Morning Herald* (22 May 2000), 9.

48. "Unions to Strike until Democracy Restored," *Sydney Morning Herald* (23 May 2000), 9.

49. "Warning to World: Do Not Meddle," *Australian* (24 May 2000), 4.

50. "Downer, Unions Put Speight on Notice," *Weekend Australia* (27–28 May 2000), 7.

51. "Kiwis Call for Rugby Final Boycott," *Weekend Australia* (27–28 May 2000), 7.

52. Fiji, Ministry of Information, press release, Laisenia Qarase, Prime Minister and Minister for National Reconciliation and Unity, "Message on Fiji Day," 6 October 2000, www.fiji.gov.fj/core/press/2000_10_06_2.html.

53. Lawson, "The Military versus Democracy."

54. Ibid.

55. Quoted in Jon Fraenkel, "Disunity Through Diversity? The Contours of Fiji's Post-Putsch Elections," *Pacific Economic Bulletin*, XVI (2001), 153.

CHAPTER ELEVEN

Haiti:
A Case of Endemic Weakness

MARLYE GÉLIN-ADAMS
DAVID M. MALONE

Haiti, the second sovereign nation in the Western Hemisphere after the United States, will celebrate its bicentennial in 2004. Yet, the main legacy of nearly two centuries of independence has been a series of crises undermining a frequently paralyzed and nearly always predatory political system, a debilitated economy, and a dilapidated judiciary. Governance in Haiti has long been associated with deep failures in public security services. Since these problems derive in large part from a traditionally weak Haitian state incapable of effectively addressing the country's needs, understanding Haiti today requires an analysis of the persisting systemic weaknesses of the state. A recent stalemate, triggered by the tainted May 2000 legislative and local elections, has heightened the country's political and socio-economic problems and has further delayed the disbursement of over $500 million in much needed international assistance.[1]

As a result of prolonged political paralysis and a lack of funds, recent governments have failed to address rampant rates of poverty, crime, violence, drug trafficking, unemployment, illiteracy, infant mortality, AIDS, deforestation, and overpopulation. Ranking 150th out of 174 countries worldwide, Haiti remains the only nation in the Americas to be classified in the "low human development" category of the United Nations Development Program's Human Development Index.[2] President Jean-Bertrand Aristide—who started a second nonconsecutive term in February 2001—announced his intention to resolve the deadlock, but a December 2001 attempted coup against his government, and

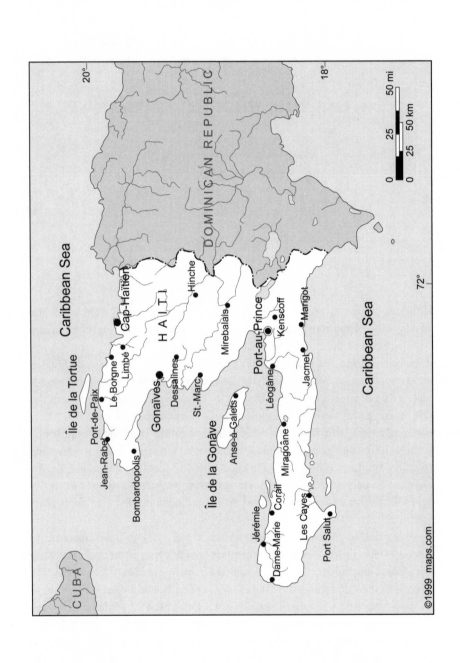

©1999 maps.com

his prime minister's resignation in January 2002, signaled that the outlook for Haiti continued bleak.[3] In the absence of viable state institutions, Haiti as a nation-state in 2002 remains as weak as ever. Indeed, Haiti may again be approaching state failure.

Haiti has remained endemically weak since independence as a nation-state. This chapter focuses on the four phases of Haiti's continuing weakness: the post-independence era from 1804 to the early 1900s, the American Occupation period from 1915 to 1934, the Duvalier dictatorships from 1957 to 1986, and the post-Duvalier era from 1986 to the present. Three central governance characteristics have been present throughout most of Haiti's history: a failure to provide basic services for the citizenry, an incapacity to generate economic development, and a high tolerance for violence and disorder. This chapter highlights how the interplay between detrimental national policies and different but equally deleterious practices by international actors have favored state weakness for nearly two centuries.

The Setting

Haiti, at 27,560 square kilometers, shares the western third of the Caribbean island of Hispaniola with the Dominican Republic and has a population of approximately 8 million inhabitants. The colonial conquest, which began in 1492 with the arrival of Christopher Columbus on this island known as Ayti by its native Taino Amerindians, led to the eradication of the original inhabitants. They were soon replaced with slaves from Africa.[4] Aided by a decline in Spanish power, France acquired the western third of the island and named it Saint Domingue. The increasing number of French settlers was accompanied by a massive importation of slaves to toil on plantations of coffee, sugar cane, cotton, and indigo. The colony became "one of the most densely populated spots in the New World at the time."[5] Saint Domingue generated more wealth than all the Spanish colonies in the Americas combined. It thus became the world's richest colony and leading producer of coffee and sugar by the 1780s.[6] While the flourishing plantation era generated enormous wealth for the colonizers, it left post-independence Haiti with severe developmental impediments, a dependency on sugar and coffee production, environmental degradation, overpopulation, and inequitable social structures.

Disagreements between absent plantation owners, colonial bureaucrats, and the emerging local elites (mulattos and whites) fueled a thirteen-year multiracial independence movement in Saint Domingue that gave birth to the Republic of Haiti on 1 January 1804.[7] This turning point in Haiti's history marked the debut of its "native" bureaucracies; however, the early regimes that succeeded colonial rule mostly reflected a continuation of past practices, including the adoption of the plantation system as a model of economic development. Failing to solve the inherited predicaments of colonialism or to address effectively other challenges that emerged from the diplomatic and economic isolation of this first independent black republic, these regimes faced a series of political and economic crises within years of independence. To date, Haiti has had twenty-one constitutions and forty-two heads of state (nine of whom declared themselves heads of state for life and twenty-nine of whom were assassinated or overthrown).

State Formation during Isolation

From the onset of independence, Haiti's relationship with the outside world has always been problematic. Haiti's daring revolution represented a major threat to the colonial powers, but also for the slave-holding United States. The United States imposed a commercial and diplomatic embargo on Haiti and withheld recognition until 1862. Apart from hindering Haiti's political, social, and economic development, its isolation—which was supported by many European nations, the emerging Latin American states, and even the Vatican—made Haiti's independence so insecure that early regimes devoted significant state resources to safeguarding sovereignty to the detriment of the population's overall welfare.[8]

Guided by their fear of foreign attacks and their haste to consolidate Haiti's sovereignty through international recognition, early leaders adopted national and foreign policies that suffocated the embryonic state. In response to threats of foreign invasions, they maintained a large army of 32,000 regular soldiers by the mid-1820s.[9] Portrayed as the guarantor of national security, on the one hand, the army's needs naturally prevailed over those of the population. That factor conveniently allowed government officials—often themselves of military background—the freedom to mismanage the country's resources and absolved them from discharging basic civic responsibilities. On the other hand, this same army primarily carried out state-sponsored violence against the population. Doing so created an ongoing climate of permissible injustice in Haiti, while forestalling the country's development.

Suffering from Haiti's isolation within the hemisphere and an obsession with sovereignty, and in hopes of attracting foreign support for Haiti's independence through trade, the production of export crops trumped the crucial need for viable institutions capable of inducing the country's development. Backed by the army's repressive tactics, attempts were made to sustain the plantation system, which relied on the exploited labor of a majority of landless citizens.

Government officials and other elite groups reproduced the parasitic colonial system by taxing all of the other crops that the population produced for its own consumption. Instead of adopting policies that could unify the diverse segments of the population, this new governing bourgeoisie (mainly composed of mulattos and a few black landowners) battled to control the state apparatus and national resources. Consequently, the temporary solidarity that had developed among members of diverse ethnic backgrounds, classes, and status during the war of liberation dissipated and was replaced by the emergence of opportunistic factions led by regional *caudillos,* who exploited racial and class differences to maximize profits and self-interest. The economic schemes that these leaders devised succeeded only in increasing Haiti's dependence on a deteriorating plantation economy and on imports of basic commodities, while deepening the economic disparity within the society and fueling tension between the wealthy and the poor.

The Authoritarian State

The majority of Haiti's governments throughout the nineteenth century and part of the twentieth century followed a pattern of military and authoritarian rule similar to the French colonial administration. "Legal authority [was] concentrated in the hands of a military governor."[10] A long-standing consequence of this tradition has been the militarization of Haitian politics. Owing to the tremendous power and wealth that this governing structure provided, destabilizing political battles intensified among a growing number of cliques in search of absolute power amidst continuing resource depletion. Hence, the tradition of "one man rule" was established in Haiti and flourished through a system of institutional corruption. It has traditionally prevented the state from meeting the public's needs. The coups d'état and political assassinations that naturally resulted, in turn worsened these leaders' shortsightedness and precluded the establishment of a social contract between the state and the disenfranchised citizenry. Accustomed to living on the margins of the national agenda, except when it came to labor requirements and mercenary tasks, the majority of the population crowded onto the least productive plots, where subsistence farming—mostly on the country's wooded mountain slopes—became a way of life. This practice, which continues today, aggravated Haiti's problems of deforestation and soil erosion and crippled the country's agricultural and environmental systems, both of which receive limited attention from the state.

As popular grievances and violent outbursts toward these regimes intensified, leaders became increasingly vulnerable in their bargaining position vis-à-vis foreign powers, which in part spurred them to mortgage their country's future. In exchange for France's support of Haiti's independence and trade opportunities, Haiti yielded to France's pressure for an indemnity of 150 million francs to compensate for the loss of French property and lives resulting from the revolution.[11] State officials then imposed additional taxes on the impoverished population to raise the money and contracted Haiti's first foreign loan to make the initial payment on the indemnity.

Foreign investment typically proved highly exploitative, largely sustaining the appalling political, social, and economic conditions in the country. Successive governments initiated few lasting developmental projects in the areas of education, health, infrastructure, or industrialization. A banking system was not established until 1880 (with French capital and under French governance). Because French trade and investment was granted preferential treatment, trade with Great Britain and the United States declined sharply, further weakening the struggling economy. Meanwhile, popular disenchantment with the state, its supporting elite groups, and foreign investors deepened.

Foreign investors succeeded, during the second half of the nineteenth century, in making Haiti into a "colonial economy" and a theater for foreign commercial rivalry. France, Germany, Great Britain, and the United States competed for dominance over Haiti's economy and intervened (militarily, at times) whenever serious disputes arose between their national proxies and local merchants or government officials, creating more instability. When seven presidents (four of whom were assassinated) in succession failed to consolidate their grip on power from 1911 to 1915, the U.S. Marines landed in Haiti in July 1915 to safeguard American interests at a time of increased international tension accompanying World War I.[12]

The American Occupation

The American occupation, which lasted until 1934, altered Haiti's political, social, and economic structures, creating a semblance of political stability and some development but failing to produce a more responsive governing system. Under its administration, the United States reinforced and expanded the existing authoritarian rule: it dissolved the Haitian parliament in 1917, rewrote the Haitian constitution, centralized political power in Port-au-Prince, promoted the expansion of a technocratic, largely black, middle class, and organized regular elections at which figurehead presidents were chosen.[13] To safeguard the new institutions, the United States formed a *gendarmerie*, the new armed forces of the state.

By 1918, the occupation authorities were utilizing the new military to neutralize political opposition, namely the caudillos, who led a guerilla campaign known as the *Cacos* rebellion.[14] At the same time, the gendarmerie compelled peasant participation in a *corvée*, or forced labor, for American-led development projects intended to attract foreign investment.[15] The Haitian army failed to maintain law and order impartially. Instead, it became a partisan institution, charged with suppressing political opposition while serving the interests of the business elite. These two functions would remain the primary tasks of the force until its demise in 1994.

Despite the health, education, and infrastructural improvements made by the Americans, the occupation further deepened the already wide economic disparities in Haitian society. The investment and developmental schemes fostered between 1915 and 1934 primarily benefited foreign investors, local proxies, state officials, and the elite groups, while ignoring the needs of most citizens. Not surprisingly, repaying Haiti's creditors—mainly American banks—remained a central economic goal during the occupation period.[16] By seizing control of the major ports and customs houses throughout the country, the Americans took over the most significant sources of state revenue and decided on expenditure priorities for the state. In addition, U.S. officials eliminated or curtailed the influence of expatriate communities (e.g., the Germans), who threatened American economic and political interests in the region.[17] Economic policy during the occupation was never primarily intended to improve the lives of ordinary citizens.

The new economic order transformed many subsistence farmers into wage earners, selling their labor to the newly built factories and re-opened plantations. Drawing on the new 1918 constitution that allowed for the right of foreign ownership, and through threats and violence, the state forced many small landholders to sell their parcels of land to foreign companies, a process that accelerated the creation of a wage earning proletariat. The exploitative conditions fostered widespread discontent within Haiti's working class. Over time, resistance to such policies fueled protests, strikes, sabotage, and riots.

The American invasion was initially welcomed by some elements in Haiti, notably the Catholic Church, which gained support in its attempt to eradicate *vodun* (voodoo), and the bourgeoisie, whose supremacy within society was reinforced.[18] Eventually, the bourgeoisie joined the popular struggle against the occupation because its traditional source of wealth and power became threatened by the tax increases that the United States imposed on the import of non-American goods. After the occupation ended in 1934, national unity degenerated as interest groups became divided over the direction and control of the state. In sum, rather than fostering responsive and accountable state institutions, the occupation spawned authoritarian regimes that continued to rely upon repression, coercion, and political machination in order to maintain their monopoly on power and the country's resources.

The Duvalier Dictatorship

Between 1934 and the election of President François (Papa Doc) Duvalier in 1957, the governing system primarily protected and promoted the interests of elite groups. The American occupation had triggered strong nationalism across the political spectrum, but the alliance only lasted so long as those groups felt that it served their interests. By 1941, the elected president, Elie Lescot, himself a mulatto, began to favor mulattoes in his administration. This policy generated a sense of exclusion within the black middle class. Lescot's fall in 1946 signaled a trend that reshaped the political landscape; for the first time in more than thirty years a black, Dumarsais Estimé, assumed the presidency. Estimé's attempts to win over the mulatto elite prevented him from implementing the more radical racial policies that his black supporters clamored for, eventually resulting in a constitutional crisis and his subsequent fall. Claiming to want to end the debilitating racial warfare, Paul Magloire, a black general, was overwhelmingly elected president in 1950. Magloire's six-year authoritarian regime generated massive unrest throughout the country, finally forcing him into exile. Five interim governments tried and failed to govern Haiti during the following eleven months, paving the way for Duvalier's election in 1957, and his subsequent long reign of terror. Duvalier's election ushered in a new era of enforced stability and the transformation of the state into a tool of personal power.

Duvalier exploited the political potential of the centralized bureaucracy created by the Americans, largely for his own personal political and economic benefits.[19] He swiftly neutralized the power of the three dominant sectors of the post-occupation political arena: the military, the black middle class, and the economic elite. Duvalier transferred a number of middle-ranking officers to diplomatic posts outside the country, exiled or murdered the most threatening figures, and forced top military leaders into retirement, replacing them with more loyal commanders drawn from the black middle class. To counterbalance the army's power, the president also created a competing paramilitary force, the Volunteers for National Security (better known as the *tontons macoutes*), that reported directly and solely to him and that he used to intimidate and coerce opponents.[20]

Given the importance that the international community, particularly the United States, attached to political stability regardless of its costs, and given the upheaval in Cuba, foreign interference in the affairs of Haiti was kept to a minimum. Duvalier succeeded in playing on Washington's fear of the potential spread of communism. The steady stream of American aid that the country received during this period underscored the strong ties between the United States and the Duvalier dictatorship.[21] Even when key international players did not directly collude with the Duvalier regime, they generally maintained silence in the face of gross human rights violations and increasing levels of corruption.

As under previous regimes, the country's development and the population's welfare were absent from Duvalier's agenda.[22] His son Jean-Claude (Baby Doc), who succeeded him upon his death in 1971, embraced his father's policies, even though he introduced a milder form of political repression in the hope of obtaining increased foreign assistance. The tenure of the Duvaliers was marked not only by massive human rights violations but also by astounding levels of corruption. Instead of boosting economic productivity, they concentrated on devising different ways of preying on the population.[23] Between 1965 and 1980, Haiti's economy only saw a 0.9 percent per capita rate of annual growth.[24] Nevertheless, the United States—relieved over the relative domestic *détente* in Haiti in the 1970s—significantly augmented developmental assistance to Haiti, which represented 40 percent of national budget revenues by 1982. Not surprisingly, however, only a small percentage of foreign aid went toward building roads, hospitals, schools, and other public services.

Though superficially effective at first, the younger Duvalier's economic and political modernization strategies could not contain growing popular discontent. The economic stagnation, oppression, and corruption that prevailed under his authoritarian regime contributed to state weakness. By curbing overt human rights violations, he made peace with the international community, which helped fund some infrastructure, assembly lines, and other labor-intensive industries. For instance, foreign aid increased from $9 million in 1970 to $106 million in 1980.[25] But since the factories were concentrated in the capital city, the resulting massive migration of the rural population to Port-au-Prince created slums and increased popular demand for social services. Consequently, further demonstrations, violent outbursts throughout the country, and an escalating flow of refugees to the United States and to other Caribbean islands induced the U.S. government to invite Duvalier to leave—which he did, for France, on 7 February 1986 on a U.S. military aircraft.[26]

The Post-Duvalier Era

Despite more democratic practices during some parts of the post-Duvalier era, the country's appalling political, social, and economic conditions persist today. Between 1986 and 1990, a series of military and military-backed regimes employed violence as a means of neutralizing the social movements that brought down the Duvalier dictatorship. The country's two other traditional powerbrokers (the business elite and the United States) often colluded with the military to curtail the emerging power of civil society. Narcotrafficking also became a major factor in fueling military power, with Colombian cocaine being transshipped with immunity into and across Haiti.

While the elite class had also lobbied for the end of the Duvalier dictatorship, its members wanted to maintain government-protected monopolies. Afraid that a popularly elected government might end these privileges, elements of the bourgeoisie financially and politically supported the army, even hiring lobbyists in Washington to represent the military regimes before American lawmakers. The financial assistance and the political tutelage that the United States provided to these regimes were crucial factors; however, its generous infusions of military aid helped stymie the development of democratic institutions and practices that it claimed to want for Haiti. During these years, hundreds of demonstrators, progressive politicians, and leaders of social movements were intimidated or killed, provoking the emergence of political alternatives.

Leaders of various social movements, among them Jean-Bertrand Aristide, transformed their protest platforms into fully fledged political parties. Partly as a result of foreign pressure, the discredited military was forced to allow their participation in the 1990 presidential and legislative elections. Aristide, a popular young priest and proponent of liberation theology who had survived assassination attempts, emerged as the frontrunner. Smaller political parties within the popular political sector joined with Aristide to form the Lavalas coalition. Under the watchful eye of the Organization of American States (OAS), the United Nations (UN), and U.S. observers, Aristide won the 1990 presidential election with 67 percent of the vote in a peaceful and fair electoral contest.[27]

As the leader of the Lavalas Family party, Aristide's victory ignited popular hope for a more responsive Haitian state. His administration's agenda for greater social justice represented a serious threat to the interests of the former governing order and provoked a fear of populism within the international community.[28] On the date of his inauguration, 7 February 1991, Aristide retired six of the country's seven highest ranking military officers and subordinated the army to the control of civilians believed to be reform-minded. But the president underestimated the entrenched interest of the officer corps in defending the privileged position of the armed forces and their elite patrons.

Aristide's government, using the limited resources at its disposal, made serious efforts to address the country's formidable challenges, with uneven skill and results. It attempted to reduce the price of staples and fuel, even though cabinet members and other supporters worried whether this policy would delay economic growth. Foreign donors were also slow in fulfilling their development aid pledges, leaving the Haitian treasury severely depleted. Faced with these numerous obstacles, Aristide's exercise of power became increasingly personalized and authoritarian.[29] His lack of finesse in pushing for change, his ambiguity with respect to reconciliation with political adversaries, and several incendiary speeches contributed to his fall. In September 1991, Raoul Cédras, Aristide's appointed commander of Haiti's armed forces, overthrew Aristide's government and forced him into exile.

Fallout from the Coup

The growing trend toward democracy in the post–Cold War period, the new Santiago Commitment to Democracy and Development, a nascent renewal of the Inter-American System, and a newly invigorated UN, thwarted the success of this coup.[30] After considerable tactical meandering involving both the OAS and the UN, Canada, France, the United States, and Venezuela took the lead in seeking to restore Aristide.[31] Nevertheless, these four countries often disagreed on strategy and specifics even though they were all essentially committed to the goal of reinstating democracy in Haiti (and, in the case of the United States, the additional goal of reversing the flow of Haitian refugees to American shores).[32]

Meanwhile, the military junta, with the support of its elite backers and para-military *attachés,* orchestrated a rampant rise in insecurity, lawlessness, weapon smuggling, and drug trafficking in Haiti, in some ways helped by international economic sanctions.[33] As the number of human rights violations and deaths increased, thousands of Haitians fled the country to escape state-sponsored terror.[34] The United States was reluctant to intervene militarily in Haiti following its October 1993 debacle in Somalia, and the importance attached by Haitians to their country's sovereignty combined to delay decisive action. Eventually, the pressure of Haitian refugee numbers and some adroit maneuvering by Aristide and his supporters in Washington convinced President Clinton to act.[35] In July 1994, the UN Security Council authorized a multinational force (MNF) to expel the military junta from Haiti, and, after some posturing, when faced with just such a U.S.-led intervention, the army leaders fled into exile. Aristide returned to power in October 1994.[36]

Stabilization and Peace-Building: Mission Impossible

At a staggering cost of over $2 billion and with an initially strong international commitment, various forms of international peacekeeping, peace-building, and human rights monitoring initiatives (which extended through February 2001) failed to achieve creditable results in Haiti. Despite international efforts to develop an independent and professional police force, filling a gap left by the armed forces that Aristide had disbanded in 1994, security sector reform remained limited in Haiti. Furthermore, the country is still largely paralyzed by divisive politics aggravated by the absence of meaningful institutional reforms. The economy has stagnated, while promised sizable international assistance, initially held up by political squabbling in Haiti, probably is no longer available, even if Aristide and his opponents do learn to compromise.

Sadly, Aristide's reinstatement in 1994, which led to the repatriation of many refugees, did not re-ignite the briefly burgeoning democratic spirit of 1990–1991.[37] As early as 1995, his loosely organized Lavalas coalition quarreled over important policies like privatization and subsequently fell apart.[38] René Préval, Aristide's hand-picked, democratically elected successor in the 1996 contest, mishandled legislative elections in 1997, triggering a political struggle between the legislature and the executive that still has not abated. Instead of resolving political battles, the multiplicity of elections that have been held as required by the 1987 Constitution (which even the most mature of democracies would have found difficult to handle) have given rise to intense ill feeling among Haiti's fractious political classes.[39]

These political conflicts have especially weakened Haiti's economy, which was already shackled by the massive looting of state revenues by the de facto military regime (1991–1994) and the economic consequences of the international sanctions against Haiti that caused its GDP to shrink by about 30 percent during this period.[40] Its economy has remained extremely weak since then; in 1995, Haiti's annual GDP per capita of only $242 was by far the lowest in the Western Hemisphere.[41] The political stalemate since 1995 has stalled modest plans for agricultural reform, and by delaying privatization has benefited inefficient and corrupt state enterprises.

Equally detrimental to Haiti's economy have been the unsuitable policies that the international financial institutions have advocated for the country. For example, given the absence of technical, infrastructural, environmental, and financial services in Haiti, market liberalization has caused a sharp decline in local food production.[42] Unable to compete with cheaper and often subsidized imports, farmers have increasingly relocated to the slums of Port-au-Prince while the country's dependence on food imports has increased steadily. In addition, the rate of unemployment, external migration, disease, child mortality, illiteracy, and environmental degradation has continued to run high, reinforcing a vicious cycle.

The prevailing political turmoil, together with the growing poverty rate, has generated a rise in crime and violence, which the police and judiciary have been unable to tackle effectively, despite some foreign-inspired and funded reforms. With assistance from the UN, the United States, Canada, and France, among others, an entirely new 5,000-strong civilian police force was created in 1995, following eighteen months of insufficient training, but insecurity has persisted due to the proliferation of drug traffickers and the prevalence of illicit weapons.[43] Although a weapons buy-back program was instituted by the MNF following the dissolution of the army, no effective disarmament took place.[44] Ineffective training, lack of equipment, long work shifts, irregular pay, the continued absence of a credible judicial system, and a lack of political will have all damaged the morale of the police force. A massive rate of absenteeism, a lack of professionalism among officers, corruption, frequent abusive conduct, and involvement in illicit trade and in the killing of civilians have all confirmed public skepticism about this supposedly reformed institution.[45] In October 1999, a total of 407 officers were dismissed for various reasons.[46] Nothing has favored effective measures to combat the rising drug trade on Hispaniola, through which at least thirty-six tons of cocaine from South America transit each year before reaching the U.S. market.[47]

Unlike the public security force, the judicial branch never received a systematic overhaul. As in previous periods in Haiti, the justice system remains inaccessible to large segments of the population, particularly in the rural areas. It lacks resources, competent judges, and the necessary credibility to serve the citizenry. Some judges appear unfamiliar with Haitian law and have admitted to not having read the country's constitution.[48] Not surprisingly, as judges face low pay, bribery, training deficiencies, and assassination threats, they often choose to protect their lives rather than uphold the law. Meanwhile, overcrowded prisons hold alleged offenders for years without trial and under appalling conditions.[49] The inability of the legal system to address the post-intervention crime wave has further alienated the population, and mob justice has often substituted for legal redress, fueling renewed cycles of violence and further testing the incapacity of an already weak state.[50]

Can This Pattern Be Broken?

The absence of effective procedures to ensure state accountability, to create institutions capable of meeting the most basic needs, and to produce effective conflict mediation processes; a tradition of repression; the lack of consensus and an absence of vision among Haiti's leaders; and the lack of legitimacy of state officials in the eyes of the Haitian population, have all contributed to weak governance in Haiti. While individuals bear a large share of the responsibility, the system has repeatedly enabled and even invited them to exploit it to their own political ends. This may be why the Lavalas regime, which started with real hope, seems to have become but another of Haiti's corrupt and self-interested cadres.

While it has often blamed international actors for all of Haiti's problems, the Haitian political class—featuring many talented individuals, sometimes drawn from the industrious and successful Haitian diaspora—has proven a disaster for the country. It displays no sense of broader national interest. Political parties are often organized around single individuals vying for absolute power. Even if the national leader in question is popular, as Aristide undoubtedly still is—although less than before—such a trend is unhealthy. One man rule and state institutions protective of the broader population are antithetical.

What of the international community? Its attention to Haiti has been often predatory and always episodic. For example, it invested tremendously in addressing Haiti's political, economic, and security crises in the early and mid-1990s, but its contributions were often poorly planned, mutually undermining (as was clear with conflicting approaches to policing urged on the new police force by France, on the one hand, and the United States and Canada on the other), and of insufficient duration. Furthermore, too often foreign policy-makers have assumed that domestic economic growth would inherently and automatically yield social and political stability without taking into account the negative impact of regional and even global economic policies on the local economy.

Unnecessary economic dislocations resulting from often experimental and unsuitable economic policies prescribed by the international financial institutions have also contributed to the incidence of internal, often violent, conflicts. Instead of adopting participatory methods to formulate achievable goals suitable to Haiti, and fostering competent institutions to achieve them, international actors have often substituted for state institutions, creating a vacuum upon their departure that in turn has served to undermine their own efforts to solve Haiti's problems.

Bringing about change in Haiti is a long-term challenge, but leading foreign capitals demonstrated repeatedly during the 1990s in Haiti and elsewhere that they suffer from attention deficit disorder. A "lessons learned" exercise identified the following conclusions for international actors.[51] Donor coordination had been problematic. The assistance provided was fragmented and lacked coherence. The relatively large programs initiated in 1994–1995 by the various donors involved significant duplication of efforts rather than complementarity and consistency. Most projects and programs were donor driven. Participatory approaches by donors were rare. Donors did not address the existence of a dual system: one strand is urban, has a hierarchical social structure, is regulated by Napoleonic law, is mainly Catholic, and uses French as the official language; the other, accounting for the vast majority of the population, is rural, with a segmented social structure, an autonomous economy based on the extended family, Creole as the popular language, and vodun as the common religion. Customary law in Haiti, reflecting social norms and beliefs, had been over-looked.[52]

The increasingly complex social conflicts associated with a growing disregard for Haitian political leaders have created a crisis of credibility within Haiti and internationally that any government will find hard to overcome. A strong and sustained commitment to build democratic institutions, to promote the rule of law through a more merit-based appointment process, and to encourage orderly and systematic contributions from civil society, all of which constitute key steps toward state-building, are urgently required.

A major ingredient in reducing endemic weakness and encouraging state-building in Haiti will be the restoration of national security, not only within the capital city but throughout the territory. In the absence of substantial improvements in the police force and judicial system, gains achieved in all other sectors will continue to fade away. Continuing support and training for an independent and more effective national police force is crucial. The need for effective cooperation in curtailing other threats to Haiti's stability, notably trafficking in drugs and small arms, will require continuous commitment from national, regional, and international players. An effort to reform Haiti's justice system is also vital to support the work of the security forces. The implementation of sound economic reforms, particularly rural developmental strategies to generate economic development and poverty reduction, is crucial.

For two centuries Haiti has lacked effective political institutions and nationally minded leadership. As a result, it has remained perpetually weak, often teetering on the brink of failure. If Haiti is to become stronger it needs better leadership as well as long-term foreign assistance. Only with that combination can Haitians begin to hope to emerge from decay and political squalor.

Notes

1. Canute James, "OAS Mission to Haiti Faces an Uphill Struggle," *Financial Times* (29 May 2001). See also The Economist Intelligence Unit (EIU), *Country Report* (July 2000); and Agence France Presse, "EU Sanctions Haiti over Non-Respect for Democracy-ACP" (6 February 2001).

2. United Nations Development Program, *Human Development Report 2000: Human Rights and Human Development* (New York, 2000).

3. Gary Pierre-Pierre, "Haitian Premier Resigns amid Mounting Pressure," *Haitian Times* (23–29 January 2002), 3.

4. See Patrick Bellegarde-Smith, *Haiti: The Breached Citadel* (Boulder, 1990).

5. James E. McClellan III, *Colonialism and Science: Saint Domingue in the Old Regime* (Baltimore, 1992), 3.

6. Ibid., 32.

7. Hurbon Laënnec, *Comprendre Haiti: Essai sur l'État, la Nation, et la Culture* (Paris, 1987), 76.

8. Michel-Rolph Trouillot, *Haiti: State against Nation, The Origins and Legacy of Duvalierism* (New York, 1990), 51.

9. David Nicholls, *From Dessalines to Duvalier: Race, Colour and National Independence in Haiti* (Piscataway, 1996), 68.

10. Ibid., 39.

11. Ibid., 62.

12. See Roger Gaillard, *Les Blancs Débarquent 1914–1915: Les Cents Jours de Rosalvo Bobo ou Mise à Mort Politique* (Haiti, 1987).

13. Nicholls, *From Dessalines to Duvalier,* 142–164.

14. See Roger Gaillard, *Les Blancs Débarquent 1914: Premier Écrasement du Cacoïsme* (Haiti, 1981).

15. Sidney W. Mintz, "Can Haiti Change?" *Foreign Affairs,* LXXV (January–February 1995), 73–86.

16. Simon Fass, *Political Economy in Haiti: The Drama of Survival* (Piscataway, 1990), 24.

17. See Hans Schmidt, *The United States Occupation of Haiti, 1915–1934* (New Brunswick, 1971).

18. Jean Price-Mars, *So Spoke the Uncle* (Washington, D.C., 1990), 103–107. See also J. Michael Dash, *Haiti and the United States: National Stereotypes and the Literary Imagination* (London, 1997).

19. Hurbon Laënnec, *Culture et Dictature en Haiti: L'Imaginaire sous Contrôle* (Paris, 1979), 82–83. See also Cary Hector, "Fascisme et Sous-Développement: le Cas d'Haïti," *Nouvelle Optique* (Montreal, 1972).

20. See Robert I. Rotberg, *Haiti: the Politics of Squalor* (Boston, 1971).

21. See Rémy Anselme, "The Duvalier Phenomenon," *Caribbean Studies,* XIV (1980).

22. Gérard Barthélemy, *L'Univers Rural Haïtien: le Pays en Dehors* (Paris, 1990), 12–19.

23. See James G. Leyburn (ed.), *The Haitian People* (New Haven, 1966).

24. See Thomas E. Weil, *Area Handbook for Haiti* (Washington, D.C., 1973).

25. Ernest H. Preeg, *The Haitian Dilemma: A Case Study in Demographics, Development, and U.S. Foreign Policy* (Washington, D.C., 1996), 17–18.

26. Marc D. Charney, "Haiti's Problem Not All Economic or Political; It's Human Tragedy," *Houston Chronicle* (13 July 1980), 17.

27. Lori Fisler Damrosch (ed.), *Enforcing Restraint: Collective Intervention in International Conflicts* (New York, 1998), 130.

28. Alice H. Henkin (ed.), *Honoring Human Rights and Keeping the Peace: Lessons from El Salvador, Cambodia, and Haiti* (Washington, D.C., 1995), 110.

29. Aristide made ministerial and judicial appointments without parliamentary approval. For more details, see Kenneth Roth, "Haiti: The Shadows of Terror," *New York Review of Books* (March 1992).

30. See OAS-AG/Resolution 1080 (XXI-0/91) of 5 June 1991. The impetus for the Santiago Declaration arose from the December 1990 coup in Surinam that deposed democratically elected President Ramsewak Shankar.

31. These four countries were known as the Friends of the UN Secretary-General for Haiti.

32. See David M. Malone, *Decision-Making in the UN Security Council: The Case of Haiti* (Oxford, 1998).

33. See *North American Congress on Latin America (NACLA) Report on the Americas*, XXVII (January–February 1994), 28–29.

34. From 31 January to 30 June 1994, 340 killings and 131 cases of abduction were reported to the Mission Civile Internationale en Haiti (MICIVIH). See MICIVIH Press Release CP/94/29 of 6 July 1994.

35. The Lawyers Committee for Human Rights, *Haiti: Learning the Hard Way: The UN/OAS Human Rights Monitoring Operation in Haiti 1993–1994* (New York, 1995), 102.

36. Dana Francis (ed.), *WPF Report 19: Mediating Deadly Conflict* (Boston, 1998), 11–15.

37. Between 17 September and 25 October 1994 alone, 7,782 refugees returned to Haiti from U.S. camps. See also UN High Commissioner for Refugees, "The State of the World's Refugees, 1995: In Search of Solutions" (London, 1995), 225–226.

38. Alex Dupuy, *Haiti in the New World Order: The Limits of the Democratic Revolution* (Boulder, 1997), 130. See also Human Rights Watch—Americas/National Coalition for Haitian Refugees, "Haiti: Human Rights after President Aristide's Return" (October 1995).

39. David Gonzalez, "U.S. to Withhold Money for Haiti's Presidential Election," *New York Times* (6 September 2000).

40. See Elizabeth D. Gibbons, *Sanctions in Haiti: Human Rights and Democracy under Assault* (Washington, D.C., 1999). See also World Bank, "Haiti Assistance Strategy Document," IBRD-15945-HA (13 August 1996).

41. See "Haiti Assistance Strategy Document."

42. Uli Locher, "Sécurité Alimentaire en Haïti," *Journal of Haitian Studies*, VII (2001), 27–28.

43. Irwin P. Stotzky, *Silencing the Guns in Haiti: The Promise of Deliberative Democracy* (Chicago, 1997), 163–175.

44. Robert Maguire, *Haiti Held Hostage: International Responses to the Quest for Nationhood 1986 to 1996* (Providence, RI, 1996), 63.

45. David Gonzalez, "Civilian Police Force Brings New Problems in Haiti," *New York Times* (11 February 2000).

46. Amnesty International, "Haiti: Unfinished Business, Justice and Liberties at Risk" (London, 2000), 10.

47. David Kidwell, "Agent's Drug Seizure Total from Boats Reaches $25 Million," *Miami Herald* (11 February 2000).

48. William G. O'Neill, "No Longer a Pipe Dream? Justice in Haiti," in Robert I. Rotberg (ed.), *Haiti Renewed: Political and Economic Prospects* (Washington, D.C., 1997), 199–214.

49. Amnesty International, "Haiti: Human Rights Challenges Facing the New Government" (London, April 2001), 27.

50. See "Haiti: Not Quite Normal," *The Economist* (27 July 1996).

51. The "lessons learned" experiment was conducted by the International Peace Academy, an independent research and policy development institution in New York. See Lotta Hagman, "Lessons Learned: Peacebuilding in Haiti" (New York, 2002), www.ipacademy.org.

52. This section is taken from the following report: International Peace Academy, "Lessons Learned Exercise Undertaken by the Emergency Response Division of the UN Development Programme" (New York, 2001). A recent World Bank report on its own programs is no less self-critical. See World Bank Report, "Haiti Country Assistance Evaluation" (22 January 2002). See also Henkin, *Honoring Human Rights and Keeping the Peace*, 83–127.

CHAPTER TWELVE

Lebanon:
Failure, Collapse, and Resuscitation

OREN BARAK

Apart from Tajikistan, Lebanon is the only state covered in this volume to fail, collapse, and later be successfully resuscitated. This chapter examines the failure of the Lebanese state before the civil war (1975–1990), its collapse during the conflict, the efforts to preserve it throughout the war, and its reconstruction in the aftermath of war.

The Lebanese state was created by the French colonial power in 1920, in response to persistent lobbying by leaders of the Maronite Christian community, which was traumatized by Ottoman excesses committed during World War I. Although Christian-dominated Mount Lebanon previously enjoyed autonomous status, other areas incorporated into the new state (the north, the south, Biqa', and the capital, Beirut) had a clear Muslim majority and strong ties to the Arab hinterland.[1] In 1943, on the eve of independence, a political compromise—the National Pact—was brokered between two prominent Lebanese leaders, a Maronite Christian and a Sunni Muslim. Together with the 1926 constitution and specific election laws, a political system based on intercommunal power-sharing was introduced, and the state's identity and regional and international orientation was agreed upon.

The inability of Lebanon's leaders to adapt the 1943 power-sharing settlement to changing political and social circumstances in the following decades, as well as the low degree of "stateness" it managed to attain, brought about its failure toward the mid-1970s and its collapse during the first phase of the civil war (1975–1976), with external forces, especially its close neighbors, exacer-

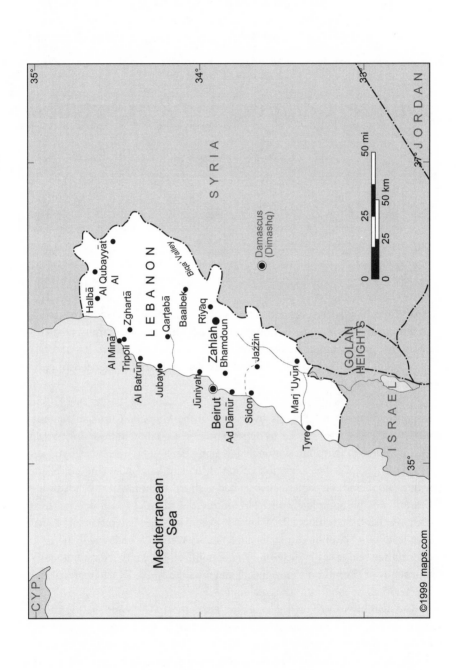

©1999 maps.com

bating its breakdown. The conflict in Lebanon, which began as a quarrel between the supporters of the political and socio-economic order, and its opponents, who demanded comprehensive reforms, was soon transformed into an all-out war involving members of all sectors of Lebanese society and regional and international players.

Efforts to resuscitate the state during the next phases of the war (particularly in 1977–1979 and 1982–1984) proved unsuccessful because the rebuilding of formal institutions was not matched by the emergence of a new internal consensus. Yet, the state continued to manifest its viability, serving as a focal point for its own society and for most political players, both domestic and foreign. After a new political compromise—the Ta'if Agreement (1989)—was reached through regional and international mediation, the war was terminated in 1990, paving the way for the state's reconstruction. Efforts to rebuild have so far concentrated on mending formal institutions, adjusting the power-sharing settlement, and rebuilding the devastated capital, Beirut. In addition, the (highly unbalanced) relationship with Syria was formalized, allowing the latter to enjoy a hegemonic position vis-à-vis its neighbor. During the most recent decade, reconstruction efforts proceeded to the point where Lebanon is now a weak state but is no longer failed or collapsed.

The debate on theoretical and practical aspects of state failure and state collapse dates back to the end of the Cold War and reflects the shift from international to internal explanations for situations of extreme political disorder.[2] During the heyday of bipolar rivalry, developing world states were generally viewed in terms of their utility for or threat to the security of each "camp." Thus, instances of disorder within states were more often than not interpreted as offshoots of global rivalries. This dominant discourse had two mutually reinforcing outcomes. Each superpower supported its clients in disordered states so as to keep them within its own sphere of influence; domestic actors had an incentive to align themselves with one of the contending blocs.[3]

The end of the Cold War served to expose these instances of disorder for what they often were: manifestations of the incapacity of many developing-world states to govern their territory effectively and to accommodate pressing political and socio-economic demands. The realization that the causes of such crises were internal encouraged a search for new analytical tools and remedies. The dramatic events of the 1990s—the disintegration of the U.S.S.R. and the struggles within its successor states, the breakup of Yugoslavia and the conflicts over its remnants, the civil war in Somalia, and the genocide in Rwanda—all reaffirmed an urgent need to change focus. The tools developed to fill this conceptual "gap" have so far concentrated on the state and its ability to perform. Thus, the term "state failure" refers to cases where the state is unable to control its territory and attend to the basic needs of its population, while the term "state collapse" applies to situations "where the structure, authority . . . law, and political order have fallen apart and must be reconstituted in some form."[4] While the former definition emphasizes the capacities of the state as the provider of security and public goods, the latter focuses on its structural, coercive, and normative aspects. A state's failure can culminate in its collapse, particularly when large-scale internal violence occurs.

Yet, in non-Western regions, the state plays an equally important role in regulating internal conflicts.[5] Unlike the centralized bureaucratic state that emerged in Europe and North America, many post-colonial states were unable to subdue powerful sectors within their own societies and had to accept their quasi-autonomous statuses.[6] Given this mode of state-society relations, it is not surprising that in several non-Western states where central authority crumbled, informal social networks stepped in and began to provide basic services, thus compensating for the state's failure.[7]

The state is the focal point of both individual and collective expectations. A failed state is a polity whose institutions and conflict regulation mechanisms do not function. Thus, failed and collapsed states can be resuscitated only when their formal institutions and conflict regulation mechanisms are revitalized.

The Lebanese Case: Markers of Failure and Collapse

That the Lebanese state failed toward 1975 and collapsed during the first phase of the conflict (1975–1976) is suggested by the following markers: the extent of the violence which rampaged throughout its territory and involved the majority of its population; the paralysis of most formal agencies and institutions, which stymied the provision of public services; the deterioration of central authority and internal security; the proliferation of armed groups and unlawful practices; the massive military intervention by outside forces; and finally, the widespread defiance of the existing political and socio-economic order by groups speaking in the name of several sectors of society, including the Shi'i and the Druze communities and leftist and pan-Arab movements.

The Lebanese conflict resulted in tremendous loss of life, displacement, emigration, and physical damage.[8] According to statistics confirmed by the government in Beirut, 144,240 persons died in the conflict and 197,506 were wounded.[9] More studies suggest that close to a third of Lebanon's pre-war population of 3.1 million left the country, including an estimated 200,000 professionals.[10] About 790,000 persons had to leave their homes, many of them more than once, and costs of damage to property reached an estimated $25 billion.[11] Given that pre-war Lebanon was a regional hub for banking and trade and a popular tourist destination, the damage to its economy as a result of the conflict was even higher.

As in earlier instances of violence in its history, the conflict in Lebanon involved members of all sectors of its pluralist (or divided) society—ethnic groups, clans, and regions—whose members were mobilized by militias (armed paramilitary groups that appealed to their collective identities). External actors also played a part in the war, including Lebanon's immediate neighbors (the Palestine Liberation Organization [PLO], Israel, and Syria), more remote players in the Middle East (Egypt, Libya, Iraq, Saudi Arabia, Iran, and the Arab League), and international powers and organizations (the United States, the U.S.S.R., France, and the UN).

The Two Years' War (1975–1976) led to the paralysis of most formal institutions in Lebanon. The president, who was the most powerful political actor in the state, controlled only his palace and its immediate surroundings. The government, when its members could meet, had little influence on the course of events. Parliament, which convened occasionally throughout the war, carried on with its routine work only in a limited way, and new elections could not be held. The work of the bureaucracy was badly disrupted and basic public services could not be provided. Finally, the state's law-enforcement agencies, including the Internal Security Forces (the police and gendarmerie), the *Surete Générale*, and the army were in a state of disarray.

The violence that ravaged most of the country, particularly the capital, Beirut (which was soon divided along communal lines), led to the rapid deterioration of internal security. Crime levels in Lebanon were on the rise in the early 1970s, and these were exacerbated by the ineffectual state law-enforcement institutions.[12] As government agencies retreated from the public sphere, "armed people" (*musallahin*) looted banks and shops; set up roadblocks and checkpoints—where passers-by were stopped, intimidated, and occasionally murdered, particularly when their identification cards revealed that they were members of the "wrong" community; kidnapped and, at times, killed members of other militias or unarmed civilians; and took over prisons and mental institutions and set their inhabitants free. Drug producing and trafficking, which were previously kept in check by the government, proliferated, and shipments of small arms and heavy weapons poured into the country by land and by sea, through a host of clandestine, militia-run ports. The state lost control over its borders, and its presence in several districts, particularly the north, south, and Biqa', was at best nominal.

Unlike in earlier periods in its independent history, Lebanon also witnessed the rise of an opposition whose criticism was directed not only at the government, but also at the regime and, in some instances, at the state itself. Toward the mid-1970s, many Lebanese came to regard their government as illegitimate and viewed the regime as biased and repressive; a large number of movements vowed to introduce radical political and socio-economic reforms. On the other hand, other groups resolutely objected to any change in the existing order, and mobilized support to this effect. In the course of the conflict, members of nearly all sectors of Lebanese society used violence in order to further their aims.

The conflict in Lebanon and the anarchy that it entailed led many of its students to view it as a "non-state state," a political entity where the central government enjoyed only nominal authority over its territory.[13] A new term—Lebanonization—was introduced into the political jargon and was used to describe instances of extreme internal disorder elsewhere.

Why Collapse?

The failure of the Lebanese state and its collapse in 1975–1976 were the products of two underlying factors. The first was the "immobilism" of the 1943 power-sharing settlement and the failure to adapt it to changing political, social, and economic circumstances in later periods.[14] The second factor was the lack of an effective institutional framework that could support the political system and keep it from falling apart, that is, the weakness of the state and its institutions. External intervention (especially after 1967) and Lebanon's post-colonial legacy are two further explanations for the state's failure.[15]

External intervention explains Lebanon's collapse only in a limited way because it was a constant feature of its political life since independence, with both constructive and destructive aspects. In 1943, several Middle Eastern and outside players (particularly Egypt and Britain) were pivotal in bringing members of Lebanon's sectors together and facilitating the settlement. Two years later, Lebanon entered the Arab League as a founding member, thus legitimizing its independence. Its generally good relations with key Arab states (especially Egypt) and the Western powers (Britain, France, and the United States) helped to sustain Lebanon's independence over the next few decades. The actions of foreign players later, especially between 1967–1976, exacerbated the state's collapse and hindered preliminary efforts to resuscitate it. But the foreign forces that were involved in Lebanon were, for the most part, patrons of local factions, whose leaders sought to use their power as leverage within the domestic arena so as to promote their own goals. Moreover, during the conflict, and particularly since the late 1980s, external players again helped to preserve the Lebanese state and facilitated its recovery. This period can be dissected to demonstrate that the behavior of certain foreign forces during specific parts of Lebanon's history was detrimental. But if foreign involvement in Lebanon is to be viewed in perspective, one must also consider its constructive aspects.

The post-colonial argument, which was voiced not too long after the outbreak of war in Lebanon, is equally problematic. It depicts Lebanon as a state with "artificial" borders, thus ignoring the fact that most states in the Middle East, as well as in other non-Western regions, have boundaries that reflect colonial, rather than indigenous, considerations. That argument also presupposes that multi-ethnic states cannot endure and are incapable of producing a viable democracy (two debatable premises). Finally, the argument leaves little room to account for the actions of Lebanon's leaders in the aftermath of its creation or for the political settlement. Indeed, it was the decisions (and indecisions) of the state's policymakers from 1943 to 1975 that prevented both the revision of the power-sharing formula and the emergence of a strong state that could have sustained it.

In political terms, Lebanon's failure and collapse represent the decline of the consensus that had been embodied by the National Pact of 1943. The pact was a dual compromise; it defined the identity and foreign orientation of the newborn state in a manner that was acceptable to most of its sectors and laid the groundwork for power-sharing between them.

The first part of the compromise stipulated that Lebanon would have an Arab face, i.e., some measure of Arab identity, and adhere to a foreign policy defined as "neither East nor West." It was not to seek an alliance with a Western power or a union with the Arab hinterland. The second part of the deal was a power-sharing settlement between Lebanese Christians (mainly Maronites, Orthodox, and Catholics) and Muslims (mainly Sunnis, Shi'is, and Druze), who were to be represented in all formal institutions according to a 6:5 ratio, respectively, and divide the state's highest posts between themselves (e.g., Maronite president, Sunni premier, Shi'i speaker of parliament, etc.). The fact that parliamentary elections were held on a regional basis ensured that the Lebanese elite would occupy the majority of seats in the assembly, as well as the office of president (elected by parliament), and hold most posts in the government (appointed by the president and subject to the approval of parliament).[16]

The rigidity of the political compromise, which was based on the results of a population census held in 1932, reflected the leaders' inability to find ways to adapt it to shifts in the demographic balance of Lebanon's population, namely, the rise in the number of Muslims compared to Christians, which was the result of birthrate patterns and emigration.[17] From the late 1960s and early 1970s, the National Pact was regarded as anachronistic by many Lebanese, especially those in Muslim communities, who began to demand a larger share of the pie. Yet most Christian leaders, who were supported by the more conservative Muslim leaders—their political allies since 1943—vehemently opposed holding a new population census and refused to give up their prerogatives. Some argued that the power-sharing settlement *already* represented a type of affirmative action in favor of the Muslims, given their lower levels of income, education, and professional skills. The proportions for handing out political and economic resources in the state were hardly adjusted until 1975.[18] By 1980, radical leaders in the Christian communities (particularly Maronites) argued that they should enjoy a "special position" in Lebanon, which would not be based on their numerical strength but on their central role in its creation in 1920, as well as on their "objective needs."[19]

This deadlock, unlike other political disputes, could not be resolved by elite accommodation or "logrolling," due to fear on all sides. It became a springboard for new Lebanese groups who wished to participate in the political game but who were barred from it due to an effective "elite cartel" of traditional leaders who monopolized the positions and resources allotted to each sector. These "newcomers" included members of the socio-economically and politically deprived Shi'i community—believed to be the largest in Lebanon—who were becoming increasingly frustrated with their traditional leadership, as well as members of the Druze community (especially the supporters of Kamal Junblat—also known as Jumblatt—who, due to his ethnic affiliation, was unable to serve in a post higher than that of government minister). They also included various leftist pan-Arab and pan-Syrian factions, whose spokesmen disapproved of Lebanon's "backward" and "reactionary" politics which, according to them, perpetuated political feudalism (the domination of public life by traditional bosses) and political sectarianism (the power-sharing settlement).[20]

This opposition undermined the legitimacy of the government and the regime. State institutions were depicted as serving the interests of "certain" segments (i.e., the Christians, and particularly the Maronites, as well as the exclusive socioeconomic elite) while ignoring the needs of the "majority" (namely, the Muslims, especially the Shi'is, and other have-nots). Unable to attain their ends within the political system, veteran parties and new groups alike felt compelled to resort to violence in order to replace what they now regarded as an oppressive political and socio-economic order. The armed presence of the Palestinian factions in Lebanon, the pledges of outside support, and the influx of arms into its territory, offered these groups the means with which to pose their challenge. Yet, this was an insufficient condition for violence to erupt and assume such great magnitude. The radical opposition groups in Lebanon, like the staunch supporters of the existing order, finally were ready to use violence to attain their ends, and there was little the government could do about it.

When looking at Lebanon's politics before the outbreak of conflict, most observers were impressed by the fact that elections were duly held, by the large measure of freedom enjoyed by the population, and by the Lebanese economy, which was among the most market oriented in the developing world. Yet political life in this state, notwithstanding its democratic features, was all too often overshadowed by what may be described as a general disregard for the law and the absence of basic norms and rules of the game among its participants. Leaders of the country's diverse sectors, who feared domination by one another and were suspicious of the central government, readily accepted power-sharing mechanisms—a grand coalition; proportionality in positions, funds, and representation; mutual veto on cardinal issues; and segmental autonomy.[21] They failed, however, to observe the obligations that are the essence of a democratic regime. Respect for the law and acceptance of shared norms was conditional, and unlawful practices, including corruption, intimidation of voters, and, at times, assassination of political opponents, were occasionally employed, particularly during elections.[22] Lebanon's "founding fathers" and members of its elite had thus adopted consociational mechanisms, which they regarded as the best means to preserve their power, but they did not always comply with the obligations that make democracy endure. This is not to say that Lebanon was not a democracy before the 1975–1990 war, but critical elements of this type of regime were lacking. This political cultural factor is significant when trying to explain the failure and collapse of states, including Lebanon.

Part of the problem, familiar in many non-Western states, was that several of Lebanon's political bosses managed to maintain their quasi-autonomous bases of power and effectively curb all national governmental attempts to assert control.[23] Formal institutions, which incorporated members of all sectors according to a proportional basis, could not act as neutral arbitrators aloof from political rivalries, a situation that proved to be exceptionally problematic as the power-sharing settlement did not put an end to all internal tensions, but rather replaced intercommunal conflicts with intracommunal struggles for hegemony, particularly on the local-regional level.[24] Since the government itself was considered not a legitimate arbiter but a reflection of Lebanon's pluralist society, the solution to domestic violence was not to assert the authority of the state but to allow all parties to manage on their own without intervention. (If worse came to worst, a compromise was mediated between the parties, with governmental institutions assuming the role of conflict managers.) The synthesis between social realities in Lebanon and the institutions of democracy, so applauded by students of the new states and the consociational school in the late 1960s and early 1970s, had thus created a lively political system, but one which was haunted by conflict.[25]

This situation, which led Nordlinger in the early 1970s to describe Lebanon as a "night watchman state," was primarily the result of decisions made by the country's leaders.[26] They envisioned the state as a mechanism to divide power between them. They thus failed to appreciate the state's crucial role in pluralist societies; unlike in ethnically homogeneous polities, where citizens have numerous spaces for mutual association, in divided societies, formal institutions (political institutions, schools, and security forces) constitute the principal, if not exclusive, meeting grounds between members of various sectors. As such, the state can promote "over-arching loyalties," which can serve to ameliorate tensions and mutual distrust and enhance intercommunal cooperation.[27]

That a strong state did not emerge in Lebanon in the wake of its independence was not a coincidence. The elite—merchants, landowners, bankers, and businessmen—who crafted the political system and monopolized it using an exceptionally effective system of patronage, viewed the state essentially as negative.[28] Michel Chiha, a wealthy banker considered the "mastermind" of Lebanon's political system, revealed a deep fear of the state:

> It is well known that foreigners visiting us think that we are a land blessed by the gods. *They see peace and plenty here, whereas we import almost everything and we export practically nothing, which seems a sort of miracle.* Work is more easily done . . . here than elsewhere, because the state has not yet got to the stage at which, in the name of would-be economic principles and rigid, harassing social theories, *the public authorities make it impossible to breathe.* Excess in this matter must be abolished forever.[29]

Lebanon's leaders, who subscribed to these and similar views, did their utmost to restrain the capabilities of the state. In the foreign arena, they believed that "Lebanon's strength lies in its weakness"; it should remain apart from regional and international conflicts and acquire a status of formal neutrality.[30] These considerations, coupled with the need to maintain a communal balance in all state institutions, led to the decision to keep law-enforcement agencies in Lebanon weak and small. The rise of army officers to power in several Arab states in the late 1940s and 1950s (particularly in neighboring Syria) and the revolutionary programs that these new leaders promulgated, encouraged the Lebanese elite to keep its own military in check to prevent it from dominating politics and from becoming embroiled in outside disputes. Thus, Lebanon was generally spared involvement in the Arab-Israeli conflict, which laid a heavy burden on most Middle Eastern economies, and managed to avoid successful coups.[31] Better still, the government did not have to raise taxes that could have hampered its *laissez-faire* economy. As a result of all these factors, Lebanon's small, under-equipped security forces were incapable of defending against serious challenges to state authority.[32]

Hanf once argued that "consociationalism is a fair weather model," a type of political settlement that functions best when a state's regional environment is peaceful.[33] In the case of Lebanon, the crisis in the political system and the decline of formal institutions took place just as external challenges to the state reached their peak. The regional system in the Middle East supported Lebanon's internal equilibrium in the wake of independence; its neighbors helped establish the National Pact, and Lebanon's leaders participated in the negotiations leading to the formation of the Arab League. From the mid-1960s, however, Lebanon's close neighbors, Palestine, Israel, and Syria, applied mounting pressure, which exacerbated Lebanon's collapse.

Lebanon was a safe haven for the Palestinian national movement, given its relatively weak government, shared border with Israel, and large community of Palestinian refugees.[34] Palestinian factions began military activity in Lebanon in the mid-1960s, though some refugees had participated individually in the 1958 crisis. But the state did not become the PLO's primary base of operations until the PLO's defeat in Jordan in 1970–1971. The Palestinian armed presence in Lebanon, and the PLO's guerrilla attacks against Israel across the Lebanese-Israeli border, put an end to the "long peace" that had prevailed since the Armistice Agreement was signed in 1949, and enforced by the Israeli-Lebanese Mixed Armistice Commission (ILMAC). A vicious cycle of Palestinian raids and Israeli counter-raids began. That cycle undermined the authority of the government in Beirut, whose role was reduced to that of a bystander.[35] Its army's credibility was also undermined. Clashes between the army and the PLO in 1969 and 1973, following Israeli commando raids on Beirut, led to the signing of the Cairo Agreement between Lebanon and the PLO, which further weakened the state's authority. This encouraged several local groups, particularly Maronite-led parties (the Phalanges and other factions), to maintain that Lebanon should prepare for an inevitably decisive clash with the Palestinians. Other movements, mostly Muslim but including Christian opposition members, were furious at the government's behavior toward the PLO. They felt that the Palestinian national movement was a natural ally for their cause, since its military power could balance the superior strength of the supporters of the prevailing order.[36]

Developments in neighboring Syria also affected Lebanon during this period. Once a vulnerable state that was a focus of incessant regional and international intervention, Syria managed to stabilize in the early 1970s, under President Hafez al-Asad's leadership, and sought to increase its influence in the region. Asad and his aides believed this policy to be necessary because of Israel's military superiority. The policy became imperative after Egypt signed a "separate" peace accord with Israel, leaving Damascus with little leverage. For the Syrian regime, dominated by members of its Alawi minority and promulgating a pan-Arab vision, Lebanon could be either an asset or a threat from geostrategic, economic, and ideological points of view. Israel could use Lebanon's territory (the Biqa') to outflank Syria's massive fortifications facing the occupied Golan—as it indeed did in 1982—and the opposition to its regime (the Muslim Brotherhood), as well as regional rivals (Iraq and the PLO), could take advantage of Lebanon's liberal politics and subvert Syria. However, bringing Lebanon under Syria's wing could keep it from following Egypt's path vis-à-vis Israel (as its leaders would attempt to do in 1983, with the blessing of the United States) and enable Damascus to exercise direct control over the PLO.

Lebanon's capitalist economy and the illicit flow of goods across the Syrian border were a threat to Syria's centralized state-controlled economy. But Syria's rapidly expanding labor force could find work in the service sector in Lebanon and provide Damascus with a steady flow of foreign currency. After Egypt's interest in the Levant waned in the late 1960s and early 1970s, Syria became determined to bring Lebanon (as well as the Palestinians and Jordan) under its influence. Accordingly, the number of its allies there—particularly President Suleiman Frangieh (1970–1976)—increased. It should be emphasized, however, that despite its pan-Arab (and, at times, pan-Syrian) propaganda, Asad's Syria favored Lebanon's existing order over all other political options, and did its utmost to preserve it.[37]

Regional and international actors' growing involvement in Lebanon's affairs in the late 1960s and early 1970s, and the intricate networks formed among local clients and foreign patrons, damaged the process of "elite accommodation" so crucial to a consociational democracy. It should be noted, however, that it was often local groups who sought to benefit from the support of outside forces and who lured them into playing a more active role in its politics. Here again, the country's politicians did not exercise restraint, paving the way for unprecedented foreign involvement in Lebanon.

When violence broke out in 1975, following a series of clashes between demonstrators supported by the opposition and the Lebanese army in Sidon, and between the Maronite-led Phalanges and a Palestinian faction in a Beirut neighborhood, supporters of the political and socio-economic order in Lebanon, who were mostly Christian but included conservative Muslim leaders as well, faced a well-armed though loosely organized opposition, whose following was overwhelmingly Muslim but which also had Christian participation.

While the government and its supporters utterly refused to consider revising the political settlement, claiming that the state's primary concern was the armed Palestinian presence and not internal reform, the opposition vowed to introduce radical change, by force if necessary. Tensions had been building since the late 1960s and early 1970s, as a result of the deterioration of Lebanese-Palestinian relations and the lawlessness that prevailed in many parts of the country. This was particularly evident in south Lebanon, where the Palestinian fighters had established a "state within a state," turning this region into a battleground between Israel and the PLO and causing tens of thousands of village dwellers, mostly Shi'is, to flee northward.[38] The clashes in Sidon and Beirut had ignited the powder keg.

The rapid deterioration of central authority—by March 1976, President Frangieh controlled only his palace in Baabda, which was bombarded by the opposition; he eventually had to flee the capital—and the vacuum in the areas of public services and internal security, led to the rapid "privatization" of these spheres. Scores of militias (paramilitary groups formed by veteran political parties and new creations) purchased, or received in exchange for patronage, large shipments of small and heavy arms, which were readily provided by Lebanon's neighbors and by dealers in the region and beyond. Soon, the militias were able to offer an alternative to the state's crumbling institutions, which were no match for the militias' size, firepower, and ruthlessness. Drawing on feelings of fear and insecurity, militia leaders effectively employed ethnic myths and symbols, as well as threats, intimidation, and extortion, to mobilize the country's sectors, vowing to provide security and launch their political and socioeconomic demands. Aiming to transform the country's ethnically mixed regions into more homogenous and defensible "cantons," the militias embarked on large-scale "ethnic cleansing" operations, causing death and destruction, displacement, and emigration. Much of this activity, and particularly the massacres of civilians (e.g., in the Tal al-Zaatar and Sabra and Shatila refugee camps, the town of Damur, and the Shuf area), was predatory, not inspired by grievance.

The militias, which were led by political bosses, their sons, their former clients, and their henchmen, as well as by newcomers to the political arena, drew their rank and file from among the lower strata of Lebanese society. Their cadres, however, came from the ranks of the state's crumbling security forces, and particularly from the army's low- and middle-ranking officers and non-commissioned officers. Given that the latter were responsible for putting together their armed units, organizing their chains of command, and devising training programs and military tactics, it is not surprising that the militias' structures often resembled that of the formal army. By the late 1980s, several of these organizations had become full-fledged private armies, accumulating huge

amounts of arms—including tanks, armed personnel carriers, and artillery bat-
teries—and, in some cases, like the Maronite-led Lebanese Forces (LF), a navy
and an air force.[39]

Although these developments did not represent a new phenomenon—
Lebanon's bosses had organized armed groups from among their supporters
during the 1958 war and extended services to their clients then and in other
periods of domestic tension—its dimensions were unprecedented. Lebanon's
economy, which was considerably damaged by the prevailing chaos, remained
active until the late 1980s, in part due to the economic activities of the militias.
Its ensuing deterioration, which plunged the country into a severe crisis, accelerated local and foreign peace-making efforts.[40]

One of the institutions most affected by the fighting was the Lebanese army.
Unlike the first civil war, when it avoided the political quarrel and could facilitate the ending of the conflict (under the motto "no victor, no vanquished"), the
army immediately became involved politically, leading to its paralysis and, to a
certain extent, fragmentation along communal and local lines. The fact that the
army's commander and some of its units supported the pro-government camp
resulted in large-scale defections of low-ranking officers and men, mostly
Muslims, culminating in an open revolt led by Lt. Ahmad Khatib (a Sunni), the
first in the army's history.[41] Syria's leaders, who were alarmed by the proximity of Khatib's forces to their border and who feared intervention by other actors (the PLO, Libya, and Iraq) in their own "backyard," fervently opposed
these developments and called for a swift political solution. But Frangieh's
utter refusal to pardon army defectors and enable them to be reintegrated into
the military ranks—as was done in 1958—and his announcement in February
1976 of a plan for limited political reform endorsed by Damascus (the Constitutional Document), led to a coup attempt by General 'Aziz al-Ahdab, who
demanded the president's immediate resignation. The result was further anarchy and the near paralysis of most state institutions. At this point, Lebanon's
partition seemed imminent, if not inevitable.

Why Did Lebanon Survive?

When attempting to apply the state failure–state collapse paradigm to the
Lebanese case, the outcome is ostensibly paradoxical. On the one hand, the
breakdown of the state during the conflict corresponds to, and perhaps epito-
mizes, the model. Yet at the same time, Lebanon was not totally destroyed by
war and remained viable enough to allow its subsequent resuscitation and reconstruction.

The discussion of Lebanon's reconstruction often emphasizes the role of foreign actors, particularly Syria, while playing down the role of domestic factors. As in earlier phases of its political history, however, Lebanon's reconstruction, like its failure and collapse, was above all an internal process that could be intensified or weakened by regional and international involvement. If a majority of the Lebanese had not been keen to preserve their state, for whatever reasons, the efforts made by others to help put it back together could never have succeeded.

The majority of actors, both domestic and foreign, involved in Lebanon's conflict viewed the state as useful, despite its apparent collapse, and preferred the Lebanese state to all other political options.[42] Lebanon's utility was appreciated in both a positive and a negative sense. A majority of Lebanese, including members of all sectors, believed that their state was irreplaceable and that its political system, based on intercommunal power-sharing, would eventually be restored.[43] But Lebanon's preservation was also the practical choice of most local actors. Apart from the Maronite-dominated LF and the Druze Progressive Socialist Party (PSP), two powerful militias that managed to establish ethnically homogeneous "cantons" in the northern and southern parts of Mount Lebanon, respectively, other groups—particularly Shi'i Amal, whose potential supporters were dispersed between the south, Biqa', and the Greater Beirut area—were incapable of creating self-supporting enclaves, and were therefore dependent on the re-establishment of a central government in which they hoped to play a part.[44] Thus, their interests overlapped the goals of the foreign forces involved in the conflict, which rejected Lebanon's partition and pushed for a political solution to the crisis, particularly in the late 1980s.

Another important factor that accounts for Lebanon's survival, and which is often overlooked, is the remarkable continuity manifested by its formal institutions during the conflict. Although paralyzed early in the war, most state agencies did not disintegrate completely and managed to perform at least some of their tasks. The president and the government, although lacking effective control over the state's entire territory, nevertheless continued to represent it both internally and externally, at least until late 1988. The same was true with regard to parliament: even though elections (last held in 1972) could not take place, its members met during the conflict, elected five presidents, debated and approved laws, and ratified and annulled agreements and treaties, including the compromise that facilitated the war's termination.[45] The army, which was considerably weakened in the Two Years' War, retained its integrity and underwent two reconstruction attempts, in 1977–1979 and 1982–1984. Its units were deployed in several regions, albeit not always successfully, and its professional capabilities proved to be indispensable during natural disasters.[46] Parts of the bureaucracy, including the ministries and the central bank, also stayed intact. Civil servants received their salaries (including army defectors) and clerks attended their jobs, despite the shelling, sniper fire, and frequent kidnappings that marked this period. The significance of this continuation became evident in late 1988, when the failed attempts to elect a new president produced a constitutional vacuum. It threatened to push the state into a political abyss.

Alternatives to the state never materialized. Despite vigorous efforts by the militias to create homogeneous "cantons" under their control, Lebanon's partition proved impossible, as was its annexation by another state. In 1976, when Lebanon seemed to be on the verge of disintegration, Syrian Foreign Minister 'Abd al-Halim Khaddam (later vice president) created a linkage between these two outcomes, warning that any attempt to divide Lebanon would prompt Syria to annex it.[47] Yet in view of the regional and international constraints on Syria's involvement in its neighbor's affairs, it could never hope to annex Lebanon. "Cantonization," the creation of a decentralized regime with loosely linked enclaves under *de facto* militia control, was rejected, as were calls to replace intercommunal power-sharing with a secular (i.e., non-sectarian) regime and/ or majoritarian democracy. In the political discourse of wartime Lebanon, the very notion of "partition" (*taqsim*), however imminent, was regarded as anathema, while "the legitimate government" (*al-Shar'iyya*), feeble though it was during most periods, remained an idea to which every actor was careful to pay allegiance, or lip service.[48]

The efforts to resuscitate Lebanon during the war included several attempts to reconstruct its formal institutions and restore law and order, thus creating a favorable climate for the revitalization of the political system. They also included attempts to reach a new political deal that would allow Lebanon's various sectors to come together. That these two tasks were closely linked and mutually dependent was not, however, clear to all parties, domestic or foreign. The first two attempts to resuscitate the state by rebuilding its army, in 1977–1979, ended in failure because a new political settlement could not be reached, while the political initiatives launched in 1975–1976 and in the first half of the 1980s proved impossible to implement due to the prevailing anarchy. Only when the restoration of central authority intersected with a new political formula could Lebanon be resuscitated effectively.

Among the external players involved in the lingering conflict, Syria proved to be the only actor capable and willing to commit itself to long-term involvement. On 1 June 1976, after its attempts to push for a political solution to the crisis backfired, and following desperate pleas by President Frangieh and his allies in the Lebanese Front (the umbrella organization of the Maronite-led parties) to intervene on their behalf, President Asad decided in favor of direct military intervention, and the Syrian army crossed the border and took control of large parts of Lebanon's territory. This move, which pitted Damascus against the radical Lebanese opposition (which had until then received support from Syria and considered the Ba'th regime its ally) and enraged Moscow (which was at the time not only Syria's patron but also the sponsor of several Lebanese opposition groups and the PLO), was, in retrospect, one of the decisive moments of the war. Fearing the spillover of intercommunal tensions into its own multi-ethnic body politic, and alarmed by the rising involvement of outside actors in the conflict and the dangers of further escalation, Syria decided to put all of its efforts into pacifying Lebanon by launching a swift military operation. It only approached its goals fourteen years later, however, after pouring massive resources into the Lebanese enterprise.[49]

In the pan-Arab summits held in Cairo and Riyad in October 1976, President Asad managed to secure pan-Arab support for Syria's move. He also coordinated its actions with Israel through the informal Red Lines Agreement, mediated by the United States and Jordan, thus averting undesirable confrontation.[50] The regional system in the Middle East thus approved a unilateral action by one of its members aimed at preventing another from falling apart, and granted Syria what amounted to a mandate to restore law and order in Lebanon.[51] It should be emphasized, however, that this authorization was by no means a *carte blanche*. Syria's future moves in and regarding Lebanon would require regional and international approval. Syria was not allowed to annex the country and had to commit to preserving it. Against this backdrop of regional and international obligations we must view Syria's role in Lebanon during the next two and one-half decades.

Between 1976 and 1982, Syria was unable, and at times unwilling, to stop the killing in Lebanon. Its *ad hoc* alliance with the Maronite-led forces broke down—although contacts between the two sides continued through various channels, and some militias, like Frangieh's *al-Marada*, maintained their alliance with Damascus. The PLO, one of the targets of Syria's operation in 1976, became a valuable ally following the Israeli-Egyptian rapprochement. Lebanon's reconstruction thus assumed a secondary place on the Syrian agenda, and this and other factors, like the staunch refusal of Israel (and the PLO) to allow the deployment of the Lebanese army in the south, hindered its success.

Israel's invasion of Lebanon in 1982, and the removal of most PLO fighters from Beirut, and later from Tripoli (after a siege by the Syrian army), paved the way for a second attempt to resuscitate the state, this time with American backing.[52] But the government in Beirut, headed by President Amine Gemayel, alienated the Druze and Shi'i communities, enabling the PSP and Amal to mobilize their members in an effective manner. First in the Shuf Mountain and then in

West Beirut, these militias overcame the ethnically mixed army brigades, pieced together since the late 1970s and trained and equipped by the United States.[53] Gemayel's attempts to ignore Syria and its role by signing an agreement with Israel under American auspices and openly calling for its withdrawal from Lebanon were equally imprudent, and encouraged Damascus to rally its local supporters and bring the state's reconstruction efforts to a halt.

In 1984, in the wake of the army's defeat by Amal and the PSP and following the American decision to disengage from Lebanon after Shi'i radicals targeted U.S. military and diplomatic personnel, Gemayel was left with no choice but to accede to Asad's demands. This result paved the way for the formation of the Government of National Unity, which included several of his rivals. From then until 1988, when the president's term expired, several attempts were made to end the conflict by reaching a political compromise. But Lebanon's leaders, first its traditional politicians (in the Geneva and Lausanne conferences of 1983 and 1984) and then the militia leaders (in the Tripartite Agreement of 1985), clung to uncompromising positions. Peace-making efforts failed. Further deterioration ensued, aggravated by an economic crisis, and a "cold war" was waged over the institutions of the state between President Gemayel and Premier Rashid Karami (assassinated in 1987) and his allies, Amal leader Nabih Berri and PSP leader Walid Junblat, who were all backed by Damascus. While Gemayel opposed the abolition of political sectarianism and rejected Syria's demands to formalize its "distinctive relations" with Lebanon, as stipulated by the Tripartite Agreement—a peace deal signed in Damascus between the LF (then led by Elie Hubeiqa), Amal, and the PSP under Syria's auspices—Karami, Berri, and Junblat pushed for comprehensive political reforms, in line with the opposition's demands. Despite this stalemate, however, contacts between all parties continued. Meanwhile, Damascus stepped up its own involvement, and tried to restore order in various regions, particularly Muslim-dominated ones, using its own army and members of the Lebanese law-enforcement agencies. But it could not pacify the entire country or find a partner in the Maronite community who would be both capable of fulfilling and willing to accept the opposition's demands for political reform and set the seal on the "distinctive relations" between the two states.[54]

The years from 1988 to 1990 were among the most brutal periods of the conflict and served, in retrospect, as a "mutually hurting stalemate" for all sides. The failed attempts to elect a new president before the end of Gemayel's term engendered a constitutional vacuum in the state's highest institution, the first since 1975. Two rival governments, a Muslim-dominated one led by Salim el-Hoss and a Christian military one headed by General Michel Aoun, commander of the Christian-led units of the army, each claimed exclusive legitimacy.[55]

Aoun, who had maintained for some time that the army could become Lebanon's savior and considered himself a candidate for president, first tried to secure Syria's support. When his efforts failed, he attempted to challenge Syria's hegemony in Lebanon by forging an alliance with its rivals—Iraq and the PLO—in hope that escalation and, possibly, foreign intervention (American, French, or Israeli) could force it to yield.[56]

The vacuum in the highest office of the state and the duality in the government had grave effects on other formal institutions. The bureaucracy virtually split in two, and the army's Christian-dominated units almost completely separated from its Muslim-led ones.[57] Of all state institutions, only the central bank, which managed to finance both sides despite the pressures applied on its director, Edmond Na'im (who was kidnapped by the lieutenants of a minister in Hoss's government after refusing the minister's financial demands), and parliament, which retained its multiethnic and interregional character but could not convene, remained intact.[58] In the regional arena, Hoss's government enjoyed Syrian support, while Iraq and the PLO backed Aoun. Until the latter's final defeat two years later, the main question was which of the two leaders would gain the upper hand in the domestic, regional, and international arenas. The possibility that both governments would endure was not contemplated.

On 14 March 1989, General Aoun declared a War of Liberation against Syria's "occupation" in Lebanon, and a confrontation ensued between his army and the Syrian forces. But this gamble backfired; Aoun's hopes that all Lebanese would rebel against Damascus and unite under his banner were dashed, and more Muslim officers and men defected from his army's ranks. Emigration—particularly of Christians—intensified, reaching unprecedented levels. The deepening internal crisis and the massive foreign involvement that threatened to disrupt regional order in the Middle East (particularly after Iraq, which ended its war with Iran, sought to settle scores with Syria, Iran's ally) caused grave concerns among several Arab League members, particularly Saudi Arabia, and peace-making efforts resumed. After several more months of violence and political deadlock, most actors began to acknowledge that their hard-line positions could not be sustained. Inter-Arab mediation commenced, this time on the highest level, and the warring parties were encouraged to agree to a cease-fire and to allow the remaining members of the Lebanese parliament to attend a conference outside the country in order to reach a new political compromise that would end the war.[59]

On 30 September 1989, 62 of the remaining 73 deputies of the 99-member parliament elected in 1972—31 Muslims and 31 Christians—convened in Ta'if, Saudi Arabia, to discuss a political agreement, the details of which had been discussed for some time by Lebanese leaders directly and through inter-Arab and American channels.[60] Although more than a decade and a half had elapsed since its members' election and despite the absence of prominent leaders, most notably the heads of the militias (PSP, LF, Amal, Hizbullah, and others), from the peace conference, the parliament was the only Lebanese political institution that included representatives of all sectors. In a session held on 22 October 1989, fifty-eight of the convening deputies endorsed a document of national understanding, known as the Ta'if Agreement.[61]

The Ta'if Agreement, which was later ratified by parliament and incorporated into the constitution, represented a turning point in the war and a critical event in Lebanon's political history. First, it was a formal document endorsed by a formal institution, and not an unofficial understanding like the National Pact, a presidential declaration like the Constitutional Document, or a deal between militia leaders like the Tripartite Agreement. Second, it settled several issues that had divided Lebanon's political community for some time. It was agreed that Lebanon was a "final homeland for all its sons," thus according the state recognition by all sectors of its society, and that it was "Arab in its affiliation and identity." Any "authority that contradict[ed] the pact of communal coexistence" was declared illegitimate, emphasizing that the agreement of the various communities to live together and share power between them was the only source of legitimate authority in Lebanon. It implied that any actor challenging the new political consensus would be removed by force.

Another important part of the agreement was a long-expected redrawing of the power-sharing formula between Lebanon's sectors. This reform, meant to adjust the political settlement so as to conform to demographic changes since 1943, appeared in one form or another in most peace-making initiatives launched during the war, but could not hitherto be implemented. Christian leaders had refused to give up any of their prerogatives, and their Muslim counterparts would not accept less than a total revision of the political settlement.[62] Among the measures agreed to in 1989: (a) executive power, earlier the prerogative of the president (a Maronite), was transferred to the government and the premier (a Sunni) and, to a lesser extent, to the speaker of parliament (a Shi'i); (b) instead of the 6:5 ratio in favor of Christians in all formal institutions, a ratio of 1:1 between Christians and Muslims was adopted for distribution of parliamentary seats and high-level posts, while other positions were to be filled according to merit; (c) a national body was to seek the end of political sectarianism, but no timetable was set. In fact, the Ta'if Agreement was once again a compromise between those demanding an end to power-sharing in Lebanon and those in favor of its preservation. However, the fact that a clause explicitly stating that political sectarianism should be abolished was added to the constitution seemed to open the door to future criticism of Lebanon's political order and elicited apprehension, particularly among hard-line Maronite activists.[63]

Reform was also enacted in the area of national security. An end was put to the prevailing ambiguity concerning the use of force in Lebanon, and law-enforcement institutions were strengthened. The army, formerly under the president's control, was subordinated to the government, which was also responsible for declaring an emergency, making war, or concluding peace, and for ordering mobilization, as well as for supervising all agencies, including the army. A Government of National Reconciliation was to devise a security plan that would expand the control of the state over all its territory, and the militias, both Lebanese and foreign, were to be dismantled.

A majority of the country's leaders, including the Maronite Patriarch Nasrallah Sfeir, Phalanges leader Georges Saadeh, and (although still not openly) LF leader Samir Geagea accepted the Ta'if Agreement. But Aoun rejected, calling it a betrayal of Lebanon's sovereignty, and vowed to resist it. After another year of bloodletting, which included an intracommunal war between Aoun's forces and the LF that ravaged East Beirut and other Christian regions, the Syrian army and Muslim-led units of the Lebanese army finally overran Aoun's last stronghold, which by now was reduced to the presidential palace in Baabda and its vicinity, finally putting an end to the civil war. The road to the implementation of the Ta'if Agreement, and toward Lebanon's resuscitation, was now open.

The Ta'if Agreement emphasized the "distinctive relations" between Lebanon and Syria, calling for agreements between the two states. Lebanon was prohibited from becoming a threat to Syria's security and a passageway or *place d'armes* for any force, state, or organization that might endanger it. This clause was a result of a prior agreement between the Arab mediators and Damascus, and the convening Lebanese deputies were unable to change it. This fact, as well as the ambiguous clauses on Syria's withdrawal, convinced several local and foreign observers that the Syrian army would remain on Lebanese soil indefinitely, and that the price of national reconciliation in Lebanon was the acceptance of certain restrictions on its sovereignty. The decade that has elapsed since the end of the conflict in Lebanon suggests that these apprehensions were not unfounded. Yet, after May 2000, when Israel withdrew its forces from Lebanon, the calls for Syria's withdrawal intensified, leading to two limited Syrian pull-outs, the first from the Beirut region in June 2001 and the second from the southern suburb of Beirut and Mount Lebanon in April 2002. Nonetheless, in August 2001, Lebanese security forces arrested 200 anti-Syrian activists, a move that elicited widespread criticism, and in 2002 Syrian troops were still positioned in many areas of the country, particularly the north and Biqa'.

Resuscitation and Reconstruction

The reconstruction of the Lebanese state, which commenced not long after the end of the conflict, has so far included efforts to revitalize formal institutions and to rebuild the state's infrastructure, in particular the devastated commercial center of Beirut. In addition, Lebanon's relations with Syria have been formalized. Regional and international legitimacy and consent for Syria's position in and vis-à-vis Lebanon, as well as the latter's own weakness, have so far enabled Damascus to serve as an alternative center supporting the new political order and to enjoy unprecedented influence over decision-making in Beirut.

On 24 December 1990, a Government of National Reconciliation was formed in Lebanon. It included most militia leaders as ministers of state. Three months later, the government decided to dissolve all armed groups in Lebanon, local and foreign (including the PLO factions and the Iranian Revolutionary Guards, who arrived in 1982), and to collect their heavy weapons. With the support and backing of Damascus, Lebanese leaders made it clear that the days of the Cairo Agreement were over, and that special arrangements with the PLO concerning its armed presence in the country would not be permitted. They did so despite claims by Palestinian officials that their weapons were "regional," namely, associated with the Middle East conflict, and not "local," and therefore did not fall under Lebanese jurisdiction.[64] Most local militias disbanded and became political parties, and their weapons were handed to the now-united Lebanese army, which also received armaments and other equipment from the United States, Britain, France, and other states. Meanwhile, the army itself went through a comprehensive process of reorganization, including the shuffling of its officers and men in order to prevent the formation of units with communal and regional allegiances, as occurred during the civil war. Although the army command initially opposed the enrollment of militia personnel in its ranks, preferring the conscription of fresh soldiers, it had to agree to include at least some of the former militiamen. (Others were referred to the other security services.) As of 1993, all Lebanese males between the ages of eighteen and thirty were subject to military draft for eighteen months' compulsory service. The army, designed to be, and regarded as, the mainstay of the Lebanese government in the post-war era, has also grown considerably. It expanded from 20,000 in 1975 to 45,000 in 1995 and to 67,900 in 1999 (including 27,400 conscripts). It is the most powerful armed force in the country.[65] With Syria's backing, the Lebanese army's units deployed in most regions, leaving intact only Hizbullah, resisting Israel's occupation of the south; and, until May 2000, the South Lebanon Army, the local militia in Israel's self-declared "Security Zone." In February 1996, in the wake of demonstrations by the labor unions, the army imposed a country-wide curfew; in 1997–1998, it crushed an uprising of a radical splinter group of Hizbullah in the Biqa'; and in 2000, it subdued a group of Islamic extremists in the north. It also performed its traditional role in facilitating the parliamentary elections of 1992, 1996, and 2000. All attempts to challenge the new political order in Lebanon were effectively put down by the national army.[66]

The "distinctive relations" between Lebanon and Syria were formalized in the Treaty of Brotherhood, Cooperation, and Coordination signed between Presidents Hafez al-Asad and Elias al-Hrawi in 1991. That agreement called for cooperation and coordination between the two states on all political, economic, and security issues, and set up a formal structure to develop and execute mutual policies. Considering the imbalance in power, as well as the presence of some 20,000–30,000 Syrian troops on Lebanese soil, some observers maintained that Lebanon had, in fact, become a Syrian satellite. Suspicions deepened as Damascus declined to establish full diplomatic relations with Beirut. Since 1991, Syria has to a large extent controlled its neighbor's foreign policy and vetoes any moves that it deems inconsistent with its own interests. However, claims that Lebanon is therefore non-existent, or that Syria controls its every political, social, and economic aspect, are exaggerated. Syrian hegemony in Lebanon is a recent phenomenon, attained after many years of endeavors and disappointments, and it remains dependent on a favorable internal, regional, and global climate.

Following the formation of the new government in Beirut, the disbanding of most militias, the deployment of the army, and the formalization of relations with Syria, politics in Lebanon slowly returned to normal. In August 1991, parliament adopted a general amnesty law for war crimes, as was done after the 1958 war, and parliamentary elections were held in 1992, putting an end to two decades without elections. Opposition parties—mostly Maronite-led groups and organizations—decided to boycott these elections, arguing that since the Syrian army had not redeployed, it might affect the outcome. But elections were held anyway, despite a low turnout of voters in the Christian regions (particularly the northern parts of Mount Lebanon). The PSP, Amal, Hizbullah, the SSNP, and other ex-militias chose to participate in the elections, thus accepting the Lebanese political system and signaling that their efforts were now shifting from trying to pull it down by force to attaining their goals from within. This is particularly significant in the case of Hizbullah, the radical Shi'i movement whose proclaimed goal has been to establish an Islamic state in Lebanon. Elections were again held in 1996 and 2000, by which time more opposition leaders were prepared to take part, and some in fact were elected.[67]

Politics in Lebanon in the post-war era reflect an increased institutionaliza-tion of power-sharing. In addition to equal representation of Lebanon's Mus-lims and Christians in all formal institutions, new mechanisms, and particularly the multi-ethnic *troika*, which includes the president, premier, and speaker of parliament, encourage intergroup accommodation.[68] Following the return of peace to Lebanon, the reemergence of formal institutions and the reestablish-ment of intercommunal power-sharing, as well as other developments (e.g., the release of Western hostages kidnapped by Shi'i militants during the war), the state has regained its status as a legitimate international player. It remains, how-ever, bound by restrictions imposed on it by the Ta'if Agreement and the bilat-eral treaties with Syria. This situation does not represent an entirely new phe-nomenon; in the aftermath of the first civil war, in 1958, Lebanon was under the heavy influence of the United Arab Republic (UAR), and was regarded by both local and foreign observers as its client.

Nor is the current relationship between Syria and Lebanon untenable. A number of groups in Lebanon, and in particular the "newcomers" to its political system (the local Ba'th party, the SSNP, Hizbullah, Amal, and several Maronite politicians), view Syria's role as crucial for maintaining the privileged position that they now have in Lebanon. Damascus, for its part, has sponsored a multi-ethnic and interregional coalition in Beirut, which was and remains a necessary condition for bidding for power there. Moreover, unlike earlier periods in its history, Syria is much more powerful than Lebanon, and there are no regional actors interested in contesting its hegemony over its neighbor. The Arab-Israeli conflict remains unresolved, allowing Damascus to present itself not only as Lebanon's foremost protector against Israeli "plots," but also as the only actor capable of bringing Lebanon to the negotiating table once a Syrian-Israeli peace agreement is reached. Finally, powerful actors in the international arena, par-ticularly the United States, but also France, view Syria's role in the Middle East as important both in the context of the Arab-Israeli conflict and in their own relationships with other actors in the region (especially Iraq and Iran, Syria's allies). They are thus reluctant to apply pressure on Damascus with regard to Lebanon.

Lebanon's Second Republic: Vulnerability and Strength

The reconstruction of the Lebanese state, which is, after 1990, referred to as the Second Republic (with the Third Republic symbolizing the non-sectarian ideal), has so far yielded mixed results. On the one hand, peace has been re-stored, most militias have been disbanded (apart from Hizbullah, which en-gaged in "resistance" against the Israeli occupation of the border area and still

maintains a significant presence there), state institutions have been reinvigo-
rated and strengthened, the power-sharing settlement has been revised, the PLO
and its factions have been subdued, and the Israeli army has withdrawn to the
international border.[69] On the other hand, the economy has not fully recovered
and still faces enormous difficulties, reconciliation is not yet fully accomplished,
and Syria's presence in the state, as well as its influence on decision-making in
Beirut, are still very much apparent.[70]

Lebanon's resuscitation efforts have so far concentrated on reinvigorating
formal institutions, adjusting the political settlement, and rebuilding the capital, Beirut. These tasks were given priority over others because the state's weakness before and during the conflict encouraged its leaders to provide an effective institutional framework to sustain the political system. In addition, the
power-sharing settlement needed to reflect the changes that had taken place in
Lebanon's society, and to complement the revitalization of its formal institutions. Finally, the reconstruction of Beirut symbolizes Lebanon's recovery, thus
helping to recapture the hearts and minds of émigrés, whose skills and capital
were needed further down the road, and attract foreign capital. These steps, as
well as others—the release of Western hostages and the arrest of members of
the Japanese Red Army who, like other foreign revolutionaries, turned parts of
the state into their base of operations—were seen as crucial if Lebanon wished
to receive foreign aid and rid itself of the "non-state" stigma that had endured
since the mid-1970s. The will to resuscitate the state was demonstrated not
only by the actions of former and current Prime Minister Rafiq Hariri, the driving force behind Lebanon's restoration, but also by the words of his rival, former
Prime Minister Salim el-Hoss:

> The end of war should underline the need to build a state of peace—one
> that can consolidate the foundations of stability and set the country on a
> steady course of orderly evolution and progress. Unless the right kind of
> state is built, with all the proper systems and institutions, the country's
> exit from violent crisis may not mean an end to the nightmares of Leba-
> non, but rather a shift from one kind of nightmare to another.[71]

Hariri, who made his fortune as a contractor in Saudi Arabia in the 1970s
and 1980s, embodies Lebanon's post-war self-image. A mathematics and business teacher who had built a multibillion-dollar financial empire, he was expected by many Lebanese to replicate his personal success at the national level.
Hariri's close links to the Saudi throne and good ties with Damascus were also
seen as helpful for Lebanon's resurgence.

As several scholars have pointed out, a process of reconciliation between
Lebanon's sectors has not been pursued, and its civil society, which was con-

siderably weakened by the conflict, has yet to recover. Khalaf alluded to the "collective amnesia" that prevails in Lebanon with respect to the civil war, and pondered how such "inglorious events" could ever be incorporated into the collective memory of its society. He also emphasized the role of ethnic identities, which came to serve as "both emblem and armor" for so many of its sons during times of conflict, making reconciliation all the more difficult.[72] Other authors have depicted the physical demolition of ruins in central Beirut as attempts to reconstruct Lebanon's history, while playwrights and film makers criticized the tendency of many in the country to pin their tragedies on others, focusing on the role of the Lebanese in the recent war.[73] Yet together, these views and the debate that they have elicited in fact represent an emerging critical discourse within Lebanon's post-war civil society, which, if pursued further, could move it closer toward reconciliation.

What about other paths to reconciliation that have been followed elsewhere? In post-war Lebanon, where members of all sectors of society can claim to be victims, it is difficult to envision reconciliation through state-sponsored projects like the South African Truth and Reconciliation Commission, which was regarded by the leaders of that country as imperative for a peaceful transition from a racist and authoritarian regime to a democracy.[74] Reconciliation in Lebanon would more likely be pursued through an open public debate, which is taking place already, or by holding a "national dialogue" between prominent figures from all sectors. The government can do its share by providing a positive climate for soul-searching, and by allowing all political factions to participate. It can also promote "over-arching loyalties" among citizens from different sectors, as it has done in the army and, to a lesser extent, in the school system.[75]

Conclusion

Democracy requires all participants in the political game to abide by a minimal set of norms and obligations if anarchy is to be averted. Warlord democratization, which Wantchekon prescribes as a remedy for several failed states in Africa and Asia, is not only an oxymoron in the sense that it produces an entirely utilitarian form of government that is devoid of any meaning—"a body without a soul"—it is also impractical because it cannot establish a viable political order.[76] As Zartman argues: "If warlords are allowed to form the new state, they ensure the return of the system that brought about its own collapse."[77] Indeed, those students of Lebanon who were impressed by its outstanding political performance before 1975 committed an error by focusing on its parliamentary and presidential elections and the frequent changes of government, while disregarding the threats, violence, and corruption that accompanied them, as well as the underlying weakness of the state. If one wishes to keep states from failing and collapsing over and over again, warlords must not be permitted to determine the rules of the post-war political game. In the case of Lebanon, it was its traditional politicians (whom Hanf called "foxes") who crafted the political system, while the warlords (the "lions") were invited to join the first post-war government as ministers of state, in order to allow the peaceful disbandment of their militias. However, the "lions" later had to become "foxes" in order to play a political role. In the general elections of 1992, 1996, and 2000, ex-warlords were forced to compete on an equal basis with other politicians and were not always successful.

The role of formal institutions during periods of state failure and state collapse is critical. In the case of Lebanon, the prevailing chaos in the state often overshadowed the routine work of its formal institutions, whose members strenuously tried to carry on with their daily tasks, however ineffectively. The army, for instance, was incapable of restoring order in the country, as expected by local and foreign actors, but nonetheless carried out limited tasks that were tremendously important for its future revitalization. Unlike the People's Army of Yugoslavia, which deteriorated into an ethnic militia in the early 1990s, sealing off the prospects of its revival as an institution shared by all sectors of society, the army in Lebanon tried—albeit not always successfully—to distance itself from the militias and remain the state's most national institution. When the institutions of failed or collapsed states, however impotent, are not totally swept away by conflict, state resuscitation may be less costly and time consuming than when the institutions completely disintegrate. After all, rather than having to establish new institutions, recruit and train their members, and inculcate them with a sense of common identity, one can mend existing structures while introducing those reforms that would enable them to perform their tasks in an uncontested manner. (In the case of the Lebanese army, these reforms included multicommunal command structures and efforts to create more ethnically balanced units.) The Lebanese case suggests, however, that when the resuscitation of formal institutions outpaces the reestablishment of political consensus, namely, when order supersedes participation, the government cannot act in a legitimate manner and is vulnerable to challenges by sectors that claim that they are discriminated against.

Lebanon's political system based on power-sharing proved to be so embedded in its social realities that all attempts to do away with it were futile. This suggests that in deeply divided societies, political settlements based on power-sharing die hard, and that even when understandings between the sectors of society fall apart, power-sharing may still be the best political option. One can broaden this observation and argue that when internal consensus exists regarding a state and its regime, even in the negative sense—namely, a refusal to consider alternatives—the question is no longer whether they will be resurrected, but when and at what cost. Here lies the difference between "doomed states," those political entities that have disintegrated and are beyond repair, since they no longer reflect the needs and aspirations of their population (e.g., the U.S.S.R. and Yugoslavia), and those polities that, however disordered, are, in a sense, "inescapable." The widespread belief that Lebanon would one day be reconstituted in a manner that would resemble the pre-war period, the stakes that key players had in the restoration of the central government, the daily work of politicians, clerks, policemen, and soldiers notwithstanding the powerlessness of their institutions, the efforts of most players, local and foreign, to avoid being tarred with the brush of partition, the adherence to the legitimate government even when its actual existence was doubtful—all these are pieces of evidence that help solve the riddle of Lebanon's extraordinary viability during the long and devastating conflict. Today's weak-but-not-failed Lebanon is far removed from its collapsed shell.

Notes

1. According to the 1932 census, the last held in Lebanon, all Christian communities formed about 51 percent of the population, and Maronite Christians were the largest ethnic group in the state (30 percent). While official statistics regarding Lebanon's current ethnic makeup are unavailable, recent estimates put all of its Muslim communities at about 70 percent, with the Shiʻis as its largest community (35–40 percent), and Maronites at about 20 percent.

2. These are also referred to as complex political emergencies (CPEs). According to Cliffe and Luckham, CPEs occur where "the state has either collapsed, been contested or been seriously weakened." Lionel Cliffe and Robin Luckham, "Complex Political Emergencies and the State: Failure and the Fate of the State," *Third World Quarterly*, XX (1999), 27.

3. The civil wars in China, Korea, Vietnam, and Afghanistan, as well as the first civil war in Lebanon, in 1958, are cases in point. As demonstrated by the case of Haiti, weak states could threaten to "switch sides" in order to extract resources from a patron. See David M. Malone and Marlye Gélin-Adams, "Haiti: A Case of Endemic Weakness," chapter 11 in this volume.

4. This is the view of several authors in this volume. A fourth term, "disrupted state," describes "unconsolidated" states, which are often in an ongoing state of entropy, as opposed to "cohesive" states, which are either Westphalian states or stable autocracies. See Amin Saikal, "Dimensions of State Disruption and International Response," *Third World Quarterly*, XXI (2000), 40; I. William Zartman, *Collapsed States: The Disintegration and Restoration of Legitimate Authority* (Boulder, 1995), 1.

5. Clifford Geertz, *The Interpretation of Cultures* (New York, 1973), 255–310; Joel Migdal, *Strong Societies and Weak States: State-Society Relations and State Capabilities in the Third World* (Princeton, 1988); Robert H. Jackson, *Quasi-States: Sovereignty, International Relations, and the Third World* (Cambridge, 1990); idem., "Surrogate Sovereignty? Great Power Responsibility and 'Failed States,'" paper read to the Failed States Conference, Purdue University (West Lafayette, April 8–11, 1999), http://www.ippu.purdue.edu/conference/Jackson.html; I. William Zartman (ed.), *Governance as Conflict Management: Politics and Violence in West Africa* (Washington, D.C., 1997).

6. By "sector" I mean any non-state actor capable of mobilizing political support by appealing to identity, e.g., ethnic group, clan, tribe, or region.

7. See, in particular, Christopher Clapham, "The Global-Local Politics of State Decay," in Robert I. Rotberg (ed.), *When States Fail: Causes and Consequences* (Princeton, 2003, forthcoming).

8. The literature on the 1975–1990 conflict is enormous. See, for example, Roger Owen (ed.), *Essays on the Crisis in Lebanon* (London, 1976); Kamal Salibi, *Crossroads to Civil War* (New York, 1976); Edward P. Haley and Lewis W. Snider (eds.), *Lebanon in Crisis* (Syracuse, 1979); Walid Khalidi, *Conflict and Violence in Lebanon* (Cambridge, MA, 1979); Marius Deeb, *The Lebanese Civil War* (New York, 1980); Edward E. Azar (ed.), *The Emergence of a New Lebanon* (New York, 1984); Itamar Rabinovich, *The War for Lebanon* (Ithaca, 1985); Samir Khalaf, *Lebanon's Predicament* (New York, 1987); Halim Barakat (ed.), *Toward a Viable Lebanon* (London, 1988); Nadim Shehadi and Dana Haffar Mills (eds.), *Lebanon: A History of Conflict and Consensus* (London, 1988); Theodor Hanf, *Coexistence in Wartime Lebanon: Decline of a State and Rise of a Nation*, (London, 1993); Elizabeth Picard, *Lebanon: A Shattered Country* (New York, 1996).

9. *Al-Hayat* (London, 10 March 1992); Augustus R. Norton and Jillian Schwedler, "Swiss Soldiers, Ta'if Clocks, and Early Elections: Toward a Happy Ending?" in Deirdre Collings (ed.), *Peace for Lebanon?* (Boulder, 1994), 64; Michael Young, "The Sneer of Memory: Lebanon's Disappeared and Postwar Culture," *Middle East Report*, XXX (2000), 42–54.

10. Boutrus Labaki, "Lebanese Emigration during the War (1975–1989)," in Albert Hourani and Nadim Shehadi (eds.), *The Lebanese in the World* (London, 1992), 610; "Situation Alarmante: L'exode des Compétences," *Magazine* (21 February 1997).

11. Hanf, *Coexistence in Wartime Lebanon*, 342–347; Sena Eken et al., *Economic Dislocation and Recovery in Lebanon* (Washington, D.C., 1995), 5.

12. *Al-Sayyad* (Beirut, 4 April 1974). According to this report, the number of weapons owned by private citizens increased during this period and included not only pistols but also machine guns. In 1973, 205 people were killed, compared to 121 in 1972; there were 123 robberies, compared to 92. In addition, fifteen Internal Security Forces personnel were killed.

13. See, in particular, Michael C. Hudson, "The Problem of Authoritative Power in Lebanese Politics: Why Consociationalism Failed," in Shehadi and Mills, *Lebanon: A History of Conflict and Consensus*, 224–239. Jackson argues that failed states are "hol-

low juridical shells that shroud an anarchical condition domestically." Jackson, "Surrogate Sovereignty?"

14. I borrow this term from Ian Lustick in "Stability in Deeply Divided Societies: Consociationalism versus Control," *World Politics,* XXXI (1979), and "Lijphart, Lakatos, and Consociationalism," *World Politics,* L (1997).

15. For the former view, see Marwan Buheiry, "External Interventions and Internal Wars in Lebanon: 1770–1982," in Laurence I. Conrad (ed.), *The Formation and Perception of the Modern Arab World* (Princeton, 1987), 129–139; Kirsten E. Schulze, *Israel's Covert Diplomacy in Lebanon* (London, 1998); Farid el-Khazen, *The Breakdown of the State in Lebanon, 1967–1976* (London, 2000); Brenda M. Seaver, "The Regional Sources of Power-Sharing Failure: The Case of Lebanon," *Political Science Quarterly,* CXV (2000), 247–271. For the latter view, see Meir Zamir, *The Formation of Modern Lebanon* (London, 1985); Elie Kedourie, *Politics in the Middle East* (Oxford, 1992).

16. Holding parliamentary elections on a regional basis worked best for the country's traditional leaders, who garnered political support by employing their locally based patronage networks and appealing to the regional, ethnic, and clan affiliations of their constituencies.

17. The birthrate among the Shi'i community has been comparatively high, while Christians, particularly Maronites, emigrated in relatively large numbers. Muslims, and particularly Shi'is, also left Lebanon, but did so in smaller numbers and often returned. Two noted examples are Prime Minister Rafiq Hariri, who emigrated to Saudi Arabia in the 1960s, and Nabih Berri, the speaker of parliament, who was born in Freetown, Sierra Leone.

18. Limited reforms were introduced by President Fouad Chehab after the 1958 civil war.

19. Itamar Rabinovich, "Arab Political Parties: Ideology and Ethnicity," in Milton Esman and Rabinovich (eds.), *Ethnicity, Pluralism and the State in the Middle East* (Ithaca, 1988), 165.

20. See Oren Barak, *The Hardships of Consociation: The Perils of Partition: Lebanon (1943–90),* Occasional Paper no. 86 (Jerusalem, November 2000).

21. Arendt Lijphart, *Democracy in Plural Societies* (New Haven, 1977).

22. See Oren Barak, "Intra-communal and Inter-communal Dimensions of Conflict and Peace in Lebanon," *International Journal of Middle East Studies,* XXXIV (November 2002), 619–644. See also the description of the 1970 presidential elections in Jonathan C. Randal, *Going All the Way* (New York, 1983), 126–128.

23. Michael C. Hudson, *The Precarious Republic* (New York, 1968), 3–13; idem., "The Problem of Authoritative Power in Lebanese Politics"; Albert Hourani, "Visions of Lebanon," in Barakat, *Toward a Viable Lebanon,* 3–11.

24. Since the quotas for representation of each community were fixed, conflict was waged primarily between leaders of these communities over the positions allotted to them. See Barak, "Intra-communal and Inter-communal Dimensions of Conflict and Peace in Lebanon."

25. Geertz, *The Interpretation of Cultures*, 293–297; Leonard Binder (ed.), *Politics in Lebanon* (New York, 1966); David R. Smock and Audrey C. Smock, *The Politics of Pluralism: A Comparative Study of Lebanon and Ghana* (New York, 1975); Lijphart, *Democracy in Plural Societies*. For criticism, see Albert Hourani, "Ideologies of the Mountain and the City," in Owen, *Essays on the Crisis in Lebanon* (Cambridge, MA, 1972), 23–31.

26. Eric A. Nordlinger, *Conflict Regulation in Divided Societies* (Cambridge, MA, 1972), 26–27.

27. Lijphart, *Democracy in Plural Societies*, 81–83.

28. Political patronage is part and parcel of the *modus operandi* of most political actors in Lebanon, old and new. Samir Khalaf, "Changing Patterns of Political Patronage in Lebanon," in Ernest Gellner and John Waterbury (eds.), *Patrons and Clients in Mediterranean Societies* (London, 1977), 185–205; Michael Johnson, "Political Bosses and Their Gangs: Zu'ama and Qabadayat in the Sunni Muslim Quarters of Beirut," ibid., 207–224; idem., *Class and Client in Beirut* (London, 1986). For a current glimpse into the workings of this system, see Michael Young, "Time to Stop the Hypocrisy on the Drug Trade and Look the Other Way," *The Daily Star* (Beirut, 7 July 2001).

29. Michel Chiha, *Lebanon: At Home and Abroad* (Beirut, 1966), 116–117 [emphasis in original].

30. Ibid. See also Nadim Shehadi, "The Idea of Lebanon: Economy and State in the Cénacle Libanais," *Papers on Lebanon*, no. 5 (Oxford, 1987). Only after Lebanon's collapse in 1975–1976 did its leaders begin to question these "dogmas." See Amine Gemayel, "The Price and the Promise," *Foreign Affairs*, LXIII (1985), 759–777 (Gemayel was president of Lebanon from 1982 to 1988). The problem was, however, that the state was unable to function either as a coercive agent or as a legitimate conflict regulator.

31. Lebanon participated in the first Arab-Israeli war, but in a very limited way. See Oren Barak, "Commemorating Malikiyya: Political Myth, Multiethnic Identity and the Making of the Lebanese Army," *History and Memory*, XIII (2001), 60–84. Between 1945 and 1975 there were two coup attempts in Lebanon, but it was a political actor, the Syrian Social Nationalist Party (SSNP), that initiated them. A few army officers did, however, take part in both episodes.

32. Despite its size, the army managed to play the role of mediator, arbiter, and maintainer of political balance, particularly in view of the ineffectiveness of other formal institutions. In the wake of the 1958 conflict, army officers called the shots in the political system, but in early 1970 the Frangieh administration purged the army and pushed it away from politics, depriving the state of its chief security apparatus and internal conflict manager. Adel A. Frieha, *L'Armée et l'Etat au Liban, 1945–80* (Paris, 1980).

33. Quoted in Hudson, "The Problem of Authoritative Power in Lebanese Politics."

34. As pointed out by René Lemarchand, "The Democratic Republic of the Congo: From Failure to Potential Reconstruction," chapter 2 in this volume, refugees and other diasporas can accelerate the process of state failure and collapse. This was also evident in the case of Jordan in 1970–1971.

35. A Lebanese journal suggested that it was merely a "chronicler." *Al-Sayyad* (24 April 1974), 18.

36. Hussein Sirriyeh, "The Palestinian Armed Presence in Lebanon since 1967," in Owen, *Essays on the Crisis in Lebanon*, 73–89; Salibi, *Crossroads to Civil War*; Rex Brynen, *Sanctuary and Survival: The PLO in Lebanon* (Boulder, 1990).

37. Fouad Ajami, "Lebanon and Its Inheritors," *Foreign Affairs*, LXIII (1985), 788–799.

38. Only recently, after Israel's withdrawal, could this population return to the area.

39. On the Lebanese militias see Frank Stoakes, "The Supervigilantes: The Lebanese Kataeb Party as a Builder, Surrogate and Defender of the State," *Middle Eastern Studies*, XI (1975), 215–236; Twefik Khalaf, "The Phalange and the Maronite Community: From Lebanonism to Maronitism," in Owen, *Essays on the Crisis in Lebanon*, 43–57; John P. Entelis, "Ethnic Conflict and the Reemergence of Radical Christian Nationalism in Lebanon," *Journal of South Asian and Middle Eastern Studies*, II (1979), 6–25; Lewis W. Snider, "The Lebanese Forces: Their Origins and Role in Lebanon's Politics," *Middle East Journal*, XXXVIII (1984), 1–33; Augustus R. Norton, *Amal and the Shi'a* (Austin, 1987); Hanf, *Coexistence in Wartime Lebanon*; Judith P. Harik, "Change and Continuity among the Lebanese Druze Community: The Civil Administration of the Mountains, 1983–1990," *Middle Eastern Studies*, IX (1993), 377–398; idem., "The Public and Social Services of the Lebanese Militias," *Papers on Lebanon*, no. 14 (Oxford, 1994); Elizabeth Picard, "Lebanon's War Economy," in Steven Heydemann (ed.), *War, Institutions, and Social Change in the Middle East* (Berkeley, 2000), 292–322.

40. Mina Toksoz, *The Lebanon Conflict: Political Shifts, Regional Impact and Economic Outlook* (London, 1986).

41. Ronald D. McLaurin, "Lebanon and Its Army: Past, Present and Future," in Azar, *The Emergence of a New Lebanon*, 79–114; Joseph A. Kechichian, "The Lebanese Army: Capabilities and Challenges in the 1980s," *Conflict Quarterly*, V (1985), 15–39. Khatib did not attract all Muslim officers and men in the army: only 15 percent of its 20,000 personnel defected and joined the militias or formed local groups to protect their towns and regions, while 10 percent remained in their positions. The remaining 75 percent went home and waited for the crisis to end. See Barak, "Commemorating Malikiyya."

42. For details, see Barak, *The Hardships of Consociation: The Perils of Partition*. For a discussion of the concept of the "usable state," see Jens Meierhenrich, "Forming States after Failure: Utility and Its Perception," in Rotberg, *When States Fail*.

43. See, in particular, Hanf, *Coexistence in Wartime Lebanon;* Edward E. Azar, "The Lebanese Case," in idem.; John W. Burton (ed.), *International Conflict Resolution* (Boulder, 1986), 131.

44. Amal attained this goal in 1992, when Nabih Berri was elected speaker of parliament.

45. The presidents were Elias Sarkis, elected in 1976; Bashir Gemayel (assassinated before assuming office) and Amine Gemayel, both elected in 1982; and René Mouawwad (assassinated shortly after entering office) and Elias Hrawi, both elected in 1989. The

National Defense Law was approved in 1979, the Cairo Agreement was annulled in 1987, the agreement with Israel was ratified in 1983 and annulled in 1987, and the Ta'if Agreement was approved in 1989 and incorporated in the constitution in 1990.

46. Juli Abi-Ghanim, *al-Jaysh al-Lubnani: al-dawr al-'akhar* [The Lebanese army: the other role] (Beirut, 1996). See also Barak, "Commemorating Malikiyya."

47. *Al-Ray al-'Am* (Kuwait, 7 January 1976).

48. See Barak, *The Hardships of Consociation: The Perils of Partition.*

49. According to Elizabeth Picard, thirty senior officers of the Syrian army tried to stand against their country's intervention in Lebanon. "Arab Military in Politics: From Revolutionary Plot to Authoritarian State," in Giacomo Luciani (ed.), *The Arab State* (Berkeley, 1990), 195. The Syrian army has suffered numerous casualties during its peacekeeping operations in Lebanon.

50. According to this understanding, the Syrian army was prohibited from coming within reach of the Israeli-Lebanese border area, and Israeli military planes could fly over Lebanese territory. Syrian fighter planes could be used in Lebanon only after notifying Israel in advance.

51. It was done through the Arab Deterrence Forces, an inter-Arab peacekeeping force whose members were primarily the Syrian forces already stationed in Lebanon.

52. On this period, see Ze'ev Schiff and Ehud Ya'ari, *Israel's Lebanon War* (New York, 1984); George P. Shultz, *Turmoil and Triumph: My Years as Secretary of State* (New York, 1993); Richard C. Parker, *The Politics of Miscalculation in the Middle East* (Bloomington, 1993); Elie A. Salem, *Violence and Diplomacy in Lebanon: The Troubled Years, 1982–1988* (London, 1993). Salem was Lebanon's foreign minister and a senior political adviser to President Amine Gemayel.

53. On the attempts to rebuild the army in this period, see its bulletins, *al-Jundi al-Lubnani* [The Lebanese soldier] and *al-Jaysh* [The army]. See also Michel Aoun, *Wa yabqa al-Jaysh huwa al-hall* [The army remains the solution] (Beirut, 1988); Kechichian, "The Lebanese Army"; McLaurin, "Lebanon and Its Army;" idem, "From Professional to Political: The Redecline of the Lebanese Army," *Armed Forces & Society*, XVII (1991), 545–568.

54. Salem, *Violence and Diplomacy in Lebanon.* See also Hani Faris, "The Failure of Peacemaking in Lebanon, 1975–89," in Collings, *Peace for Lebanon?* 17–30. After signing the Tripartite Agreement, Hubeiqa was quickly deposed by the hard-liners in the LF, led by Samir Geagea, with Gemayel's support. He was assassinated in January 2002.

55. Aoun's government was supposed to include three Muslim officers as well, but they refused to assume their ministerial posts.

56. See, in particular, Aoun, *Wa yabqa al-Jaysh huwa al-hall.* See also Dominique Sigaud, "L'Armée Libanaise: Éclatement ou Destin National?" *Les Cahiers de l'Orient*, XI (1988), 47–68.

57. Given the taboo on "partitionist" measures, the contending governments resorted to euphemisms in order to avoid criticism by the other side and the general public. Thus, they refrained from "appointing" (*ta'yin*) their supporters to jobs "vacated" by the rival

government's followers (who continued to perform their duties under their own government), preferring to "commission" (*taklif*) them to these jobs instead. See Barak, *The Hardships of Consociation: The Perils of Partition.*

58. Salim el-Hoss, *'Ahd al-qarar wa al-hawa* [The era of decision and caprice], (Beirut, 1991); Karim Baqraduni, *La'nat watan: min harb Lubnan ila harb al-khalij* [A cursed homeland: from the Lebanon war to the Gulf war], (Beirut, 1991). The latter was deputy commander of the LF and was elected President of the Phalanges in October 2001.

59. Antoine N. Messarra, "The Hostage State in the Modern International System," in Leila T. Fawaz (ed.), *State and Society in Lebanon* (Oxford, 1991), 7–17; John T. McCarthy, "Lebanon and the Arab League: Success Story in the Making," *Mediterranean Quarterly*, II (1991), 37–44. McCarthy was the American ambassador in Lebanon. See also Sarkis Na'um, *Mishal Awn: hilm aw wahm* [Michel Aoun: dream or delusion?], (Beirut, 1992).

60. For the talks and some of the drafts they produced, see Hoss, *'Ahd al-qarar wa al-hawa;* Salem, *Violence and Diplomacy in Lebanon*, 275–279; *al-Nahar* (17 March 1987, 19 December 1988); *al-Hawadith* (London, 10 March 1989).

61. *Tishrin* (Damascus, 24 October 1989). For an English translation, see *Beirut Review*, I (1991). For an analysis of the Ta'if Agreement, see Joseph Maila, "The Document of National Understanding: A Commentary," *Prospects for Lebanon*, no. 4 (Oxford, 1992). Maila was an adviser to President Amine Gemayel. See also Hanf, *Coexistence in Wartime Lebanon.*

62. For a comparison between the major proposals, see Collings, *Peace for Lebanon?* 312–313.

63. See, for example, Joseph Abu Khalil, *Lubnan . . . limadha* [Lebanon . . . why?] (Beirut, 1993). Abu Khalil was editor of *al-'Amal,* the mouthpiece of the Phalanges. See also Walid Phares, *Lebanese Christian Nationalism: The Rise and Fall of an Ethnic Resistance* (Boulder, 1995). Phares was a senior member of the LF.

64. The PLO's weakness in the wake of the Gulf War helped to tip the scales in Lebanon's favor.

65. International Institute for Strategic Studies, *The Military Balance, 1999–2000* (London, 1999), 138–139.

66. In addition to the army bulletins from this period, see Sean Boyne, "Lebanon Rebuilds Its Army," *Jane's Intelligence Review*, VII (1995), 122–125; Riad Taqi al-Din, *Ihyaa' jaysh, 1988–1994* [An army revived, 1988–1994] (Beirut, 1998). Taqi al-Din, an army officer who joined the PSP militia during the war, served as chief-of-staff of the army during the period of its reconstruction.

67. President Hrawi's term was extended by three years, and General Emile Lahoud, the commander of the army, who led the efforts to reconstruct the Lebanese military, replaced him in 1998.

68. This is also evident in the field of national security, where multi-ethnic bodies (the Army Command, the Military Council, and the Higher Defense Council) create power-sharing, or "command-sharing." In addition, members of different Lebanese communities are in charge of the state's security forces.

69. In the wake of Israel's withdrawal, Hizbullah sought to evade the need to decommission its militia by claiming that the Shebaa farms, which form part of the Israeli-occupied Syrian Golan, are in fact occupied Lebanese territory that ought to be liberated. Since then, it has launched numerous attacks on Israeli positions in this area. It refrained, however, from attacking Israeli positions along the Israeli-Lebanese border (the "Blue Line") delineated by the UN in 2000, and at times prevented other factions, particularly Palestinians, from launching such attacks.

70. A detailed discussion of Lebanon's post-war economy is outside the scope of this chapter. In 2002, the economy was still in recession; the budget deficit in 2000 stood at 46 percent of the expenditure, compared with 37 percent for the corresponding period in 1999, and foreign investments dropped by 13 percent. The per capita gross domestic product (GDP) in Lebanon in 2000 was estimated at $4,700, and unemployment was around 20 percent. Lebanon also had a public debt of $22 billion (140 percent of GDP). U.S. Department of State, *Country Reports on Human Rights Practices: 2000,* Bureau of Democracy, Human Rights, and Labor (2001).

71. "Lebanon: Back to Business," *Time International* (19 December 1994); Salim el-Hoss, "Prospective Change in Lebanon," in Collings, *Peace for Lebanon?* 249.

72. Samir Khalaf, "Culture, Collective Memory, and the Restoration of Civility," in Collings, *Peace for Lebanon?* 273–285; idem., "From a Geography of Fear to a Culture of Tolerance: Reflections on Protracted Strife and the Restoration of Civility in Lebanon," in Paul E. Salem (ed.), *Conflict Resolution in the Arab World* (Beirut, 1997), 354–383.

73. See, for example, Saree Makdisi, "Reconstructing History in Central Beirut," *Middle East Report*, XXVII (1997), 23–30. Notable examples are the play *Film Amriki Tawil* [A long American film] by Ziyad Rahbani and the films *Civilisées* (1999), *West Beirut* (2000), and *In the Shadow of the City* (2000).

74. Young, "The Sneer of Memory," 45; George E. Irani and Nathan C. Funk, *Rituals of Reconciliation: Arab-Islamic Perspectives* (Notre Dame, 2000), 12.

75. On its efforts in the army, see Barak, "Commemorating Malikiyya." The Ta'if Agreement stipulated increased state supervision over Lebanon's (mostly private) educational system, as well as efforts to reach "uniformity in textbooks in the field of history and national education." Although several "integrative" textbooks were published in the 1990s, reconciling the conflicting narratives of Lebanon's communities remains an onerous task.

76. Leonard Wantchekon, "Democratization as a Result of Civil War," unpublished paper for the Harvard Failed States Project (Cambridge, MA, 2001).

77. Zartman, *Collapsed States*, 269.

Contributors

Oren Barak is Assistant Professor in the Department of Political Science and the Department of International Relations at the Hebrew University of Jerusalem. He is the author of several articles on the history and politics of the modern Middle East and is working on a book on the Lebanese army.

Walter Clarke is a senior consultant on political-military planning and multidisciplinary issues pertaining to complex humanitarian emergencies. During his thirty-six years in the U.S. Foreign Service, he served in Africa, Latin America, and Europe. He has written broadly on African political matters and peacekeeping issues in academic and military professional journals. Clarke and Jeffrey Herbst co-edited *Learning from Somalia: Lessons of Armed Humanitarian Intervention* (Boulder, 1997).

Nasrin Dadmehr is a doctoral candidate at l'Institut d'Etudes Politiques de Paris. In 1999–2000 she was a fellow at the Harvard Center for Middle Eastern Studies and Harvard's World Peace Foundation Program on Interstate Conflict, and a Fulbright grantee.

Marlye Gélin-Adams is a Senior Program Officer at the International Peace Academy, where she has worked on its peace-building program in Haiti. She wrote "Holding Up Democracy," *The World Today* (May 2000), 14–16.

Rachel Gisselquist is a doctoral student in political science at MIT and a former program associate with the World Peace Foundation.

Robert Gosende is Associate Vice Chancellor for International Programs at the State University of New York. He was with the U.S. Foreign Service until 1998, serving in Uganda, Libya, South Africa, Poland, and Russia. He was President Clinton's Special Envoy for Somalia in 1993.

Erin Jenne was a WPF/ISP Research Fellow at the Kennedy School's Belfer Center, 2000–2002. She is an Assistant Professor in International Relations at the Central European University, Budapest.

Harvey J. Kline is a Professor of Political Science at the University of Alabama. He wrote *State Building and Conflict Resolution in Colombia, 1986–1994* (Tuscaloosa, 1999), *Latin American Politics and Development* (Boulder, 2000, 5th ed.), and *An Introduction to Latin American Politics and Development* (Boulder, 2001).

Stephanie Lawson is Professor of International Relations in the School of Economic and Social Studies, University of East Anglia. She has written several books, including *The New Agenda for International Relations: From Polarization to Globalization in World Politics* (Cambridge, 2002) and *The Failure of Democratic Politics in Fiji* (Oxford, 1997).

René Lemarchand is Professor of Political Science, Emeritus, at the University of Florida. His book, *Rwanda and Burundi* (Westport, 1970), received the Herskovits Award of the African Studies Association. He has previously taught at Smith College, Brown University, Concordia University, University of California, Berkeley, the University of Bordeaux, and the University of Copenhagen.

Michael S. Malley is Assistant Professor in the Department of Political Science at Ohio University. He is the author of *Indonesia beyond Suharto: Polity, Economy, Society, Transition* (Armonk, 1999).

David Malone is President of the International Peace Academy, on leave from the Canadian Foreign Service, where he was Director General of the Policy, International Organizations, and Global Issues Bureaus of the Canadian Foreign and Trade Ministry.

Gérard Prunier is a journalist and historian. His many books include *The Rwanda Crisis: History of a Genocide* (New York, 1995).

William Reno is Associate Professor of Political Science at Northwestern University. He wrote *Corruption and State Politics in Sierra Leone* (Cambridge, MA, 1995) and *Warlord Politics and African States* (Boulder, 1998).

Robert I. Rotberg is President of the World Peace Foundation, Director of the Program on Intrastate Conflict, and Adjunct Professor at Harvard's Kennedy

School of Government. He is the author and editor of numerous books and articles on U.S foreign policy, Africa, and Haiti, most recently *Ending Autocracy: Enabling Democracy* (Washington, D.C., 2001). He co-edited *Truth v. Justice: The Morality of Truth Commissions* (Princeton, 2000), and edited *Creating Peace in Sri Lanka: Civil War and Reconciliation* (Washington, D.C., 1999) and *Burma: Prospects for a Democratic Future* (Washington, D.C., 1998).

Index

Abdiqassim Salad Hasan, 129–30, 154
Abdulrahman Tur, 153
Abraham, Arthur, 86
Abshir, Mohammed Musa, 134, 153–54
Aceh: political transition, 197–201; separatist wars, 14
Adow, Abdullahi Ahmed, 154
Afar and Issas, 135
Afghanistan, 6, 10, 13, 20, 23, 260
African Unity, Organization of. *See* Organization of African Unity
Aga Khan, 253
Aga Khan Foundation, 256
Aideed, Hussein, 147, 152
Aideed, Mohamed Hassan Farah, 140–47, 153, 155
AIDS, 287; HIV infection rates, 15
Akandwanaho, Jovia, 56
Akol, Lam, 105
Al-Asad, Hafez, 316, 327
Al-Azhari, Sayed Ismail, 114
Albania: a weak state, 222
Al-Banna, Hassan, 116
Al-Bashir, Omar Hassan Ahmed, 107
Albright, Madeleine, 44
Al-Halim Khaddam, 'Abd, 320
Alianza Nacional Popular (ANAPO), 166
Alliance des Forces Démocratiques pour la Libération du Congo (AFDL), 32–34, 43, 45, 50, 53, 66n
Alliance of Democratic Forces (ADF), 60

All Peoples Congress (APC), 78, 80–82, 85, 90–91
Al-Mahdi, Mohamed Ahmed, 111
Al-Mahdi, Sadiq, 113, 117, 119
Al-Mirghani, Mohamed Osman, 117–18
Al-Turabi, Hassan, 107, 117–18
Al Qaeda, 209, 257
Ambon: Muslim-Christian conflict in, 14
Anarchy: causes of, 6
Angola, 6, 10, 13, 22, 123, 135, 233; civil war, 46; involvement in the Congo, 30
Animism, 110, 208
Annan, Kofi, 152
Anyanya II, 104
Aoun, Michel, 322–23, 325, 337n
Arab Deterrence Forces, 337n
Arab-Israeli conflict, 328, 335n
Arab League, 114, 129, 152, 310, 315
Aristide, Jean-Bertrand, 18, 287, 296–98, 300, 302n
Armed Forces of Liberia, 74
Armed Forces Ruling Council (AFRC), 88–89, 91–92, 99n
Armée Nationale Conglaise (ANC), 67n
Arta group, 129
Authoritarian state: in Haiti, 291–92
Autodefensas Unidas de Colombia (AUC), 173–74
Autonomist pressures: in Indonesia, 210–12
Averting state failure in Sri Lanka, 231–39; the civic solution, 235–36; a composite

solution, 236–39; external solutions, 233–35

Baba, Tupeni, 280
Bainimarama, Frank, 279
Bakongo people, 46
Bandaranaike, Sirimavo, 23
Bandaranaike, Solomon West Ridgeway D., 23, 227
Bangilima people, 43
Banyamulenge people, 31, 39, 43–46, 48–51, 60; a genocide waiting to happen, 49–52; history of, 65–66n
Banyarwanda people, 42–43
Barak, Oren, 10, 17, 341
Baramoto, Philemon Kpama, 40
Barco, Virgilio, 167, 170, 177
Basmachi, 260n
Bavadra, Timoci, 272, 282
Belarus, 5; a weak state, 222
Belgium, 12, 29, 31, 34, 42, 57, 63
Bemba, Jean-Pierre, 30, 47, 56, 60
Berri, Nabih, 322
Betancur, Belisario, 170
Bir, Cevic, 156n
Bisengimana, 42
Blackhawk Down debacle, 145
Bockarie, Sam, 94
Bogor, Hagi Musa, 134
Bolivia, 17
Bond, Karl I., 39
Borama Conference, 150
Bose Levu Vakaturaga, 273–75, 278–79, 281–83
Bosnia, 20
Botero, Jorge Enrique, 172
Boutros-Ghali, Boutros, 140
British legacy: in post-independence Sudan, 112–13
British Somaliland, 136
Buddhism, 224–25, 242n
Bugera, Deogratias, 45
Bula Matari kingdom, 33–34
Bulgaria: arms bazaar in, 58
Bureaucratic state: failure of in Sierra Leone, 76–78
Burkina Faso, 19
Burundi, 10, 13, 36; involvement in the Congo, 30
Bush, George H. W., 141, 157n
Butadroka, Sakeasi, 277

Cacos rebellion, 292
Cairo Agreement, 315, 337n
Cali group, 172, 181n
Camacho, Alvaro, 181n
Cambodia, 5, 19

Camdessus, Michel, 188
Canada, 63, 297–99; Harker commission, 106; a strong state, 222
Cano, Alfonso, 172
Carter, Jimmy, 135
Castaño, Fidel, 173
Castillon, 101
Causes of state failure, 1–25; human, 22–24
Cédras, Raoul, 297
Central African Republic, 73, 108
Central banks, 39, 83; desirability of, 3
Central Intelligence Agency, U.S. (CIA), 38, 40
Ceylon, 23. See also Sri Lanka
Chad, 19, 24n, 108
Chaudhry, Mahendra, 272, 277–78
Chemical weapons, 107
Chevron Oil Company, 116
Chiha, Michel, 314
Chile, 165
China, 101
Christopher, Warren, 143
Civil Defense Forces (CDF), 95
Civil wars: Angola, 46; in failed and collapsed states, 5; foreign intervention, 139–45; Somalia, 139–45; Sudan, 104–08; Tajikistan, 249–51
Clan families, 132
Clarke, Walter, 11, 23, 341
Climatic disasters, 8–9, 18–19
Clinton, Bill, 297
Cocaine, 168, 296
Cokonauto, Ratu Tu'uakitau, 278
Cold War: Somalia and, 130–31, 135; post–Cold War terrain, 2; aftermath in the Congo, 37–38
Collapsed states, 7, 9–10, 27–158, 283n; causes and indicators, 1–25; civil wars in, 5; contagion, 35; contemporary, 10–13; resuscitating themselves, 10, 128–58; strengths and weaknesses, 2–5
Collectif d'Actions pour le Développement des Droits de l'Homme (CADDHOM), 50
Colombia, 11, 15–16, 160–82, 222, 233; drug dealers, 168–70; elite political game, 164–65; failure of state, 174–79; a fragmented state, 222; guerrilla groups, 166; human rights violations, 171–72; new challenges, 165–70; paramilitary groups, 166–67; recent presidencies, 171–74; violence in politics, 163–64; weakening of state, 170–74
Colonial states, 242n; Fiji, 268–71; Sierra Leone, 79
Commission on National Reconciliation, 250
Commonwealth of Independent States (CIS), 256, 258

Communal conflicts in Indonesia, 204–10; Kalimantan, 208–09; Maluku, 205–07; Sulawesi, 209–10
Complex political emergencies (CPEs), 332n
Congo. See Democratic Republic of the Congo
Congo-Brazzaville, 24n, 73
Congolese Armed Forces (FAC), 36, 45
Constitutionalism: failure of independent Fiji, 271–81
Control: over violence lacking in Tajikistan, 255–56; territorial, 222, 241n
Copper mining, 37
Corruption, 8, 15, 17–18; Corruption Perception Index, 4
COSLEG, 57, 68n
Côte d'Ivoire, 17, 74
Council of Europe, 240
Council of Trade Unions, 280
Crime, 3, 75–76; an indicator of state failure, 6, 18
Cuba, 105, 135–36; Cuban missile crisis, 166
Culture: cohesiveness: in Somalia, 132–33; heterogeneity in Sudan, 110–11
Cunningham, James, 93

Dadmehr, Nasrin, 16, 341
Dangerously weak states, 159–262
Defense, U.S. Department of, 142–44
Democrat Party of Tajikistan, 249–50
Democratic Republic of the Congo (DRC), 10, 28–69, 73, 222, 283; aborted transition to multiparty democracy, 38–40; anatomy of disaster, 32–35; the Banyamulenge, 49–52; costs of self-cannibalization, 37–38; essence of failure, 58–59; a failed state, 13, 222; failure of security forces, 40–41; Hema-Lendu tragedy, 48–49; infrastructure breakdown, 7; from integral to shell state, 37–38; Kabila's son, 52–54; Kivu emergency, 41–43; mineral resources, 54–58; 1998 rebellion and its aftermath, 45–46; the 1996 watershed, 43–45; paths to reconstruction, 59–63; regional context, 35–36; trajectories of collapse, 38–58; from Zaire to DRC, 43–45
Democratic Unionist Party (DUP), 118
Democratization: in Indonesia, 191–212
Development Unity Party, 187
Diamond mining and marketing, 55–56, 74, 78–80; illicit, 79–80, 82, 85
Difaa esh-shabiyya, 122
Dinka people, 104
Disarmament: not attempted in Somalia, 149
Disintegration of the state: in Indonesia, 191–212
Dispute resolution, 3

Division of state: Colombia, 160–82; Fiji, 264–86
Division Spéciale Présidentielle (DSP), 40–41
Djibouti, 152–53
Doe, Samuel, 23, 92
dos Santos, Jose Eduardo, 22, 46, 52, 60
Downer, Alexander, 280
DRC. See Democratic Republic of the Congo
Drug trafficking: Colombia, 168–70; Haiti, 18; narcotraficantes, 176; Tajikistan, 245
Druze community, 308
Dutch East Indies, 196
Duvalier, François (Papa Doc), 294–95
Duvalier, Jean-Claude (Baby Doc), 295

East Timor: independence, 2, 185–86, 196–98; political transition, 196–97
Economic issues: crisis in Indonesia, 186–95; global context and failure in Sierra Leone, 83–84; policy and state weakness in Tajikistan, 248–49
Ecuador, 17
Egal, Mohammed Haji Ibrahim, 134, 153
Egypt, 13, 107; Ottoman, 101, 108–9, 122
Ejército de Liberación (ELN), 166, 173–74
Ejército Popular de Liberación (EPL), 166–67
Elections: early elected government in Somalia, 133–35; and state legitimacy, 251–52
El-Hoss, Salim, 329
Elite political games: in Colombia, 164–65
Entrepreneurial capability, 3, 7
Eritrea, 105, 108, 114
Estimé, Dumarsais, 294
Ethiopia, 108, 135–36, 152
Ethiopian People's Revolutionary Democratic Front, 105
Ethnic war, 20; ethnic ideology fomenting, 49
European Union (EU), 63, 240, 280; European Commission efforts in Somalia, 151–52
Executive Outcomes, 87–88
External forces: in Somalia, 139–45; in Tajikistan, 256–57
ExxonMobil, 199–200

Failed states, 5–9, 27–158, 222; Afghanistan, 10, 13; Angola, 10, 13; Burundi, 13; causes and indicators, 1–25; characterizing, 2; civil wars in, 5; Colombia, 174–79; considerations for intervention, 147–51; contemporary, 10–13; defined, 4; Democratic Republic of the Congo, 10, 13, 32–35, 58–59, 222; economic opportunity offered by, 7–8; Lebanon, 305–39; Liberia, 10, 13, 222; Sierra Leone, 10, 13, 70–100, 222; Somalia, 13, 128–58, 222; strengths and weaknesses in, 2–5; the Sudan, 10, 13, 101–27

Failure of public authorities: vs. failure of states, 73–76
Failure of public order: role of outsiders in Sierra Leone, 92–96
Fiji, 17, 264–86; colonial state, 268–71; a failing state, 281–83; failure of constitutionalism at independence, 271–81; recommendations, 275–76; state system, 267–68
Fijian Association Party (FAP), 277–78
Fijian Nationalist Party, 277
Fiji Development Fund, 280
Fiji Labour Party, 272
Fiji Public Service Association (FPSA), 272
Fiji Trade Union Congress (FTUC), 272
Food shortages, 8, 21, 103
Forces Armées Rwandaises (FAR), 36
Forces Armées Zairoises (FAZ), 36, 41
Forces pour la Défense de la Démocratie (FDD), 31, 56
Forces Républicaines Fédéralistes (FRF), 31, 50
Forum for the Reconciliation of Irian Jaya Society, 202
Fragmentation: in the Congo, 32–35
Fragmented states: Colombia, 160–82, 222; Georgia, 222; Indonesia, 183–218, 222; Philippines, 222; Sri Lanka, 219–44, 222
France, 31, 63, 101, 133, 292, 297–99, 328; a strong state, 222
Frangieh, Suleiman Bey, 317, 320–21, 335n
Free Aceh Movement (GAM), 198–200
Freedom of the World Report (Freedom House), 4
Free Papua Organization (OPM), 201
French Guinea, 79
French Somaliland, 135
Front de Libération du Congo (FLC), 30, 49
Fuerzas Armadas Revoluciónarias de Colombia (FARC), 166–67, 172–75

Gandhi, Rajiv, 228
Garang, Colonel John, 104–6
Garde Civile (GC), 40
Garreton, Roberto, 44, 48, 58
Gaviria, César, 170–71, 175, 177
Geagea, Samir, 325
Gécamines, 57
Gélin-Adams, Marlye, 18, 341
Gemayel, Amine, 321–22, 336n
Gemayel, Bashir, 336n
Genocide: impending among the Banyamulenge, 49–52
Georgia, 19; a fragmented state, 222
Germany, 57, 106; a strong state, 222
Ghana, 19
Gisselquist, Rachel, 13, 341
Gorbachev, Mikhail, 249

Gordon, Arthur, 269–70
Gordon, Charles, 108
Gosende, Robert, 11, 23, 342
Gouled Aptidon, Hassan, 152
Grands Lacs Metals, 56
Great Britain, 12–13, 57, 63, 72, 79, 90, 95, 101, 108–13, 124–25n, 224–25, 229
Great Council of Chiefs, 273–75, 278–83
Guerrilla groups in Colombia, 166
Guinea, 19, 73
Guinea-Bissau, 74
Gulamali, Aziza Kulsum, 56
Guurti, 149

Habibie, Bacharuddin Jusuf, 189, 202, 210
Haiti, 10, 18, 145, 287–304; American occupation, 292–93; authoritarian state, 291–92; breaking the pattern, 299–301; drug trafficking, 18; Duvalier dictatorship, 294–95; fallout from coup, 297; impossibility of stabilization and peace-building, 297–99; post-Duvalier era, 295–97; context, 289–90; state formation during isolation, 290–91
Hakmatyar, Gulbuddin, 23
Harakat al-Ikhwaan al-Muslimin, 116
Hariri, Rafiq, 329
Harker commission, 106
Hawiye clan, 137–38, 146
Haz, Hamzah, 191
Hema-Lendu tragedy, 48–49
Historical antecedents of Sudanese state, 108–12; cultural heterogeneity, 110–11; political ambiguity, 109; territorial imprecision, 111–12
Hizbullah, 326–28, 339n
Hobbes, Thomas, 75
Holland, 57, 224
Howe, Jonathan, 143
Hrawi, Elias, 327, 336n, 338n
Human Development Index, 4, 72, 258–59
Human rights violations, 24n, 106; Colombia, 171–72
Human Rights Watch (HRW), 49, 173
Hunger: Hunger Triangle, 106; widespread, 8, 15, 21; starvation, 24n
Hutu people, 35–36, 43

India, 57, 280; intelligence service (RAW), 227
Indian Peace Keeping Force (IPKF), 234–35
Indicators: of failure, 19–22; of failure and collapse in Lebanon, 308–10; of strengths and weaknesses, 2–5
Indonesia, 11, 14–16, 183–218, 222; autonomist pressures, 210–12; communal conflicts, 204–10; from democratization to

disintegration, 191–212; from economic crisis to political transition, 186–91; economic signals of failure, 21; a fragmented state, 222; political transition, 195–204; post-Soeharto era, 15; separation issues, 14, 195–204
Indonesian Bank Restructuring Agency (IBRA), 193
Indonesian Democracy Party, 187, 191
Infant mortality rates, 18, 20
Inga-Shaba power line, 37
Instability, internal: in Tajikistan, 256–57
Institutions, flawed, 6, 22
Instrumental disorder: in Sierra Leone, 78–82
Interahamwe, 31, 36, 60
Inter-American Commission on Human Rights, 180n
Inter-American System, 297
Intercommunal tensions, 4–5
Intercongregational Commission of Justice and Peace, 180n
Intergovernmental Authority on Development (IGAD), 106, 152
Internally displaced persons (IDPs), 136, 138, 146
Internal Security Forces, 309
Internal Security Unit (ISU), 80, 85
International Confederation of Trade Unions, 280
International Crisis Group (ICG), 52, 107, 201
International Monetary Fund (IMF), 32, 63, 84, 185, 188, 193, 240
International Rescue Committee, 29
Intervention: considerations of in a failed state, 147–51; in Somalia, 139–45; in Tajikistan, 256–57
Iranian Revolutionary Guards, 326
Iraq, 5, 323; potential for failure, 16; a weak state, 222
Islamic Movement of Uzbek (IMU), 262n
Islamic Rebirth Party, 249–50
Island states, 267–68
Israel, 309, 327–29
Israeli-Lebanese Mixed Armistice Commission (ILMAC), 315
Issaq clan, 136, 138

Ja'far Umar Thalib, 206–7
Japan, 329; a strong state, 222
Jebha al-Mithaq al-Islamiya, 117
Jenne, Erin, 5, 14, 16, 342
Jess, Ahmed Omar, 139
Johnson, Prince, 23
Joint Chiefs of Staff, U.S. (JCS), 141–42
Jonas, James, 140
Jonglei canal, 116
Junblat, Kamal, 312

Junblat, Walid, 322

Kabarebe, James, 45, 55
Kabbah, Ahmed Tejan, 88–89, 95
Kabila, Joseph, 29–31, 53–54, 57–59
Kabila, Laurent-Désire, 30–33, 40, 43–46, 50–54, 66n
Kadogo, 54
Kagame, Paul, 30, 43, 45, 51, 53, 66n
Kainerugabe, Muhoozi, 56
Kalimantan: communal conflicts, 208–09; xenophobic outbursts, 14
Kamajor militias, 87–88, 90
Kapend, Eddy, 52–53
Karaha, Bizima, 45, 50
Karami, Rashid, 322
Kazini, James, 55
Kenya, 17, 108, 151
Khatib, Ahmad, 318
Kinship, 40; kin country syndrome, 35
Kinyarwanda speakers, 35, 45, 49
Kirundi speakers, 35
Kivu emergency, 41–43
Kline, Harvey F., 15, 342
Koromah, Johnny Paul, 88–89, 92
Kumaratunga, Chandrika, 231
Kuwait: Iraqi invasion, 140
Kyrgyzstan, 17
Kyungu wa Kumwanza, Gabriel, 65n

La Violencia, 164–67, 176–77
Lahoud, Emile, 338n
Lake, Anthony, 143
Laos, 19
Laskar Jihad, 203–9
Lavalas Family party, 296–99
Lavalie, Alpha, 87
Lawlessness: in Colombia, 160–82
Lawson, Stephanie, 17, 342
Lebanon, 10, 13, 17, 305–39; economic signals of failure, 21; factors in collapse, 310–18; markers of failure and collapse, 308–10; reasons for survival, 318–26; resuscitation and reconstruction, 326–28; Second Republic, 328–30; Syrian intervention, 10, 17–18
Legitimacy of states, 9, 37–38; and elections, 251–52
Lemarchand, René, 13, 342
Lendu people, 48–49
Lescot, Elie, 294
Liberation theology, 296
Liberation Tigers of Tamil Eelam (LTTE), 14, 23, 221, 223, 228–39
Liberia, 20, 23, 73, 92–93; a failed state, 10, 13, 222
Libya, 4; a weak state, 222

Lomé peace agreement, 89, 94–95
Luba immigrants, 39
Lumumba, Patrice, 31
Lusaka accords, 51, 59, 61

Machar, Riek, 105
Mafiosi, 169
Magloire, Paul, 294
Mahavamsa, 224, 228
Mahdi, Ali, 148
Mahdiyya, 108, 110
Mahidin Simbolon, 203
Mahjoub, Mohamed Ahmed, 113
Mai-Mai faction, 30, 47–48, 51, 54–55, 58–60
Malaysia, 57
Malley, Michael, 14, 342
Malone, David M., 18, 342
Maluku islands, 14, 205–07
Mammy Cokerism, 77
Mara, Kamisese, 277, 279–80
Marijuana, 168
Masire, Ketumile, 31, 53, 59
Massaquoi, Gibril, 72
Matanitu Vanua (MV), 282
Matos, Jogo Baptista de, 52
Médecins sans Frontières, 256, 259
Medellín, 175
Megawati Sukarnoputri, 191–92, 194, 197, 200, 203
Mengistu Haile Mariam, 105
Michelsen, Alfonso López, 163, 169
Mijertein clan, 136
Military rule, 6–7, 17
Mission creep, 143
Mobutu Sese Seko, 6, 12–13, 22, 30–44, 61, 64n
Modern states: expectations of, 3
Mohamed, Ali Mahdi, 142, 153–54
Mohamed, Jamil, 83, 87
Moldova, 19
Momoh, Joseph, 84–86, 92
Montgomery, Thomas, 143, 156n
Morgan, Said Hersi, 137, 153
Mouawwad, René, 336n
Mouvement de Libération du Congo (MLC), 30, 46, 56, 60
Mouvement Populaire pour la Révolution (MRP), 37
Mouvement Révolutionnaire pour la Libération du Congo (MRLC), 30, 46
Movimiento *19* de abril, 166
Mubarak, Hosni, 107
Muerte a Secuestradores (MAS), 169
Mugabe, Robert Gabriel, 57
Mugisha, Adele, 49
Muhammad 'Ali, 108
Muleliste insurrection, 32, 40, 50, 59

Multiparty democracy in the Congo, 38–40
Museveni, Yoweri, 51, 53, 56
Muslim Brotherhood in Lebanon, 316
Muslim Brotherhood in Sudan, 104, 112, 116–22, 126–27n
Muslims, 13–14, 110, 318
Mussallaha al-wataniya, 117
Mutabazi, Shweka, 50

Na'im, Edmond, 323
Namibia: involvement in the Congo, 30
Nasser, General Abdul, 114
National Awakening Party, 191
National Congress (NC), 103–04, 107, 127n, 170
National Defense Law, 337n
National Democratic Alliance (NDA), 103, 106
National Federation Party (NFP), 271–72, 277
National Front, 164–65
National Islamic Front (NIF), 103, 107, 118–20
National Pact, 315, 324
National Patriotic Front of Liberia (NPFL), 93
National Provisional Ruling Council (NPRC), 86–87
National reconciliation conferences for Somalia, 150–51
National Sovereign Conference (CNS), 32, 39–40, 42, 44
National Transition Assembly (NTA), 154
Native Lands Trust Board, 270
Ndogboyosoi uprising, 90
Nepal, 16
New Guinea, 17
New Zealand, 280
Nganda, Masasu, 52
Ngbandi people, 40–41
Niger, 19
Nigeria, 10, 17, 21, 73
Nimeiry, Gaafar, 107, 116–17
Nindaga, Masasu, 53
Nongovernmental organizations (NGOs), 153; performing state functions in Tajikistan, 256
Norman, Hinga, 88
Northern Alliance, 257
North Korea, 5; potential for failure, 16; a weak state, 222
Norwegian Refugee Committee, 204
Nueva Granada, 162
Nur, Hassan Mohamed, 153
Nyamwisi, Mbusa, 30, 47, 49
Nyarugabo, Moise, 45
Nzimbi, Etienne Nbgale Kongo, 40

Oakley, Robert, 142

Obasanjo, Olusegun, 17
Oleghankoy, Joseph, 44
Olympic Hotel raid, 148
Open Society Foundation, 256
Operation Clean Sweep, 85
Operation Clear All, 85
Operation Desert Storm, 141–42
Operation Lifeline Sudan, 103
Operation No Living Thing, 88
Operation Pay Yourself, 80
Operation Provide Relief, 141–42
Operation Restore Hope, 142–43, 148
Organisation of African Unity (OAU), 115,
    129, 152
Organization of American States (OAS), 296
Oryx Zimcom, 57
Ottoman empire, 2, 109; Egypt, 101, 108–
    09, 122

Pacific island states, 267–68
Palestine Liberation Organization (PLO), 309,
    315, 323, 326
Pantoja, Zambrano, 164
Papua: political transition, 201–04; separatist
    wars, 14
Papua New Guinea, 204
Paraguay, 17
Paramilitary groups: in Colombia, 166–67
Party of National Unity (PANU), 277
Pashtun people, 23
Pastrana, Andrés, 170–74
Patrimonial rule, 6
Patronage-based systems, 6, 12
Peace-building: in Haiti, 297–99
People's Coalition, 277
People's Consultative Assembly (MPR), 189–
    91, 197
People's Democratic Party of Tajikistan, 251
People's Liberation Organization of Tamil
    Eelam (PLOTE), 229
People's Power Committees (PPCs), 44
People's Regional Assembly, 115
People's Self-Defence Force (FAP), 44
Persian Gulf region, 138
Pescas milagrosas, 173
Philippines, 17; a fragmented state, 222
Pinilla, Gustavo Rojas, 166
Plural society syndrome, 271
Pol Pot, 4
Politics: ambiguity in current Sudanese state,
    109; civilian techniques in Somalia, 148–
    49; political goods, 2–3, 24n; use of vio-
    lence in Colombia, 163–64. See also Com-
    plex political emergencies; Elite political
    games
Popular Movement for the Liberation of
    Angola, 53

Popular Movement of Rastokhiz, 249
Portugal, 224
Poso II and Poso III, 209
Post-state society: and warfare in Sierra Leone,
    70–100
Potemkin pretense: 12
Powell, Colin, 141–42
Power structure in Tajikistan: government
    dependency on one group, 253–54; and
    parallel forces, 252–55; warlords, 254–55
Predatory regimes, 6
Préval, René, 298
Progressive Socialist Party (PSP), 319
Prunier, Gérard, 13, 101–27, 342
Public services, provision of, 222, 241n
Puntland, 152–53
Pweto, 30, 46, 59

Qarase, Laisenia, 279–83
Quasi states, 10
Qur'anic law, 254

Rabani, Burrhan ul-din, 23
Rabuka, Sitiveni, 266, 273–78
Rahanwein Resistance Army (RRA), 153
Rakhmonov, President Emomali, 251
Rassemblement Congolais pour la Démocratie
    (RCD), 30, 40, 45–53, 60, 62, 67n
Rastokhiz, 250
Raznajatovic, Zeljko (Arkan), 91
Reconstruction: in Lebanon, 326–28; paths to
    in the Congo, 59–63
Red Berets, 136–37, 139
Red Lines agreement, 321
Reddy, Jai Ram, 277
Refugees, 13, 24, 35–36
Regime breakdown: in Indonesia's political
    transition, 188–91
Regionalism: in Tajikistan, 245–62
RENAMO, 92
Reno, William, 12, 23, 342
Resistance: homogenization of political in Si-
    erra Leone, 89–92
Restrepo, Carlos Lleras, 167, 175
Resuscitation: of collapsed state in Somalia,
    128–58; in Lebanon, 326–28
Revenge killings, 47
Revolutionary Council, 134
Revolutionary United Front (RUF), 71–72, 77,
    82, 85–96
Ridgepoint, 57
Rodríguez Orejuela brothers, 172
Rojas Pinilla, Gustavo, 166
Roman Catholic Church, 176, 180n, 293
Rotberg, Robert I., 183, 265, 342–43
Royal Fiji Military Forces, 271, 273
Ruberwa, Azarias, 50

Ruhimbika, Manasse Muller, 31
Rujigiro, Tibere, 56
Russia, 18, 57, 114, 256–57
Rwanda, 35–36, 145
Rwanda Metals, 56
Rwanda Patriotic Army (RPA), 30, 33, 36,
   45–56
Rwanda Patriotic Front (RPF), 39, 43

Saadeh, Georges, 325
Saddam Hussein, 140
Sadirov, Rizvan, 255
Safely weak states, 263–339
Sahnoun, Mohamed, 140
Saleh, Salim, 55–56
Samanid Empire, 261n
Samper, Ernesto, 170–73
Sankoh, Foday, 80, 87–88, 93–94
Santiago Commitment to Democracy and
   Development, 297, 303n
Sarkis, Elias, 336n
Saudi Arabia, 323
Save the Children, 256
Savimbi, Jonas, 46
Selassie, Haile, 115
Self-cannibalization: in the Congo, 37–38
Separation issues: in Indonesia, 14, 195–204
September 11, 108
September Laws, 119
Sesay, Issa, 94
Sfer, Nasrallah, 325
Shaba insurrections, 40
Shakur, Tupac, 91–92, 99n
Shari'a, 254
Shell state, 37–38
Shermarke, Abdirashid Ali, 133
Shi'i community, 308, 312, 328, 334n
Shir, 149–50
Siad Barre, Mohammed, 11–12, 23, 130, 134–
   39, 147, 150, 157n
Sierra Leone, 12, 23, 70–100, 219, 222, 233,
   236; a failed state, 10, 13, 222; failure of
   bureaucratic state, 76–78; failure of pub-
   lic order sustained by outsiders, 92–96;
   failure of states vs. of public authorities,
   73–76; global economic context and fail-
   ure, 83–84; homogenization of political
   resistance, 89–92; under Siaka Stevens, 6;
   town and bush rebels, 84–89; violent commerce and instrumental disorder, 78–82
Sierra Ore and Mineral Company, 77
Sierra Rutile, 77
Singapore: a strong state, 222
Smalls, Biggie, 91, 99n
Social contract, 9, 23
Société Miniere de Bakwanga (MIBA), 57
Société Miniere et Industrielle du Kivu, 55

Socio-economic development: in Tajikistan,
   257–59
Soeharto, 14, 186–89, 192, 201, 205, 210
Solomon Islands, 17
Somalia, 11–12, 20, 23, 74, 128–58, 219, 222,
   233, 236, 283; Arta initiative, 152–54;
   civil war and foreign intervention, 139–
   45; and Cold War, 130–31; decline and fall
   of state, 135–39, 145–47; early elected
   government, 133–35; European Commission's efforts to restore local and regional structures in, 151–52; a failed state,
   13, 222; failures of international
   intervention in, 147–51; lessons learned,
   155–56; seemingly cohesive culture,
   132–33
Somaliland, 10
Somali National Army (SNA), 136, 138
Somali National Movement (SNM), 136–
   37, 139
Somali Patriotic Movement (SPM), 137
Somali Salvation Democratic Front (SSDF),
   136
Soqosoqo Duavata ni Lewenivanua (SDL),
   282
Soqosoqo ni Vakavulewa ni Taukei (SVT),
   274, 276–77
South Asian Forum, 237
Soviet Socialist Republic of Tajikistan
   (SSRT), 247
Soviet Union, 2, 105, 130, 135–36, 332
Speight, George, 266, 278–80, 282, 286n
Sri Lanka, 14, 23, 219–44, 222; averting state
   failure in, 231–39; external factors, 227–
   31; a fragmented state, 222; governance,
   242–43n; institutionalizing the divide,
   229–31; path to fragmentation, 223–27;
   post-independence era, 225–27
Sri Lanka Freedom Party (SLFP), 227
Sri Lankan Peace Accord, 228
Stabilization: impossibility of in Haiti,
   297–99
State, U.S. Department of, 143, 173
Statehood, 267–68
States, 222, 267–68; authoritarian, 291–92;
   broadcasting power, 34, 138; bureaucratic,
   76–78; collapsed, 1–158, 283n; colonial,
   79, 242n, 268–71; contagion of collapsed,
   35; dangerously weak, 159–262; disintegration of, 191–212; disrupted, 332n; division of, 160–82, 264–86; failed, 1–158;
   integral, 37–38; landlocked, in Africa, 2;
   modern, 3; quasi, 10; safely weak, 263–
   339; shell, 37–38; strong, 222; typology
   of health, 222; weak, 1–25, 159–339
Steel production, 37
Stephen, David, 152

Stevens, Siaka, 6, 12, 23, 73, 77–87
Strasser, Valentine, 86
Strong states: Canada, 222; defined, 3–4; France, 222; Germany, 222; Japan, 222; Singapore, 222; United States, 222
Successful failure: in Sudan, 101–27
Sudan, 10, 13, 74, 101–27, 233; historical antecedents of current state, 108–12; Muslim Brotherhood and, 116–22; pattern of post-independence politics, 112–16; pre-*2001*, 6; second civil war and current failure, 104–08
Sudan Defense Force, 115
Sudanese People's Liberation Movement/Army (SPLM/A), 101, 103–06
Sulawesi: communal conflicts, 209–10; Muslim-Christian conflict, 14
Sun City (South Africa), 62, 69n
Surete Générale, 309
Sweden, 63
Syria, 309; intervention in Lebanon, 10, 17–18, 325, 328, 333n

Ta'if Agreement, 305, 324–25, 328, 339n
Tajikistan, 10, 13, 16, 245–62; external forces and internal instability, 256–57; independence and civil war, 249–51; lack of state control over violence, 255–56; lack of state legitimacy, 251–52; power structure and parallel forces, 252–55; socio-economic development, 257–59; sovereignty and state weakness, 248–49; Soviet elements of state weakness, 247–49; UN and NGO's state functions, 256
Tajik people, 23
Taliban, 6, 23; Taliban-inspired militarism, 257
Tanzania, 74
Taylor, President Charles, 23, 74–75, 92–93
Tibasima, Ateenyi, 56
Tibasima, John, 49
Togo, 24n
Tonko Limba Chiefdom, 92
Tontons macoutes, 294
Treaty of Brotherhood, Cooperation, and Co-ordination, 327
Triangle of death, 146
Tripartite Agreement, 322, 324
Truth and Reconciliation Commission, 330
Tshisekedi, Etienne, 33, 38–39, 62
Turkiyya, 108–9
Tutsi people, 31, 36, 39, 47, 49
Two Years' War, 309, 319

Uganda, 105, 108; involvement in the Congo, 30

Uganda People's Defense Forces (UPDF), 30, 47, 49, 54–55
UN Development Fund for Women (UNIFEM), 256
UN Development Program (UNDP), 256, 258; Human Development Index, 4, 72, 258–59
UN General Assembly (UNGA), 129
UN High Commissioner for Refugees (UNHCR), 138, 141, 256, 258
UN Human Rights Commission, 48
Uniao Nacionale para a Independencia Total de Angola (UNITA), 46, 52, 60
Unified Task Force (UNITAF) operation in Somalia, 131, 142–44, 147–50, 156n
Union des Fédéralistes et Républicains Indépendents (UFERI), 39, 65n
Union pour le Progrés Social et la Démocratie (UPSD), 38–39, 62
United Arab Republic (UAR), 328
United Fijian Party, 282
United Generals Party (UGP), 277
United National Party (UNP), 226, 235
United Nations (UN): enforcing peace agreements, 234, 237–40, 297–99; facilitators appointed by, 31, 56; Millennium General Assembly, 129; multinational force in Haiti, 297, 299; peacekeeping forces, 12, 96; performing state functions in Tajikistan, 256; Resolution *1132*, 94; secretary-general, 49, 140, 152; Security Council, 63, 89, 93, 107, 142, 297; supervising referenda, 186, 296
United Somali Congress (USC), 137, 139–40
United States, 31–32, 63, 280, 297–99, 328; a strong state, 222
United Tajik Opposition (UTO), 250, 257, 261n
UN Mission in Sierra Leone (UNAMSIL), 72, 89, 94, 96
UN Mission in the Congo (MONUC), 59
UN Mission of Observers in Tajikistan (UNMOT), 256
UN Observer Mission in Sierra Leone (UNOMSIL), 72, 88
UN Office for Project Services (UNOPS), 256
UN Operations in Somalia (UNOSOM I and II), 131, 148–49
U.S. Committee for Refugees, 106
U.S. Liaison Office: in Somalia, 147, 149
U.S. Marines, 292
U.S. Rapid Deployment Joint Task Force, 138
Uzbekistan, 247–48, 260

Valencia, Guillermo León, 167, 175
Venezuela, 297
Victoria Group, 56

Vietnam War, 144–45
Violence: in commerce in Sierra Leone, 78–82; an indicator of state failure, 6, 22; lack of state control over in Tajikistan, 255–56; in Colombian politics, 163–64, 178
Vodun, 293
Volunteers for National Security, 294
Vouchergate trial, 73

Wahid, Abdurrahman, 190–93, 199
Wamba dia Wamba, Ernest, 30, 46–47, 49
Warfare: in post-state Sierra Leone, 70–100; fatigue in Somalia, 155
Warlords, 6, 9–10, 131; in the Congo, 30; democratizing, 330–31; in modern civil wars, 146; in Tajikistan, 254–55
Warsame, Ahmed, 137
Weak institutions, 6, 18
Weak states: Albania, 222; appearing to be strong, 5; Belarus, 222; Burkina Faso, 19; Cambodia, 19; causes and indicators, 1–25; Chad, 19; Colombia, 160–82, 222; contemporary, 10–13; dangerously weak, 159–262; defined, 3–4, 10–11; Fiji, 264–86; Georgia, 19; Ghana, 19; Guinea, 19; Haiti, 287–304; Indonesia, 183–218, 222; Iraq, 222; Laos, 19; Lebanon, 305–39; Libya, 222; Moldova, 19; Niger, 19; North Korea, 222; safely weak, 263–339; Sri Lanka, 219–44; strengthening, 1; Tajikistan, 245–62

Weapons buy-back programs, 298
Weber, Max, 241n
Western Somali Liberation Front (WSLF), 136
West Side Boys, 72, 91–92, 95
Wickremesinghe, Ranil, 232, 235
Widner, Jennifer, 24n
World Bank, 32, 63, 188, 194, 238–39, 304
World Food Program (WFP), 141, 256
World Trade Organization (WTO), 195

Yemba, Adolphe Onusumba, 30
Yugoslavia, 91, 283, 307, 331–32
Yusuf, Abdullahi, 153–54

Zaire: becoming DRC, 43–45; under Mobutu Sese Seko, 6, 12. *See also* Democratic Republic of the Congo
Zairian Armed Forces (ZAF), 33, 40
Zartman, I. William, 24n
Zaruq, Mubarak, 115
Zimbabwe, 8, 10, 15–16, 23; economic signals of failure, 21; involvement in the Congo, 30
Zimbabwe Defense Forces (ZDF), 57–58
Zinni, Anthony, 200
Ziyayov, Mirzo, 255
Zvinavashe, Vitalis, 57
Zvinavashe Investment, 57